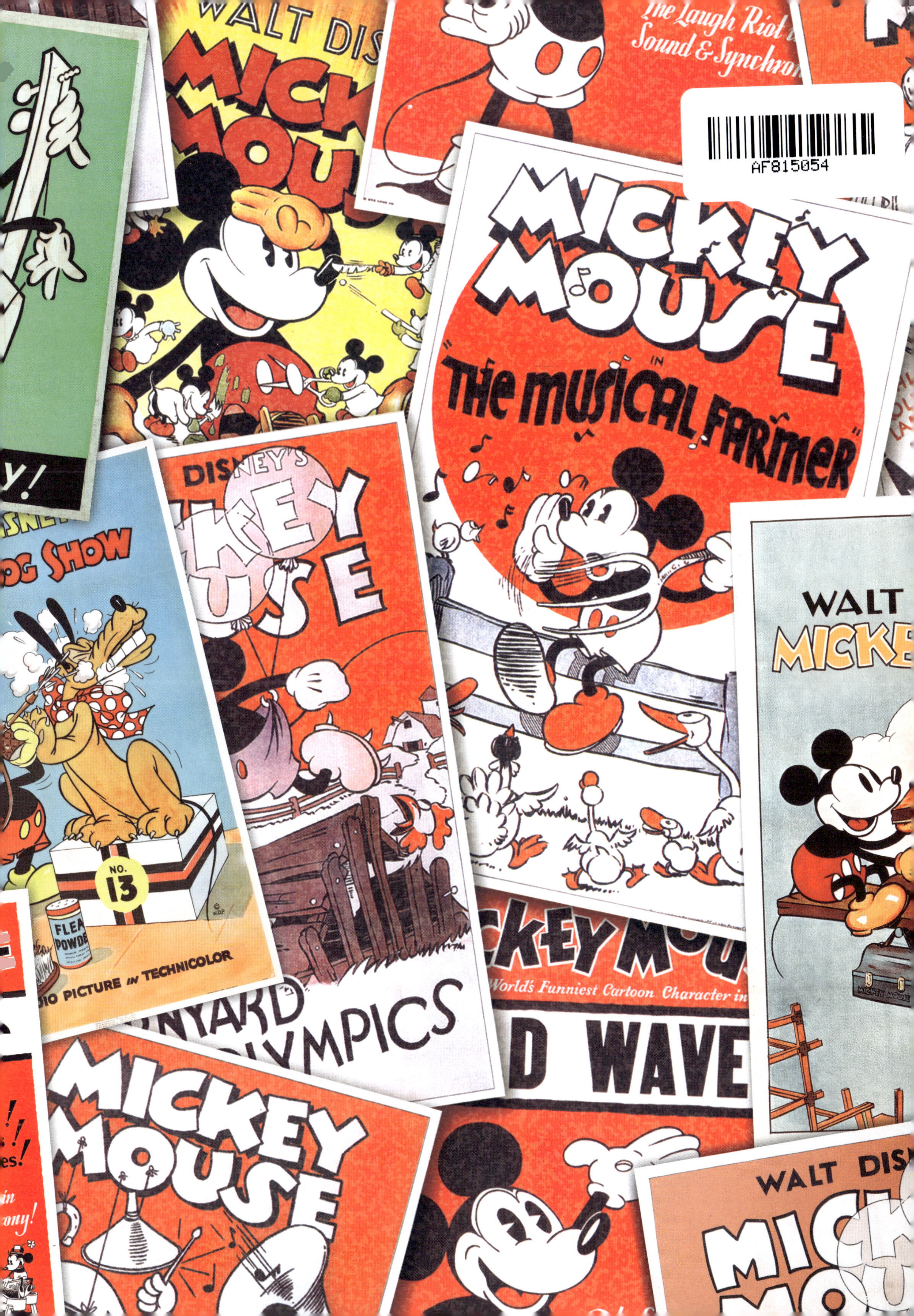
WALT DIS
The Laugh Riot
Sound & Synchron
MICKEY MOUSE
IN
THE MUSICAL FARMER
DISNEY'S
OG SHOW
NO. 13
FLEA POWDE
DIO PICTURE IN TECHNICOLOR
NYARD
OLYMPICS
CKEY MOU
World's Funniest Cartoon Character in
D WAVE
WALT
MICKE
MICKEY MOUSE
WALT DIS

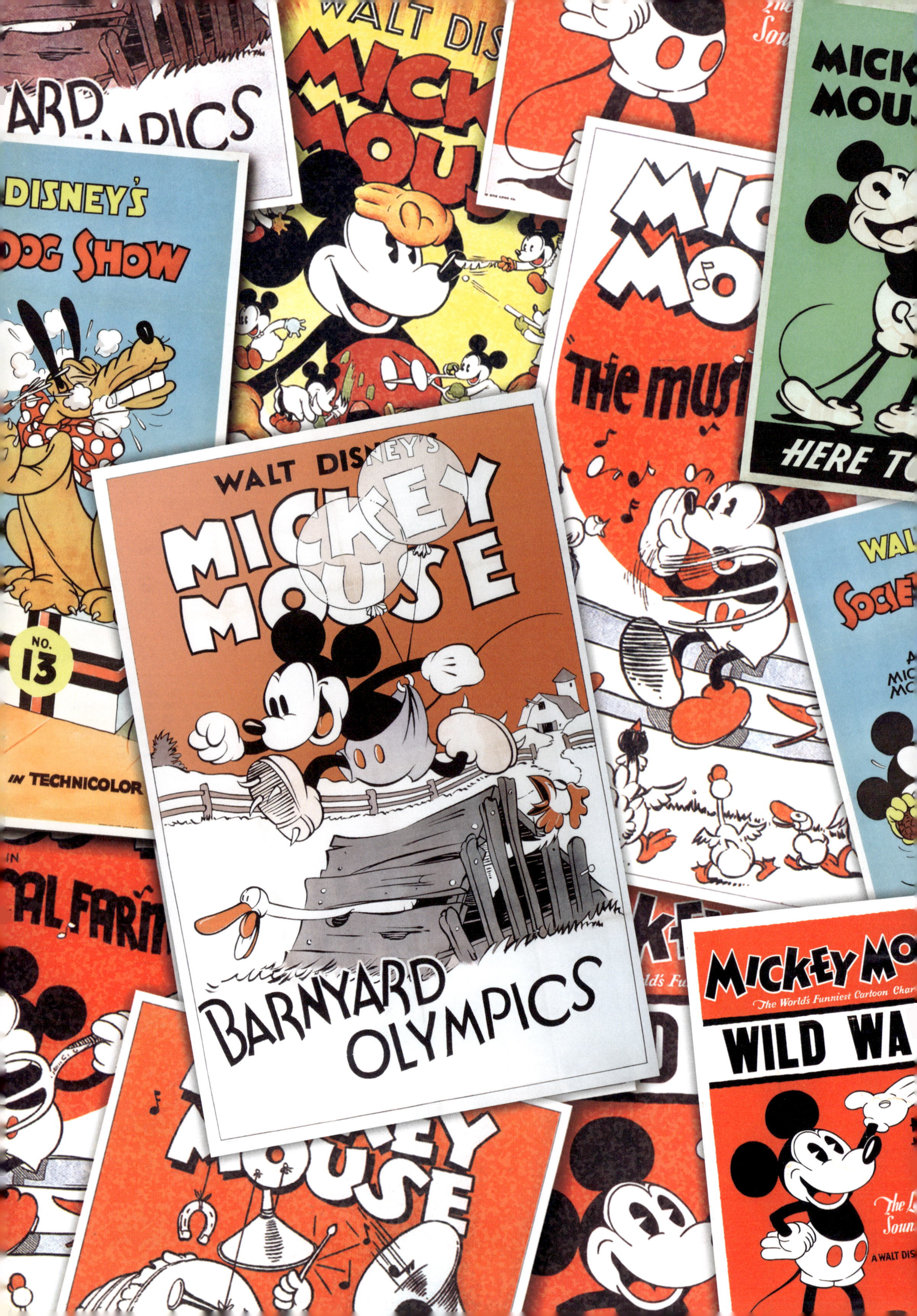
WALT DISNEY'S
MICKEY MOUSE
BARNYARD OLYMPICS
NO. 13
IN TECHNICOLOR

LEARN TO DRAW
MICKEY MOUSE
& FRIENDS
THROUGH THE DECADES

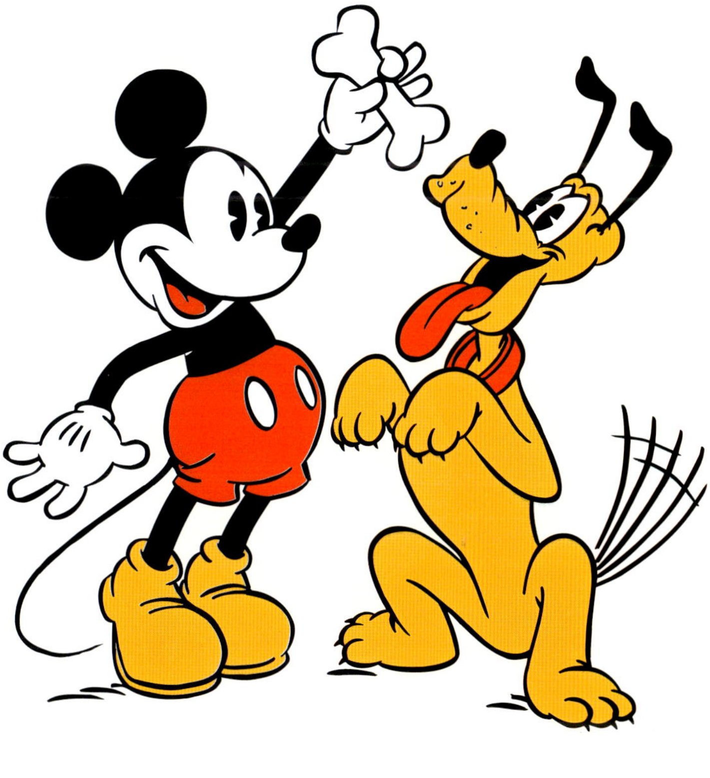

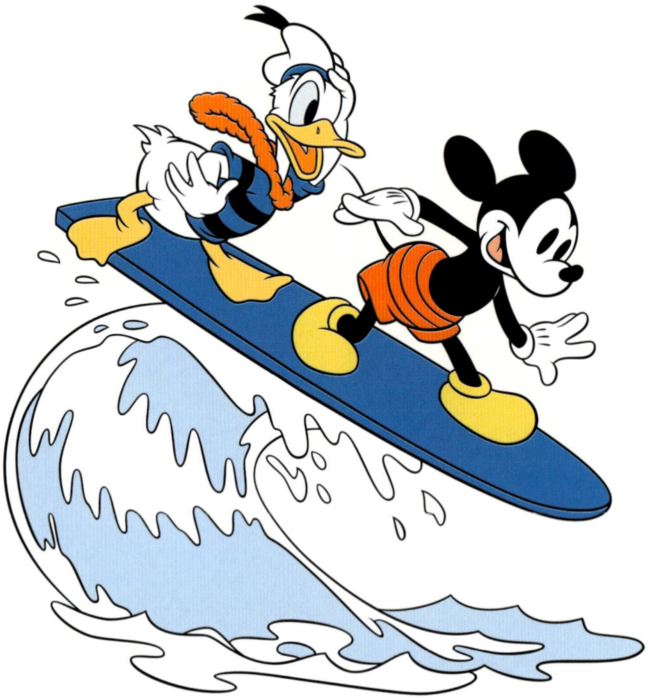

Written by David Gerstein. Illustrated by John Loter and the Disney Storybook Artists.
Text on pages 6 and 8 written by Jennifer Gaudet.

6 Orchard Road, Suite 100
Lake Forest, CA 92630
quartoknows.com
Visit our blogs at quartoknows.com

Printed in China

5 7 9 10 8 6

MIX
Paper from responsible sources
FSC® C016973

LEARN TO DRAW MICKEY MOUSE & FRIENDS

THROUGH THE DECADES

WRITTEN BY DAVID GERSTEIN

ILLUSTRATED BY JOHN LOTER
AND THE DISNEY STORYBOOK ARTISTS

TABLE OF CONTENTS

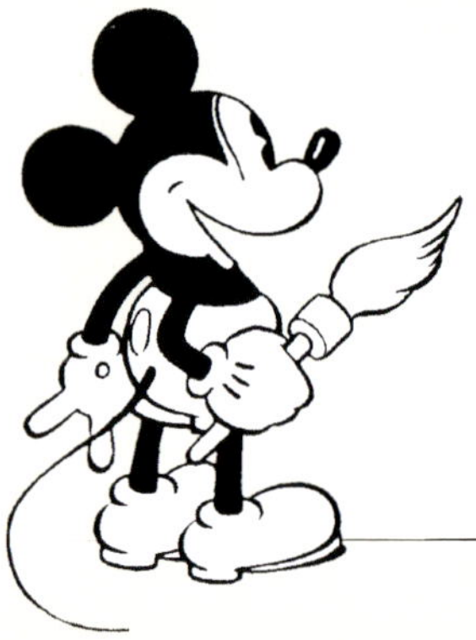

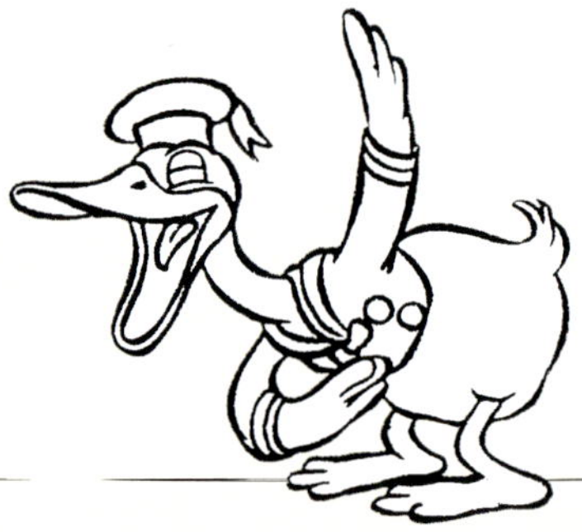

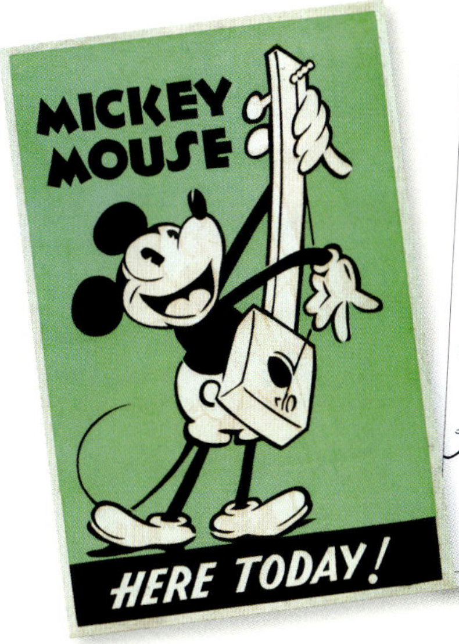
MICKEY MOUSE
HERE TODAY!
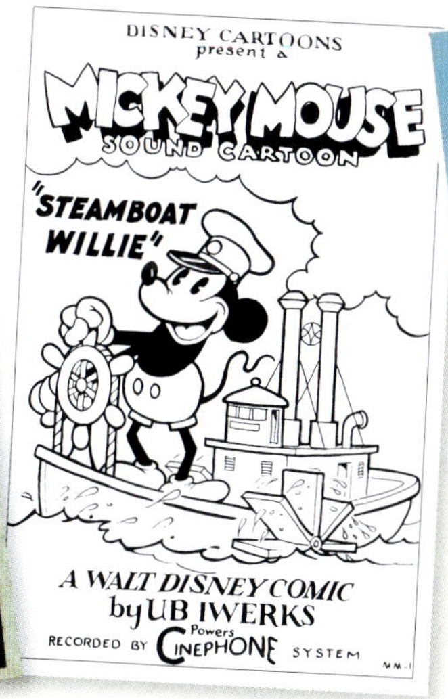
DISNEY CARTOONS present a
MICKEY MOUSE
SOUND CARTOON
"STEAMBOAT WILLIE"
A WALT DISNEY COMIC
by UB IWERKS
RECORDED BY Powers CINEPHONE SYSTEM
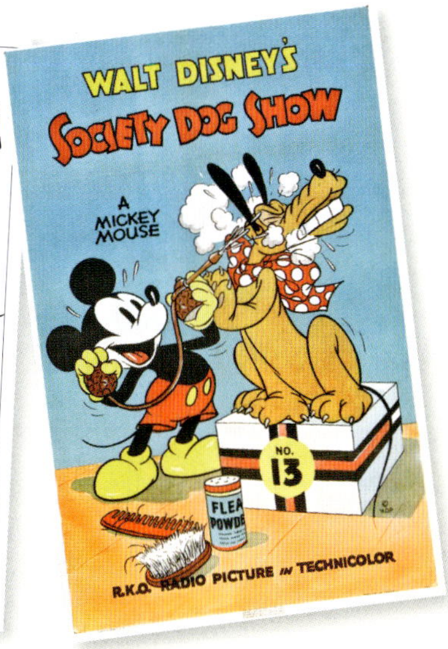
WALT DISNEY'S
SOCIETY DOG SHOW
A MICKEY MOUSE
NO. 13
FLEA POWDE
R.K.O. RADIO PICTURE IN TECHNICOLOR

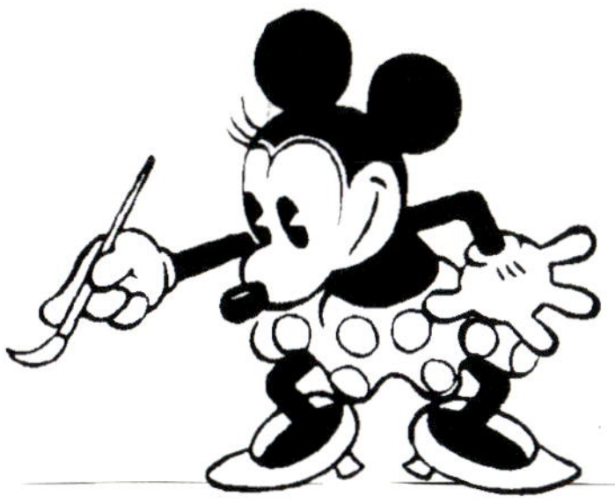

ABOUT THIS BOOK

In the pages of this book you'll learn how to recreate Disney's most celebrated characters as they originally appeared in animation from the 1920s, 1930s, 1940s, and beyond. Simply follow the step-by-step instructions, as shown below.

Each section features beautiful vintage images from the Disney archives and historical anecdotes that capture the spirit of what makes Mickey Mouse and Friends so beloved to generations of fans.

1

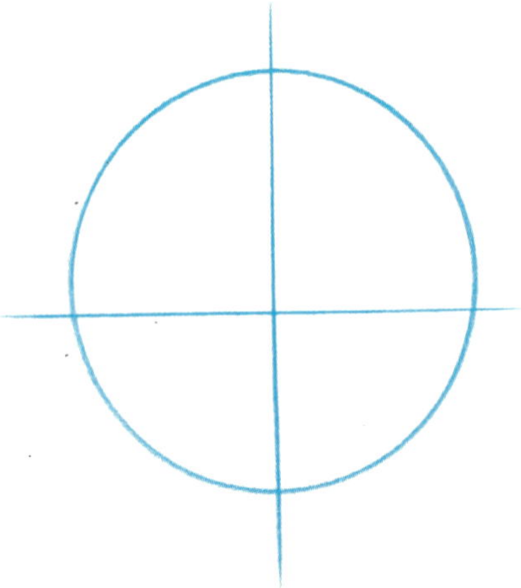

FIRST DRAW GUIDELINES TO HELP POSITION THE CHARACTER'S FEATURES.

2

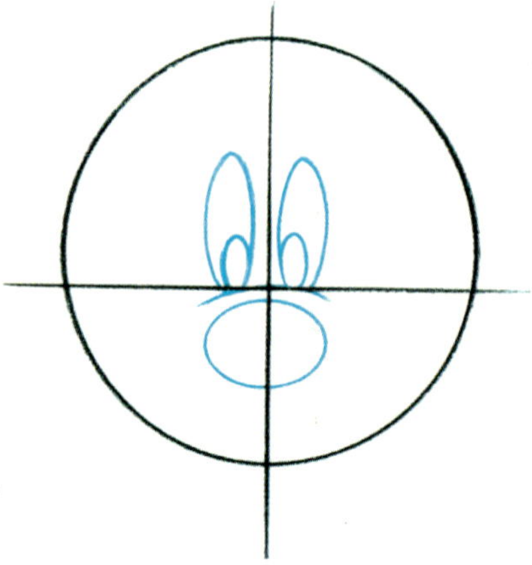

FOLLOW THE STEPS TO ADD THE DETAILS.

3

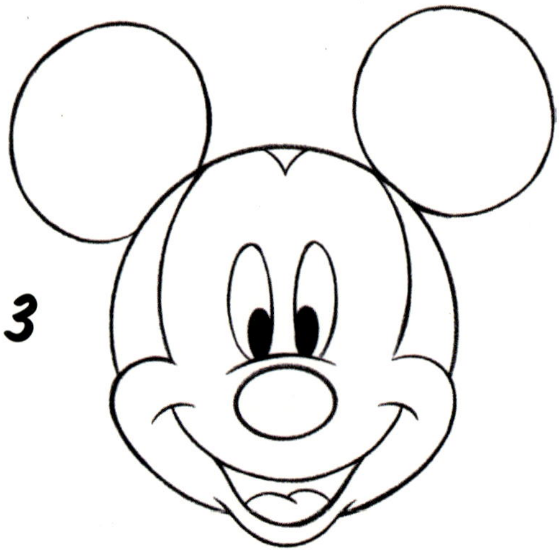

WHEN YOU FINISH ADDING THE DETAILS, ERASE YOUR GUIDELINES. THEN DARKEN YOUR FINAL SKETCH LINES WITH A PEN OR A MARKER.

4

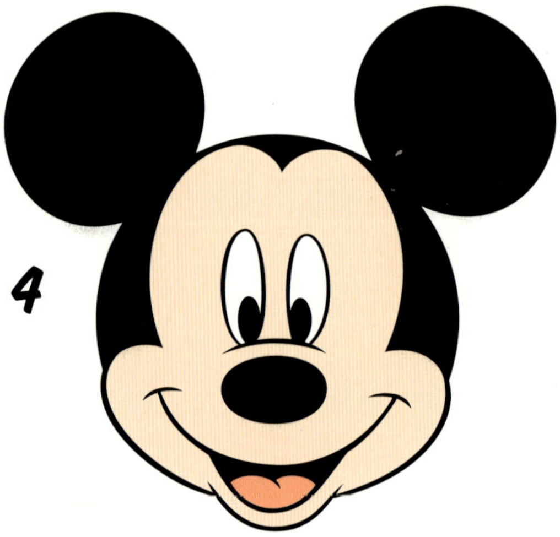

ADD COLOR.

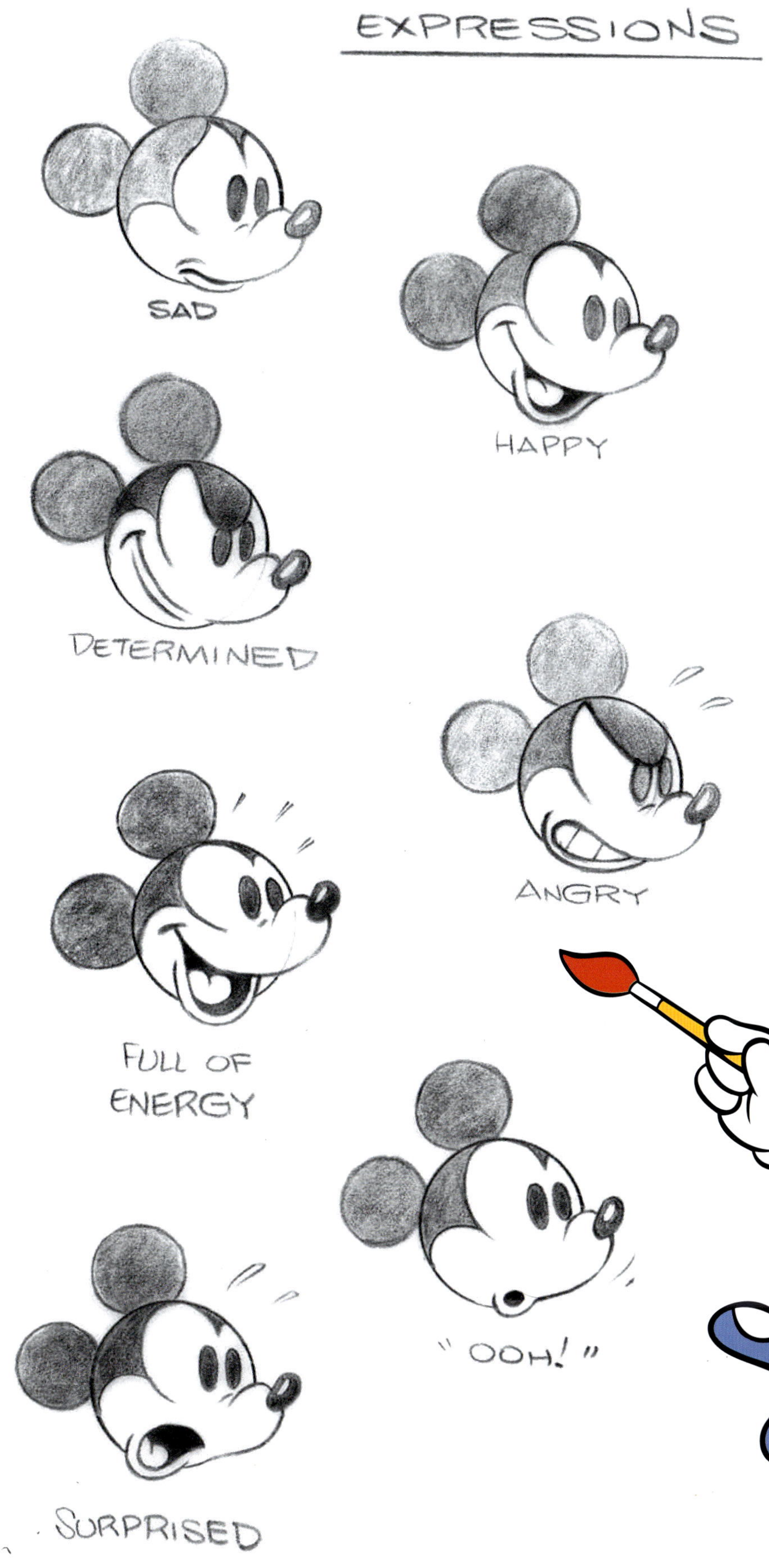

USE THIS MICKEY MOUSE MODEL SHEET FROM THE 1930s FOR INSPIRATION.

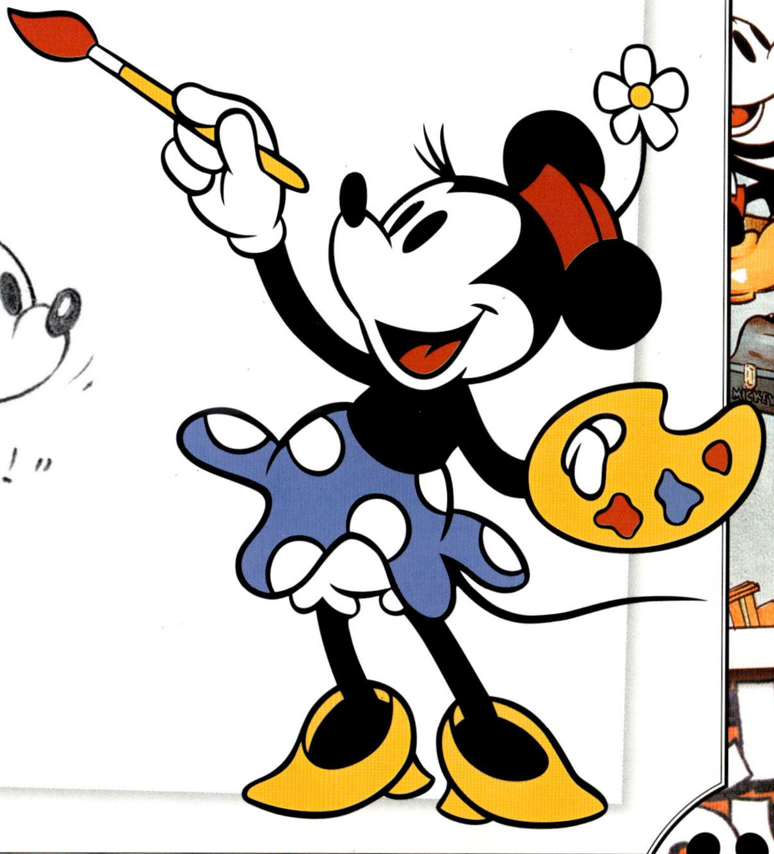

INTRODUCING DISNEY'S CLASSIC CHARACTERS

In 1932, Walt Disney was awarded a special Oscar® for the creation of the world's most beloved animated character—a mere four years after Mickey Mouse was introduced. From his debut to the present day, Mickey hasn't skipped a beat, adventuring his way into the hearts and homes of audiences everywhere. As a well-known public figure, Mickey paved the way onscreen for a gang of friends that became Disney's biggest stars. Minnie Mouse made her debut alongside Mickey in 1928, and the two have since enjoyed one of the strongest and longest-running courtships in animation history. The characters Disney introduced thereafter not only supported Mickey's role, but became icons in their own right, with their own set of memorable quirks and personalities—from Donald Duck's fiery temper to Goofy's good-natured silliness. Mickey, Minnie, Donald, and Goofy, along with loyal, playful Pluto and sassy yet sophisticated Daisy, have entertained generations of fans for more than 75 years, while Mickey alone has appeared in more than 130 film shorts, features, and featurettes. The dress, style, and shape of these characters have reflected the times and evolved with cultural and historic events; however, their inherent charm has proven timeless. In the pages that follow, you will discover how these beloved characters have become, and why they undoubtedly always will remain, an impactful, innovative part of cartoon animation history.

MICKEY MOUSE
U.S. PATENT OFFICE REGISTERED

OPPOSITE PAGE: THE DRAWING DESK (AS PRESERVED AND DISPLAYED BY THE WALT DISNEY COMPANY TODAY) OF ARTIST FLOYD GOTTFREDSON, WHO DREW MICKEY MOUSE IN COMIC STRIPS EVERY DAY FOR 45 YEARS. GOTTFREDSON IS CREDITED WITH PERFECTING THE 1930S MICKEY DESIGN THAT IS STILL IN USE TODAY.

PHOTO COURTESY OF KEN SHUE

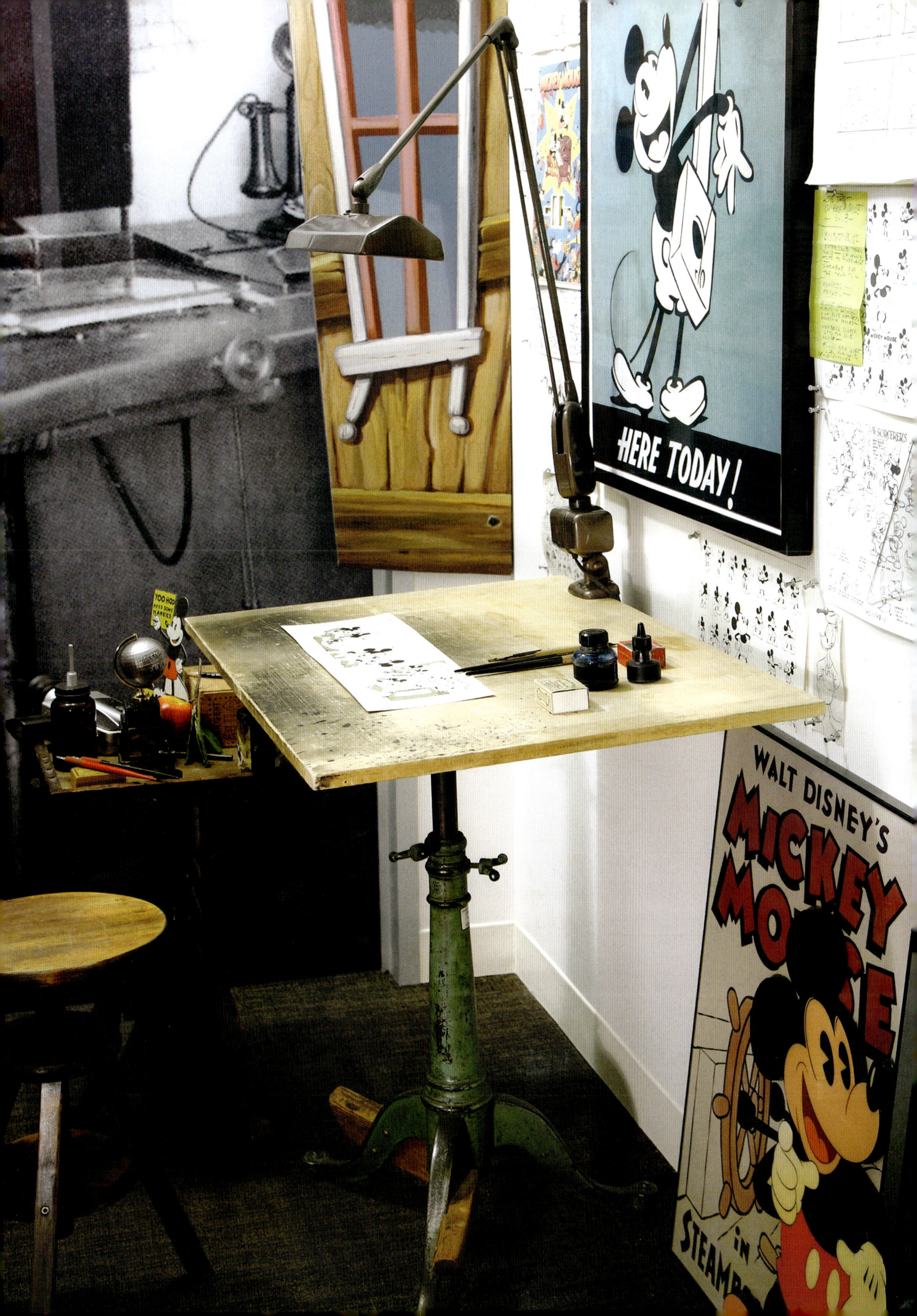
HERE TODAY!
WALT DISNEY'S
MICKEY MOUSE
in
STEAMB

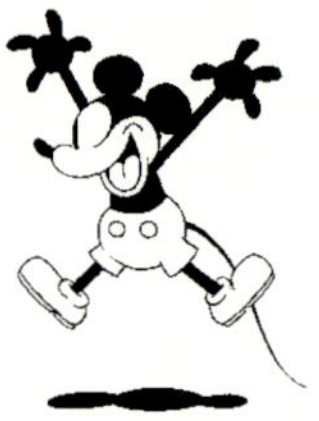

THE 1920s

THE BEGINNING

"I only hope we never lose sight of one thing," Walt Disney liked to say over the years. "It all started with a mouse."

But did it? As much as we celebrate Mickey—adventurer, mischief-maker, hero, and dynamo—the classic Disney styles of art and storytelling didn't quite begin with him. Instead, they were a natural outgrowth of earlier cartoon history. As early as 1910, for instance, George Herriman's comic character Krazy Kat set a trend for black-furred, white-faced animal heroes. In 1913, John R. Bray's Colonel Heeza Liar starred in the first adventure cartoons. Otto Messmer's Felix the Cat was animation's first great emotive figure. And Disney's own Oswald the Lucky Rabbit pioneered cartoon speed, rhythm, and squash-and-stretch motion.

OPPOSITE PAGE: 1929 PROMOTIONAL POSTER FOR WILD WAVES

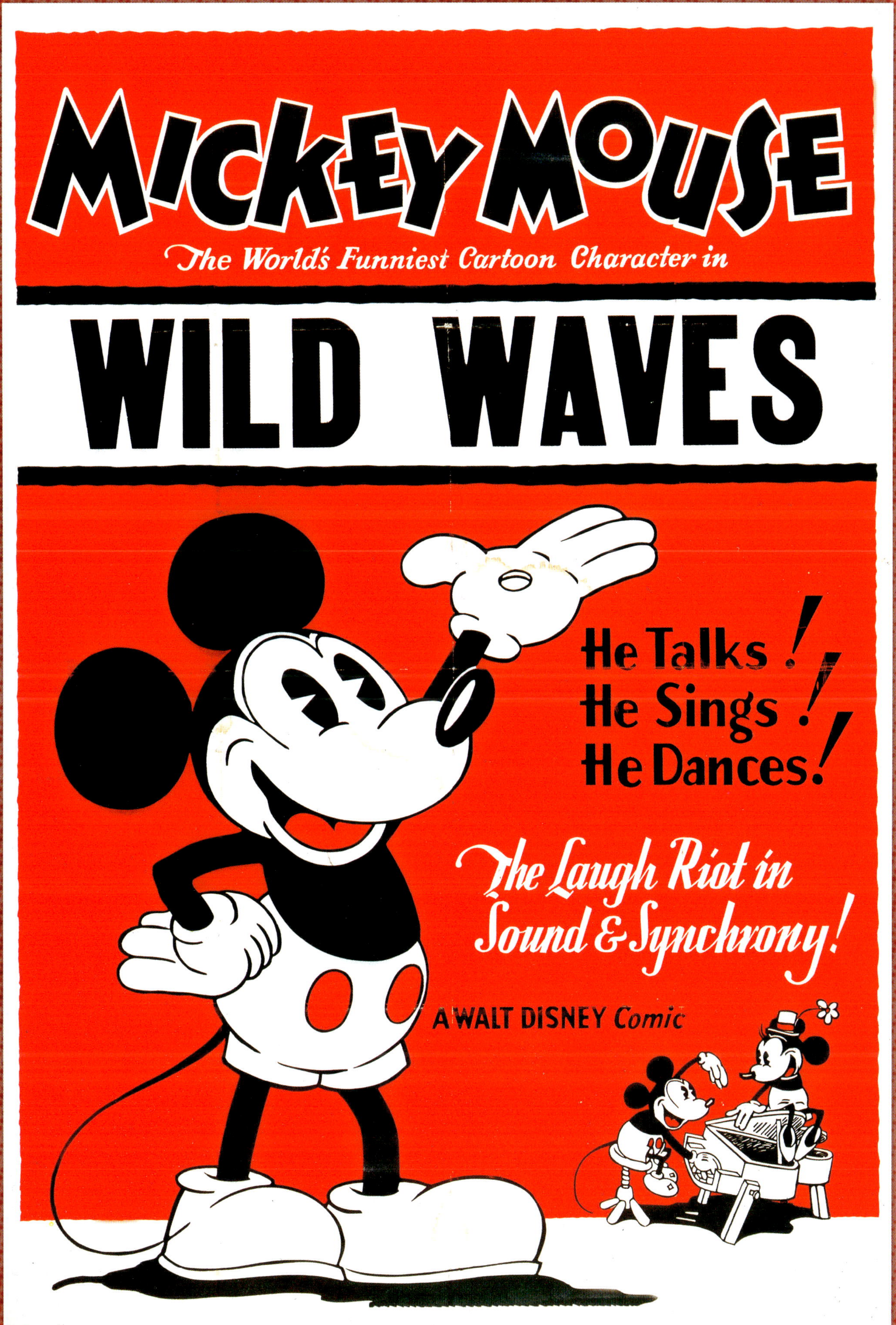
MICKEY MOUSE
The World's Funniest Cartoon Character in
WILD WAVES
He Talks!
He Sings!
He Dances!
The Laugh Riot in Sound & Synchrony!
A WALT DISNEY Comic

So what made Mickey stand out in 1928? His edge lay in how perfectly he combined his precursors' innovations: funny, animal-adventure cartoons with rhythm and music, moving at wild speed; no film product had ever shared all of these elements. And Mickey's black-and-white face went a step beyond Krazy's coloration and Felix's emotion; the Mouse's uniquely round features made him a special kind of eye magnet.

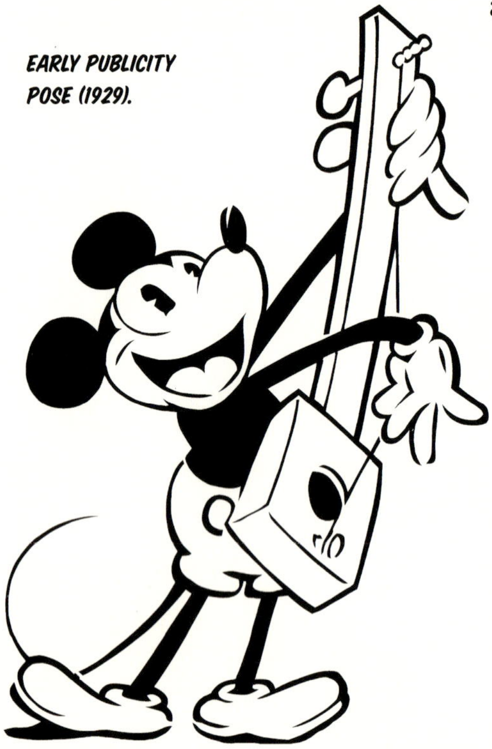

EARLY PUBLICITY POSE (1929).

In short, when "it all started" with Mickey, it wasn't the start of Disney or the start of exceptionally funny animals. But it was the start of an exceptional spirit of innovation: a deliberate effort by Walt and his animator partner, Ub Iwerks, to do better at absolutely everything.

Was it also the spirit of the Jazz Age? The brassy 1920s were a time when anything seemed possible

1920s ANIMATION TIMELINE

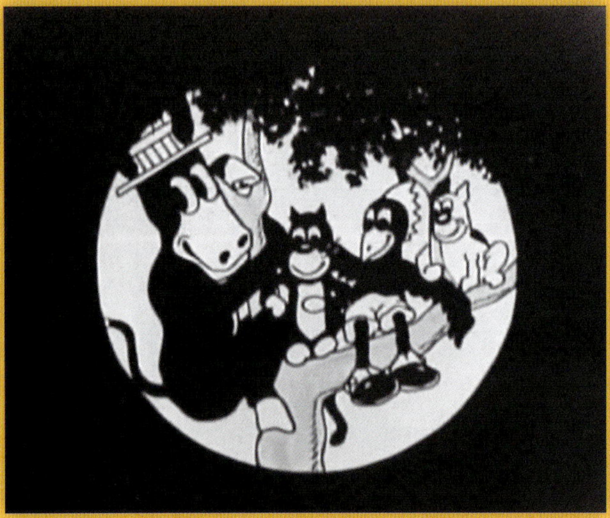

1922

LAUGH-O-GRAM "FOUR MUSICIANS OF BREMEN"

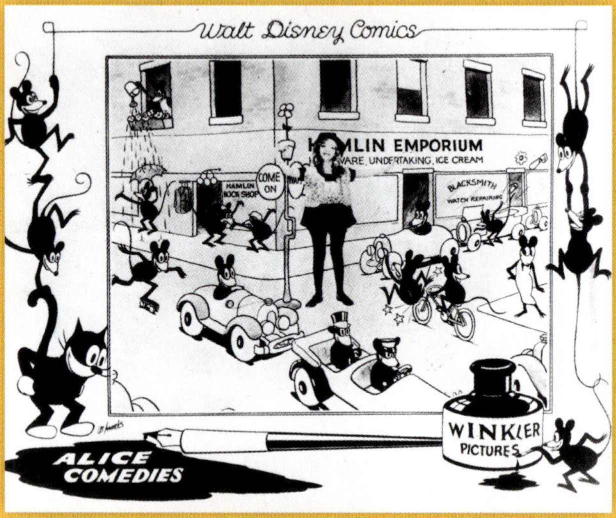

1924

THE ALICE COMEDIES (PUBLICITY STILL FOR "ALICE THE PIPER")

in pop culture. As a sign of this confidence, perhaps, Mickey was born with a girlfriend—Minnie—from the start. While Felix and Oswald had loved and lost varying leading ladies, high-stepping Mickey had a feisty fellow high-stepper from the outset.

The earliest Mickey of 1928 was called a "demon hero" by a reviewer in *Film Daily*.[1] Character designer Ub Iwerks compared this Mouse to Douglas Fairbanks: "the superhero of his day, always winning, gallant and swashbuckling."[2] And Iwerks's design bears this out. In direct contrast to the thick-limbed Oswald before him, Mickey is lean and scrawny, an active figure reduced to its most vital form.

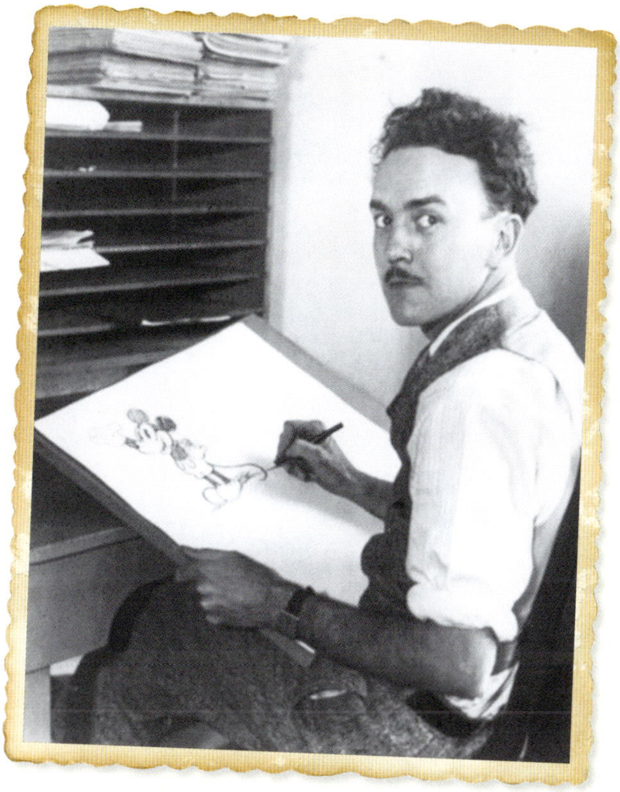

UB IWERKS DRAWING MICKEY MOUSE.

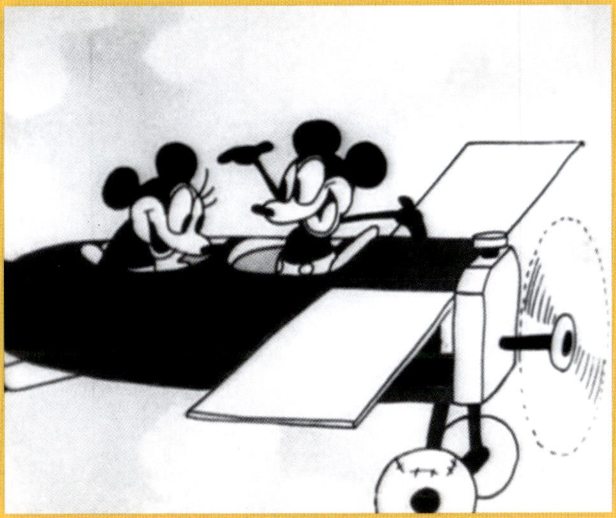

1928

PLANE CRAZY
(FIRST MICKEY MOUSE CARTOON.
ORIGINALLY SILENT; RELEASED WITH SOUND IN 1929.)

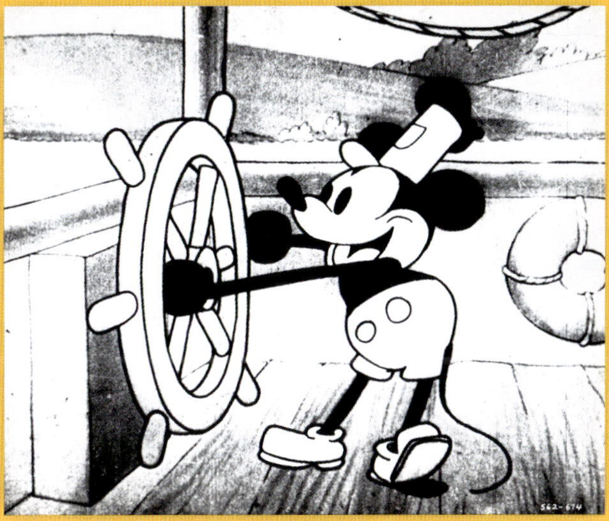

1928

STEAMBOAT WILLIE
(THIRD MICKEY MOUSE CARTOON; FIRST TO GO INTO GENERAL RELEASE. DISNEY'S FIRST SOUND CARTOON.)

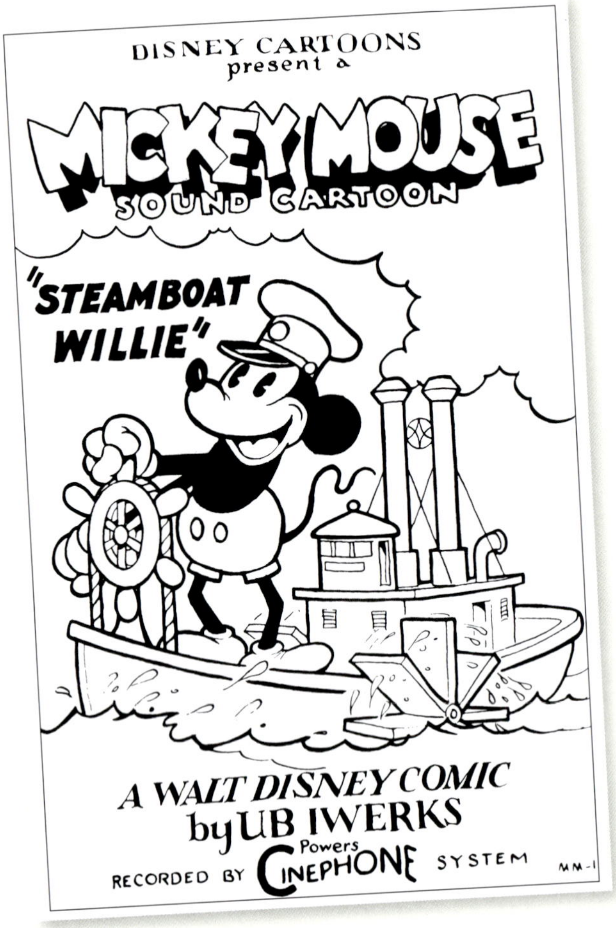

The very first Mickey Mouse was gloveless, shoeless, and goggle-eyed. The design shown on pages 16 and 17—based on a model sheet for the recent "retro" short *Get a Horse!* (2013)—evolved several months into the series. Squarish shoes bring weight as a counterpoint to long arms ready for action. The goggle eyes are gone, but an eyebrow line remains, adding a slightly saucy edge to many of his expressions.

And where an expressive Mickey goes, so does rotten-hearted Pete, and Minnie, who was around this time described

STEAMBOAT WILLIE *PROMOTIONAL POSTER (1928). ART BY UB IWERKS.*

1920s ANIMATION TIMELINE

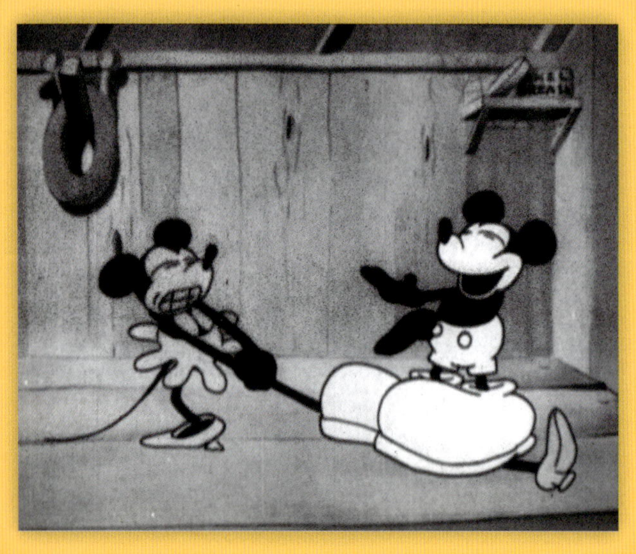

1928

THE BARN DANCE

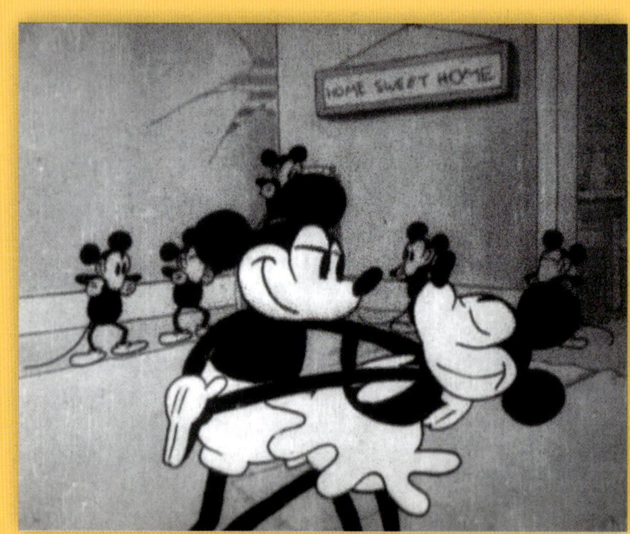

1929

WHEN THE CAT'S AWAY

as "Mickey's fickle, frivolous flapper."[3] Rather than the demure, gentle girl she would later become, Jazz Age Minnie needs no excuse to show off, show Mickey up, or sing at the top of her lungs! The Minnie pose—cleaned up for us via another *Get a Horse!* model sheet—originates in *The Plowboy* (1929), where she enjoys a tune break while skipping breathlessly through the farmyard. Meanwhile, Pete—having none of this foolishness—comes straight from *Steamboat Willie* (1928), the whole gang's first sound cartoon. (The big lummox probably complained about all the noise...)

[1] "Short Subjects—Sound." *Film Daily* (January 6, 1929), 11.

[2] Interview with Iwerks by George Sherman (July 30, 1970), Walt Disney Archives.

[3] Walt Disney, Mickey Mouse promotional comic strip (1929). (The actual Mickey Mouse comic strip began January 13, 1930; early promos were created beforehand.)

EARLY PUBLICITY POSE (1929) INCLUDES MINNIE WITH A SHOWY TOP HAT AND BRASSIERE, BOTH WORN AT TIMES IN THE EARLIEST FILMS.

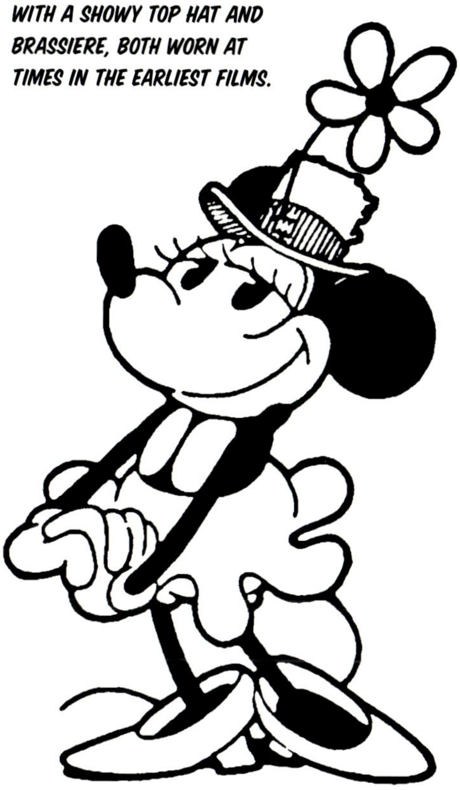

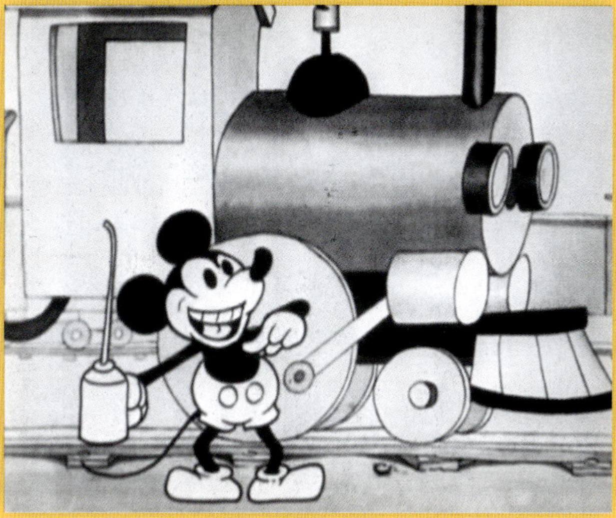

1929

MICKEY'S CHOO-CHOO

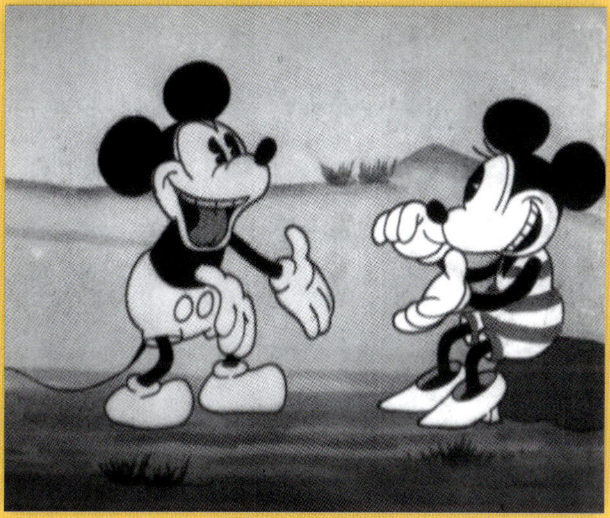

1929

WILD WAVES

1920s

MICKEY MOUSE

GET A HORSE!

WHILE THIS PROJECT FEATURES THE GLOVELESS EARLY MICKEY WITH FOUR FINGERS, HE WAS PICTURED WITH FIVE IN SOME 1928 CLOSE-UP SHOTS—AND BEFORE MICKEY, DISNEY CHARACTERS ROUTINELY HAD FIVE FINGERS.

1

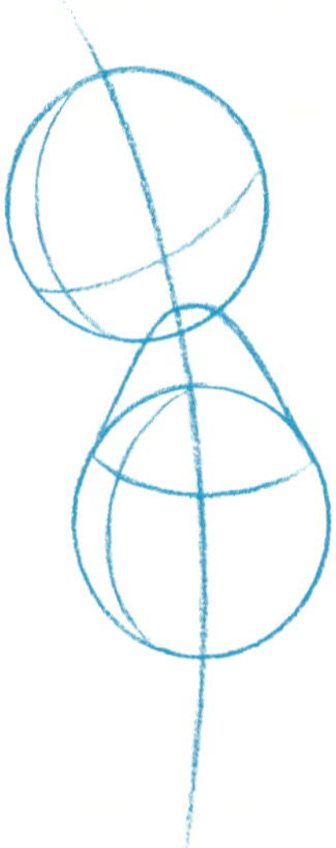

2

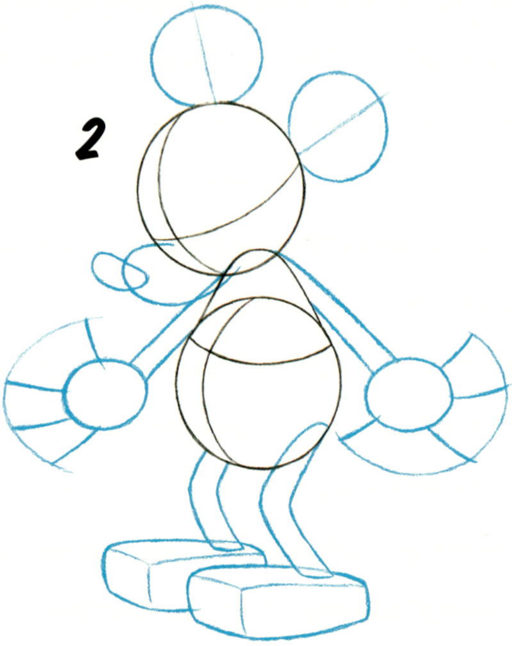

3

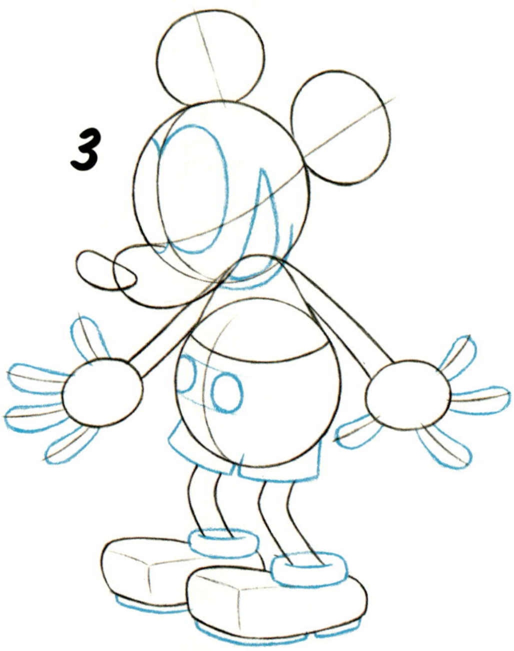

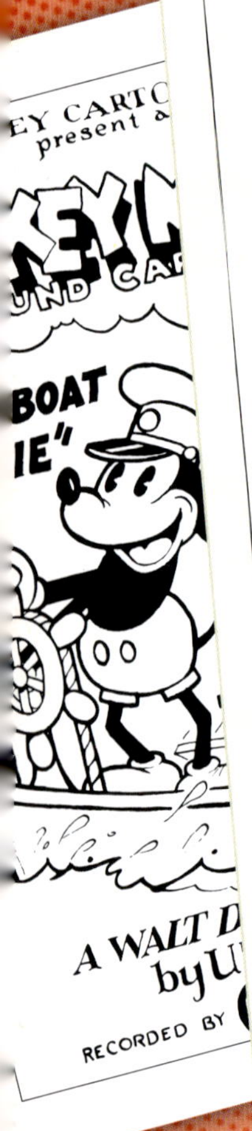

4

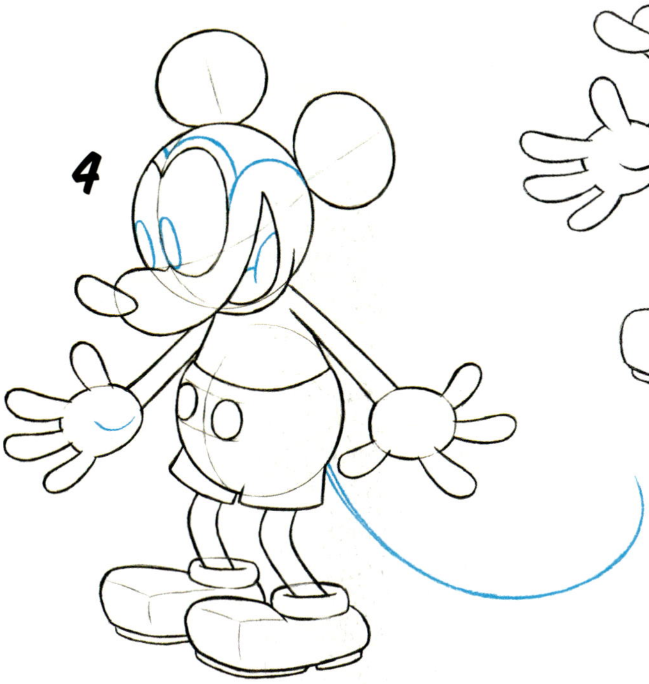

5

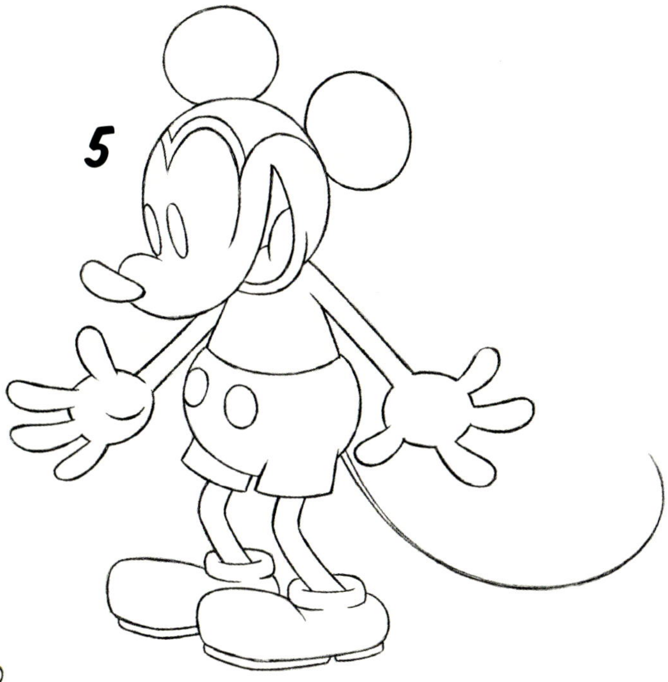

6

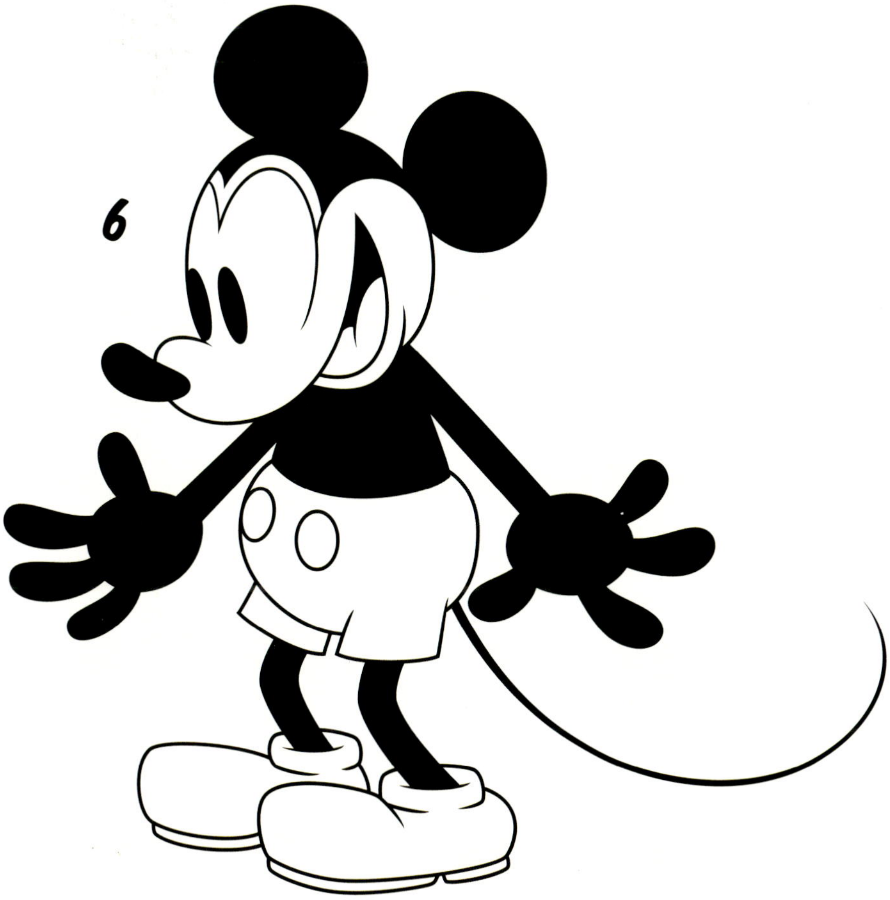

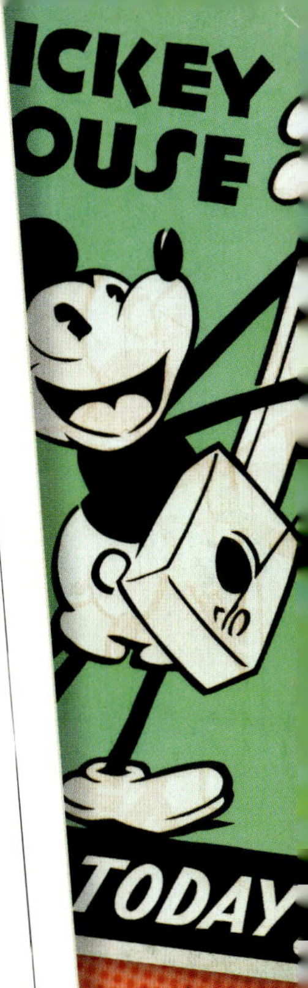

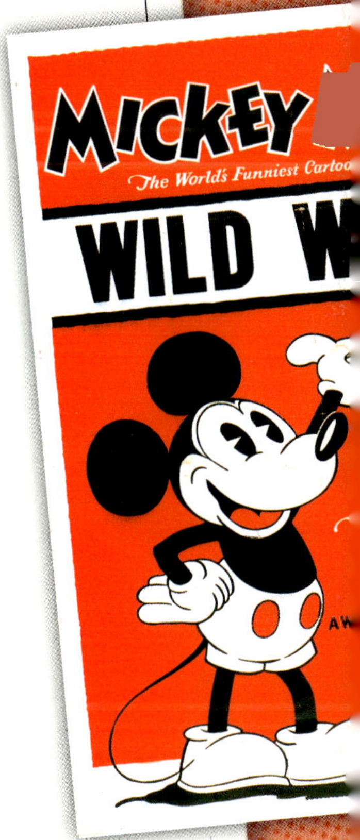

1920s

MINNIE MOUSE

THE PLOWBOY/GET A HORSE!

1

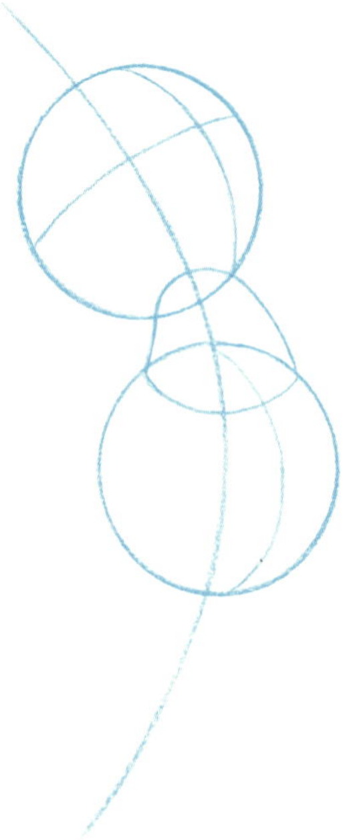

2

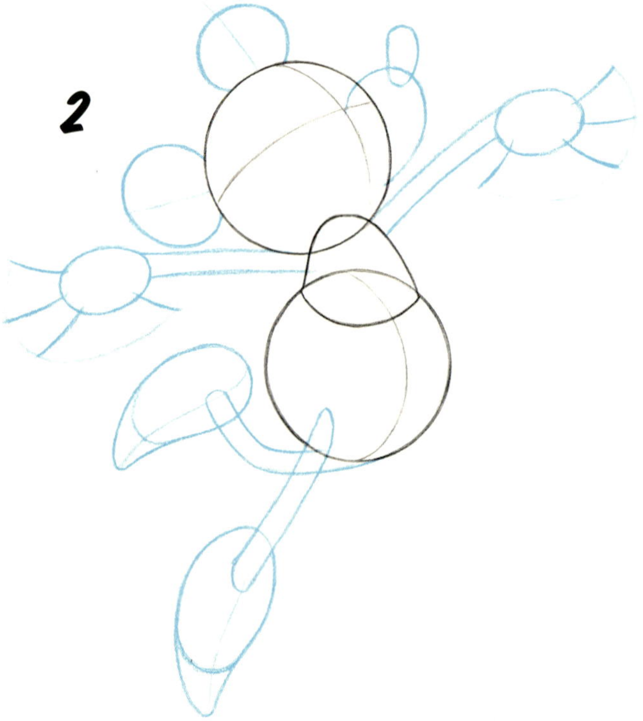

3

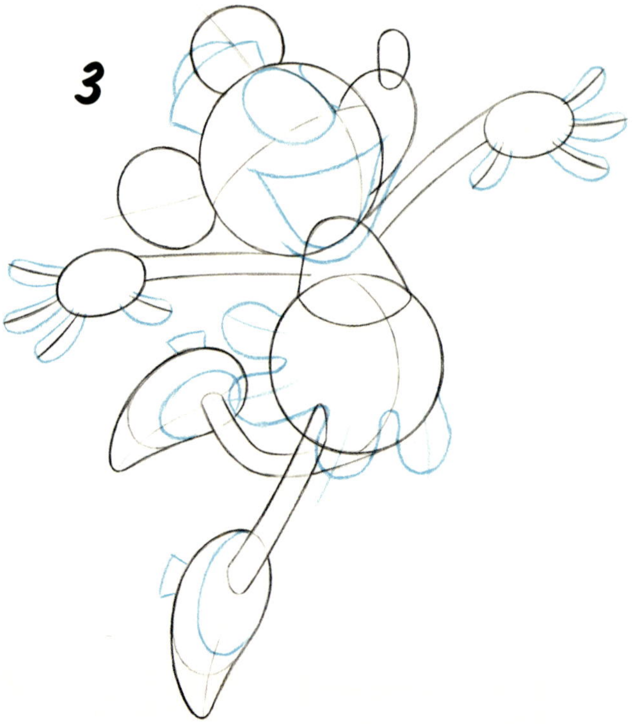

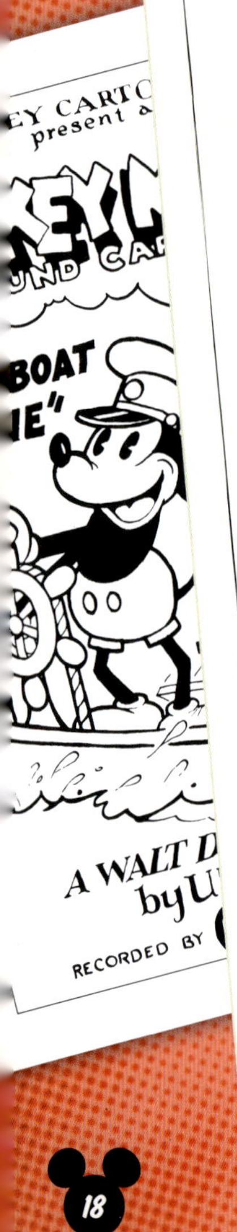

MINNIE GREETED MICKEY WITH A "YOO-HOO" SO OFTEN THAT IT BECAME HER CATCHPHRASE; IN 1931, ROY DISNEY SINGLED OUT A RIVAL STUDIO'S MOUSE CHARACTERS FOR STEALING THE EXPRESSION.

4

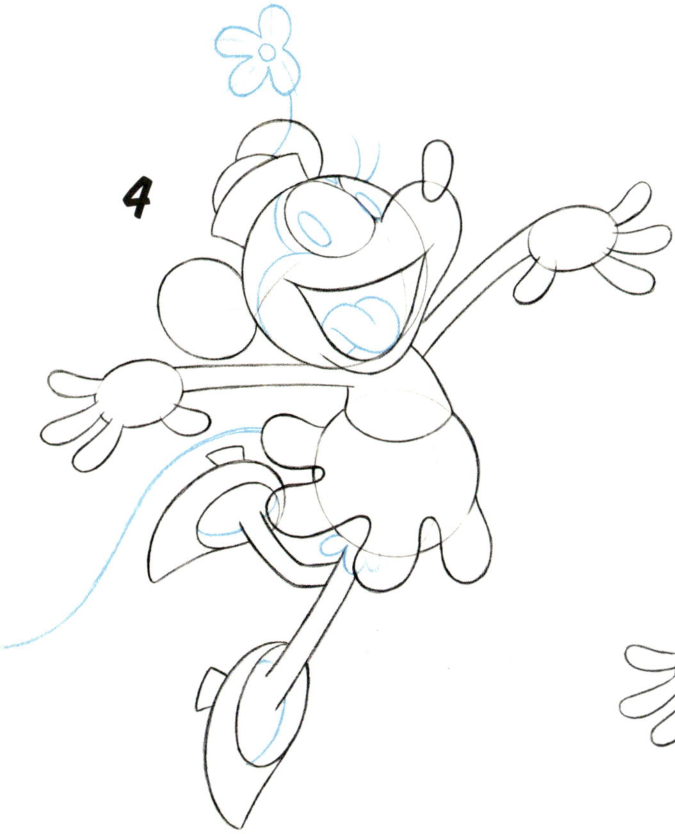

5

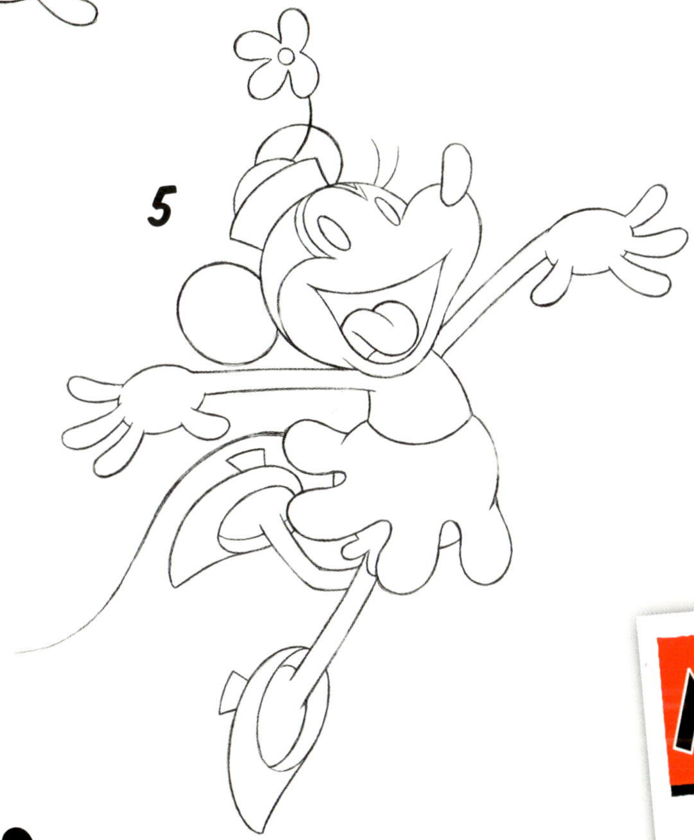

6

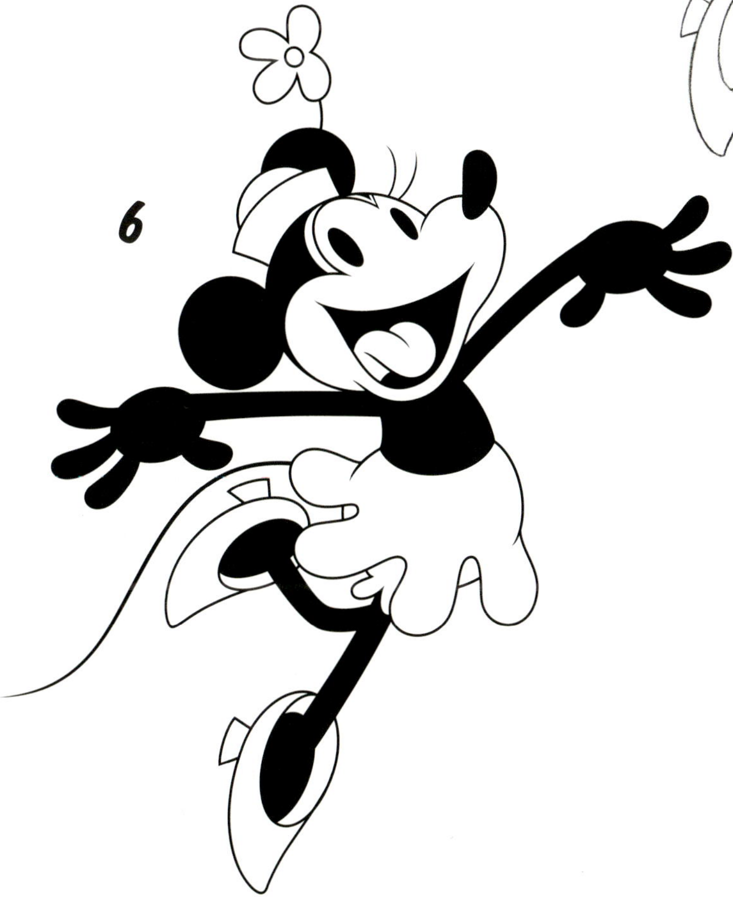

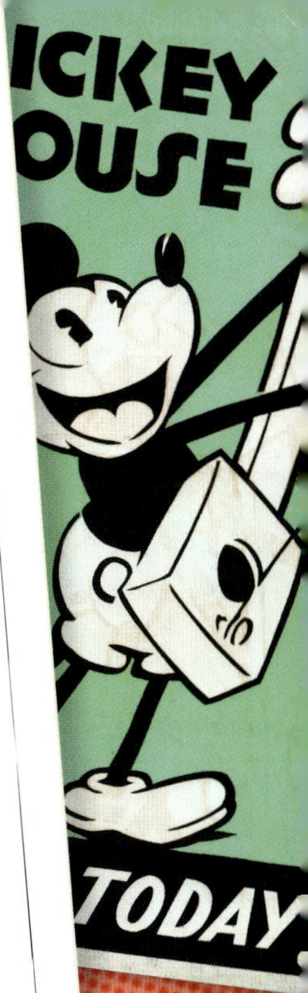

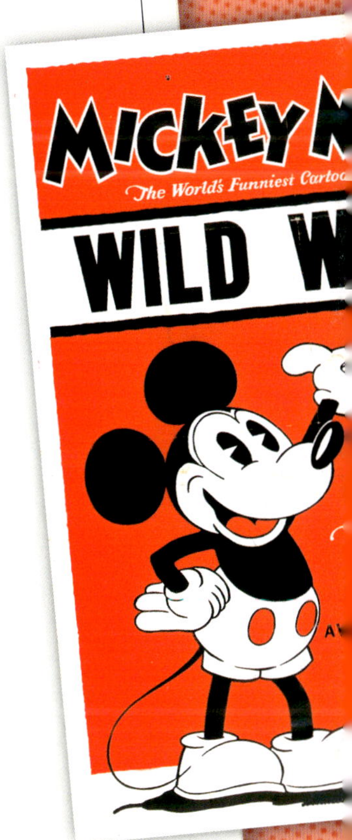

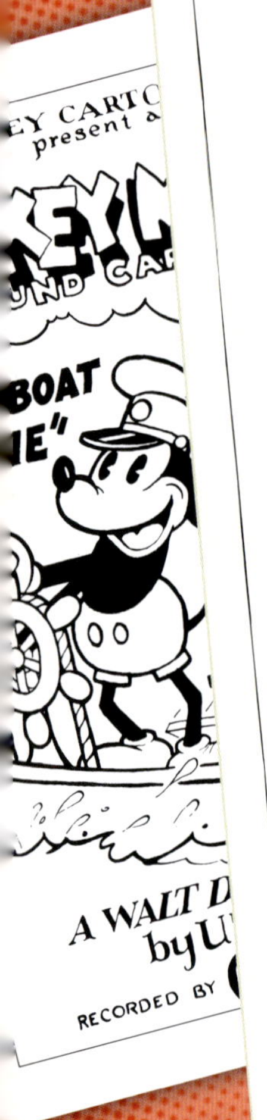

1920s

PETE

STEAMBOAT WILLIE

1

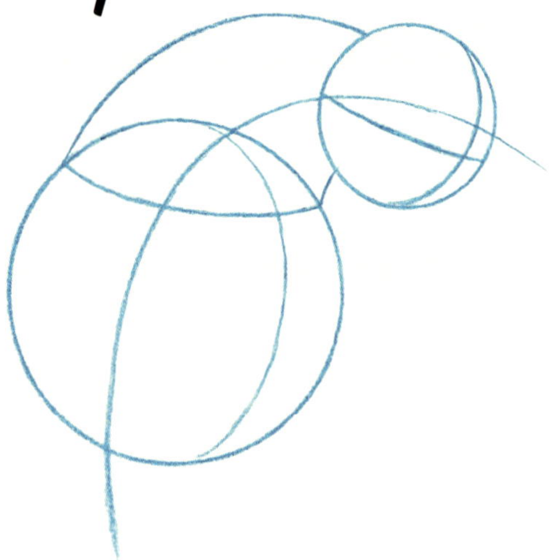

2

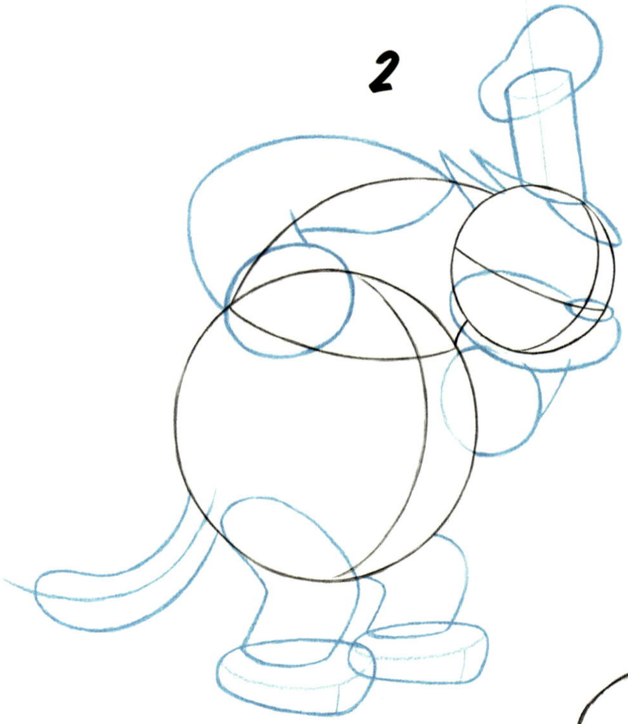

3

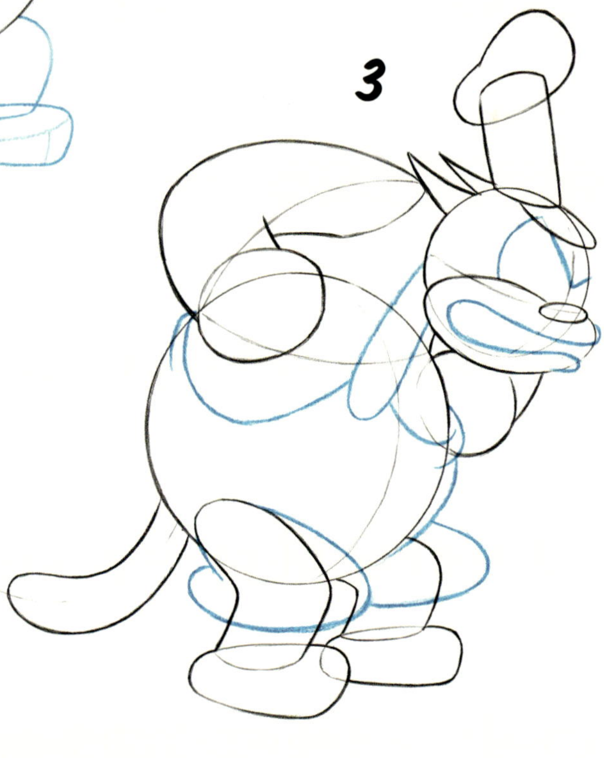

4

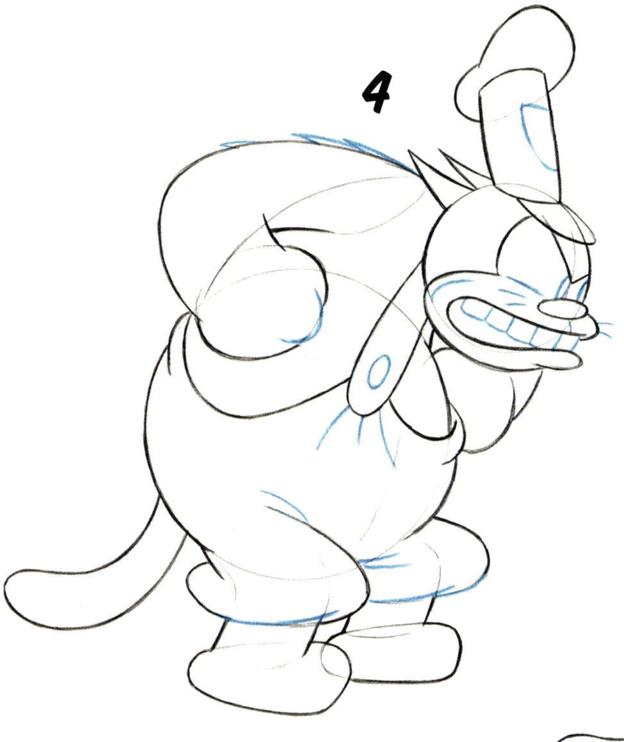

5

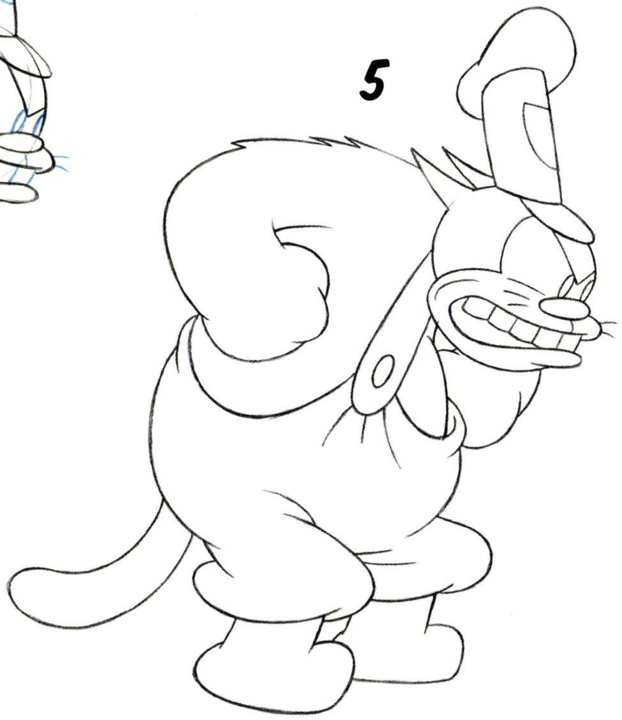

6

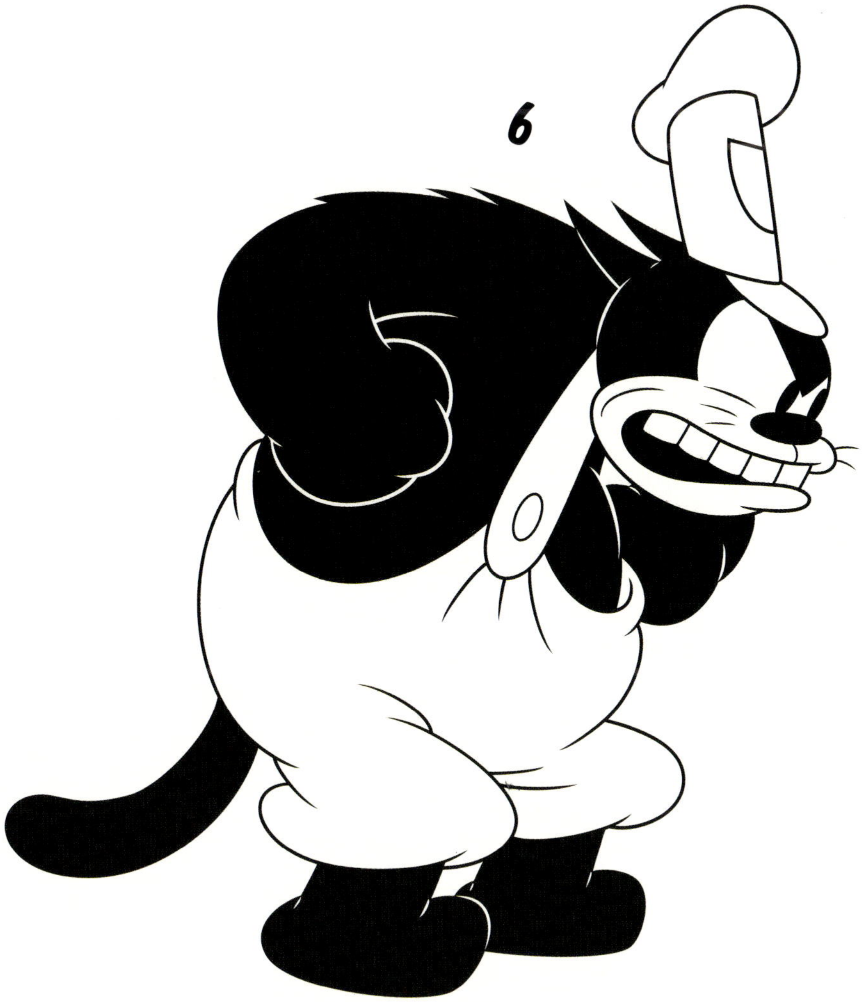

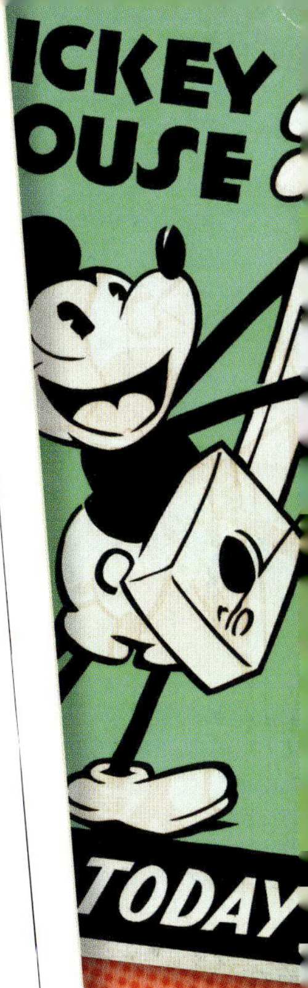

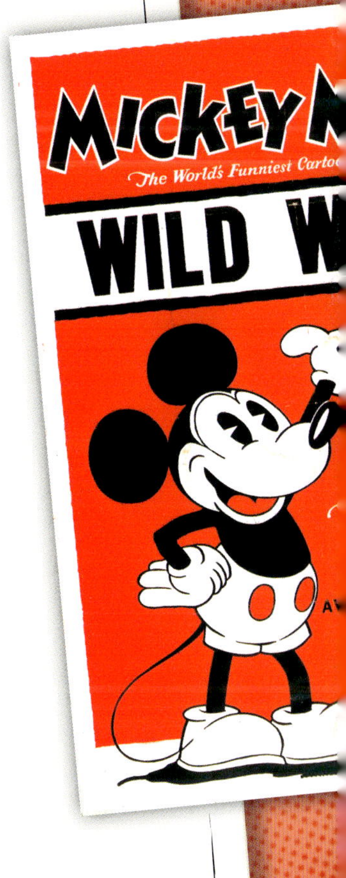

INSIDE STORY

PEGLEG PETE: THE CAT'S ME-OUSE!

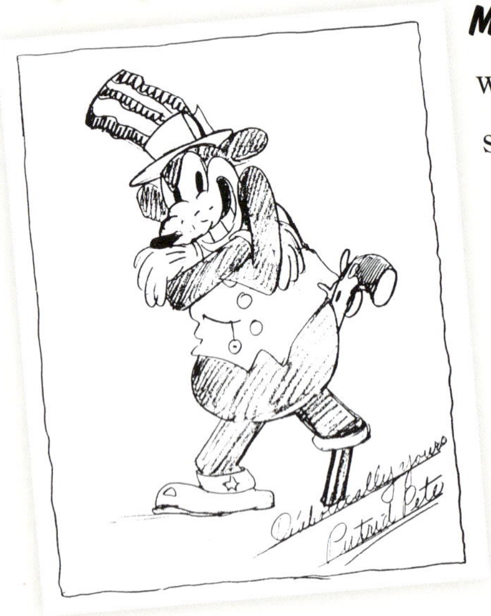

(ABOVE) PETE IN HIS BEARFACED PRE-MICKEY DESIGN. EARLY PUBLICITY DRAWING ATTRIBUTED TO UB IWERKS (1927).

MICKEY AND PETE ARE NOTORIOUS ENEMIES—and fans wouldn't have it any other way. No foe feels quite as right for a spunky, heroic mouse as a brutish, overbearing, criminal cat.

Or *is* he a cat?

The answer is...not always! Pete actually debuted years before Mickey, in Disney's silent film *Alice Solves the Puzzle* (1925)—and at the start, Pete was drawn as a big bad *bear*. It must have seemed natural: Pete's early good-guy foes were a human kid named Alice, a cartoon cat named Julius, and Oswald the Lucky Rabbit. A bear was naturally bigger than all three. But a cat? Well, Julius was *already* a cat.

Bear Pete went though various redesigns—fat, slim, peg-legged—before Mickey took his first bow. And then, in 1928, came the species change; for as we said, no foe is quite as suitable for a mouse as a cat. However, even post-Mickey, Pete's weight, prostheses, and scruffy chin size varied a little from film to film.

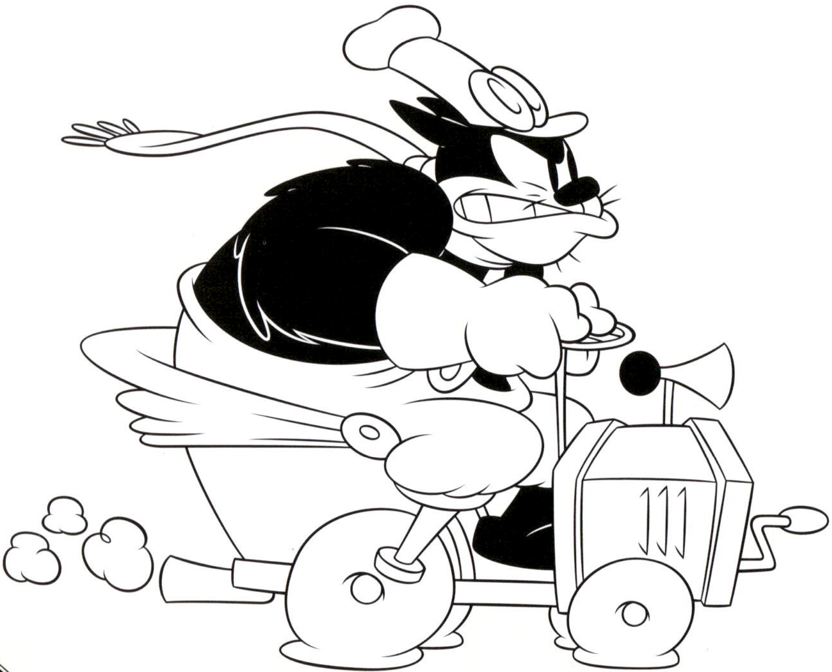

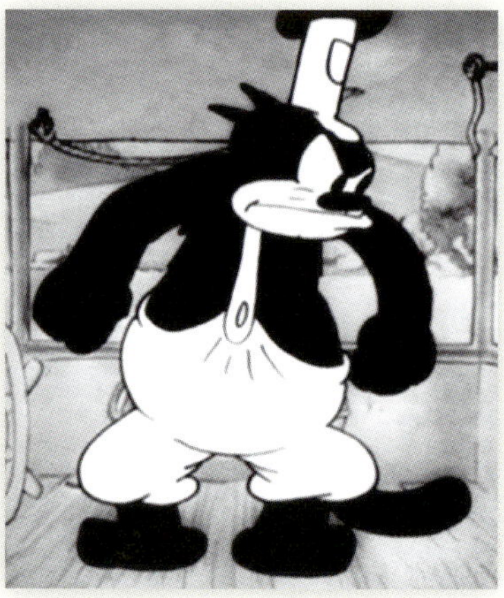

ANIMATION FROM STEAMBOAT WILLIE (1928).

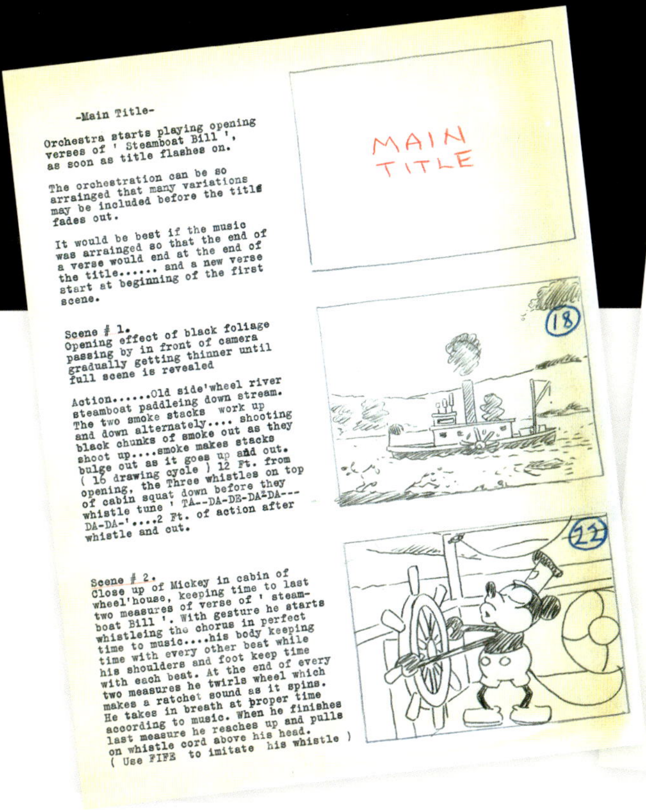

-Main Title-

Orchestra starts playing opening verses of ' Steamboat Bill ', as soon as title flashes on.

The orchestration can be so arrainged that many variations may be included before the title fades out.

It would be best if the music was arrainged so that the end of a verse would end at the end of the title...... and a new verse start at beginning of the first scene.

MAIN TITLE

Scene # 1.
Opening effect of black foliage passing by in front of camera gradually getting thinner until full scene is revealed

Action......Old side'wheel river steamboat paddleing down stream. The two smoke stacks work up and down alternately.... shooting black chunks of smoke out as they shoot up....smoke makes stacks bulge out as it goes up and out. (16 drawing cycle) 12 Ft. from opening, the Three whistles on top of cabin squat down before they whistle tune ' TA--DA-DE-DA-DA--- DA-DA-'....2 Ft. of action after whistle and out.

Scene # 2.
Close up of Mickey in cabin of wheel'house, keeping time to last two measures of verse of ' steamboat Bill '. With gesture he starts whistleing the chorus in perfect time to music....his body keeping time with every other beat while his shoulders and foot keep time with each beat. At the end of every two measures he twirls wheel which makes a ratchet sound as it spins. He takes in breath at proper time according to music. When he finishes last measure he reaches up and pulls on whistle cord above his head. (Use FIFE to imitate his whistle)

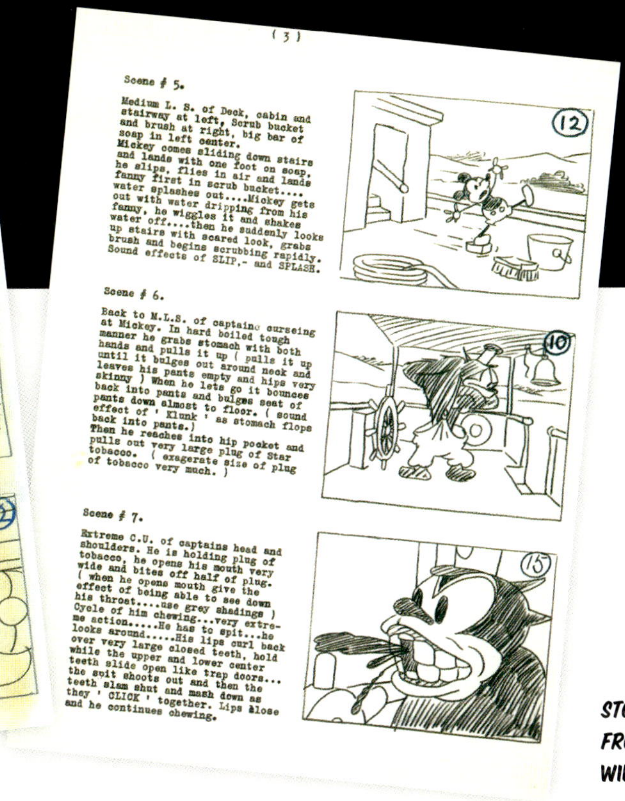

(3)

Scene # 5.

Medium L. S. of Deck, cabin and stairway at left, Scrub bucket and brush at right, big bar of soap in left center. Mickey comes sliding down stairs and lands with one foot on soap, he slips, flies in air and lands fanny first in scrub bucket.... water splashes out....Mickey gets out with water dripping from his fanny, he wiggles it and shakes water off....then he suddenly looks up stairs with scared look, grabs brush and begins scrubbing rapidly. Sound effects of SLIP,- and SPLASH.

Scene # 6.

Back to M.L.S. of captains curseing at Mickey. In hard boiled tough manner he grabs stomach with both hands and pulls it up (pulls it up until it bulges out around neck and leaves his pants empty and hips very skinny) When he lets go it bounces back into pants and bulges seat of pants down almost to floor. (sound effect of ' Klunk ' as stomach flops back into pants.) Then he reaches into hip pocket and pulls out very large plug of Star tobacco. (exagerate size of plug of tobacco very much.)

Scene # 7.

Extreme C.U. of captains head and shoulders. He is holding plug of tobacco, he opens his mouth very wide and bites off half of plug. (when he opens mouth give the effect of being able to see down his throat....use grey shadings) Cycle of him chewing...very extreme action.....He has to spit...he looks around.....His lips curl back over very large closed teeth, hold while the upper and lower center teeth slide open like trap doors... the spit shoots out and then the teeth slam shut and mash down as they ' CLICK ' together. Lips close and he continues chewing.

STORY SKETCHES FROM STEAMBOAT WILLIE.

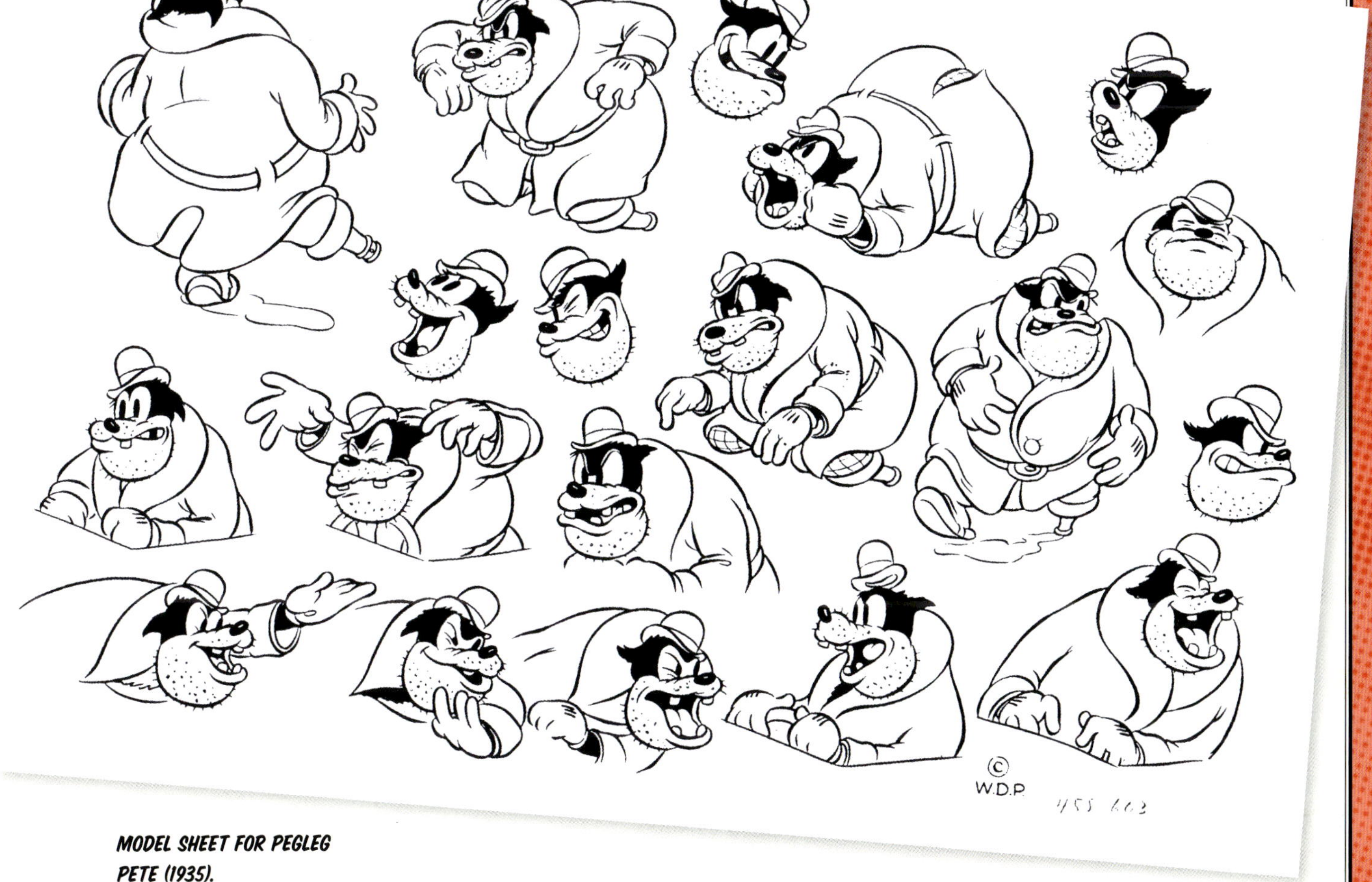

MODEL SHEET FOR PEGLEG PETE (1935).

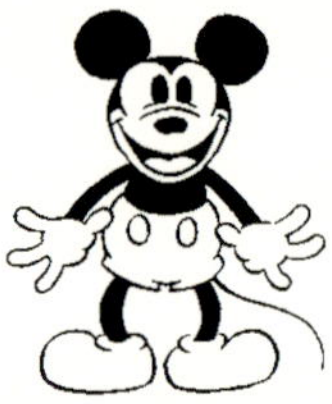

THE 1930s

ICONIC FRIENDS

The high life of America's Jazz Age ended in October 1929, when a legendary stock market crash sent the nation sliding into the Great Depression. Over the years of pain and unemployment that followed, cartoons and comics brought warmth to those with little other joy. One might call it Mickey's greatest good deed.

But animation wasn't fully an escape from the Depression; art always reflects its era, and hard times made for different cartoons. This meant unavoidable changes to Disney's leading lights. Minnie Mouse evolved rapidly from flapper to farm girl; Mickey, while always heroic, developed a knee-jerk humility and nervousness that made him funnier in stressful situations.

***OPPOSITE PAGE: 1933 PROMOTIONAL POSTER FOR* BUILDING A BUILDING**

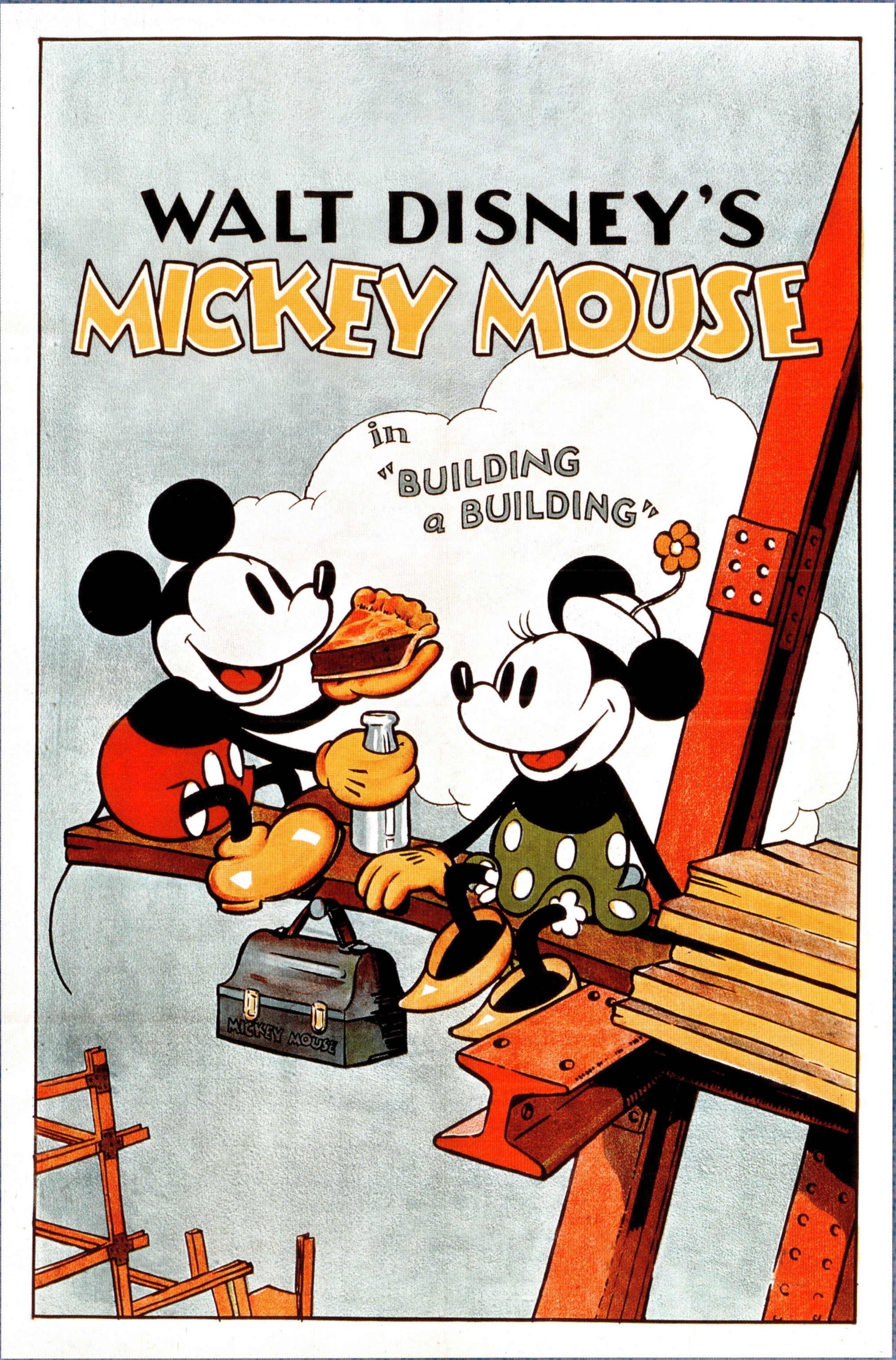
WALT DISNEY'S
MICKEY MOUSE
in "BUILDING a BUILDING"
MICKEY MOUSE

Soon animators were piling on the stress, trying to make this new Mickey crack. In 1932, artist Charles Philippi created Dippy Dawg, an endearing bumpkin costar who reliably caused chaos.[1] Originally clad in nothing but a hat and vest, Mickey's goofy new pal later adopted a goofier wardrobe, a goofier philosophy of life, and a goofier name—Goofy!

Other new costars caused additional chaos. Mickey's bloodhound, Pluto, whelped in 1930, was the first somewhat realistically designed animal in the cast. Animator Norm Ferguson developed myriad ways in which Pluto's behavior exaggerated real doggy doings, such as sniffing into trouble and fighting a carnival of neighborhood critters.

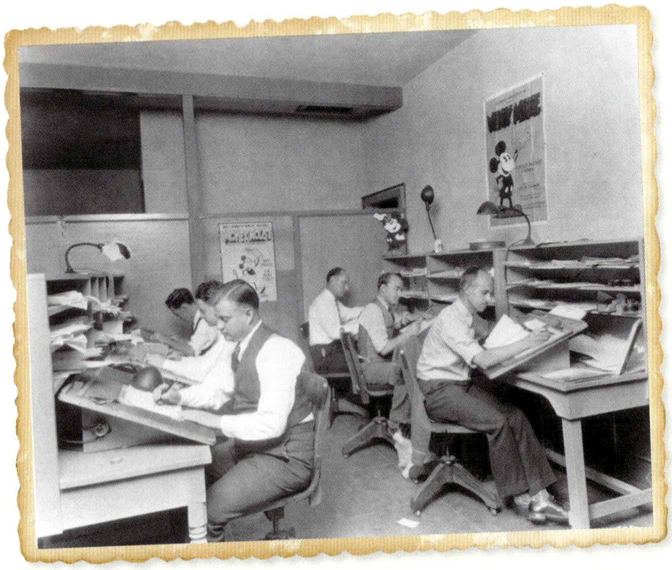

FROM FRONT LEFT: JACK KING, NORM FERGUSON & DICK LUNDY. FROM FRONT RIGHT: BEN SHARPSTEEN, MERLE GILSON & BERT GILLETT.

1930s ANIMATION TIMELINE

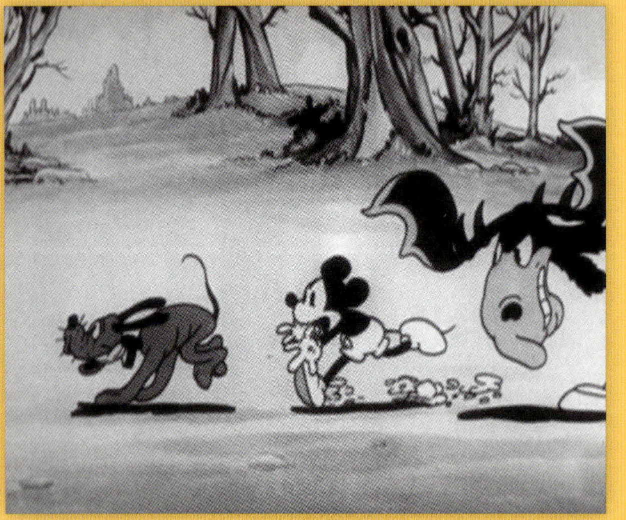

1930

THE MOOSE HUNT (FIRST APPEARANCE OF PLUTO BY THAT NAME, AND AS MICKEY'S DOG)

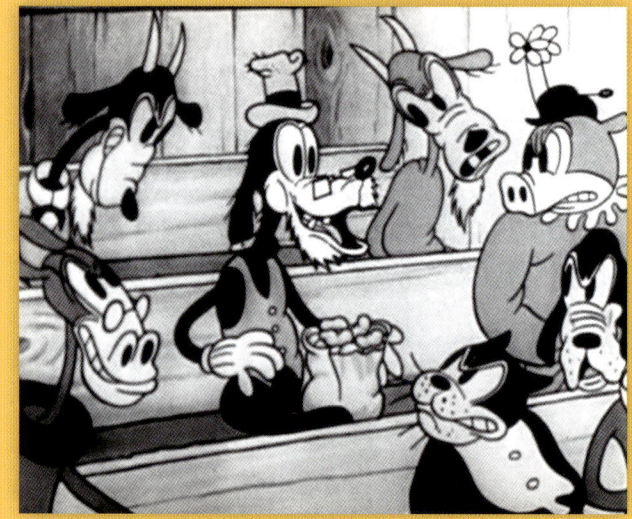

1932

MICKEY'S REVUE (FIRST APPEARANCE OF GOOFY, THEN CALLED DIPPY DAWG)

But the craziest critter of all emerged from Disney's one-shot series, Silly Symphonies. As hatched in *The Wise Little Hen* (1934), Donald Duck started out as the fairy-tale loafer who refused to help Mrs. Hen plant corn. But Donald swiftly acquired further bad habits—an eager ego and a titanic temper—and became an ideal opposite number for the stressed-out Mickey. "Donald Duck is just as vital and animate in my imagination as…Tom Sawyer," said writer Dana Burnet in *Pictorial Review*.[2]

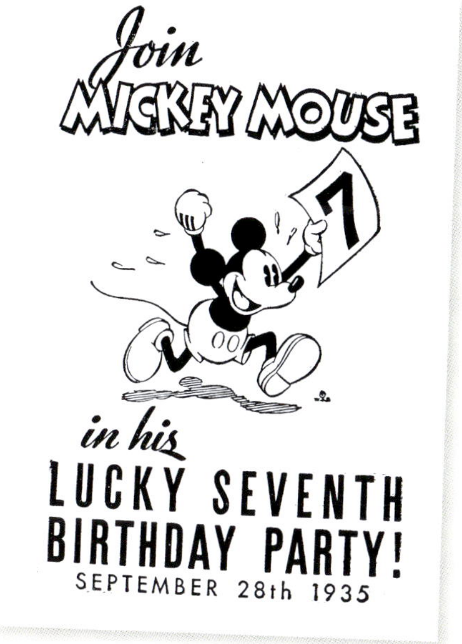

In the late 1930s, Mickey's propensity for stress resulted in an arguably misguided rethinking of his persona. While increasingly cast as the grown-up leader of his gang, Mickey now behaved less as an adult, and more as a shy "young

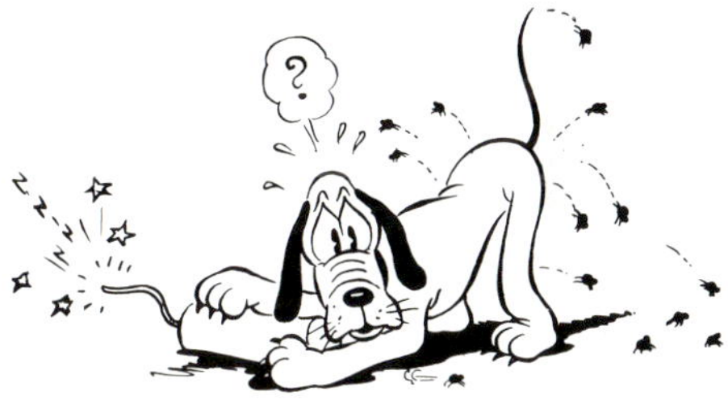

1931 PUBLICITY DRAWING FOR THE DELIVERY BOY. (DON'T WORRY... NO CARTOON CHARACTERS WERE HARMED WHEN THE GIANT FIRECRACKER WENT OFF.)

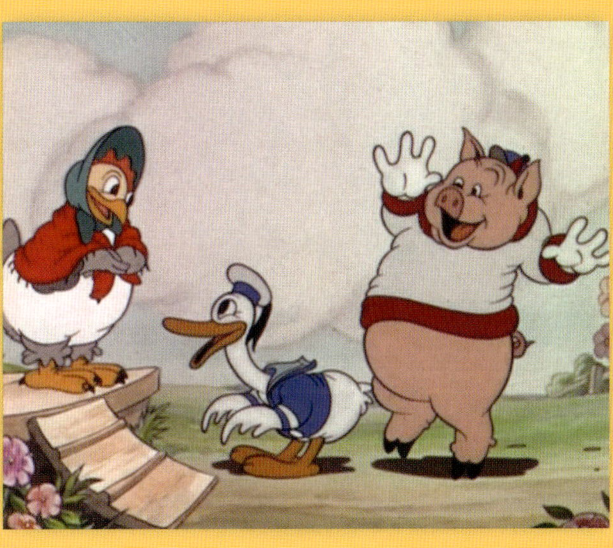

1934

SILLY SYMPHONIES THE WISE LITTLE HEN (DONALD DUCK'S FIRST APPEARANCE)

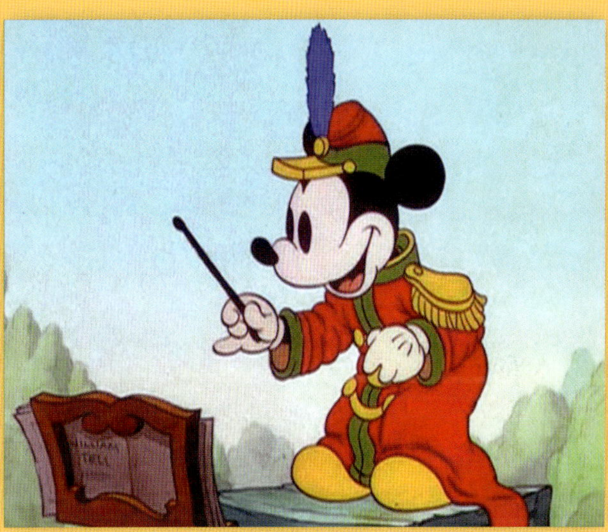

1935

THE BAND CONCERT (FIRST COLOR MICKEY MOUSE ANIMATION)

boy," overwhelmed by all and sundry.[3] While such a Mouse could still be funny, his passivity allowed dynamic Donald, Goofy, and Pluto to steal the show. The trend lasted in cartoons for years—even as in the comics, Mickey stayed an adventure star. This is why Mickey's print fans tend to know him as a fighter—while animation aficionados see him as a shrinking violet!

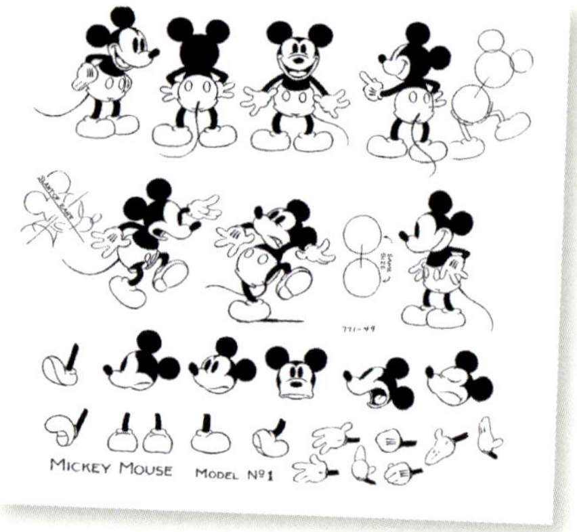

1931 MICKEY MOUSE ANIMATION MODEL SHEET.

The changes to Mickey's personality also affected his look. The 1930s drawing models on pages 30-35 reflect the influence of animator Fred Moore, whose pear-shaped, more realistically structured Mickey reflected his more domesticated persona. Minnie, too, stopped showing off and started baking cakes!

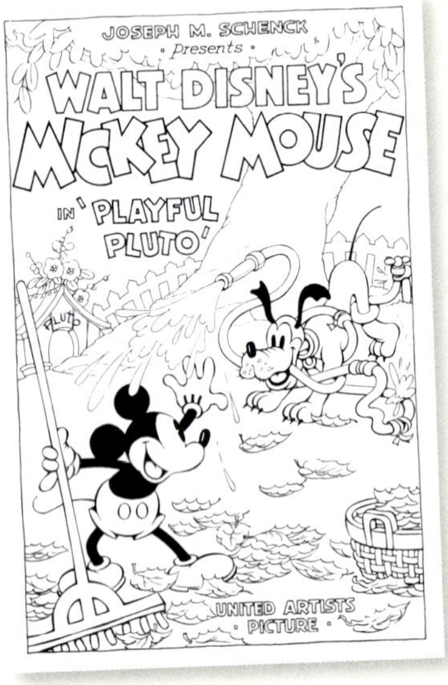

PROMOTIONAL POSTER FROM PLAYFUL PLUTO. ART BY TOM WOOD.

1930s ANIMATION TIMELINE

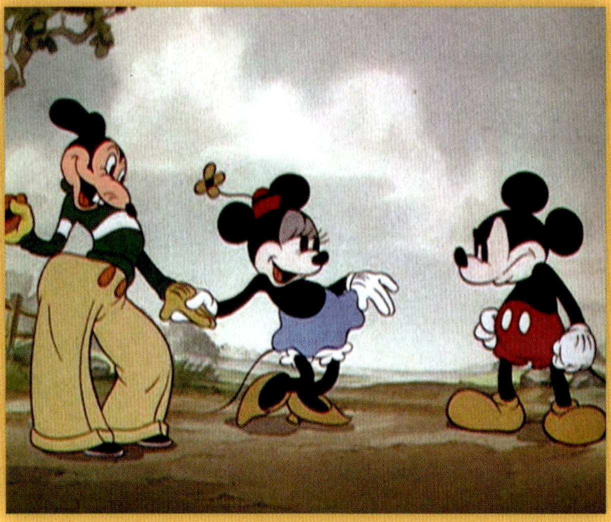

1936

MICKEY'S RIVAL
(FIRST APPEARANCE OF MORTIMER MOUSE)

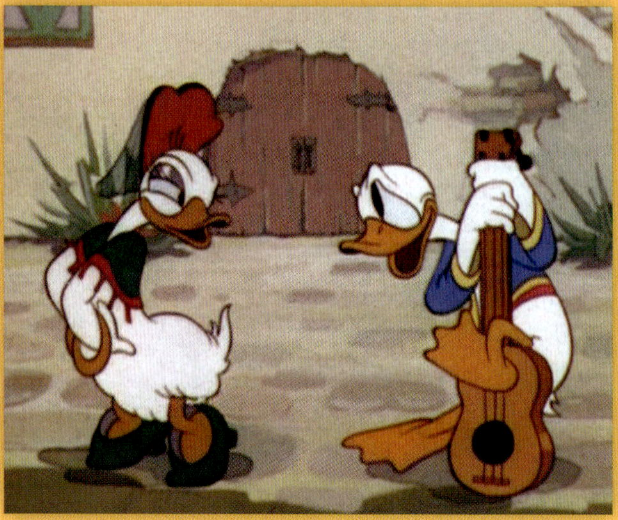

1937

DON DONALD
(FIRST APPEARANCE OF DONNA DUCK, LATER KNOWN AS DAISY DUCK)

But maybe domesticity was just par for the course, given the restrictive nature of Depression home life. Before the 1930s were out, even Donald became less an active pest to Mickey and more a homebody himself, bedeviled by other pests. His nephews Huey, Dewey, and Louie, created by comic strip team Ted Osborne and Al Taliaferro, made the jump to animation…and jumped all over "Unca Donald," too.

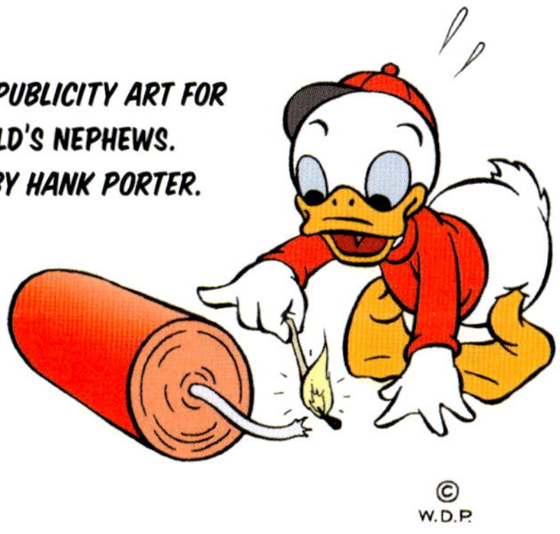

1938 PUBLICITY ART FOR DONALD'S NEPHEWS. ART BY HANK PORTER.

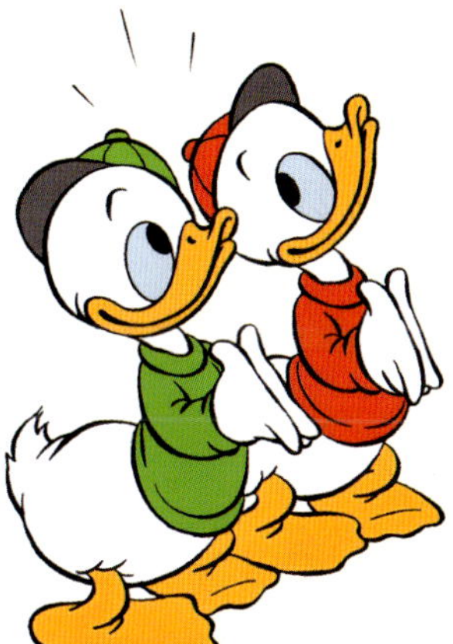

The drawing models on pages 48-51 of these three dirty little ducks come from *Donald's Nephews* (1938), their film debut. They're almost more wildly behaved than they would ever be again—can you hold them down long enough to draw them?

[1]On Philippi's creation of the character: Floyd Gottfredson to David R. Smith, *Mickey Mouse in Color*, Deluxe Edition (Prescott: Another Rainbow, 1988), 167.

[2]Dana Burnet, "The Rise of Donald Duck." *Pictorial Review* (October 1935).

[3]Ted Sears, "Mickey Mouse." Character Analysis (1935), 1.

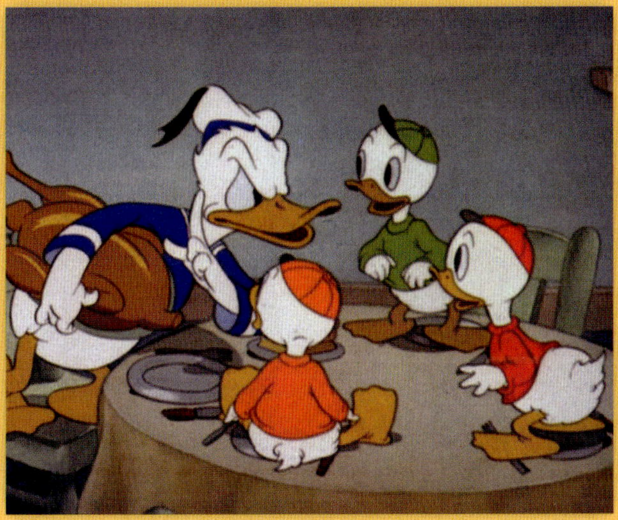

1938

DONALD'S NEPHEWS
(FIRST ANIMATED APPEARANCE OF HUEY, DEWEY, AND LOUIE)

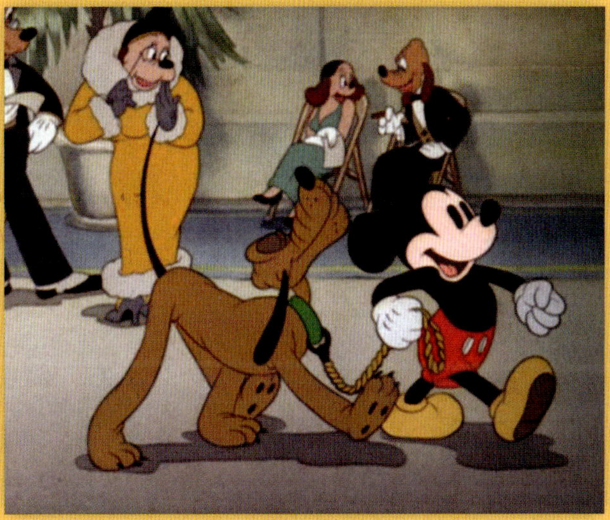

1939

SOCIETY DOG SHOW
(LAST APPEARANCE OF MICKEY WITH BUTTON EYES)

1930s

MICKEY MOUSE

HEAD POSE

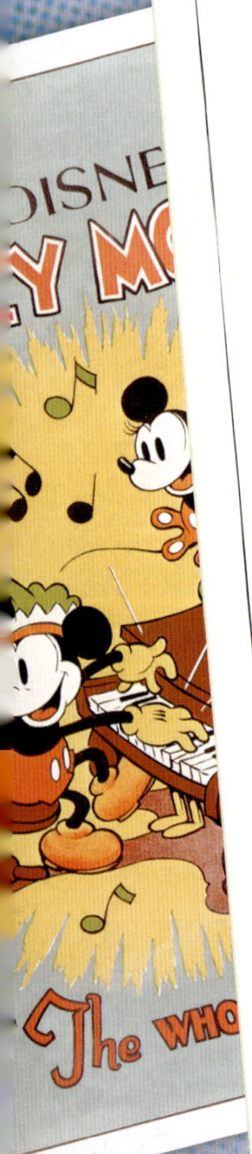

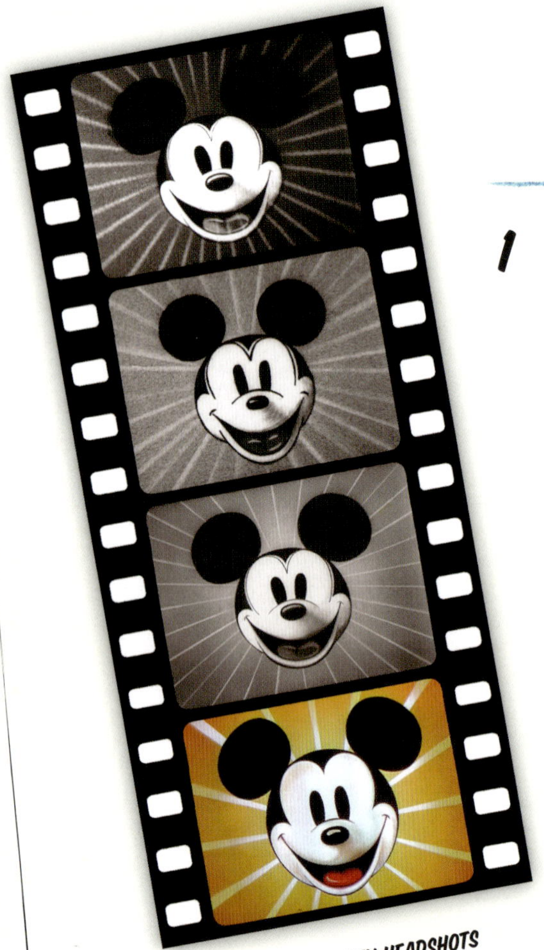

CHRONOLOGICAL MICKEY HEADSHOTS FROM EARLY CARTOON OPENINGS (1932, 1933 [TWO], 1935). THIS DRAWING MODEL IS A SLIGHTLY MODIFIED 1937 DESIGN.

1

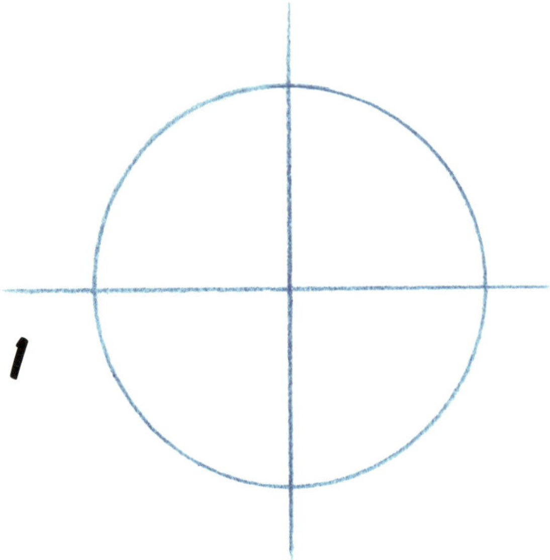

2

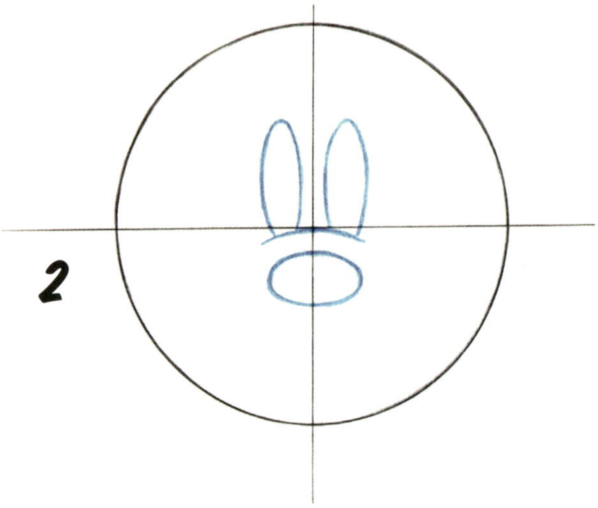

3

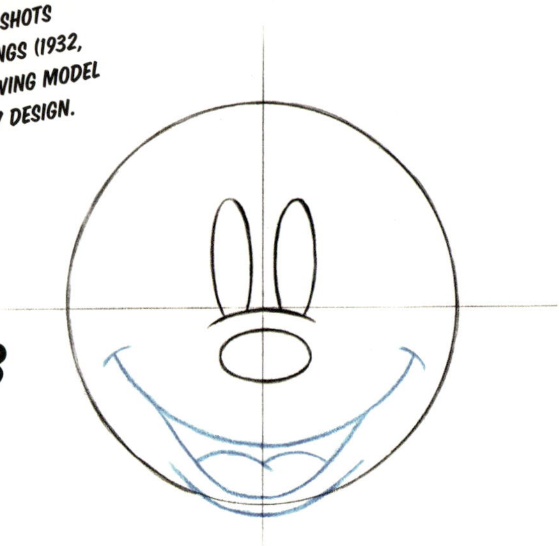

4

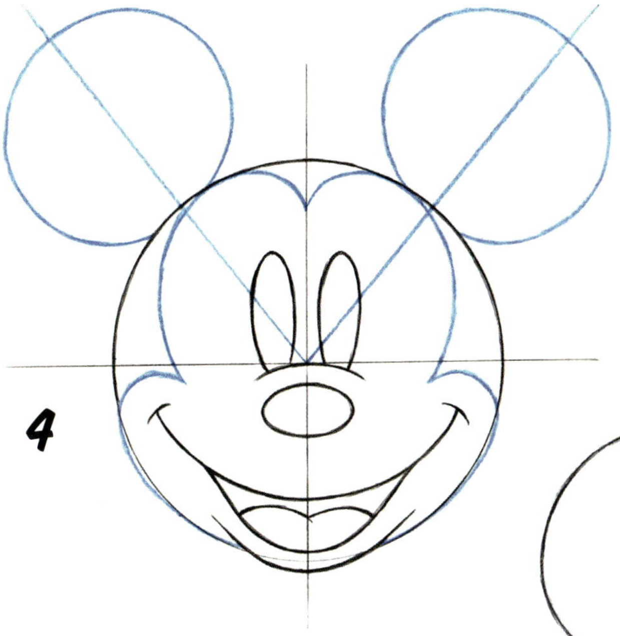

5

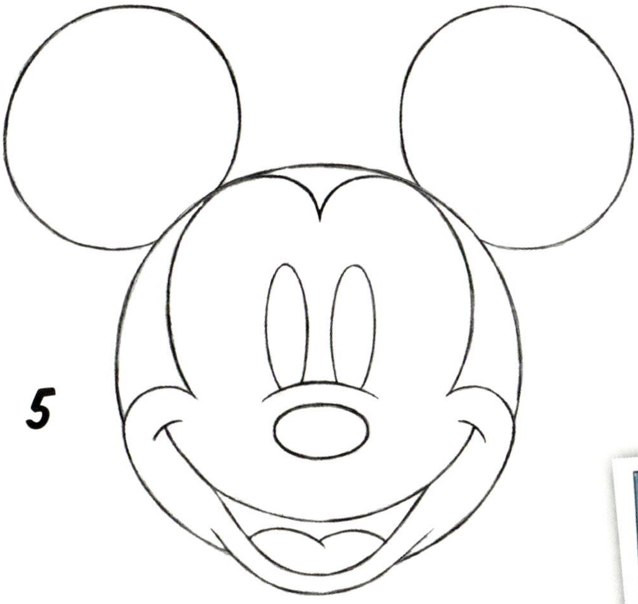

6

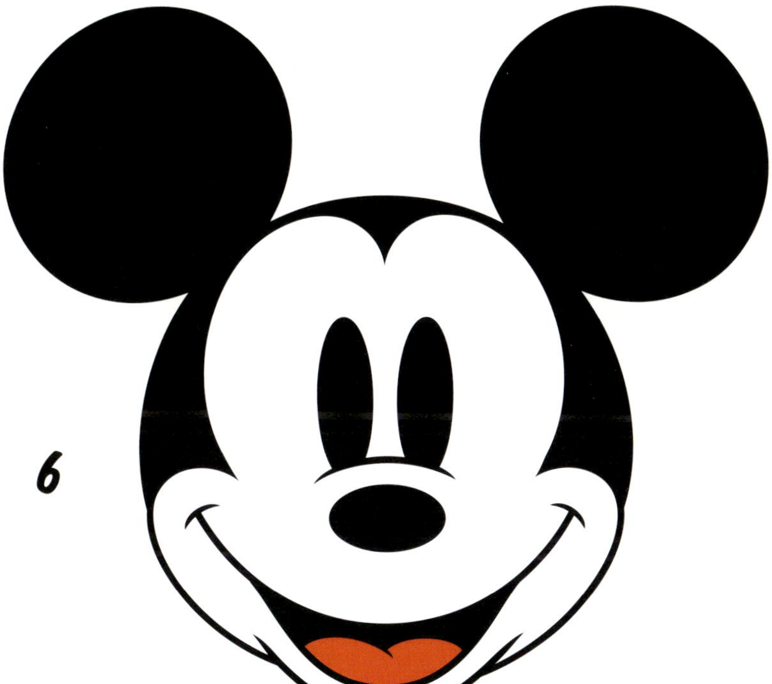

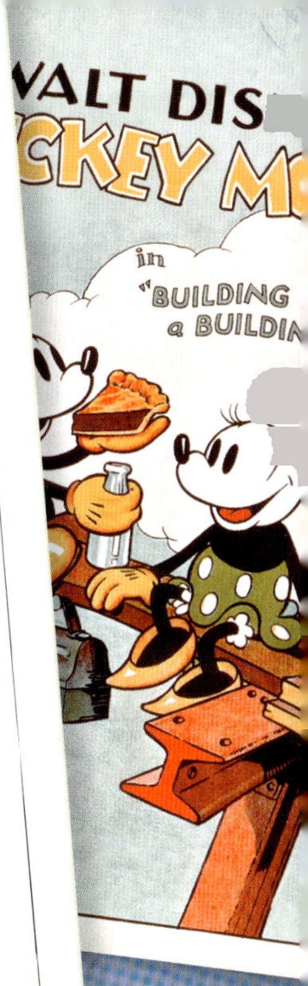

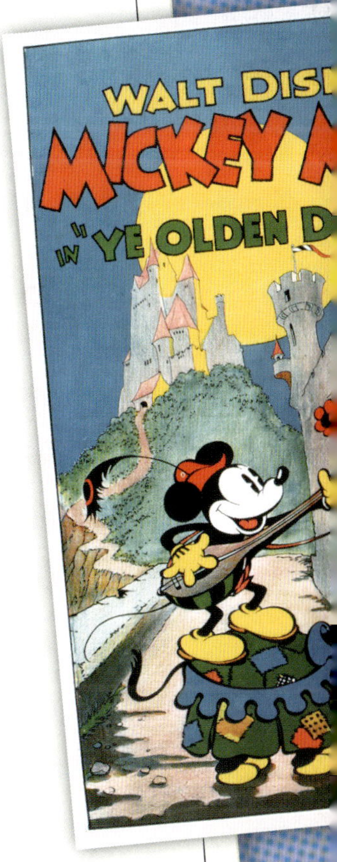

1930s

MICKEY MOUSE

BODY POSE / PUPPY LOVE

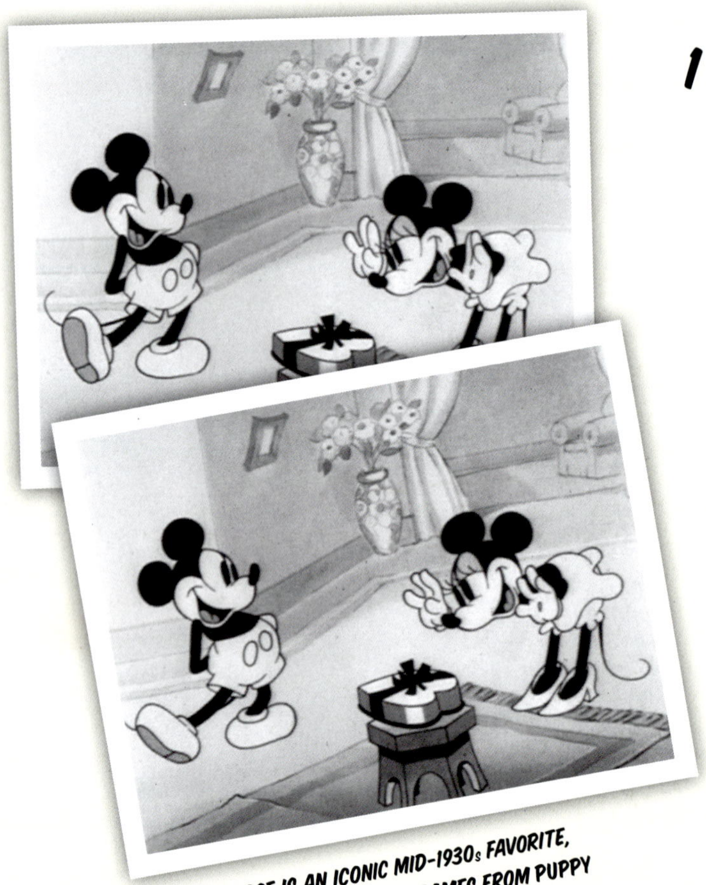

THIS BODY POSE IS AN ICONIC MID-1930s FAVORITE, COMBINING ELEMENTS OF TWO FRAMES FROM PUPPY LOVE (1933). ANIMATION BY FRED MOORE.

1

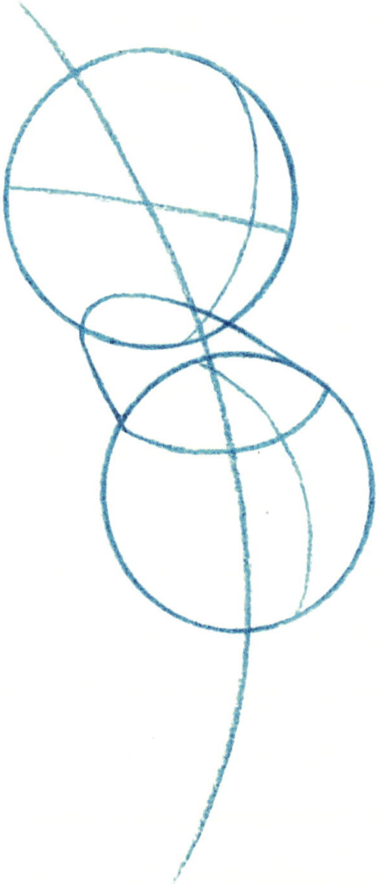

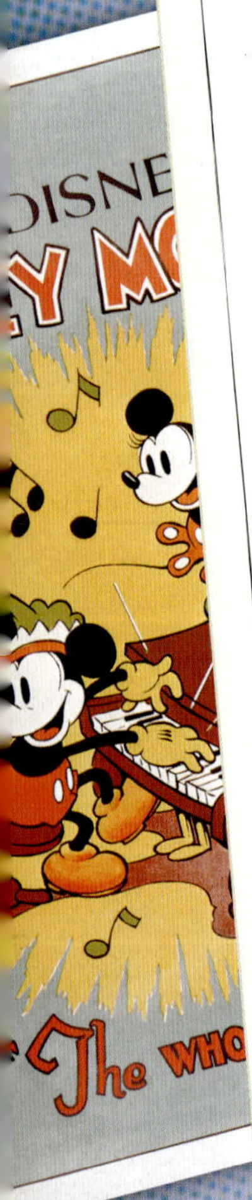

PERSONALITY PLUS

"MICKEY'S A NICE FELLOW WHO NEVER DOES ANYBODY ANY HARM, WHO GETS IN SCRAPES THROUGH NO FAULT OF HIS OWN, BUT ALWAYS MANAGES TO COME UP GRINNING." —WALT DISNEY

2

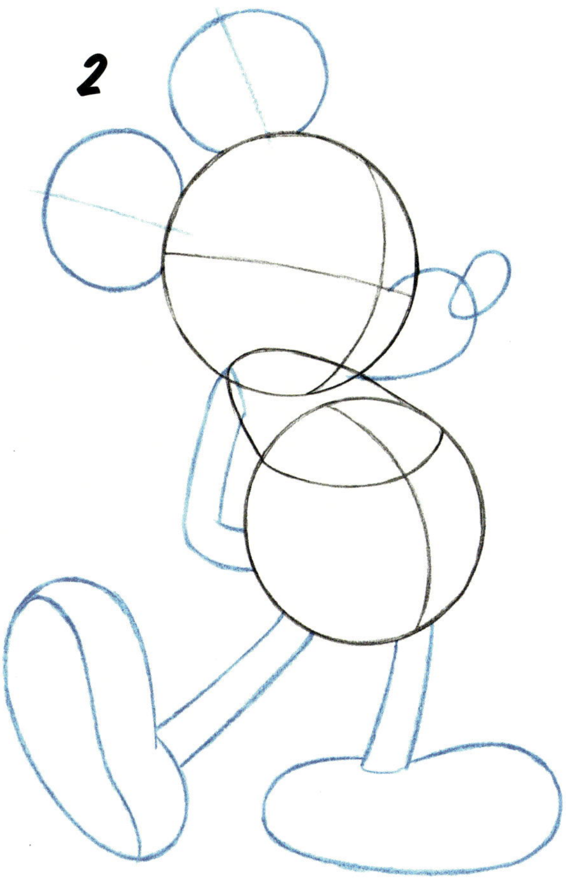

3

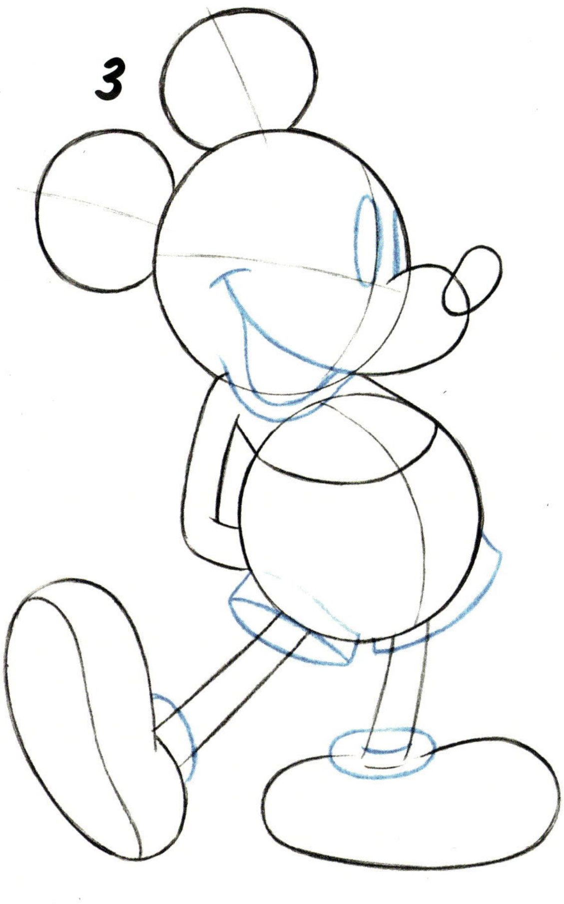

MICKEY'S POSES

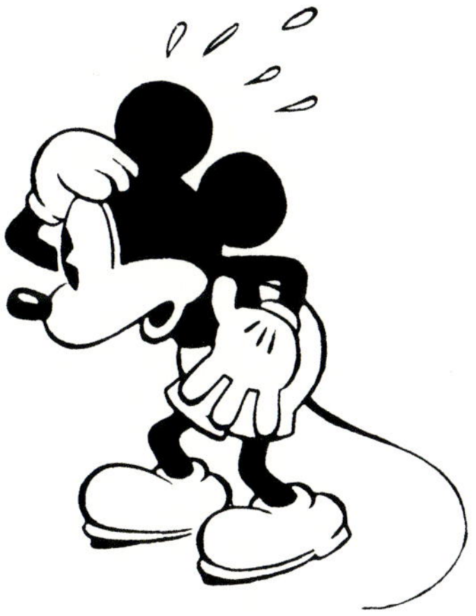

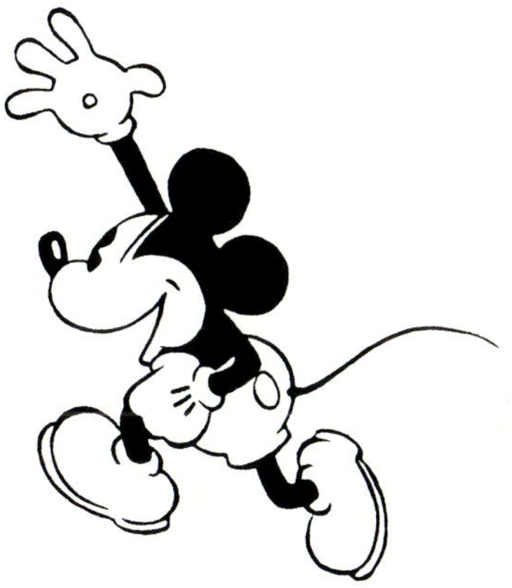

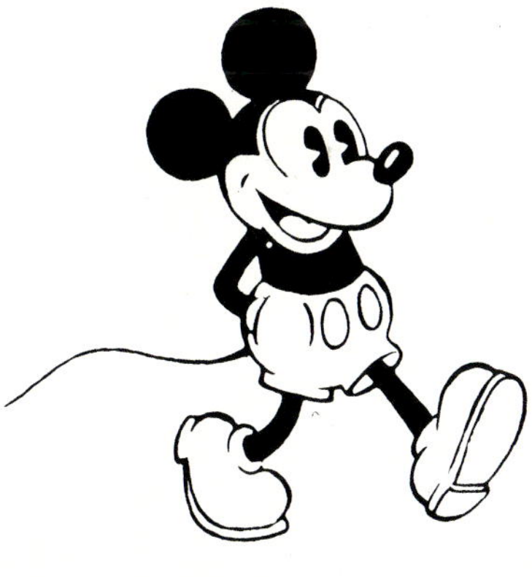

THE SMALL, "PIE-EYE" STYLE OF THE MICKEY AND MINNIE POSES ON THIS PAGE AND PAGES 35, 39, AND 41 WERE DRAWN FOR 1931 MARKETING MODEL SHEETS BY COMIC ARTISTS FLOYD GOTTFREDSON AND AL TALIAFERRO.

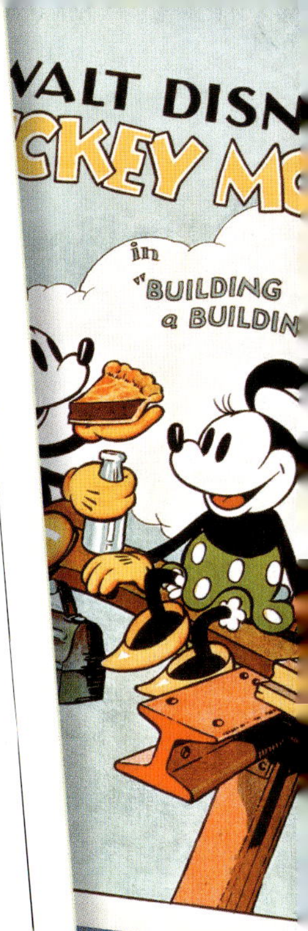

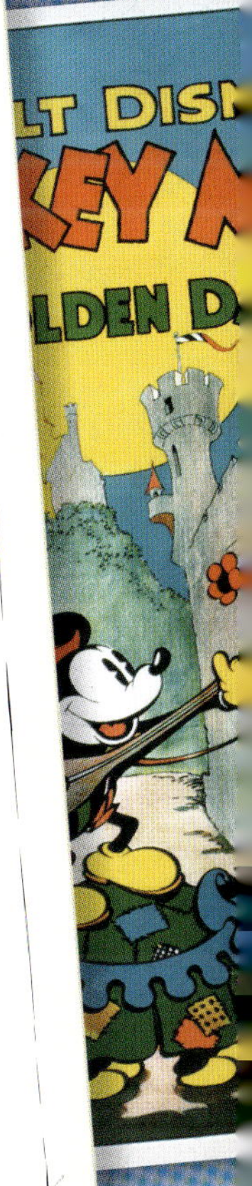

4

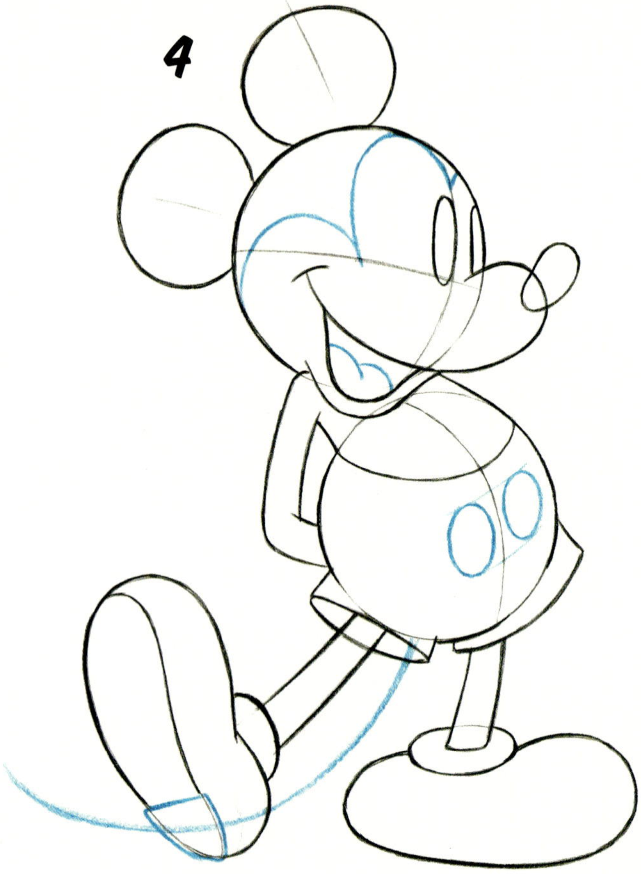

MICKEY'S 1930s DESIGN WAS MARKED BY SOLID, "BUTTON"-SHAPED EYES, A SAME-SIZED HEAD AND BODY, AND TUBULAR ARMS AND LEGS.

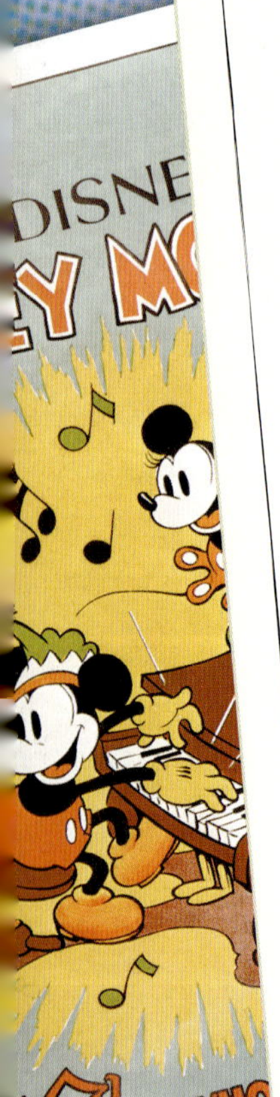

5

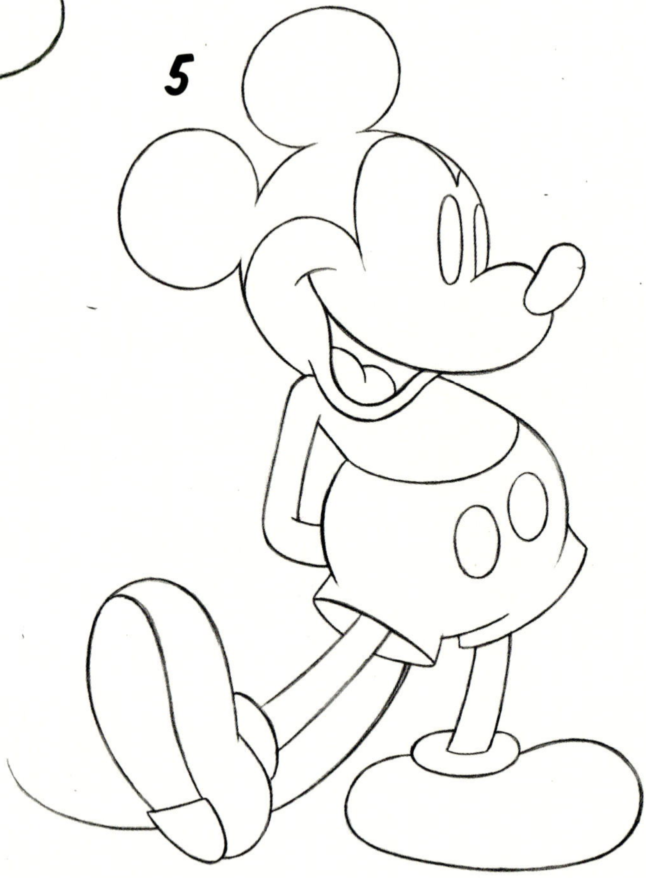

6

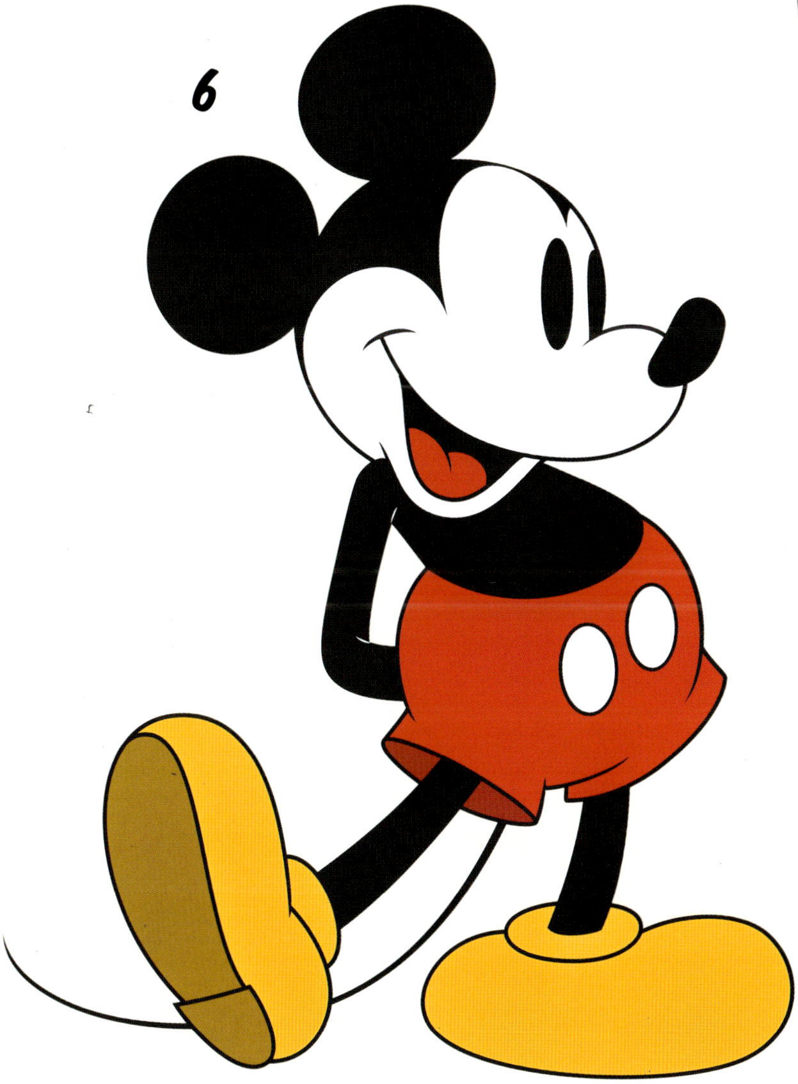

MICKEY'S POSES

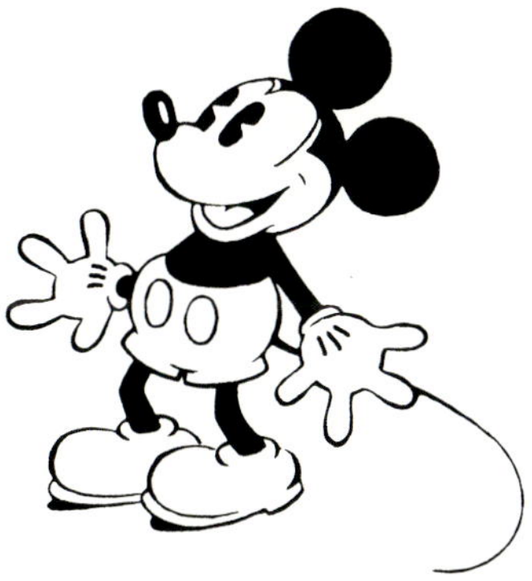

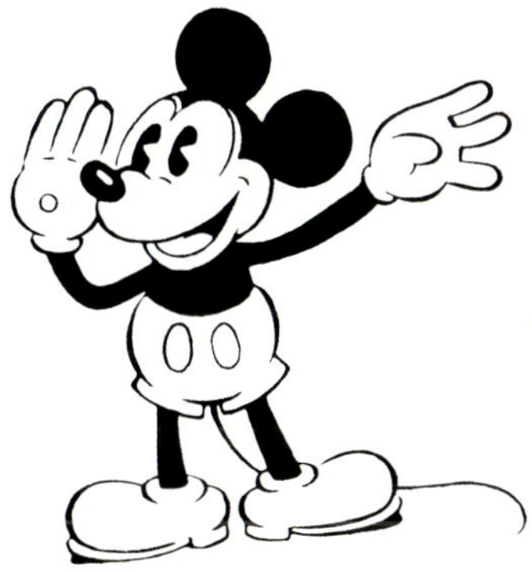

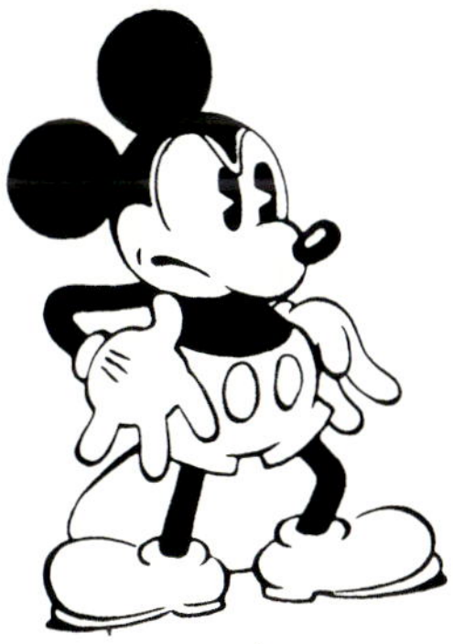

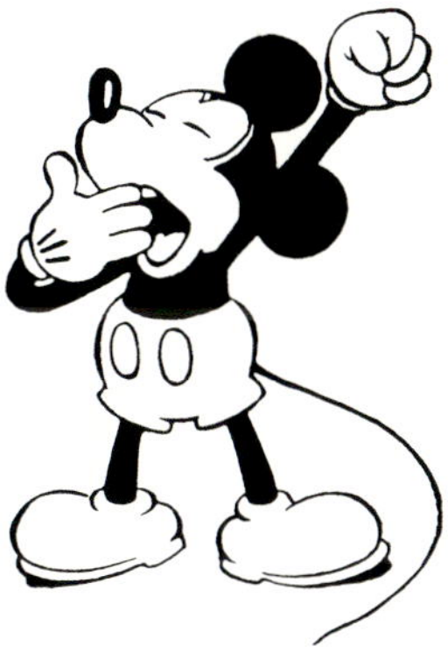

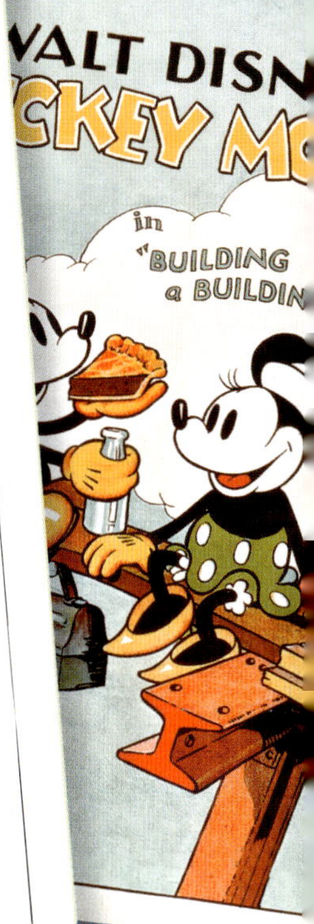

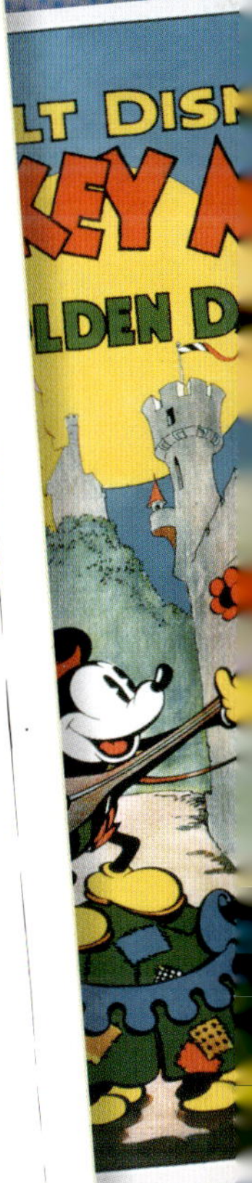

1930s

MINNIE MOUSE

HEAD POSE

1
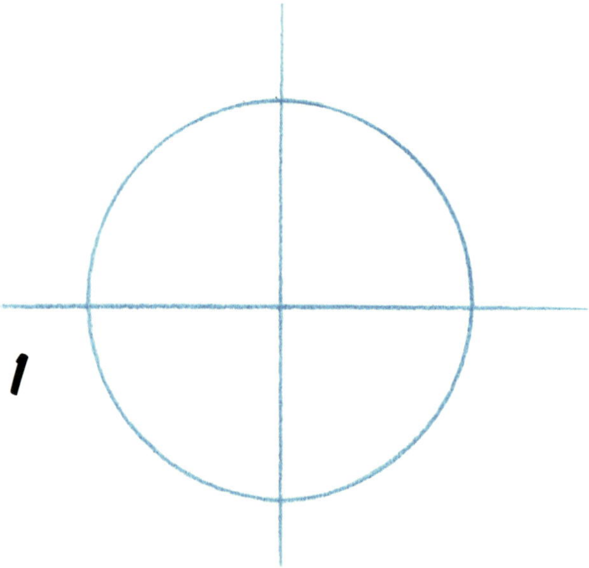

2
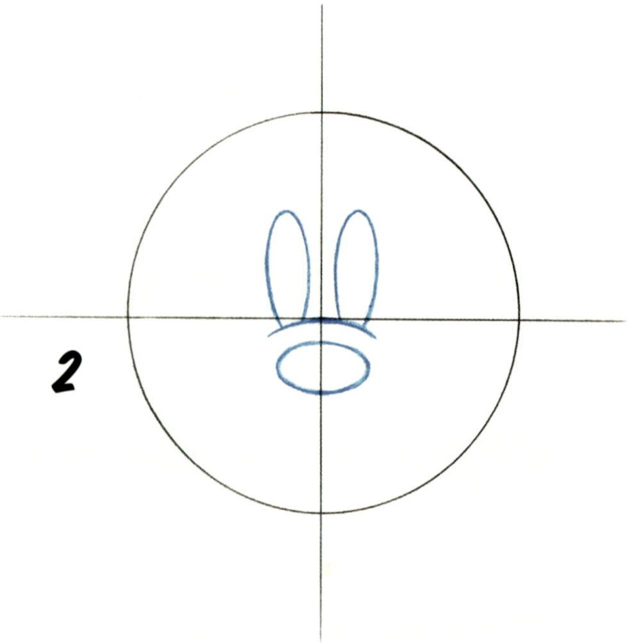

3
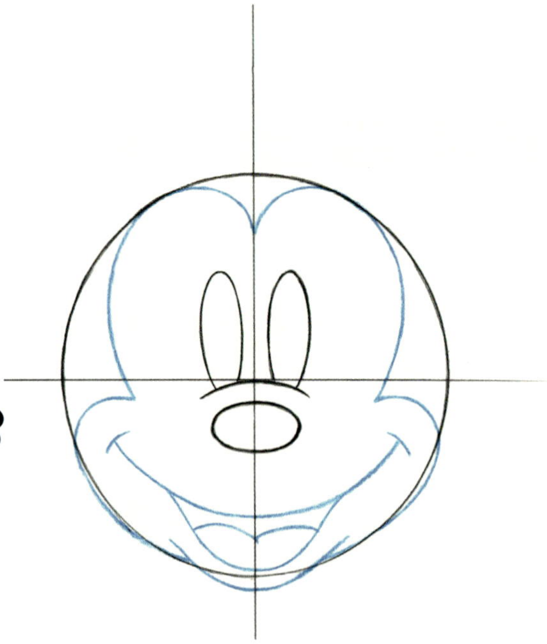

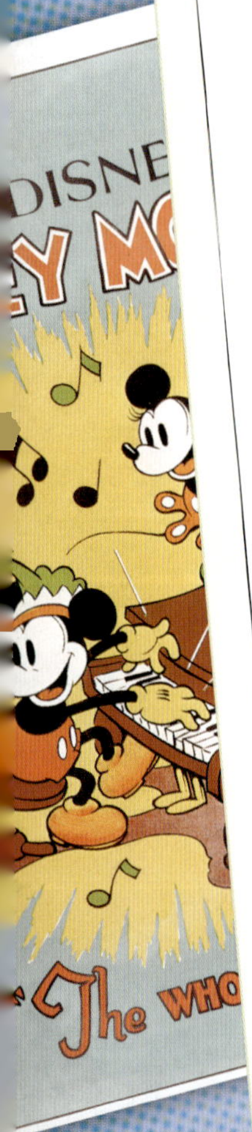

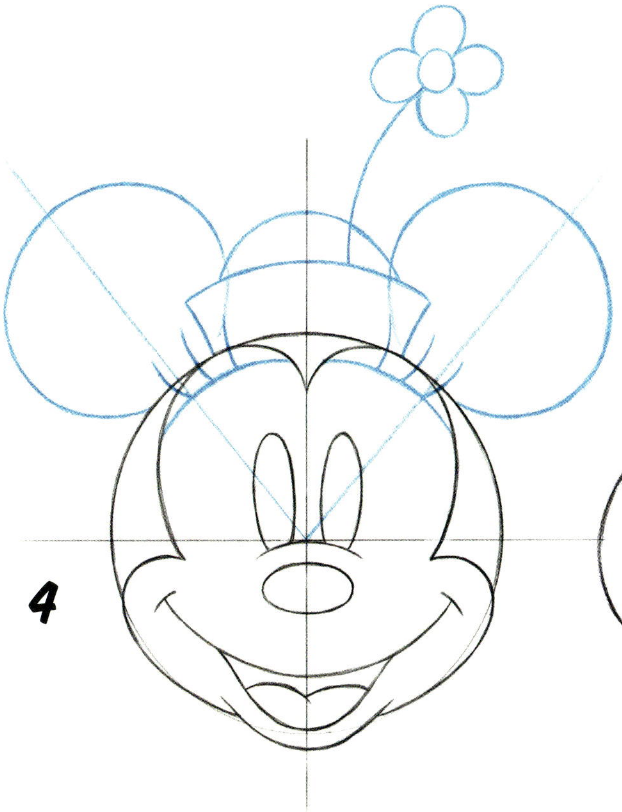

4

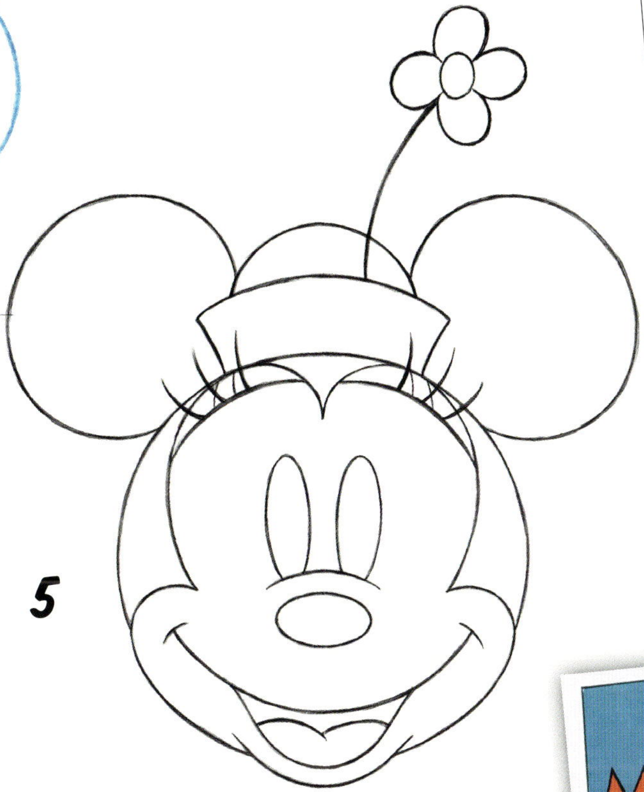

5

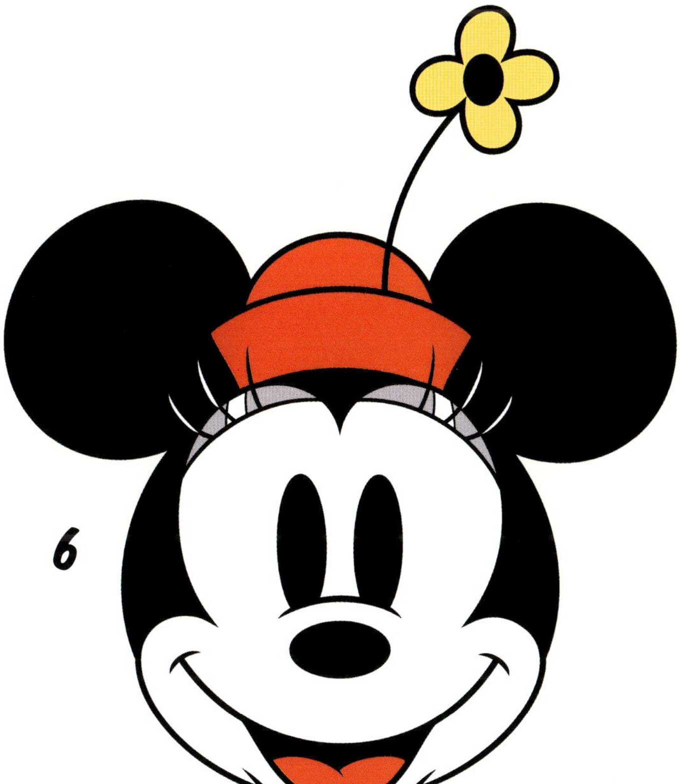

6

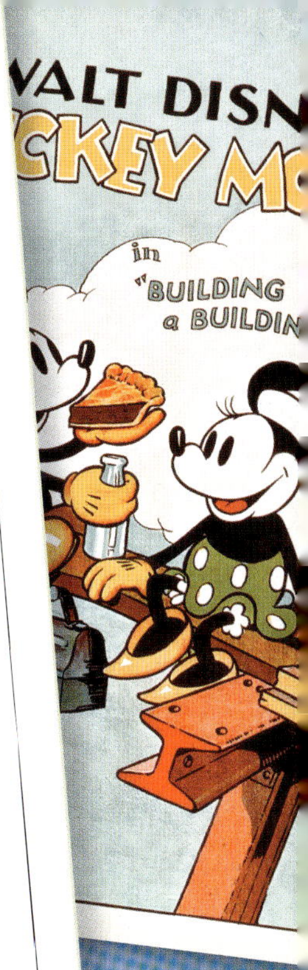
WALT DISN
CKEY MO
in
"BUILDING
a BUILDIN

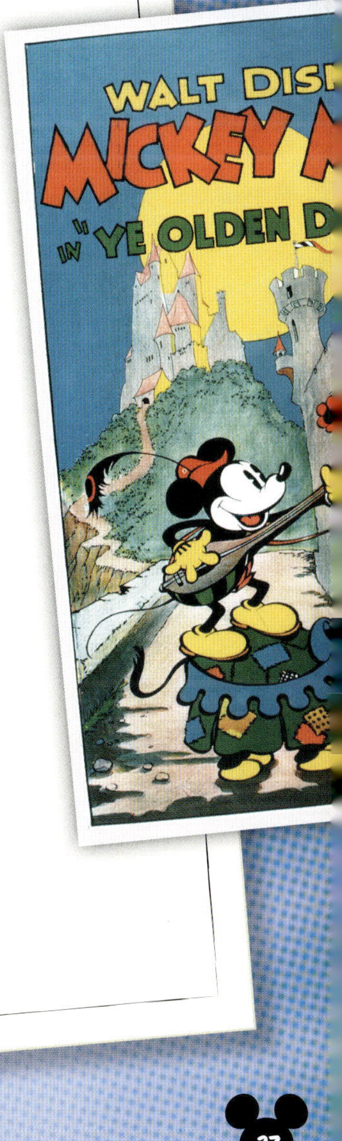
WALT DISN
MICKEY M
IN "YE OLDEN D

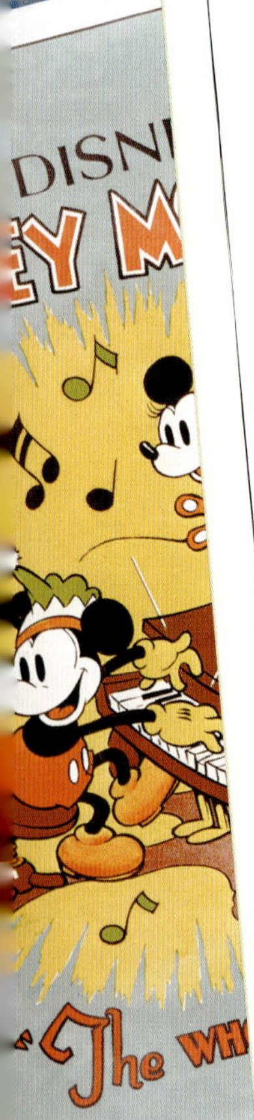

1930s

MINNIE MOUSE

BODY POSE / MICKEY'S RIVAL

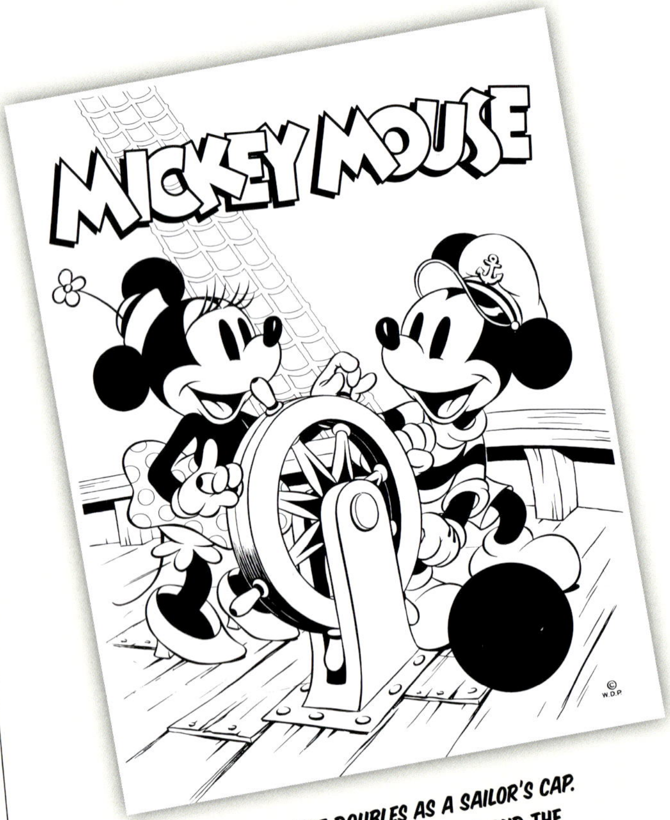

MINNIE'S PILLBOX HAT DOUBLES AS A SAILOR'S CAP. COVER TO THE STORY OF MICKEY MOUSE AND THE SMUGGLERS, 1938.

1

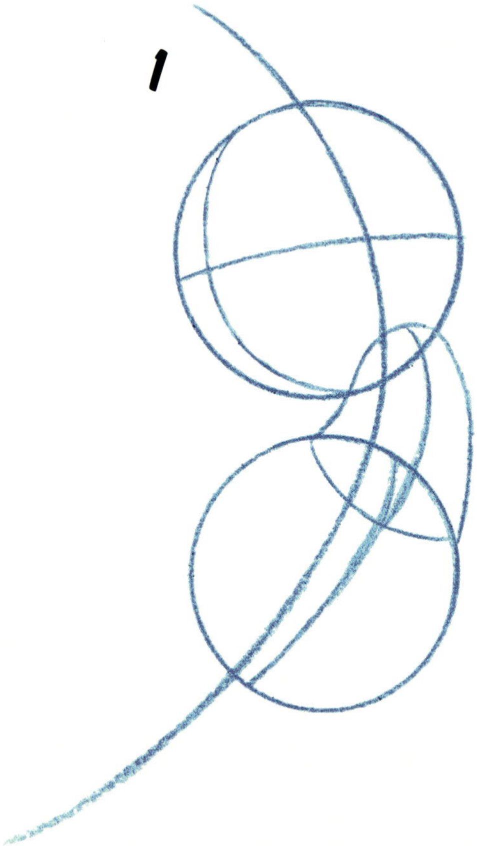

PERSONALITY PLUS

"AS [MICKEY] ENTERS [MINNIE'S HOME], SHE EXPANDS; SHE BECOMES SIMPLE, TENDER, BRAVE AND STRONG, AND HER COQUETTERIE IS OF THE DELIGHTFUL TYPE–WHICH NEVER CONCEALS ITS OBJECT. AH, THAT SQUEAK OF GREETING!"–E.M. FORSTER, 1934

2

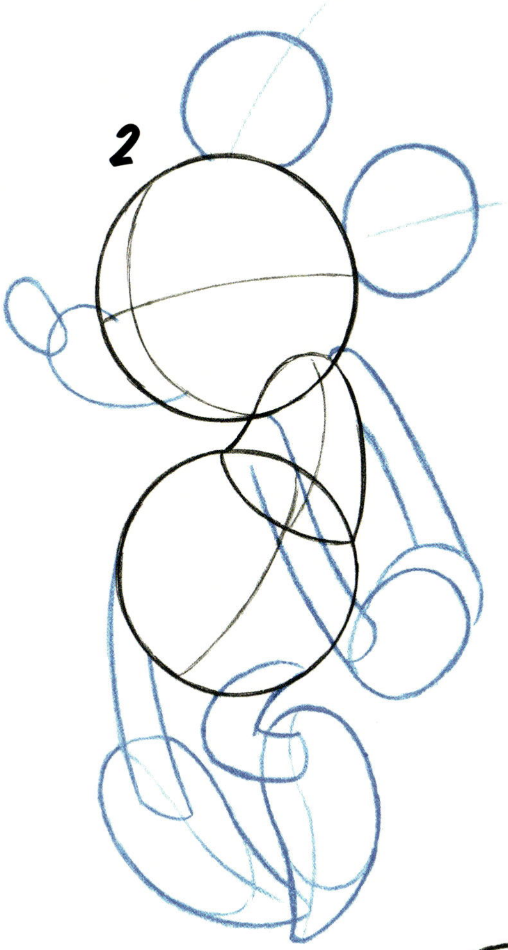

3

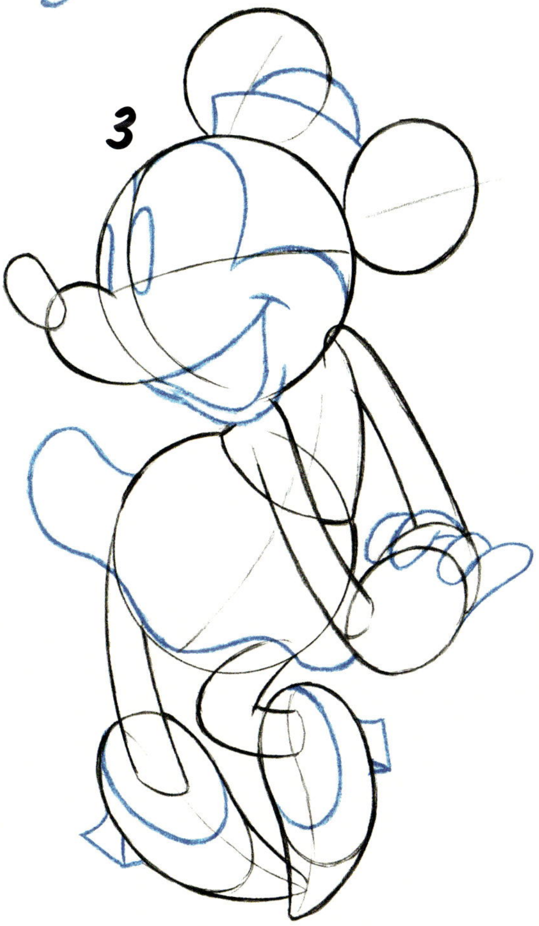

MINNIE'S POSES

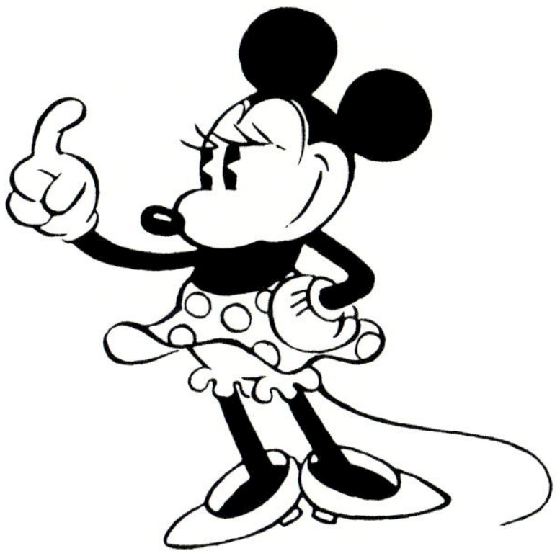

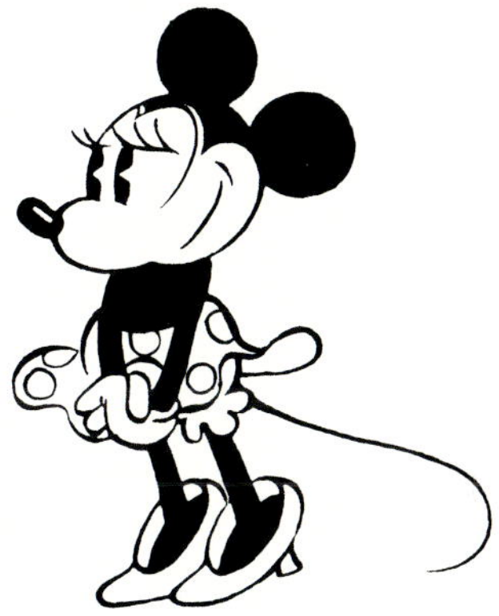

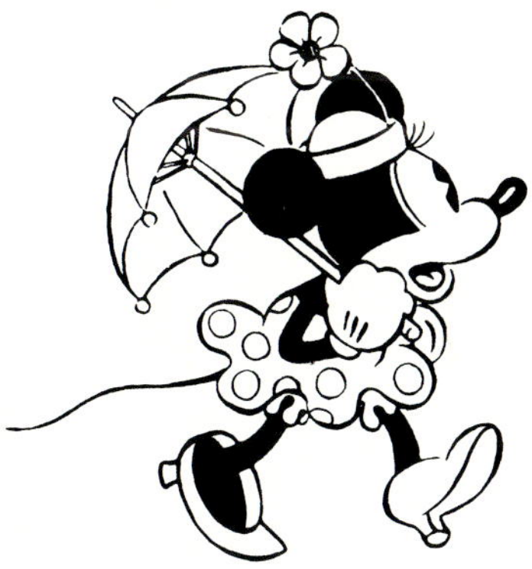

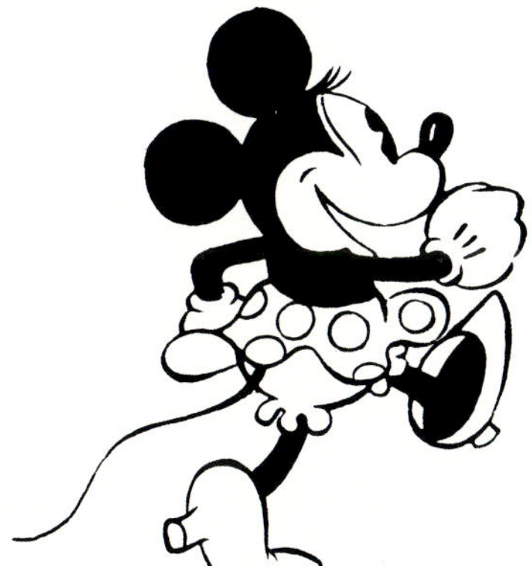

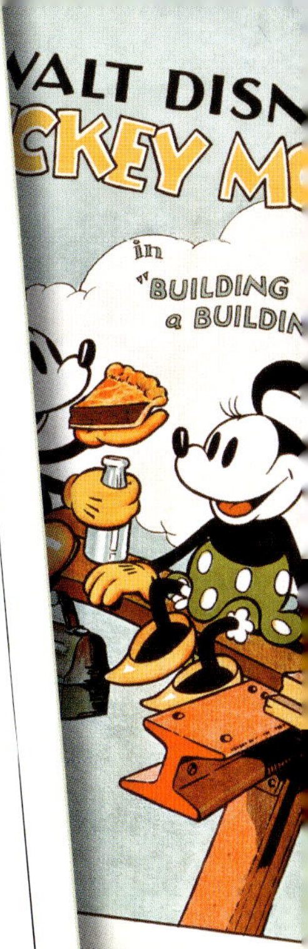

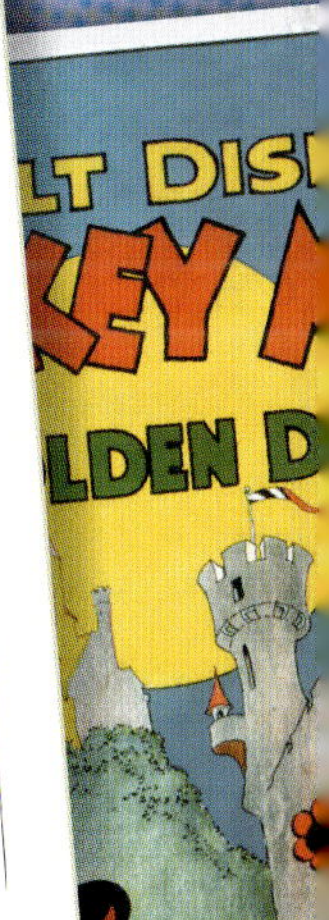

4

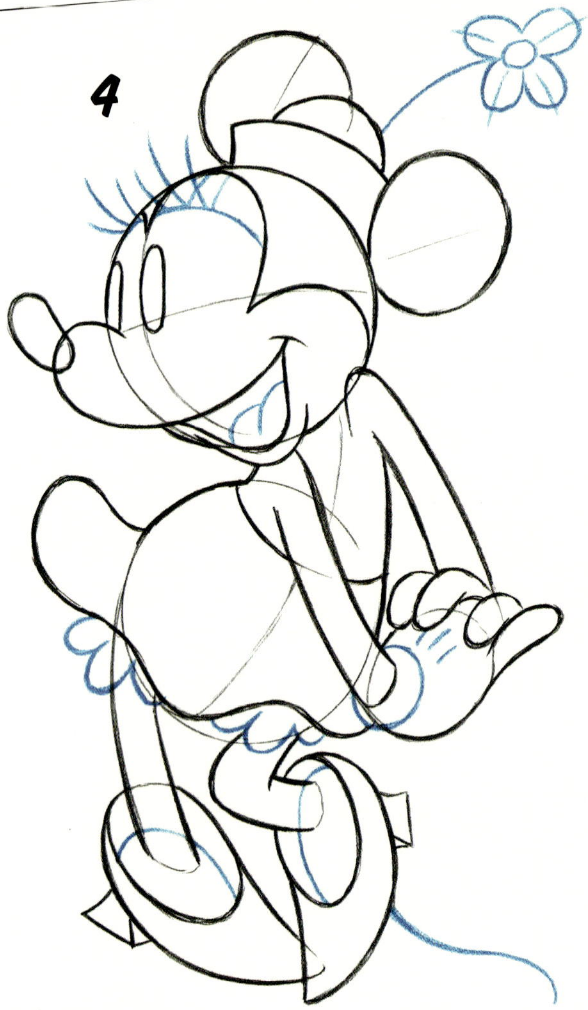

5

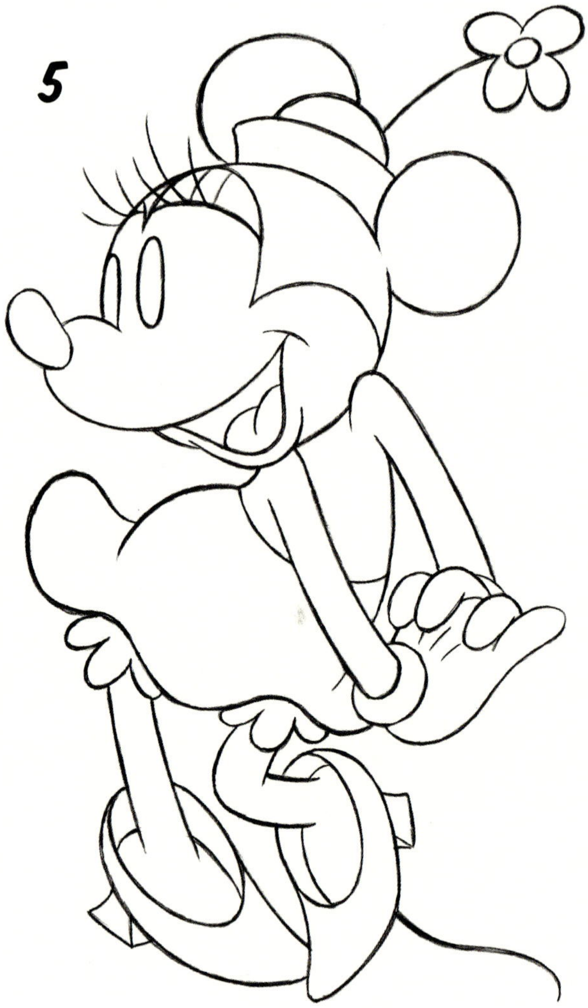

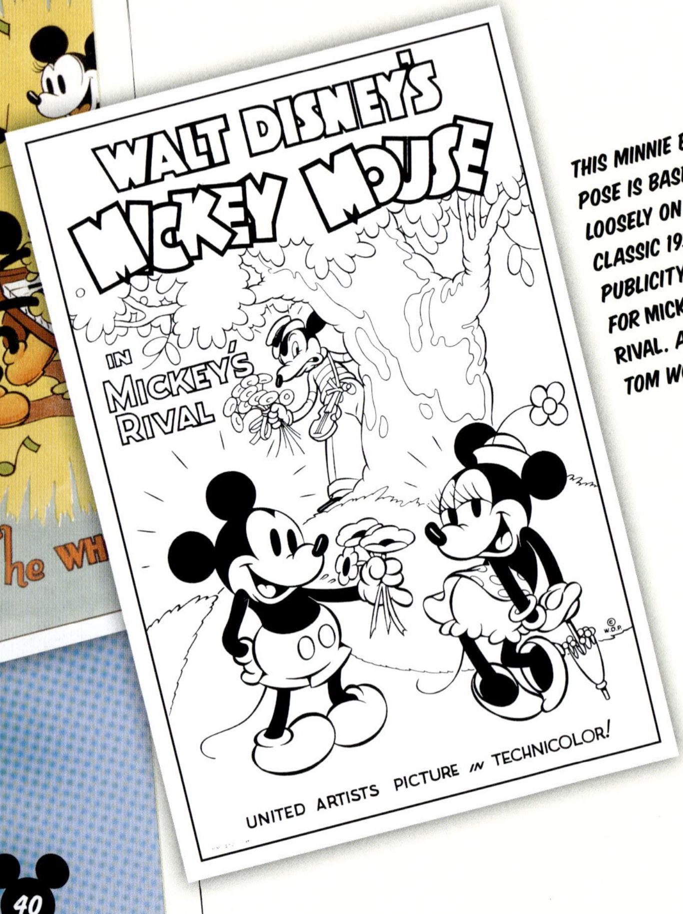

THIS MINNIE BODY POSE IS BASED LOOSELY ON THIS CLASSIC 1936 PUBLICITY POSTER FOR MICKEY'S RIVAL. ART BY TOM WOOD.

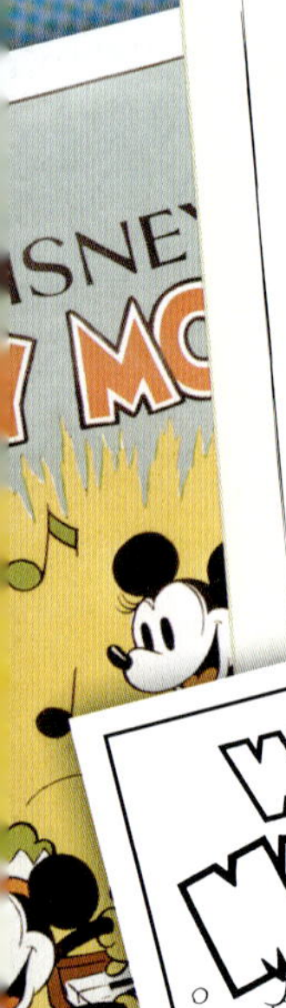

6

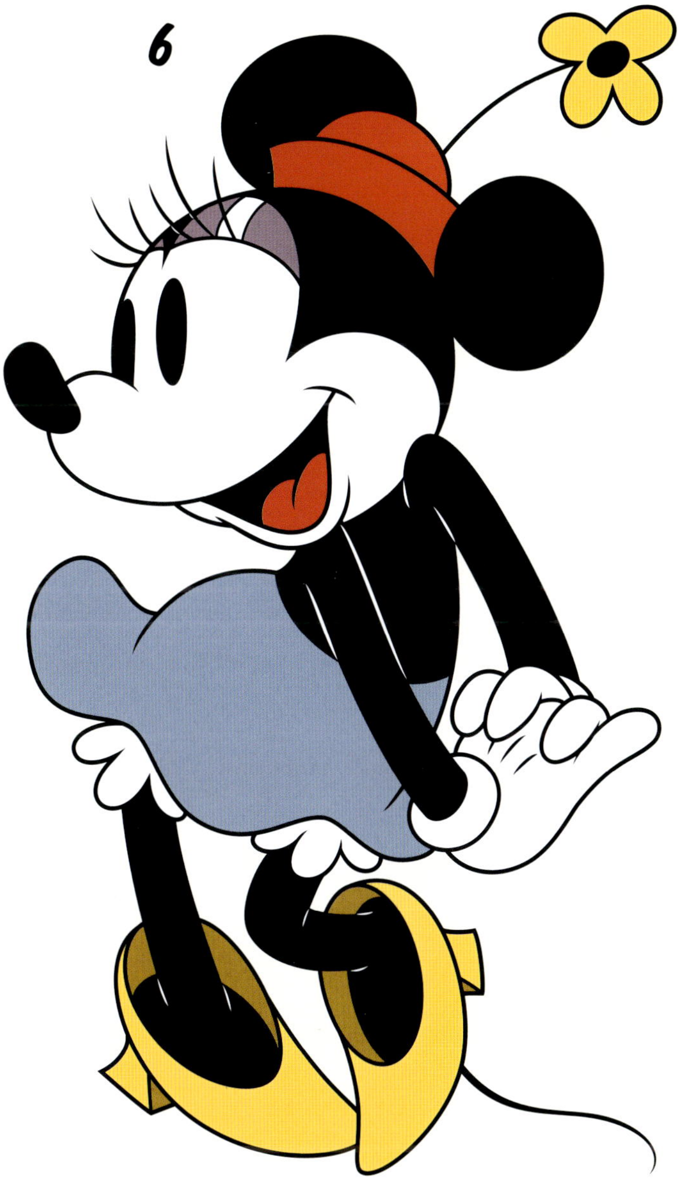

MINNIE'S POSES

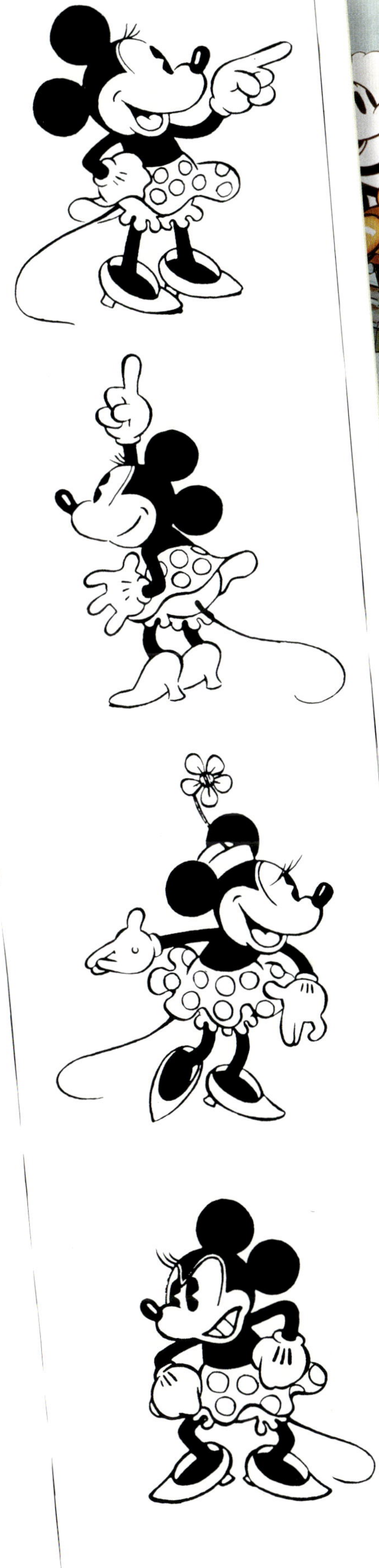

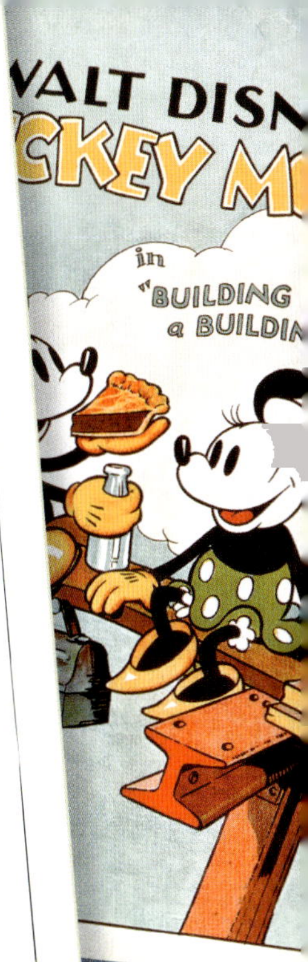

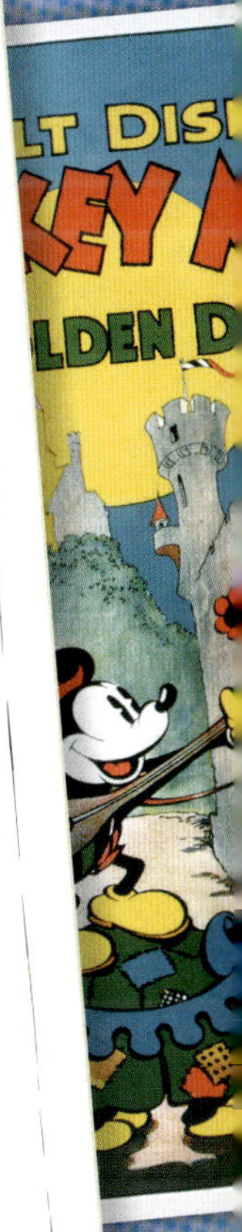

1930s

DONALD DUCK

EARLY APPEARANCE

1

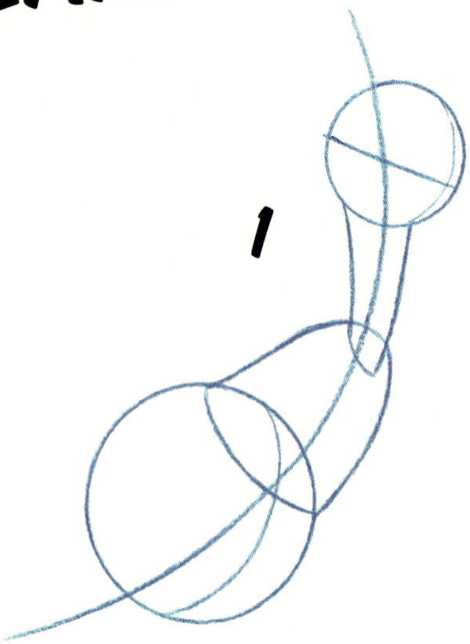

2

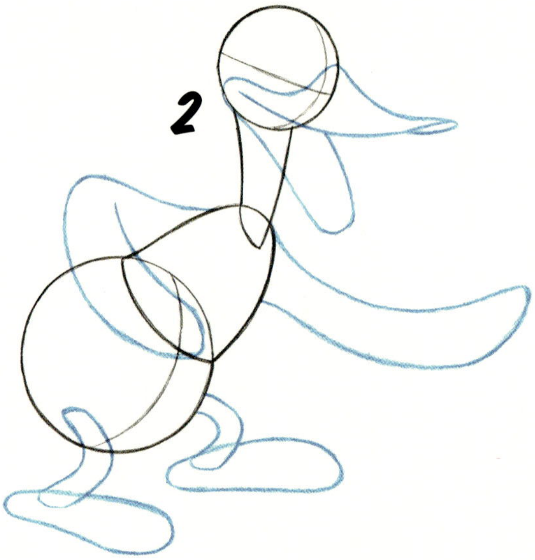

3

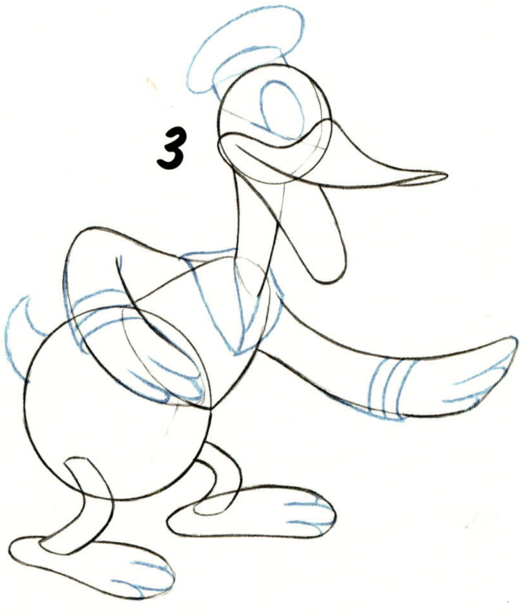

4

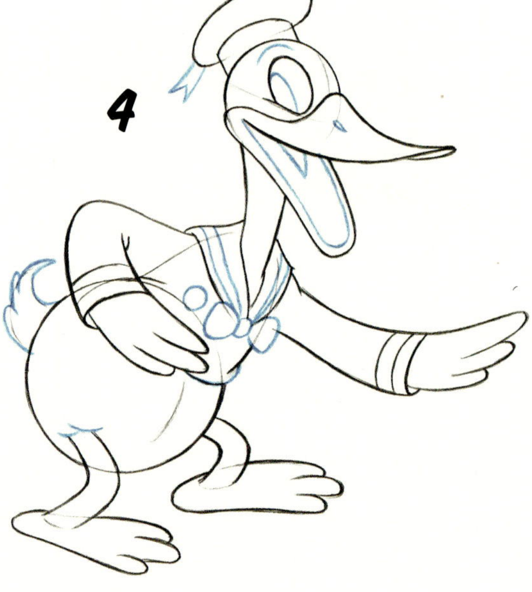

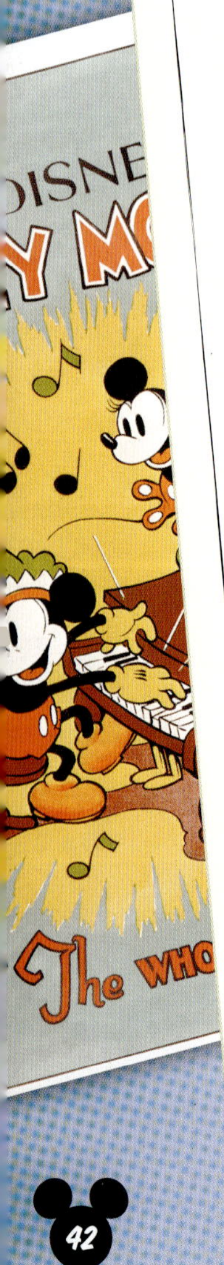

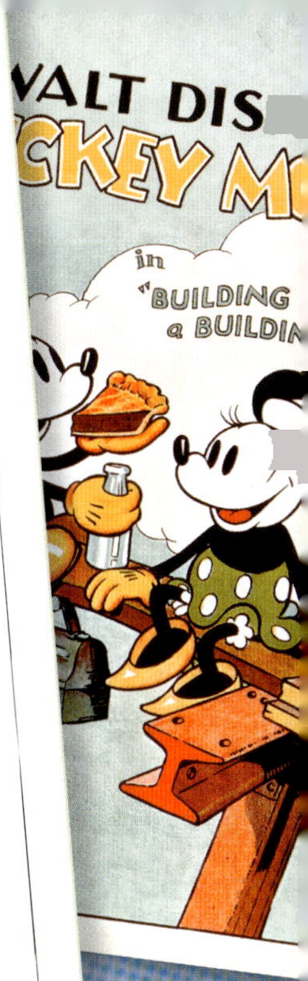

DONALD'S POSES

5

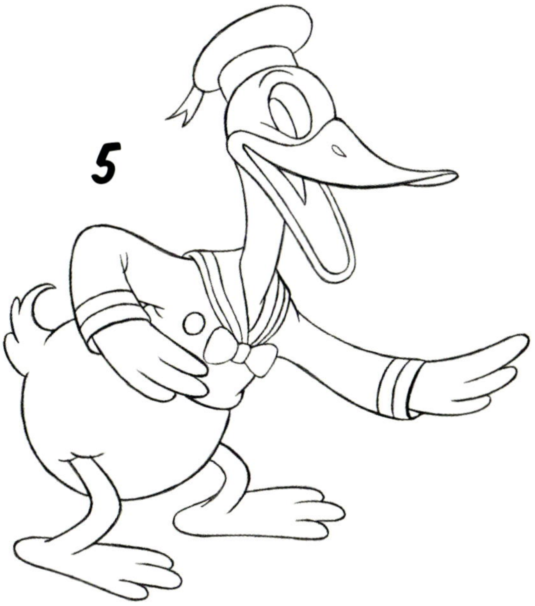

6

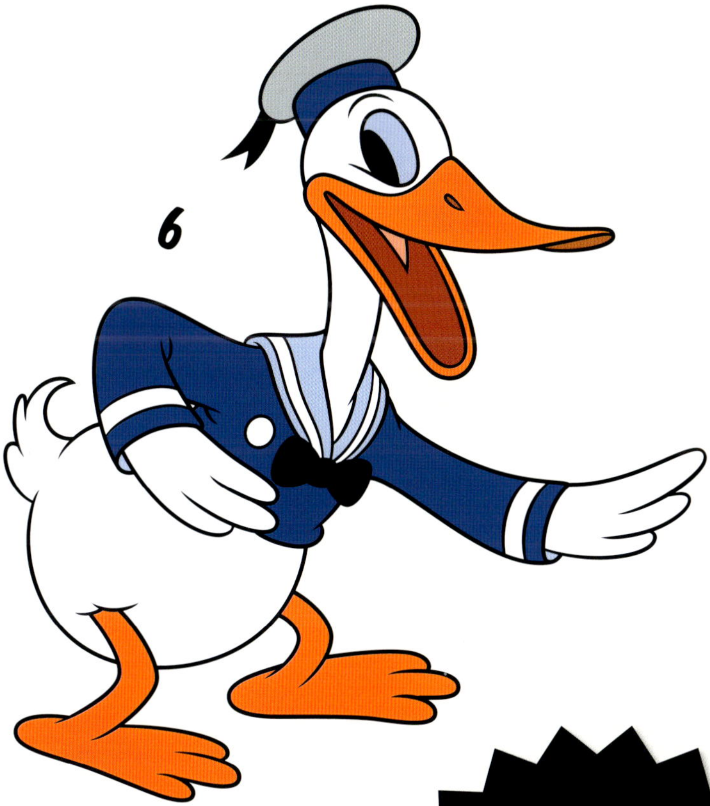

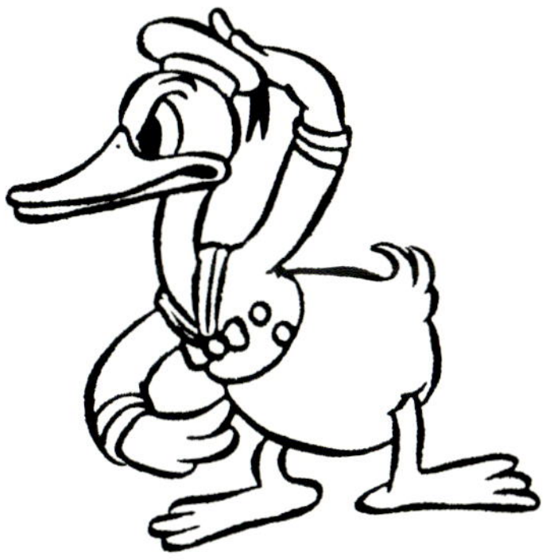

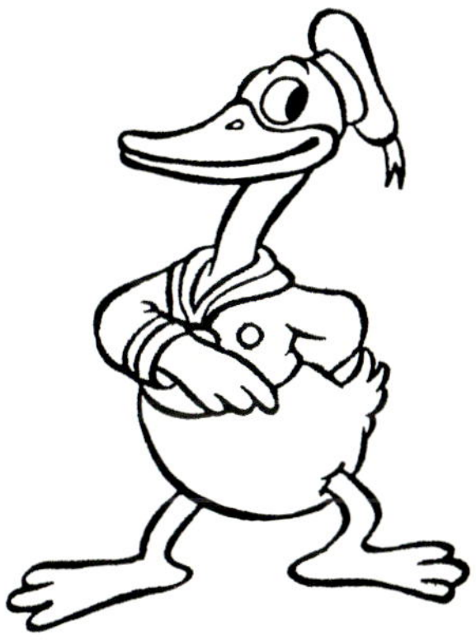

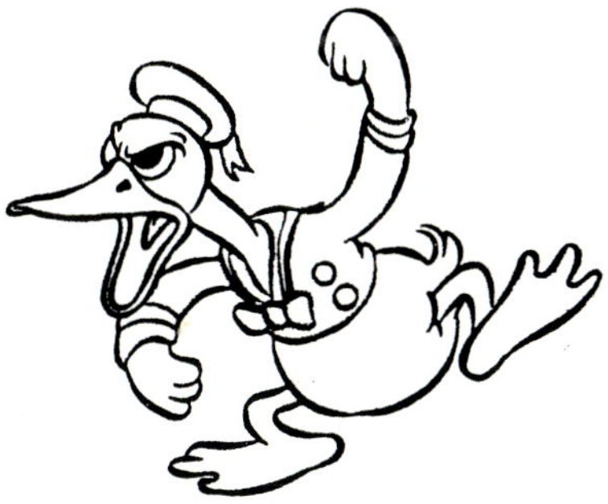

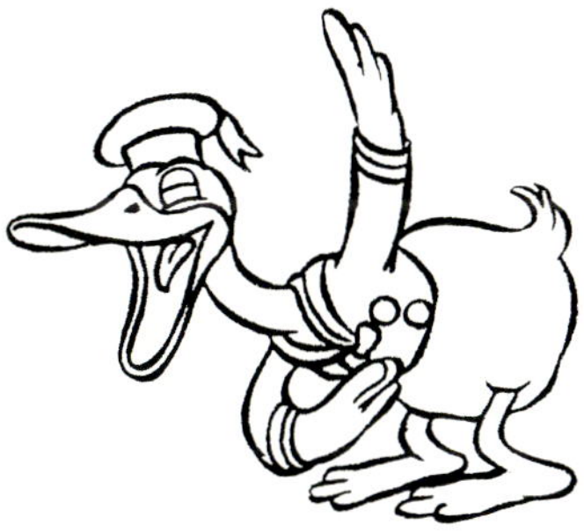

DONALD'S FIRST PERFORMANCE WAS A SUPPORTING ROLE IN THE 1934 FILM SHORT, THE WISE LITTLE HEN.

1930s

DONALD DUCK

LATER 1930s APPEARANCE

1

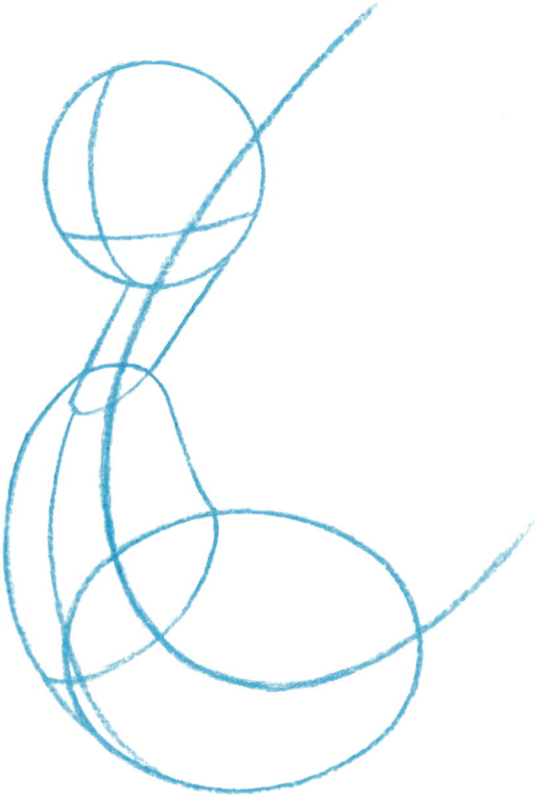

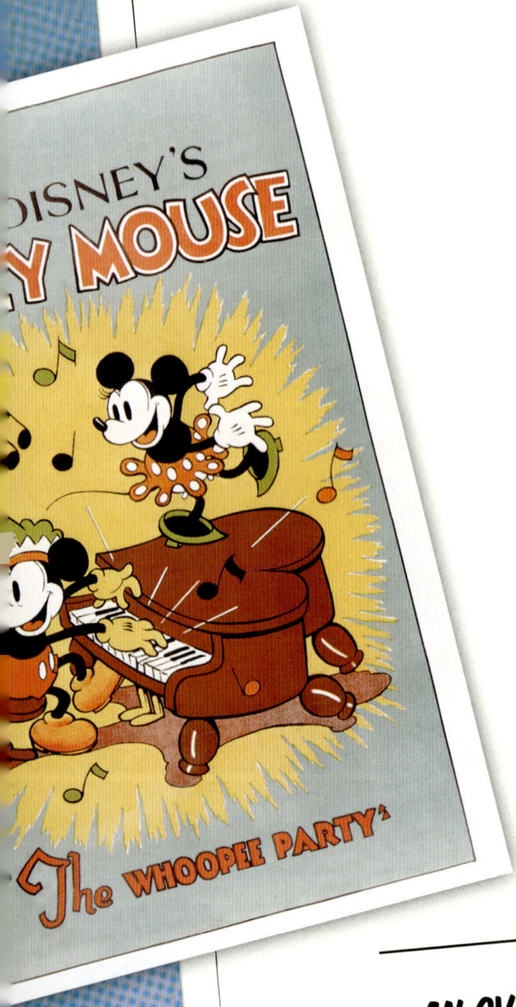

PERSONALITY PLUS

AN OVERLY CONFIDENT DUCK, DONALD THINKS SO HIGHLY OF HIS OWN TALENTS THAT HE WILL CHASE WILDLY AFTER THE LIMELIGHT, EVEN IF HE'S NOT THE RIGHT CANDIDATE FOR THE JOB. BUT DESPITE HIS WAYS, IT'S HARD NOT TO LIKE HIM.

2

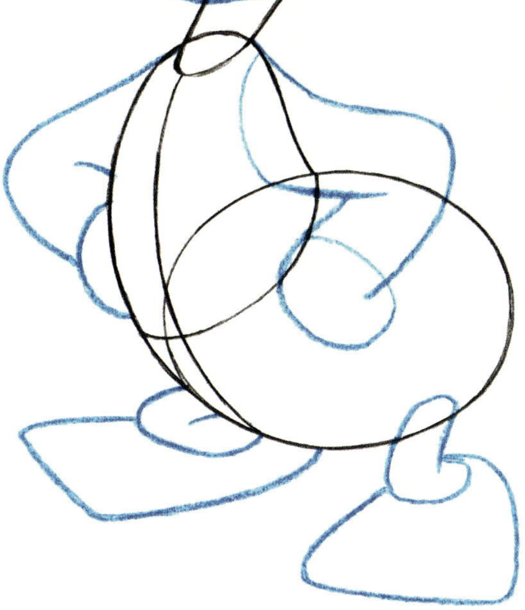

3

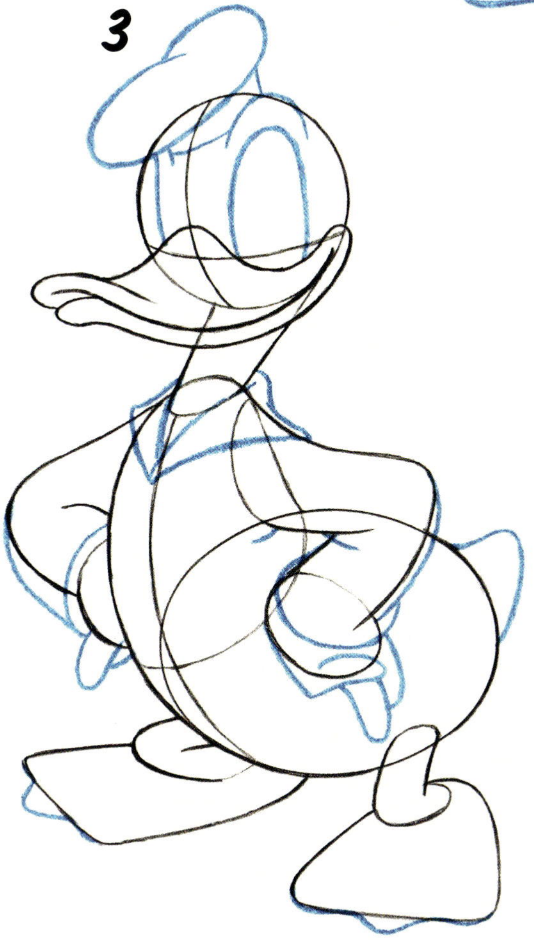

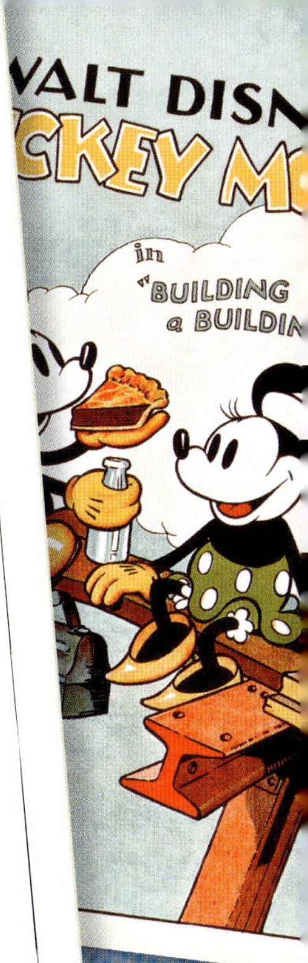
WALT DISN
CKEY MO
in
"BUILDING
a BUILDIN

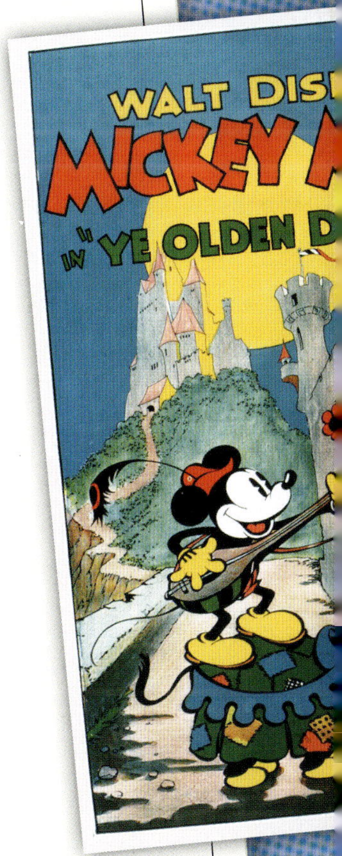
WALT DIS
MICKEY M
IN "YE OLDEN D

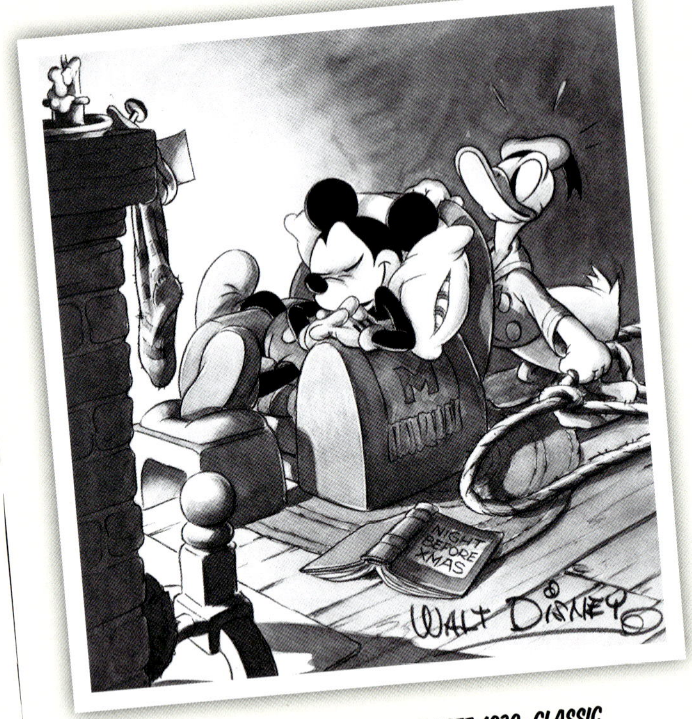

GO-GETTER DONALD AWAITS SANTA IN A LATE-1930s CLASSIC DISNEY CHRISTMAS CARD. ART BY HANK PORTER.

4

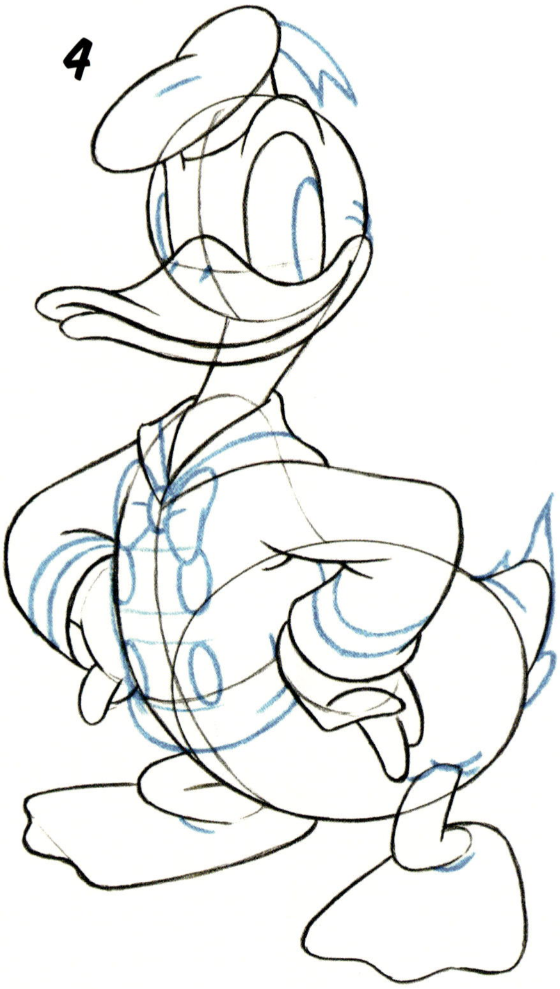

5

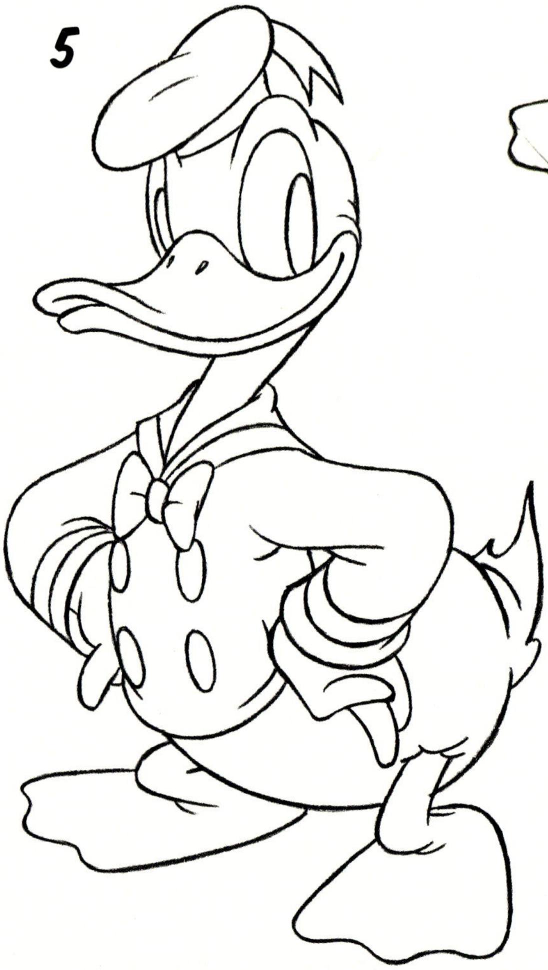

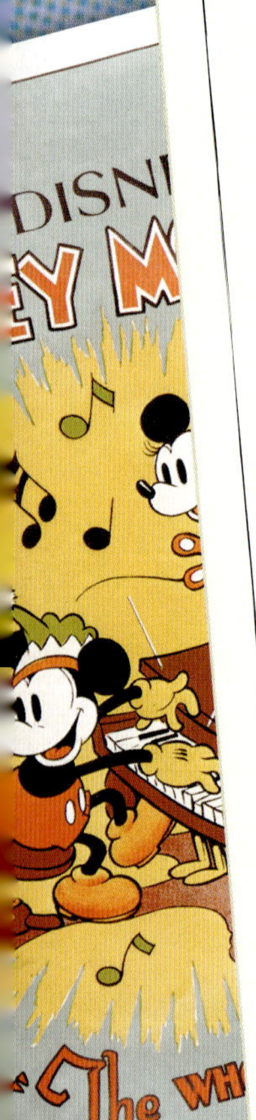

6

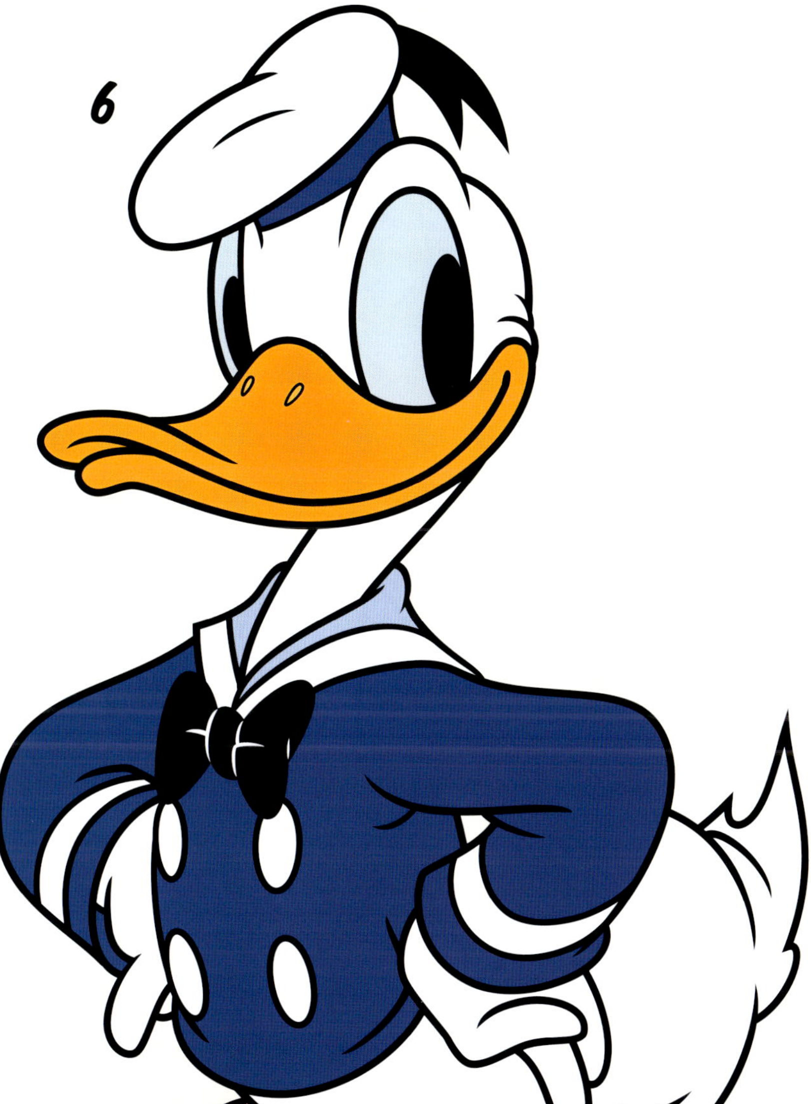

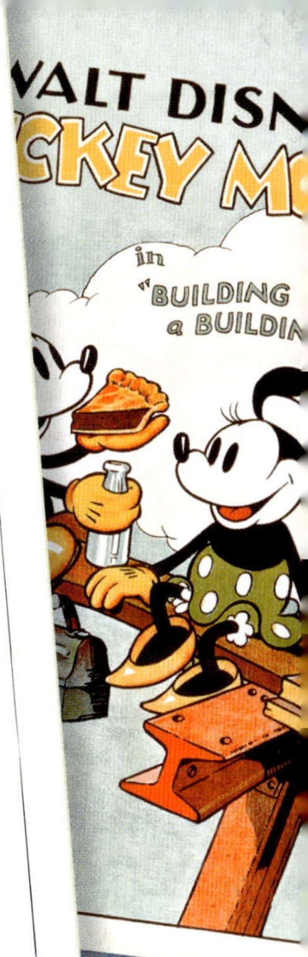

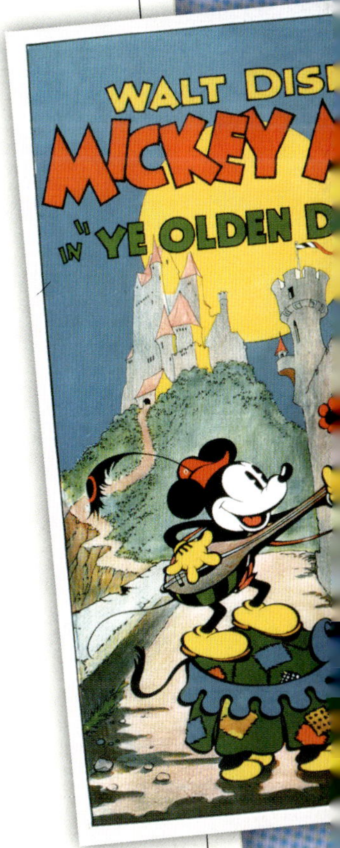

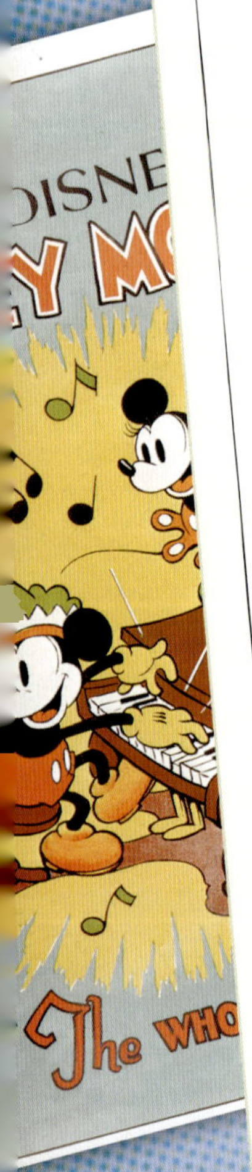

1930s

HUEY, DEWEY & LOUIE

1

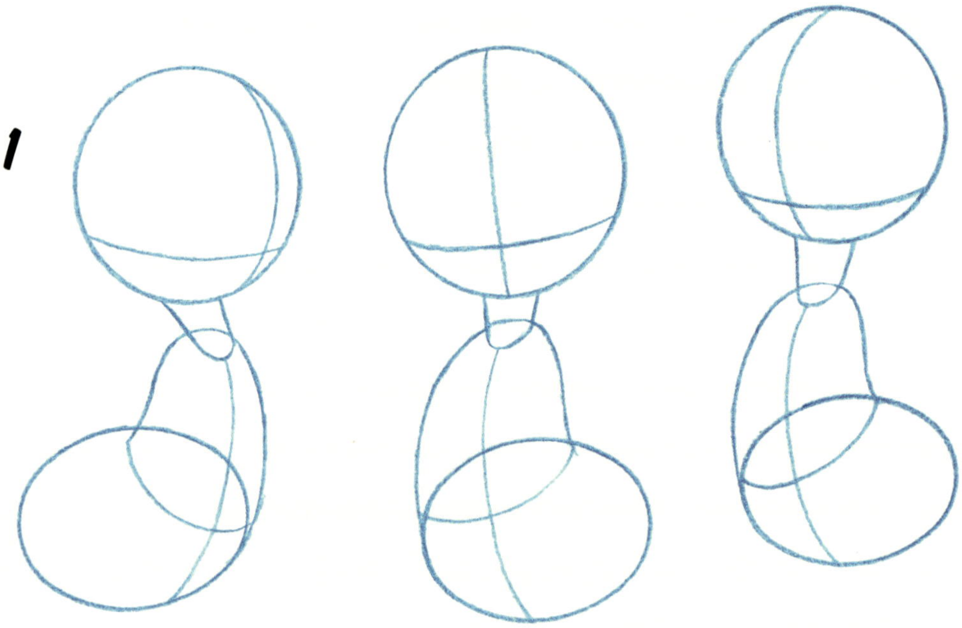

PERSONALITY PLUS

IN THEIR FIRST FEW APPEARANCES, THE IDENTICAL TRIPLETS DIDN'T YET LIVE PERMANENTLY WITH DONALD; THEIR MOTHER SIMPLY SENT THEM TO VISIT FOR SHORT PERIODS OF TIME. BUT STARTING WITH THE DONALD DUCK COMIC STRIP IN 1938, THEY TOOK UP RESIDENCE WITH DONALD FOR GOOD.

2

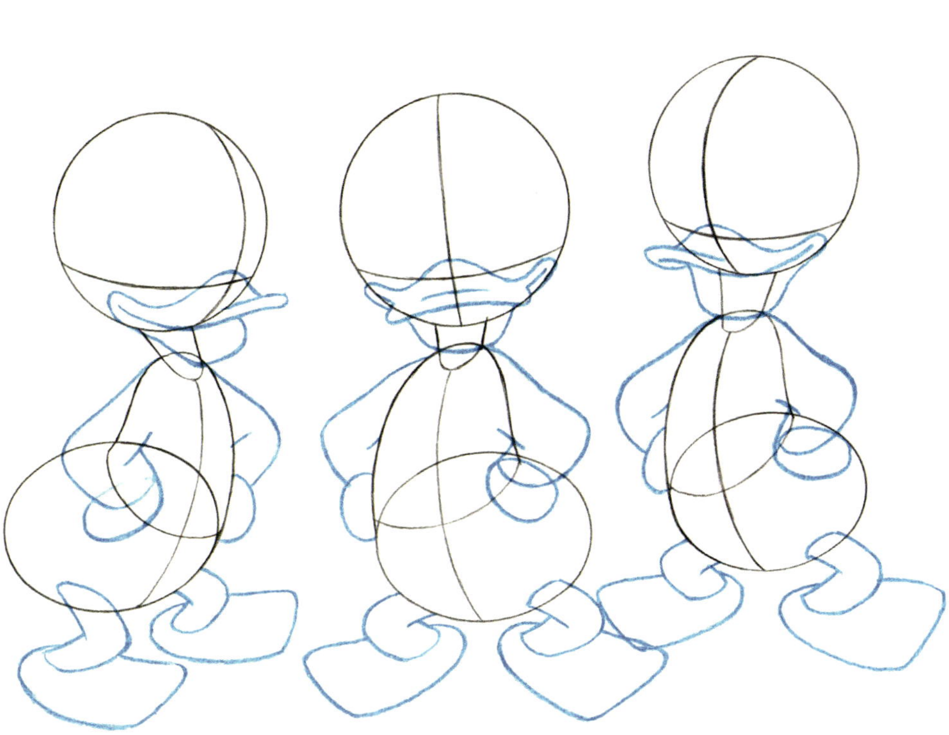

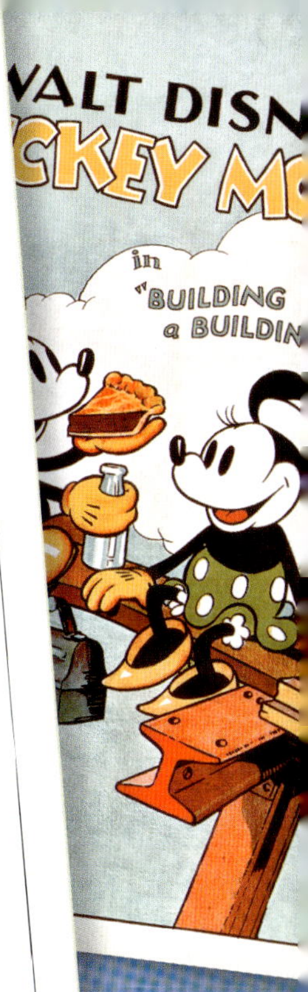

3

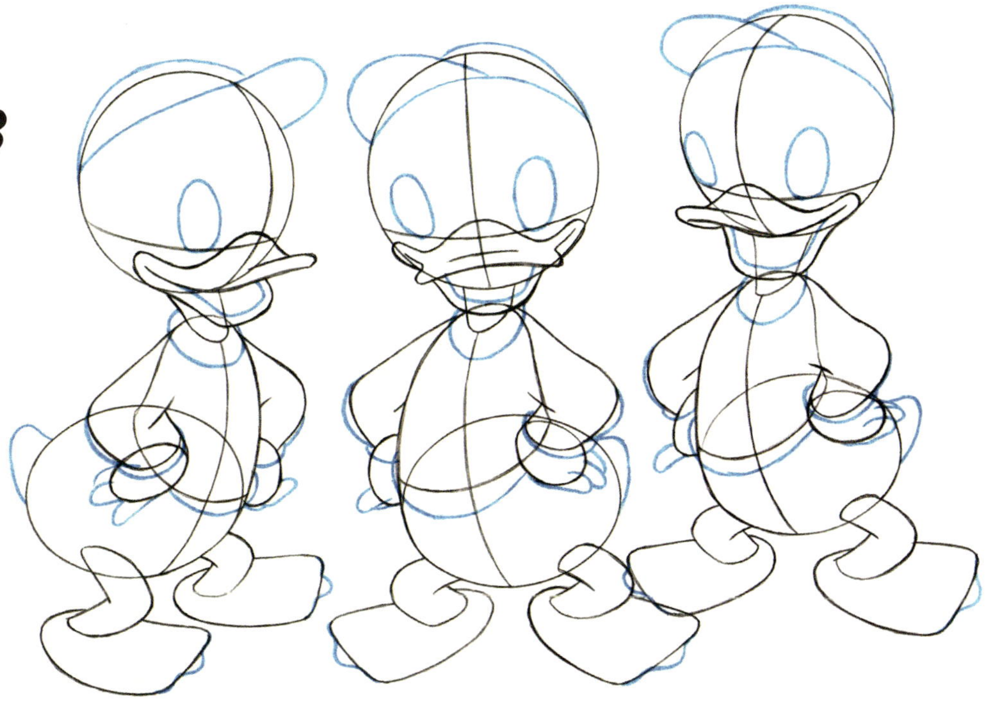

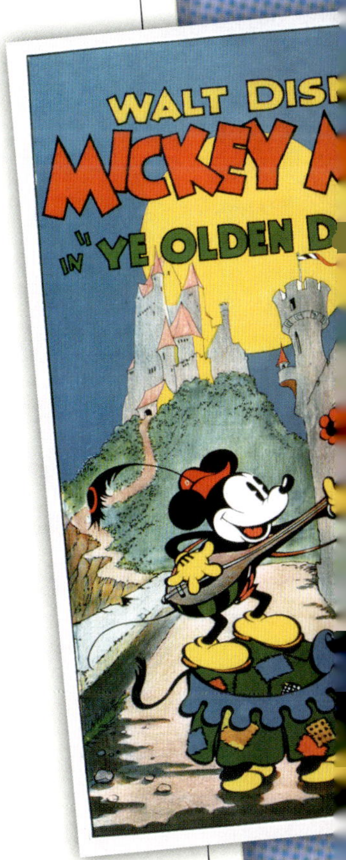

4

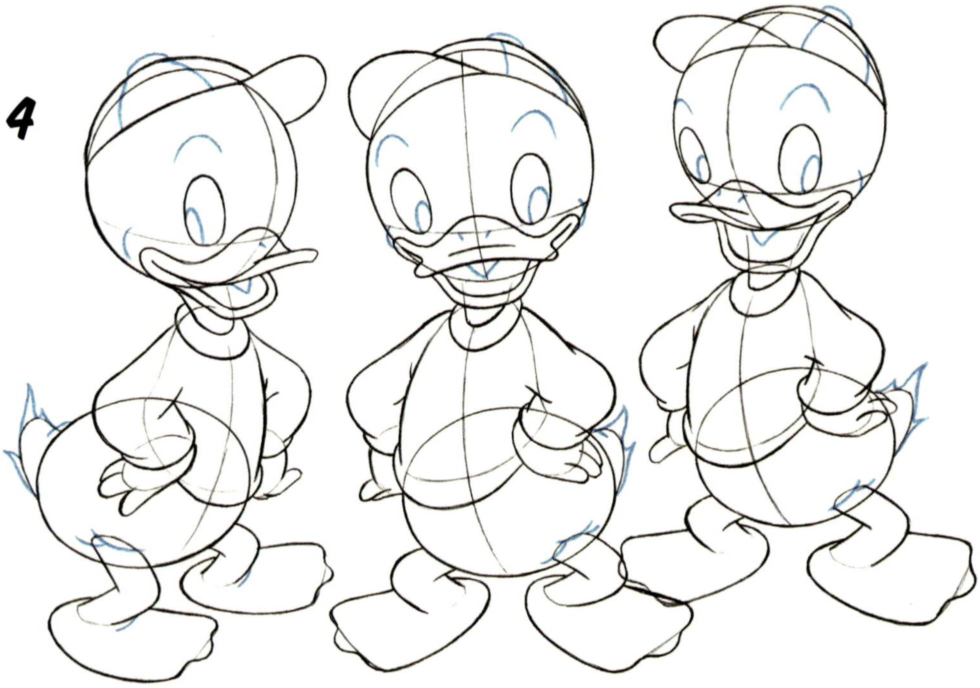

5

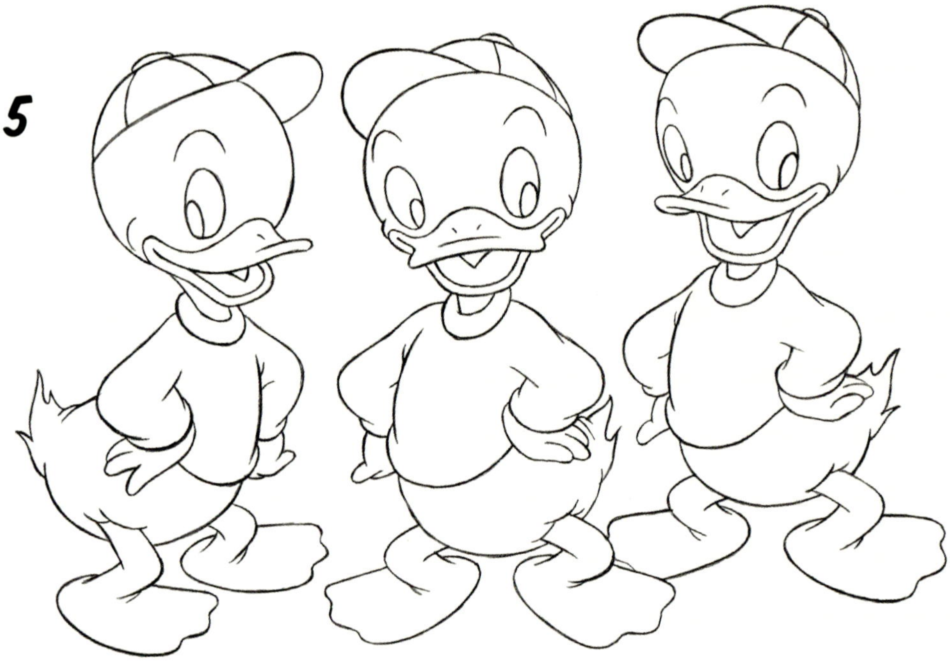

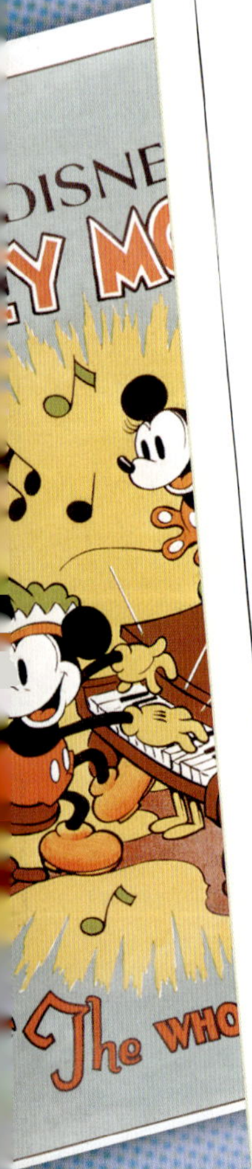

FOR THE 1987 TV SERIES DUCKTALES, THE TRIPLETS RECEIVED THEIR MODERN COLORS: RED, BLUE, AND GREEN. EARLIER, THE DUCKLINGS OFTEN WORE DIFFERENT COLORS OR IDENTICAL OUTFITS. IT WAS ASSUMED THAT THE SIBLINGS SHARED EVERYTHING—EVEN THEIR CLOTHES!

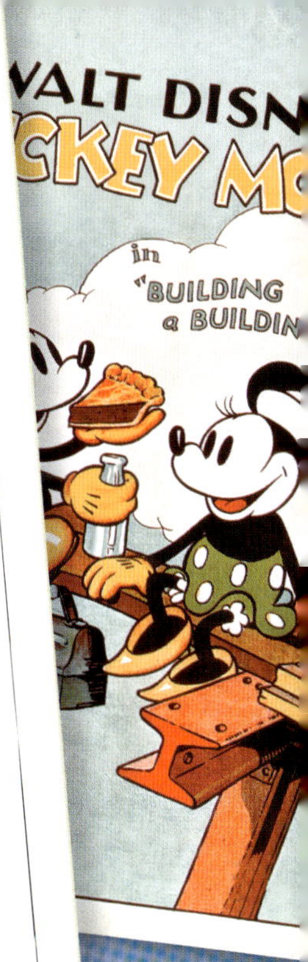

6

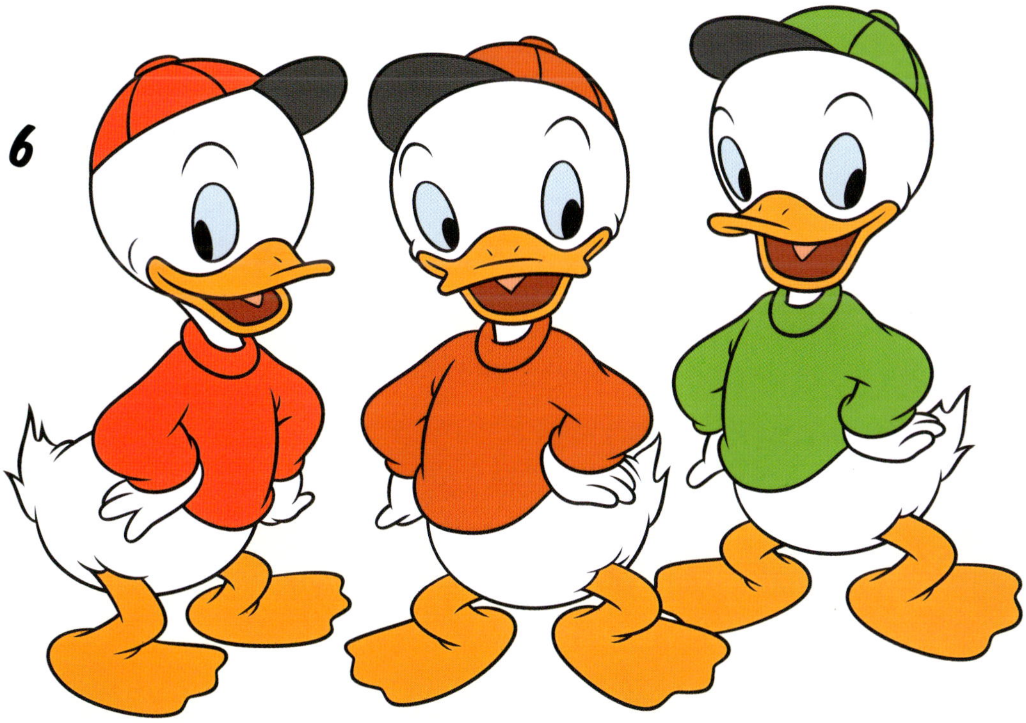

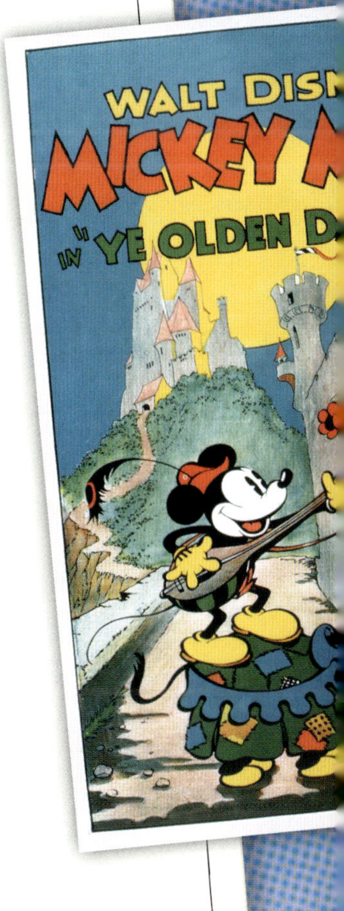

INSIDE STORY

THE WHOLE DUCK FAMILY

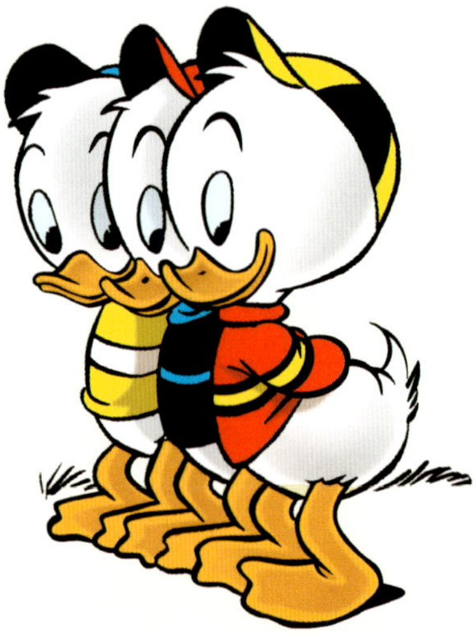

ALL DUCK CHARACTERS ON THIS SPREAD, EXCEPT WHERE NOTED: ART BY CARL BARKS.

"DONALD DUCK...IS NOT RELATED TO ANYONE IN PARTICULAR," a 1934 Disney press release stated—and it was one of several puff pieces to make this claim.[1] The earliest, rowdiest Donald was quite often portrayed as having been disowned by his family. All the better to show that his temper was definitely trouble!

Over time, however, a new meme emerged. Rather than a distant family, Donald was given a close-knit, extensive one. For if they were to really tick off Donald's temper, and vice versa, wouldn't it be fun to *see* that?

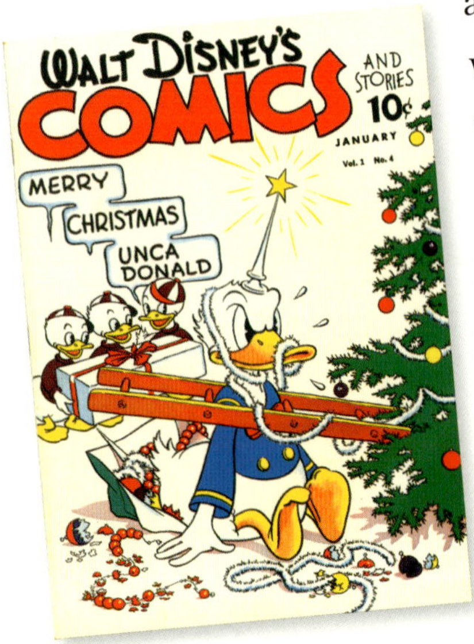

Nephews Huey, Dewey, and Louie, created by artist Al Taliaferro, came first. They were inspired by Mickey's "orphans," pesky mouselings with whom Donald had battled previously onscreen. Taliaferro deduced that a fight with unruly brats would be funnier if Donald bore familial responsibility for the kids.

And soon even more ducks were introduced to bear responsibility for Donald! Stern farmer Grandma Duck,

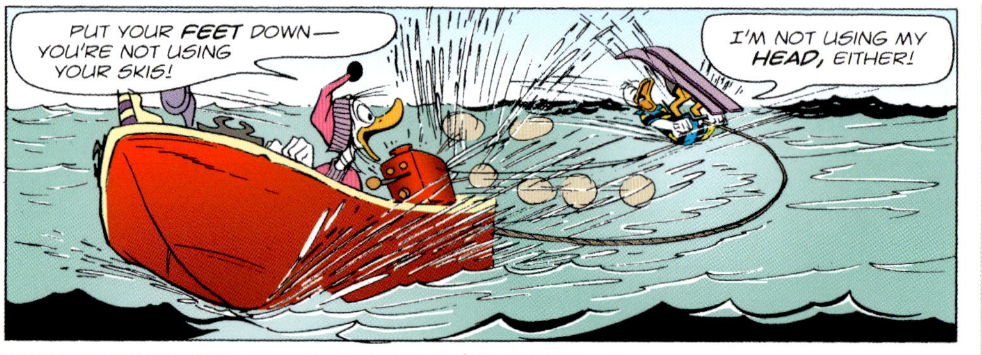

ABOVE: WALT DISNEY'S COMICS AND STORIES FEATURING HUEY, DEWEY, AND LOUIE AND DONALD DUCK (JANUARY 1941). ARTIST UNKNOWN.

RIGHT: GEEKY COUSIN FETHRY DUCK HAS A NEW HOBBY EVERY WEEK. ART BY AL HUBBARD.

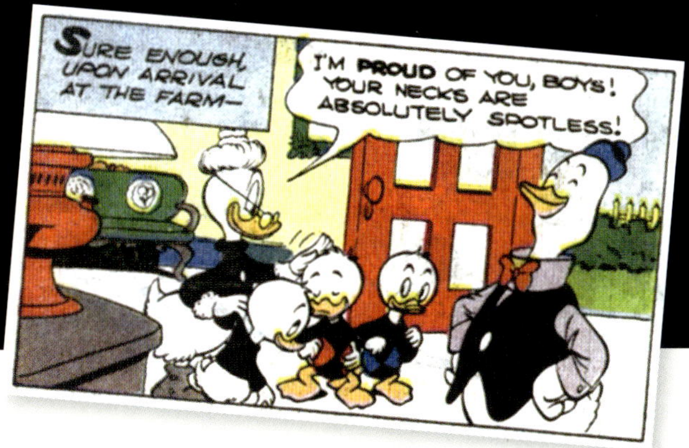

COMIC FEATURING GRANDMA DUCK; HUEY, DEWEY, AND LOUIE; AND GUS GOOSE.

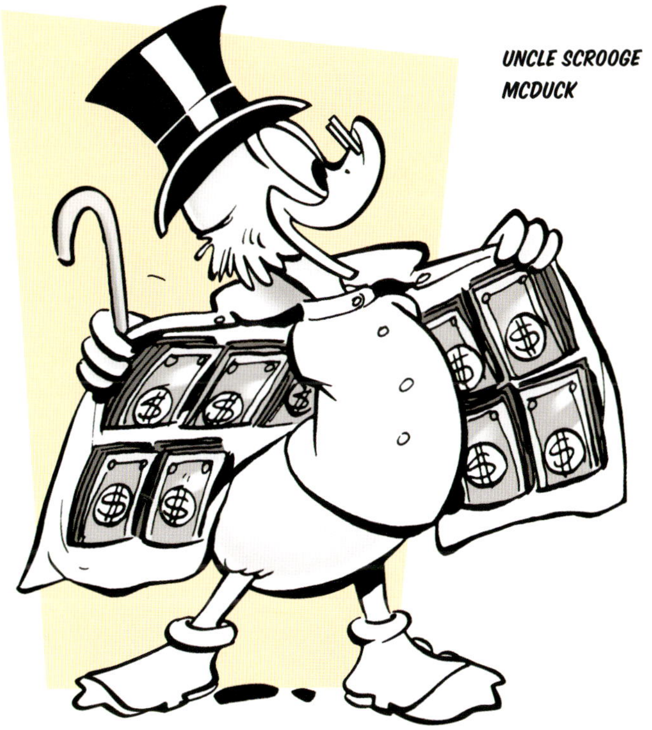

UNCLE SCROOGE MCDUCK

another Taliaferro creation, emerged in 1940; in 1947, writer/artist Carl Barks created rich, adventurous Uncle Scrooge McDuck.

Other relatives flocked in for later films and comics. Who doesn't recognize gluttonous Gus Goose, annoyingly lucky Gladstone Gander, egotistical expert Ludwig Von Drake, or faddist Fethry Duck? With the exception of tubby Gus, all of the ducks evolved from Donald's own visual design; so if you can draw Donald, you can learn to draw the rest.

Donald is proud of his family—even if the whole cranky clan still ticks off his temper.

1. The Walt Disney Company, "Any Pork in a Storm!" from publicity for *Walt Disney's Silly Symphony*, "The Wise Little Hen" (Beverly Hills: United Artists Corporation, 1934), 3.

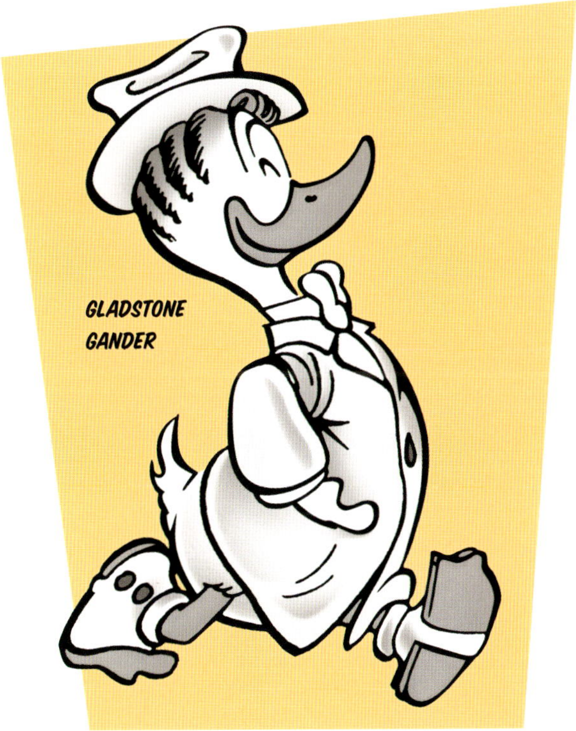

GLADSTONE GANDER

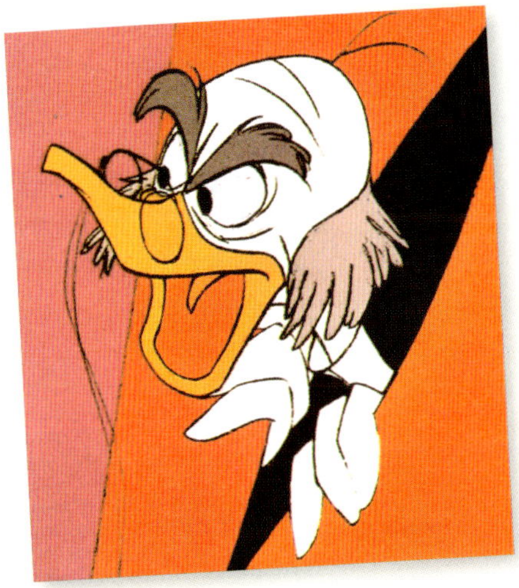

LUDWIG VON DRAKE IS A MADDER-THAN-USUAL SCIENTIST IN AN ADVENTURE IN COLOR (TV, 1961).

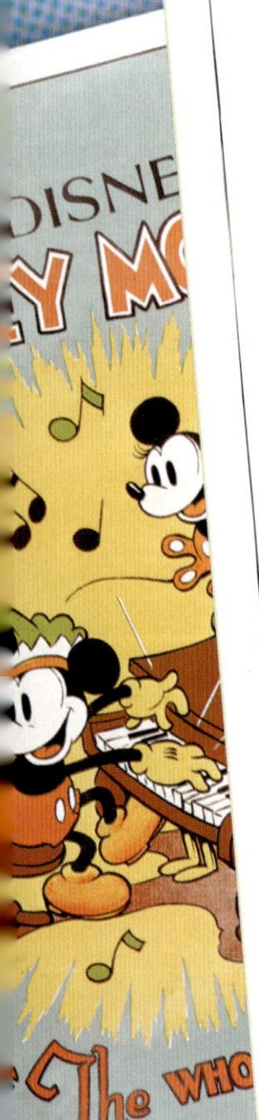

1930s

PLUTO

EARLY APPEARANCE

PLUTO FIRST APPEARED IN 1930 AS AN UNNAMED DOG IN THE CHAIN GANG.

1

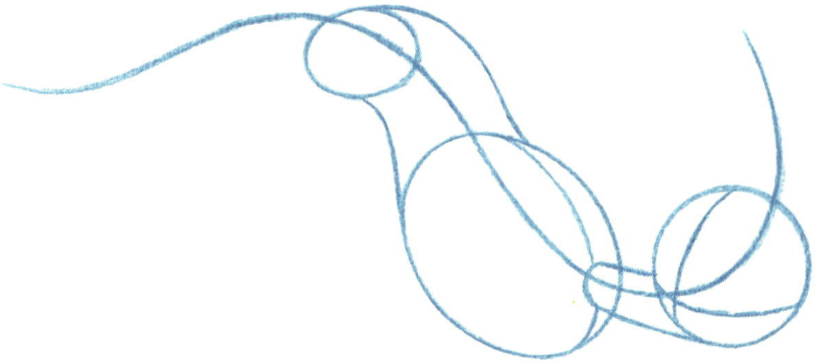

2

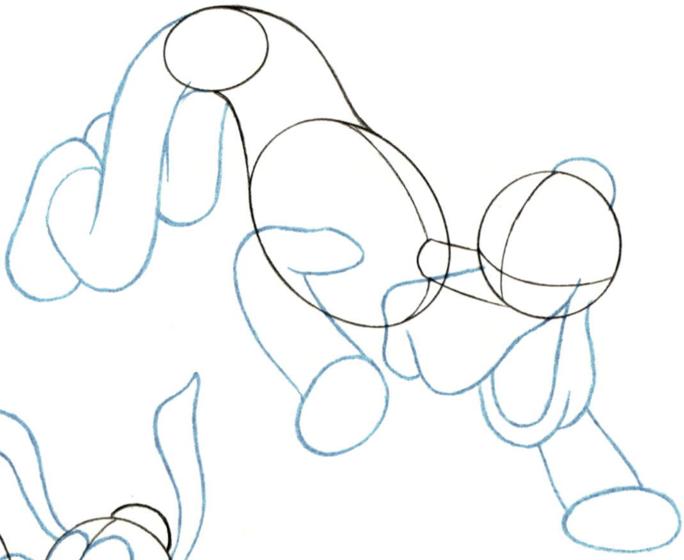

3

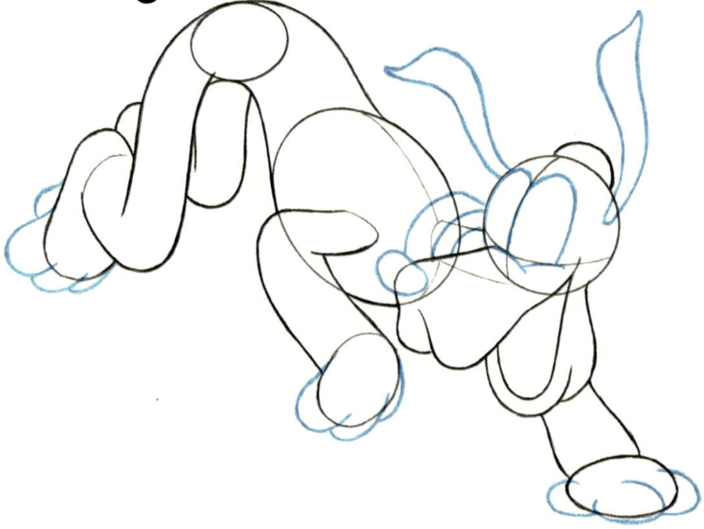

4

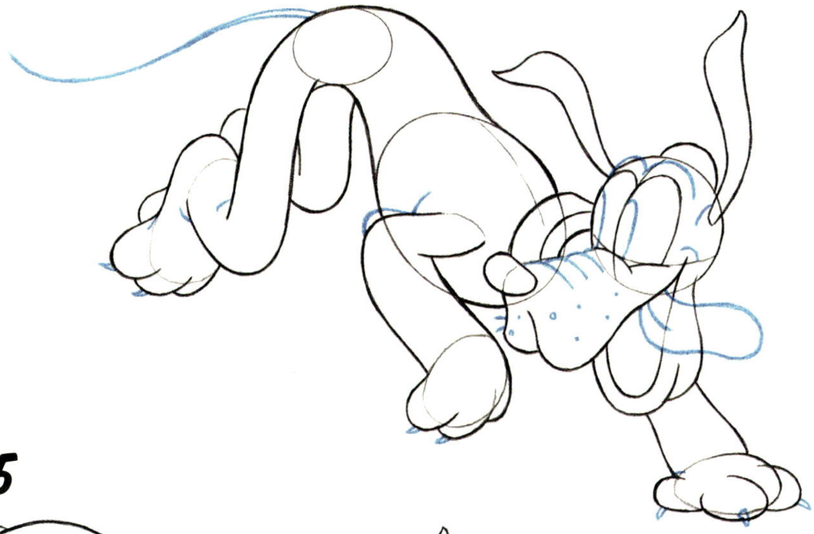

5

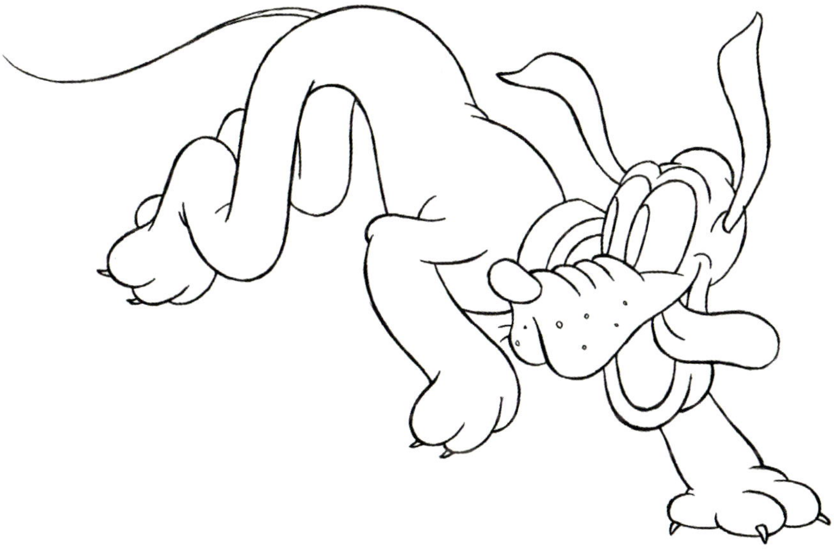

6

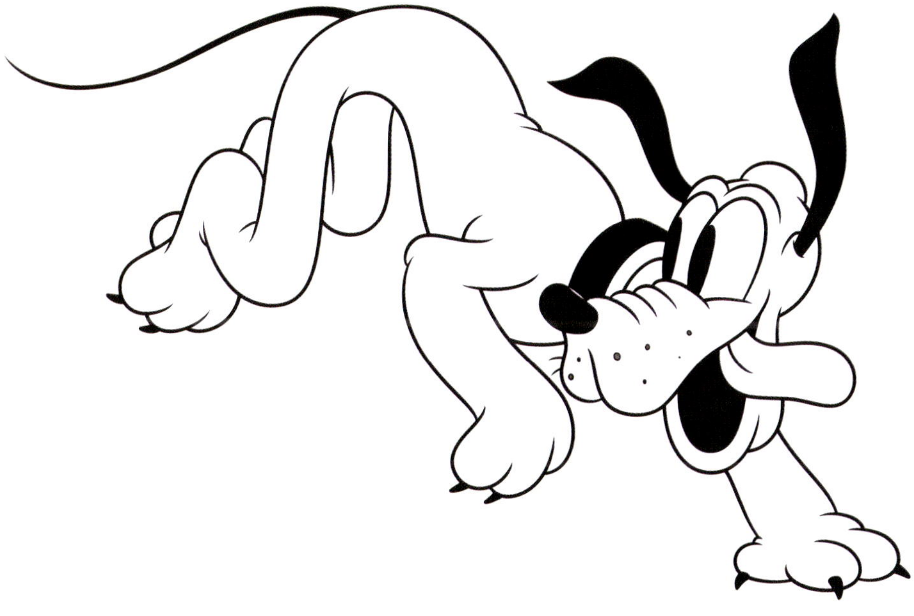

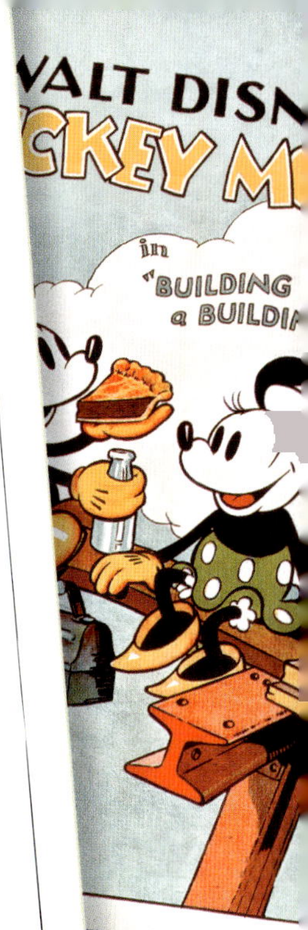
WALT DISN
CKEY M
in
"BUILDING
a BUILDI

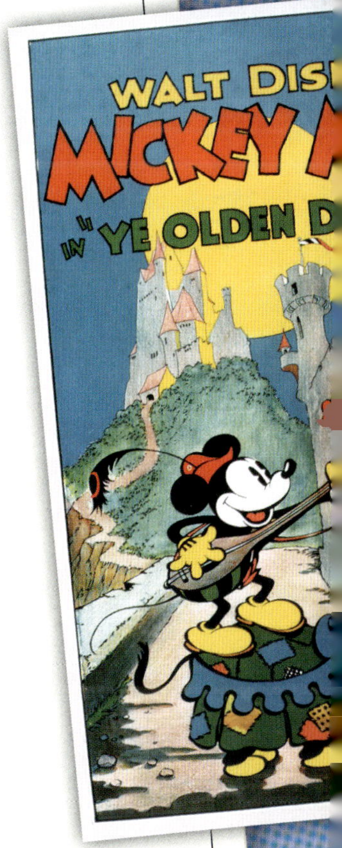
WALT DIS
MICKEY M
IN "YE OLDEN D

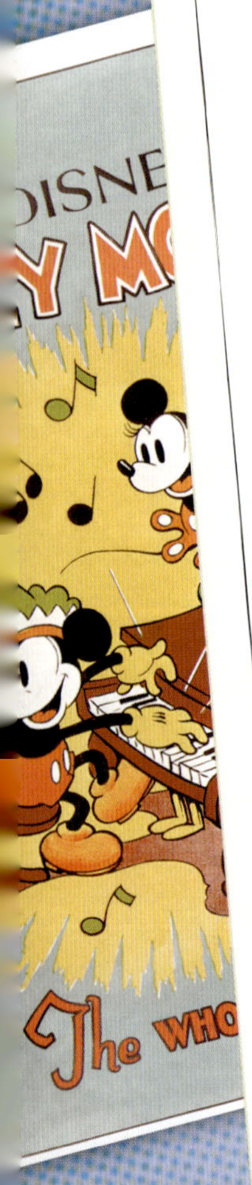

1930s

PLUTO

LATER 1930s APPEARANCE

1

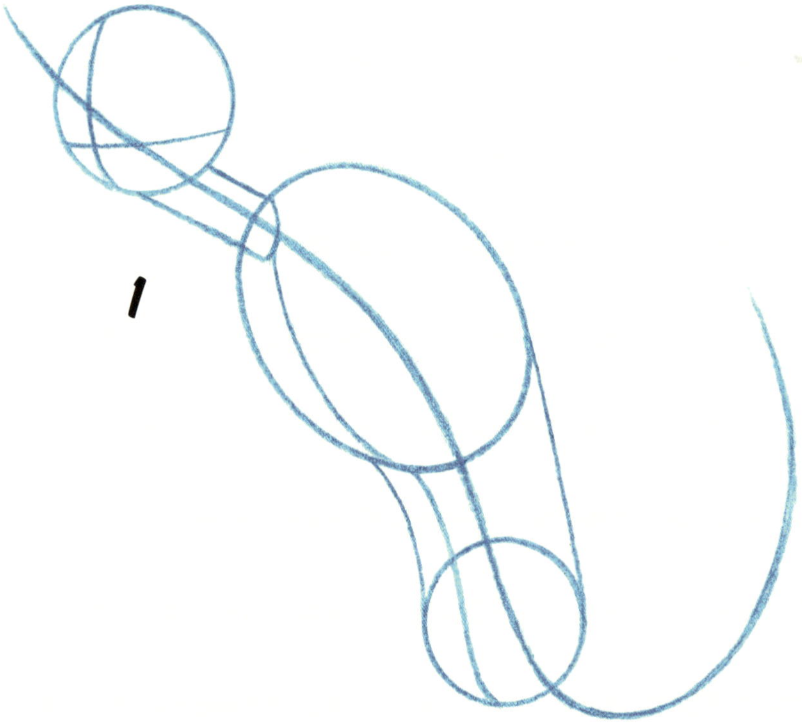

PERSONALITY PLUS

PLUTO IS 100% CANINE. FUN-LOVING AND PLAYFUL, PLUTO IS FULL GROWN, BUT HE HAS THE SPIRIT OF A PUPPY. HE IS A LOYAL COMPANION AND IS ALWAYS THERE FOR MICKEY.

IN 1931, PLUTO APPEARED AS HIMSELF IN THE FILM SHORT, THE MOOSE HUNT.

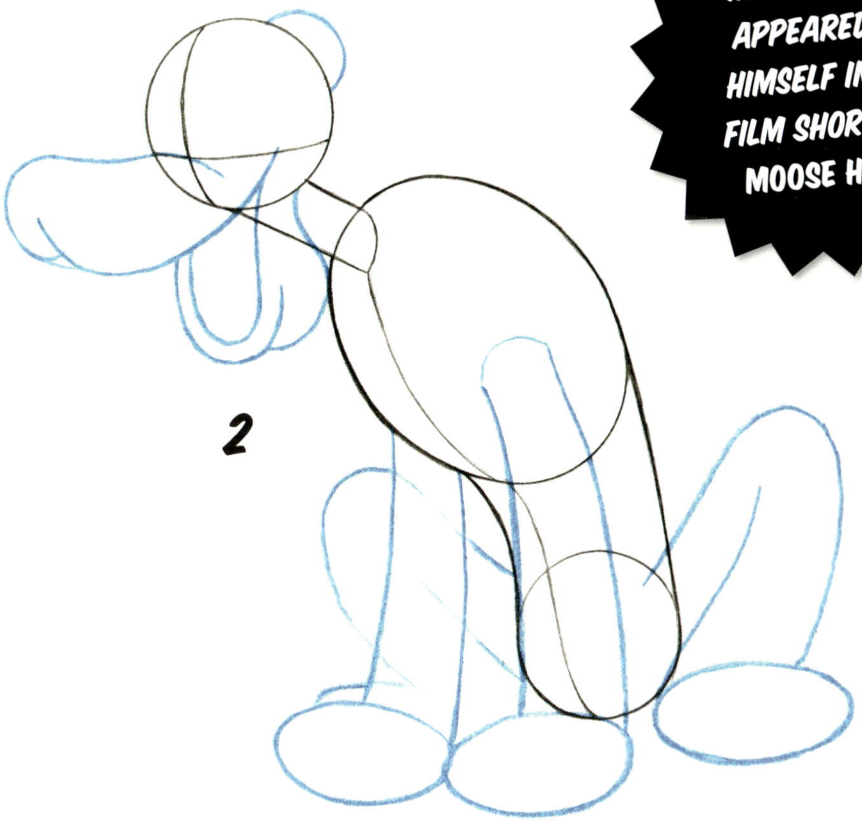

2

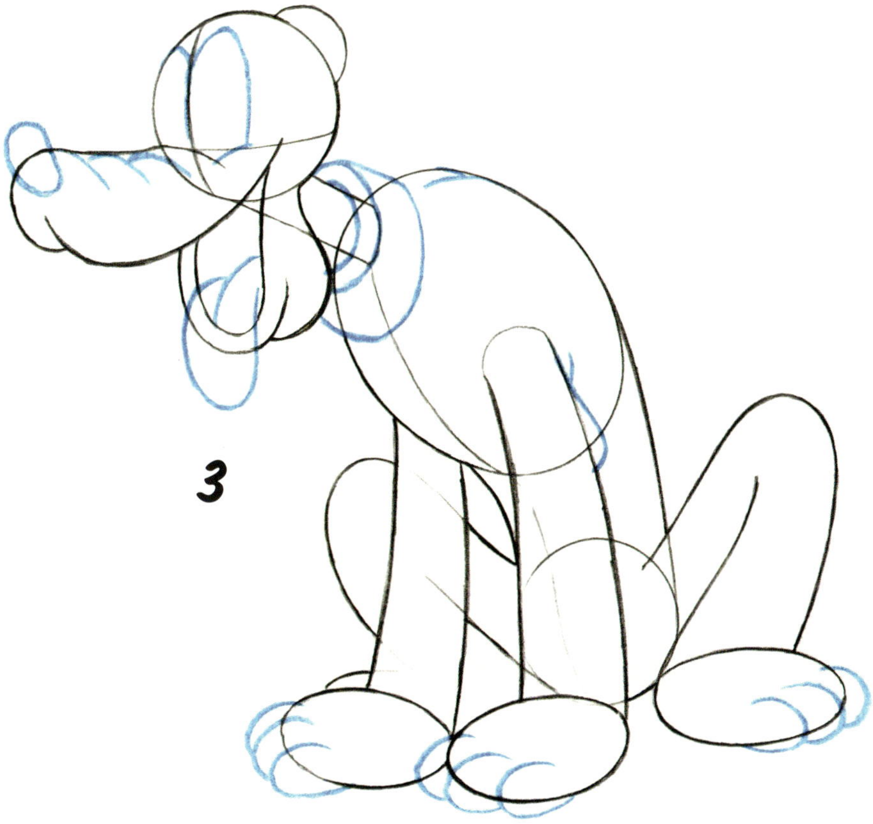

3

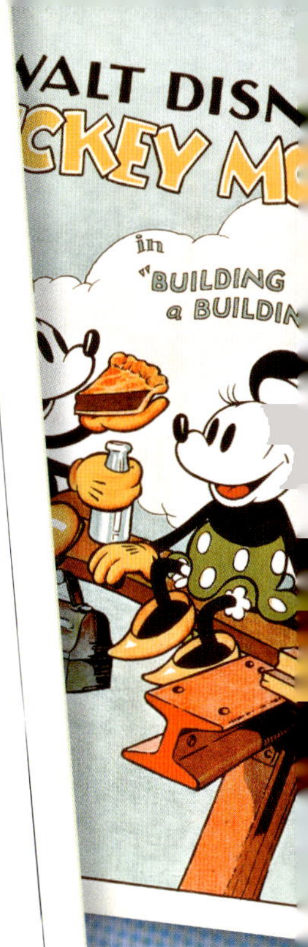

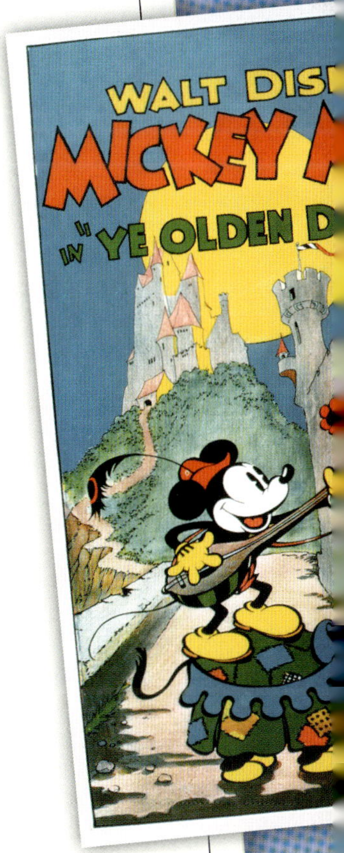

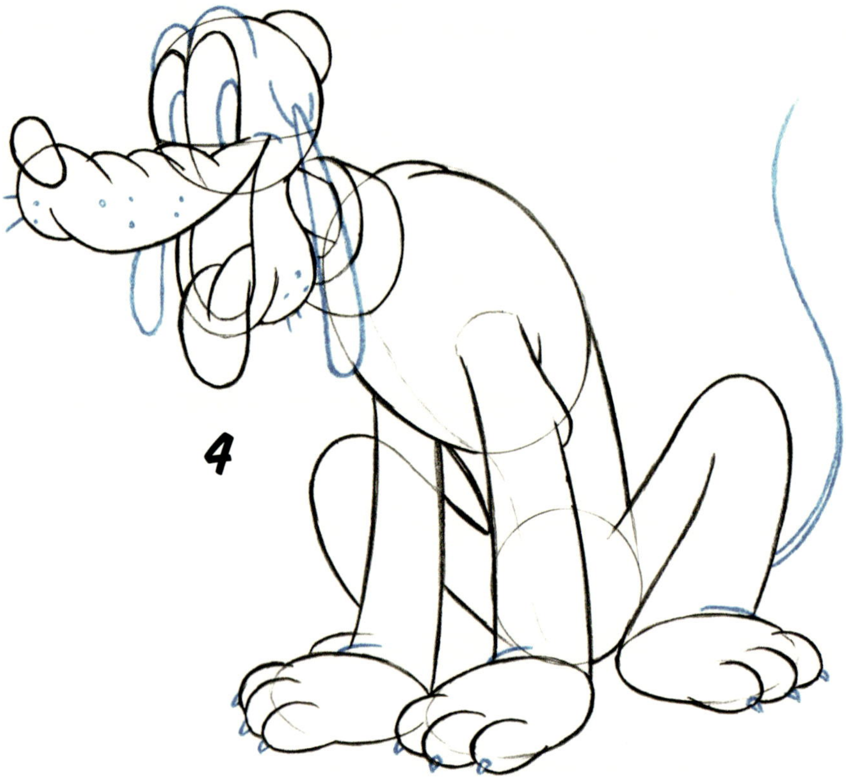

4

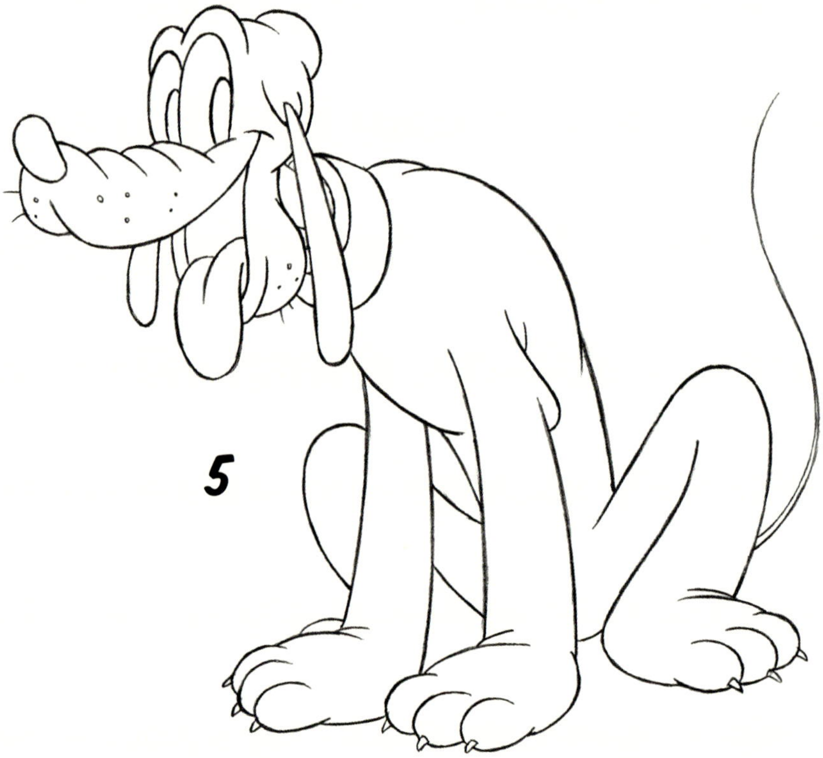

5

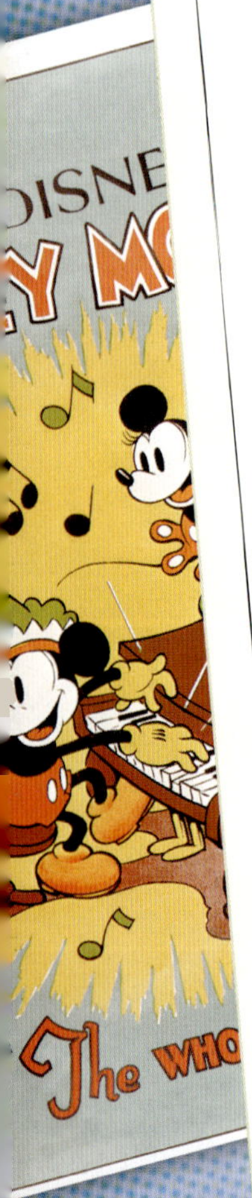

PROMOTIONAL POSTER FOR SOCIETY DOG SHOW (1939). IMAGE COURTESY OF HERITAGE AUCTIONS.

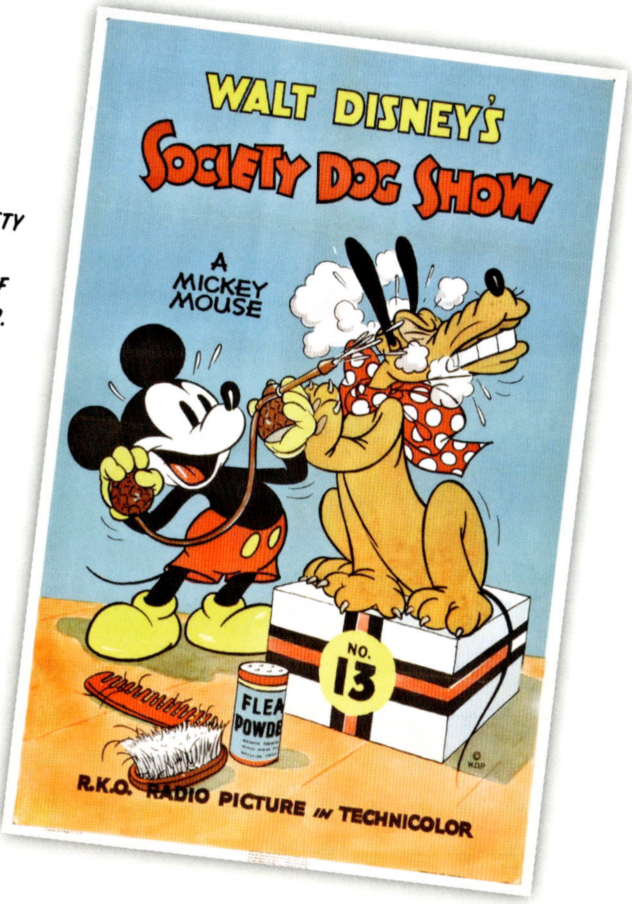

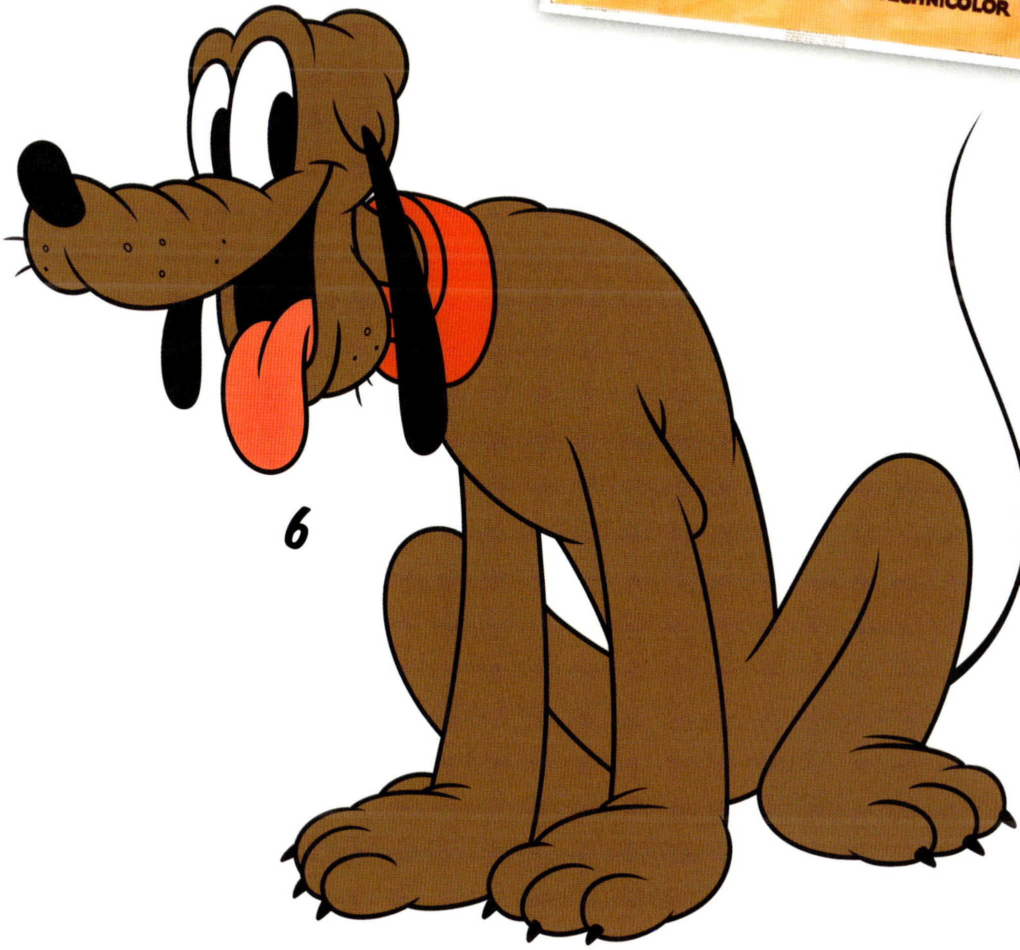

6

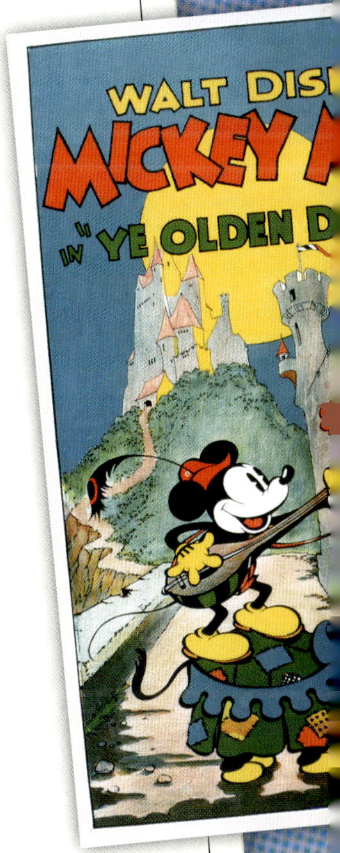

1930s

GOOFY

EARLY APPEARANCE

1

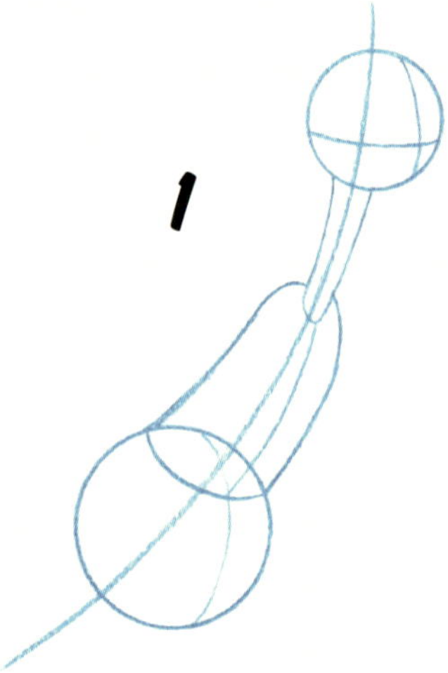

2

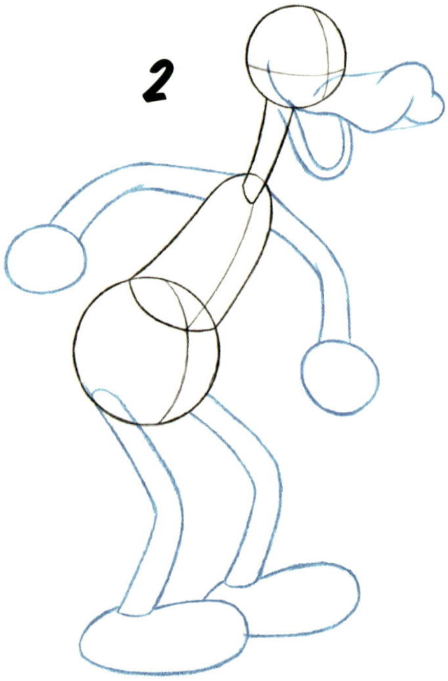

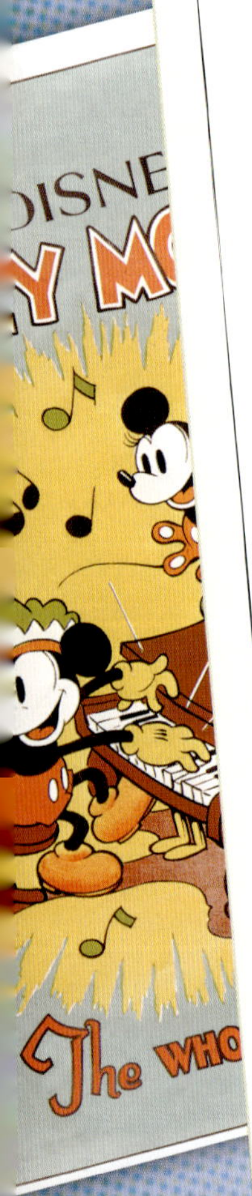

3

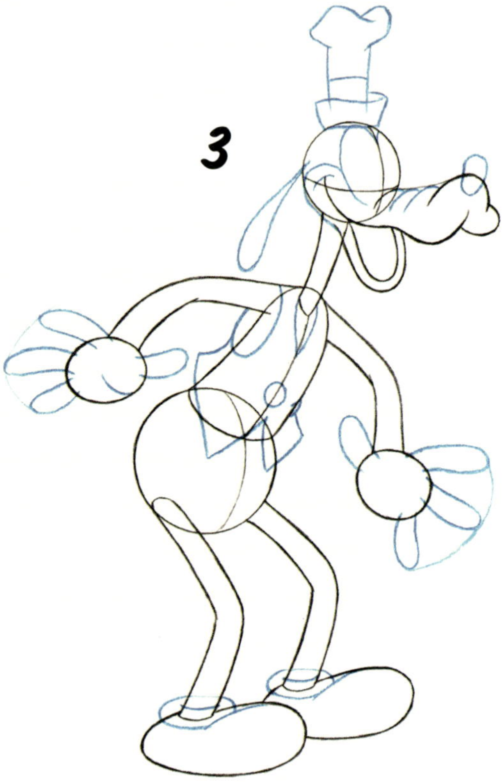

GOOFY'S ORIGINAL VOICE ARTIST, PINTO COLVIG, JOKINGLY CALLED HIMSELF AN "OREGON APPLEKNOCKER," A TERM FOR HILLBILLIES THAT LIVED IN HIS HOME STATE.

4

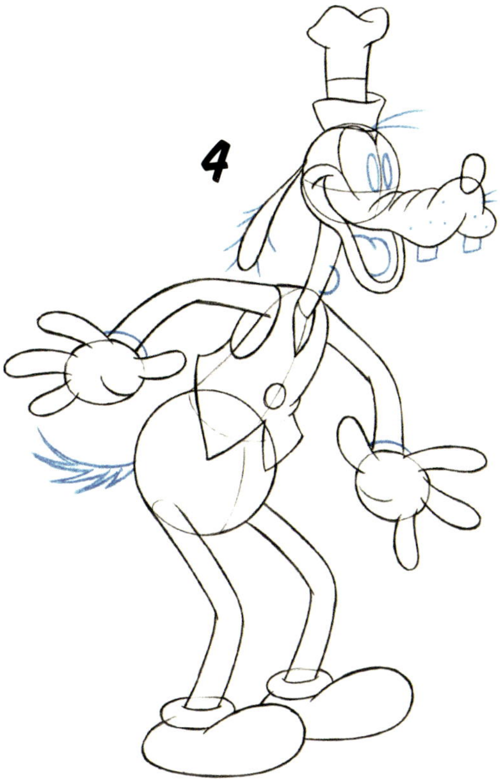

5

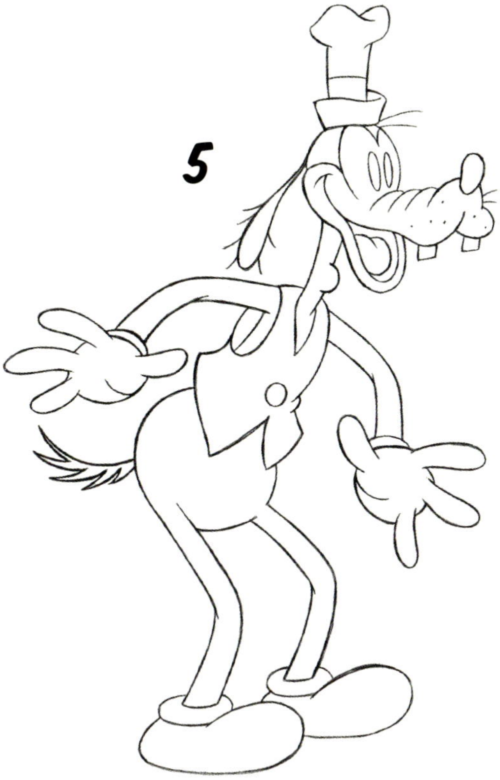

6

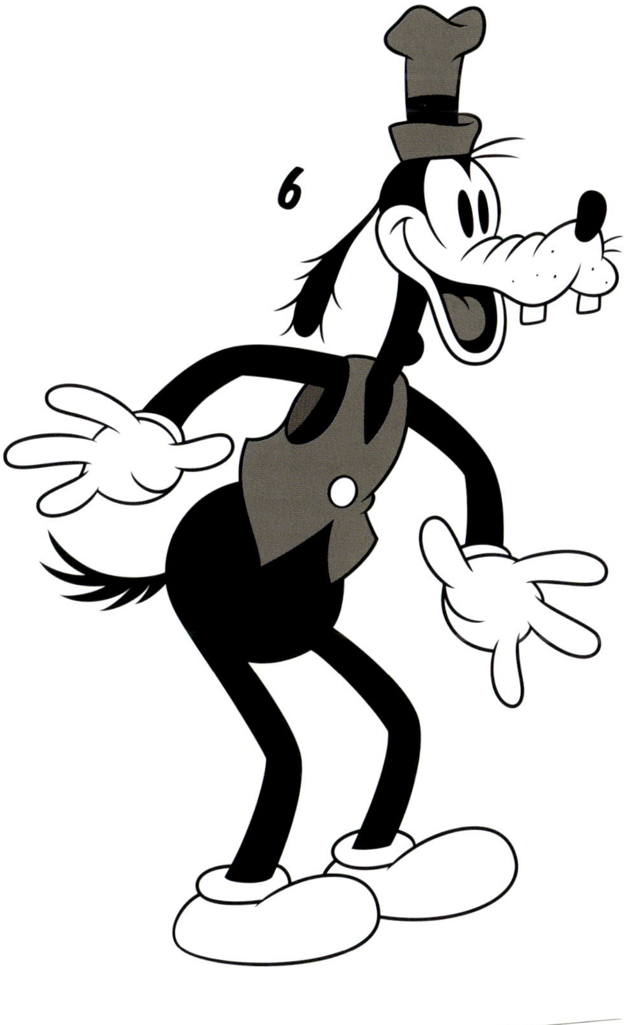

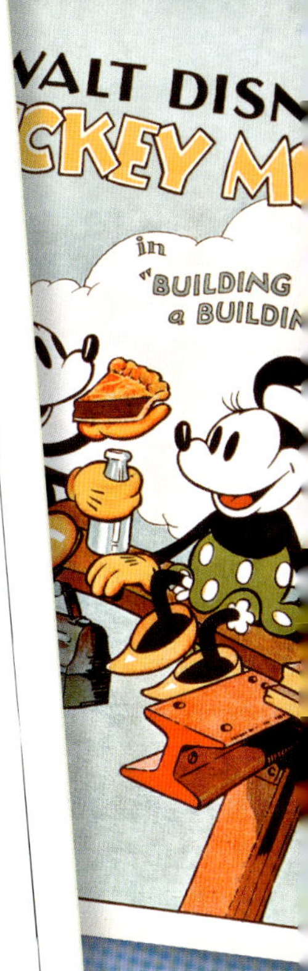
WALT DISN
CKEY M
in
"BUILDING
a BUILDIN

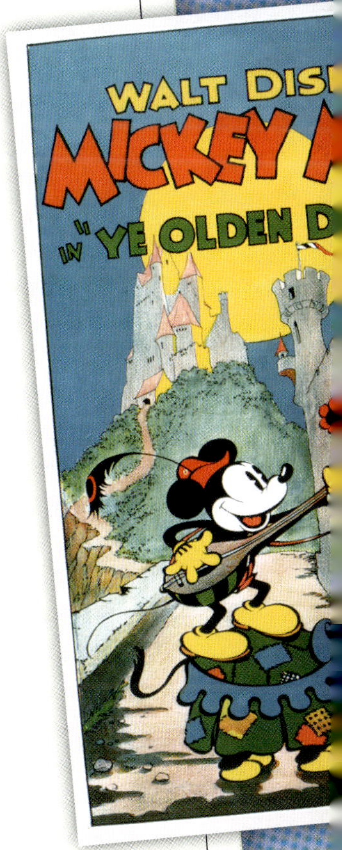
WALT DIS
MICKEY M
IN "YE OLDEN D

1930s

GOOFY

LATER 1930s APPEARANCE

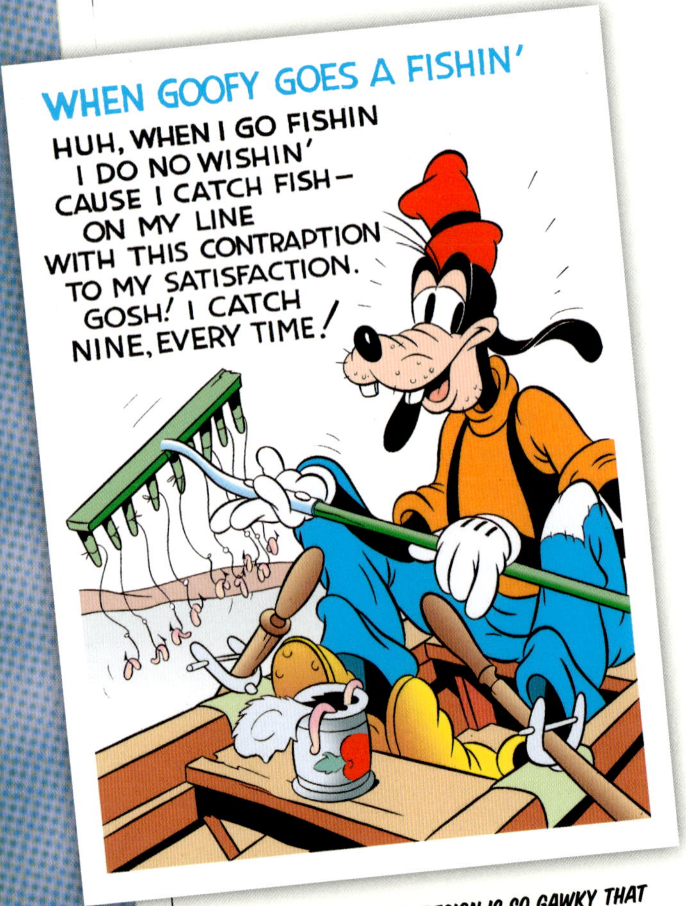

GOOFY'S LATE-1930s DESIGN IS SO GAWKY THAT HE CAN'T EVEN SIT STRAIGHT! ART BY BOB GRANT FROM MICKEY MOUSE MAGAZINE 59, 1940.

1

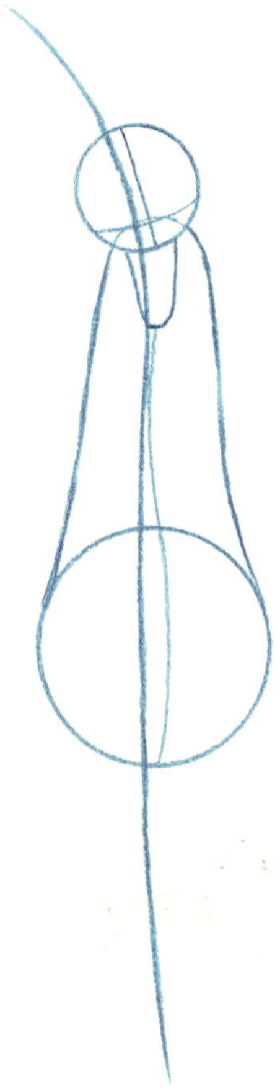

PERSONALITY PLUS

GOOFY'S HIGH SPIRITS AND GOOD HUMOR ARE INSPIRATIONAL. NO MATTER WHAT CHAOS GOOFY GETS HIMSELF INTO, HE ALWAYS MANAGES TO COME UP SMILING.

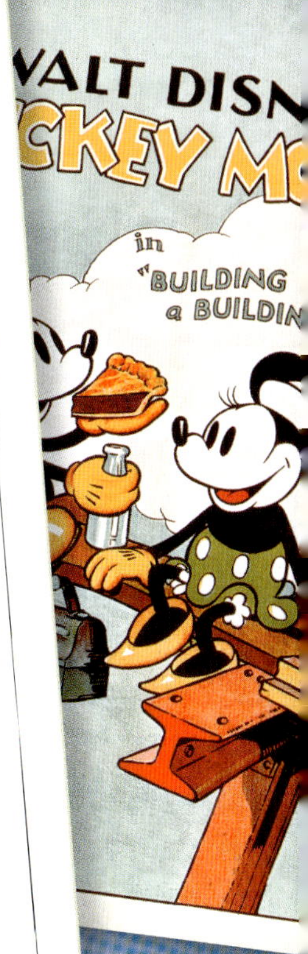
WALT DISN
CKEY MO
in
"BUILDING
a BUILDIN

2

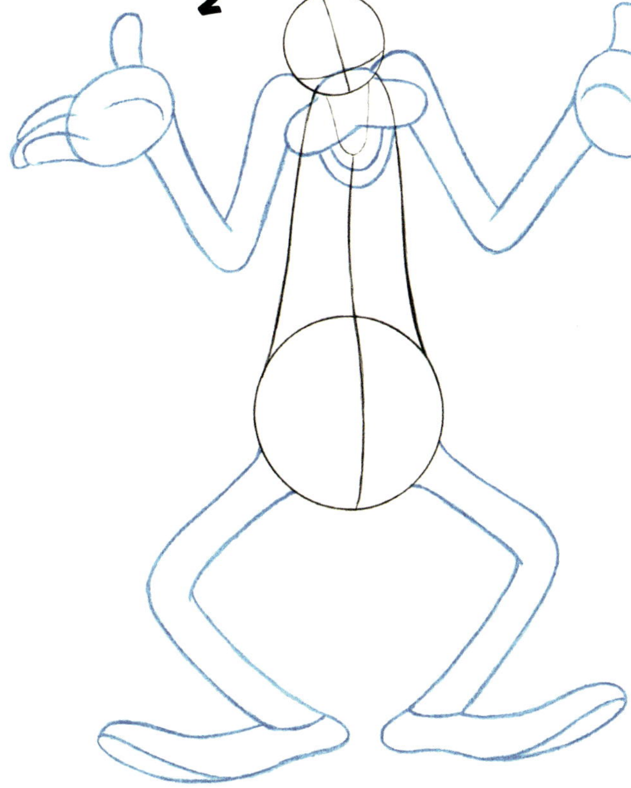

3

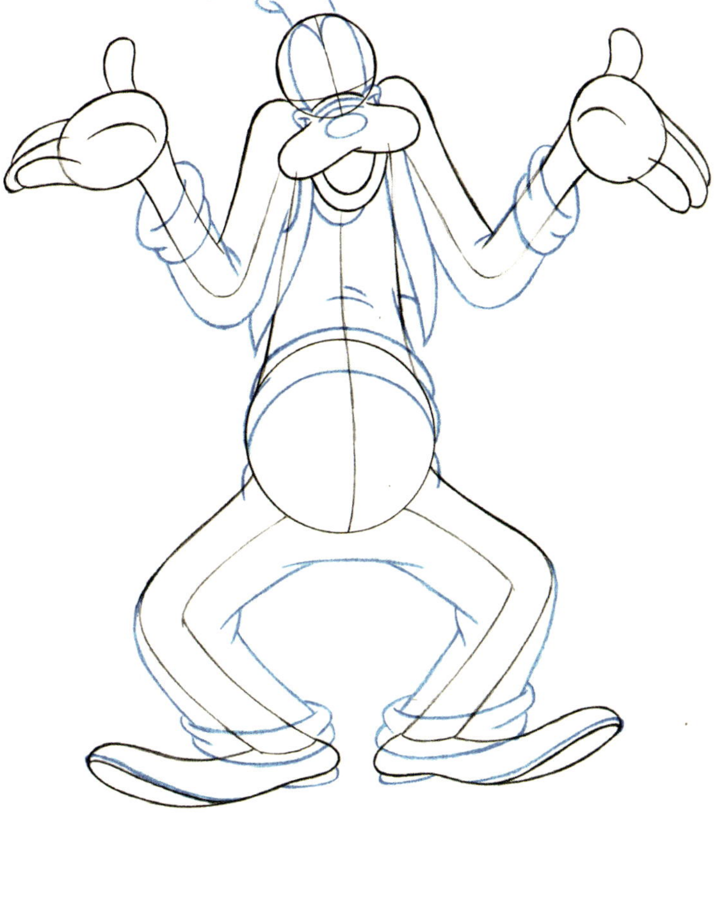

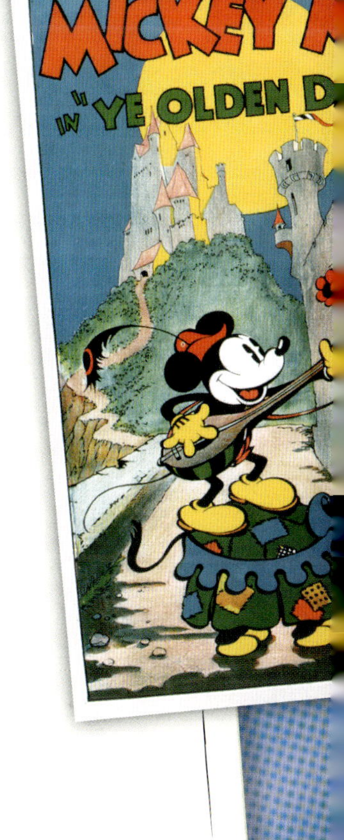
WALT DISN
MICKEY M
IN "YE OLDEN D

4

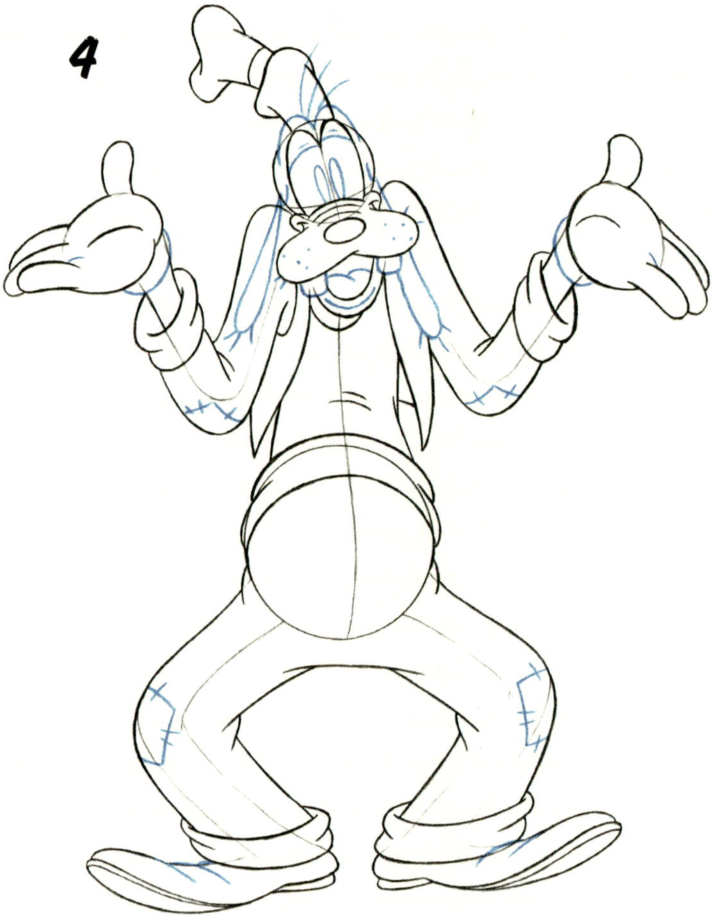

5

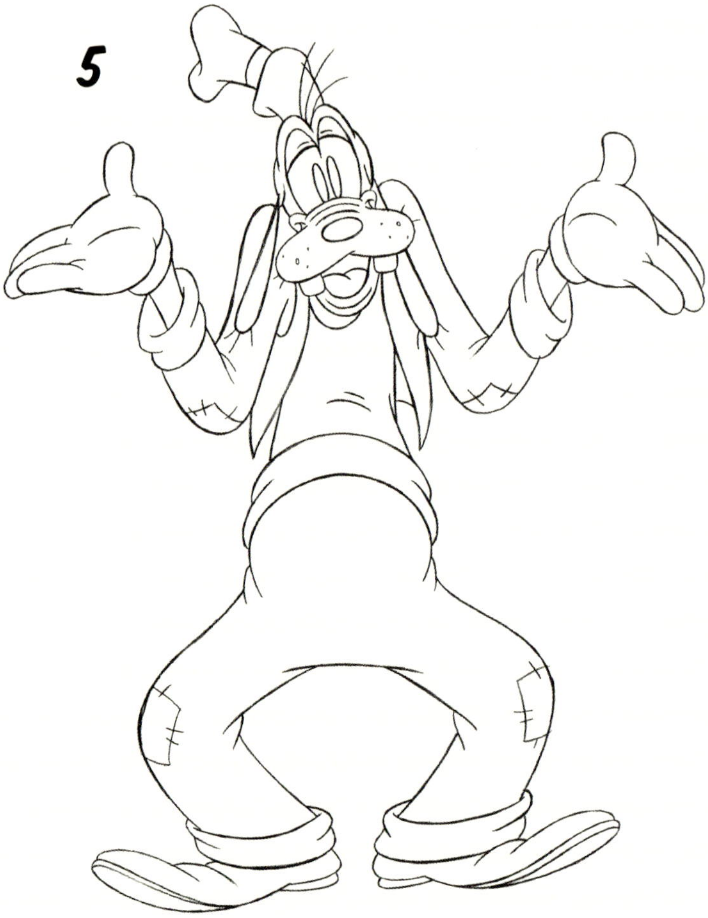

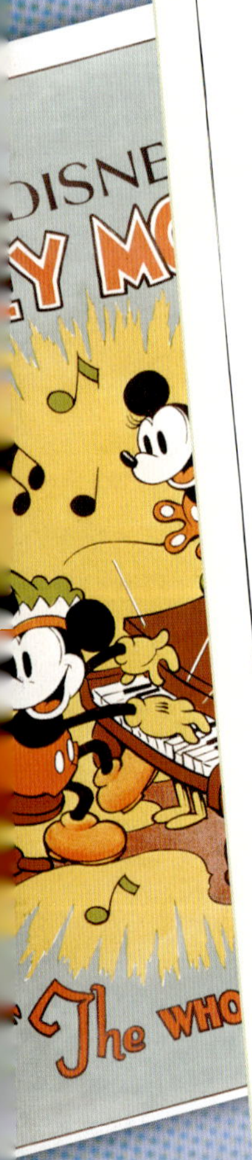

6

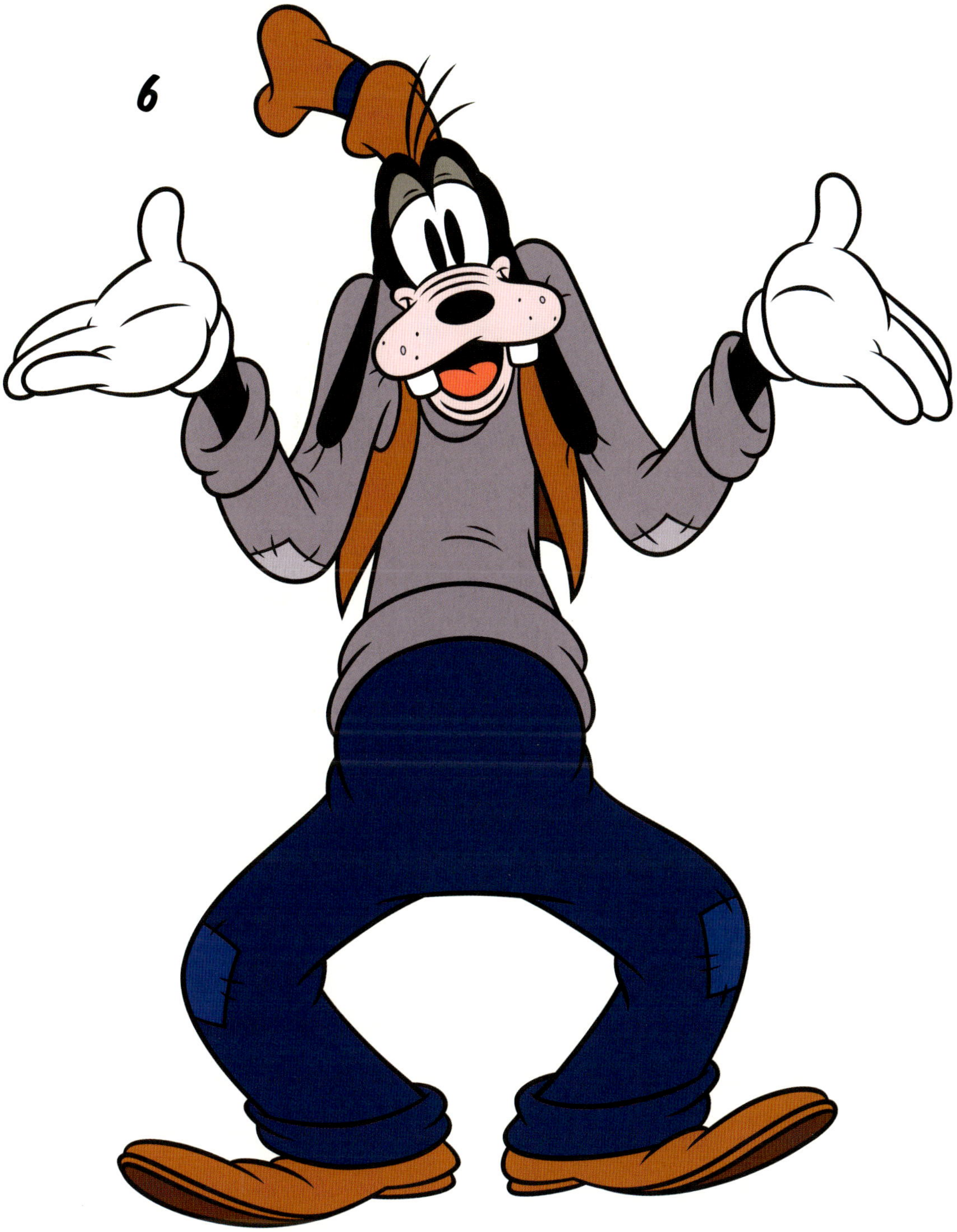

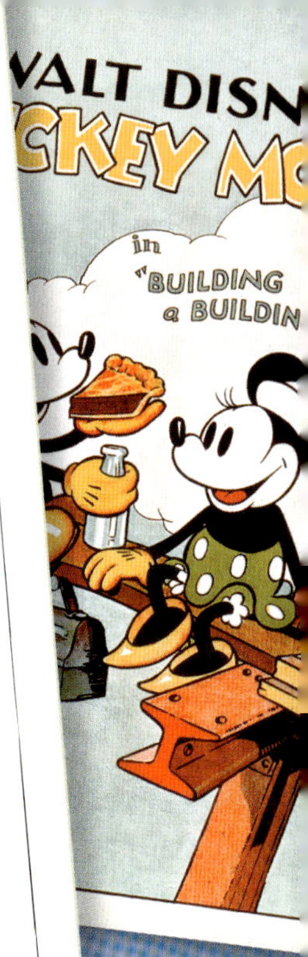
WALT DISN
CKEY MO
in
"BUILDING
a BUILDIN

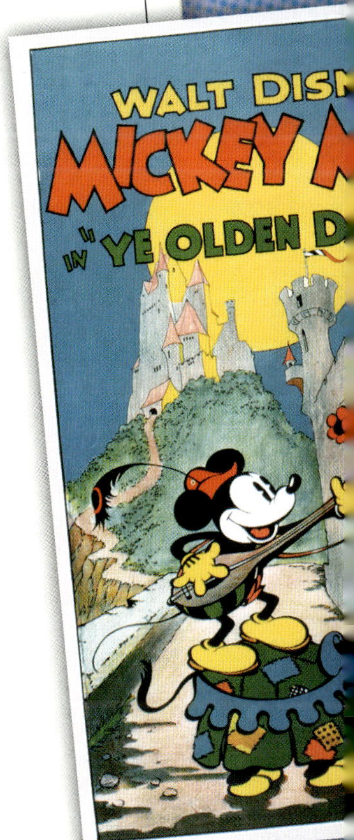
WALT DISN
MICKEY M
IN "YE OLDEN D

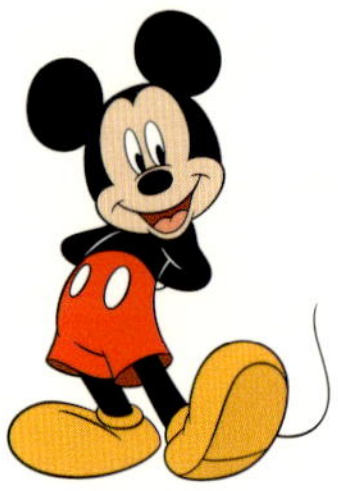

THE 1940s & BEYOND

THEN & NOW!

The seeds of the modern Mickey Mouse were planted in 1937. That was the year *Snow White and the Seven Dwarfs* marked Disney's move into feature films—and an upswing in the studio's drive toward cartoon realism. The dwarfs, supervised in part by Mickey's own Fred Moore, possessed boyish eyes and cheeks that were lifelike without being overdetailed: a design milestone at the time. Mickey and Minnie seemed old-fashioned by contrast, even after their mid-1930s Moore overhaul. Most tellingly, the whites of their eyes still covered their entire upper faces, a vestige of 1920s animated abstraction.

OPPOSITE PAGE: 1940 PROMOTIONAL POSTER FOR TUGBOAT MICKEY, *IMAGE COURTESY OF HERITAGE AUCTIONS*

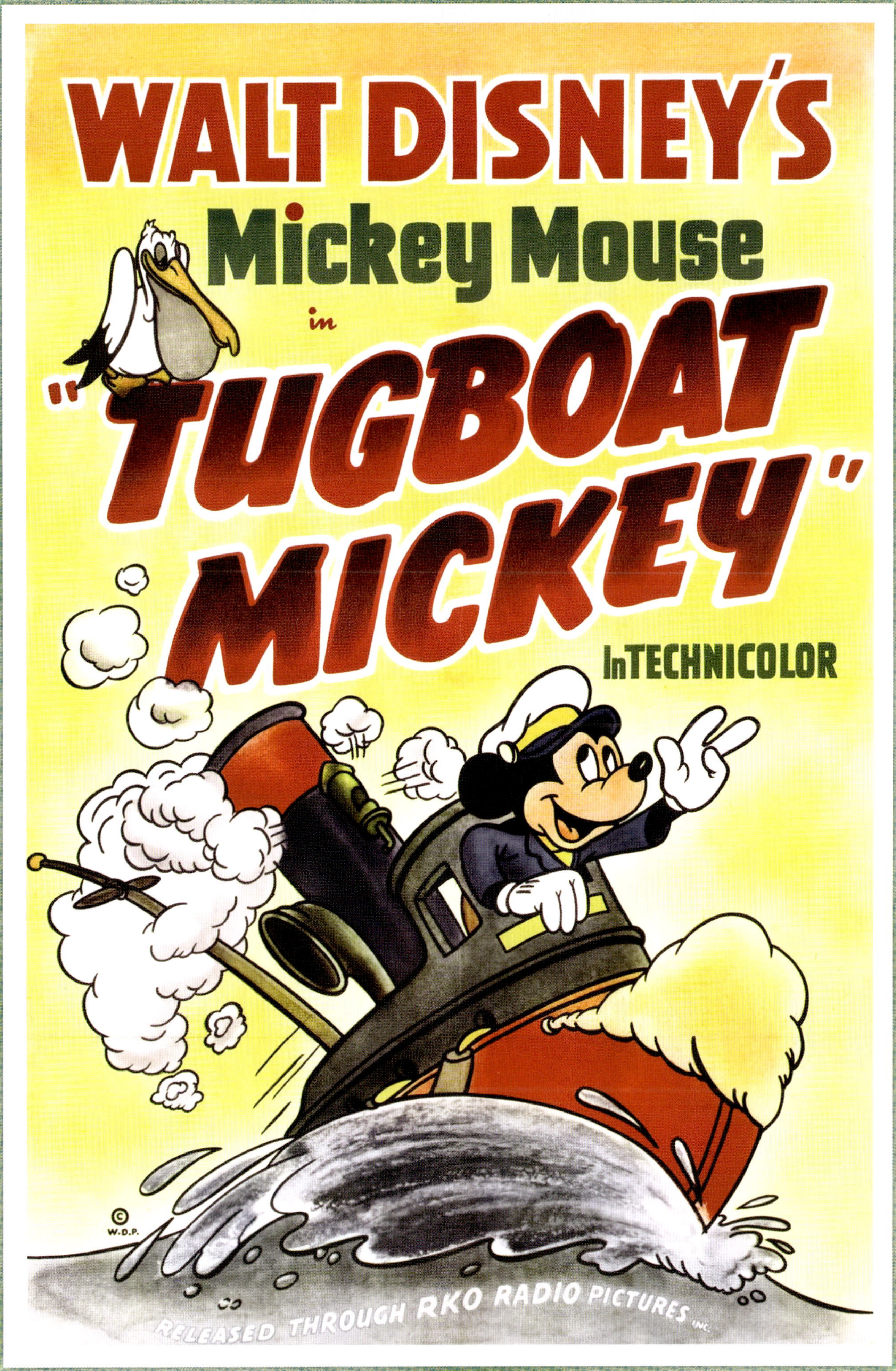

WALT DISNEY'S
Mickey Mouse
in
"TUGBOAT MICKEY"
In TECHNICOLOR
© W.D.P.
RELEASED THROUGH RKO RADIO PICTURES INC.

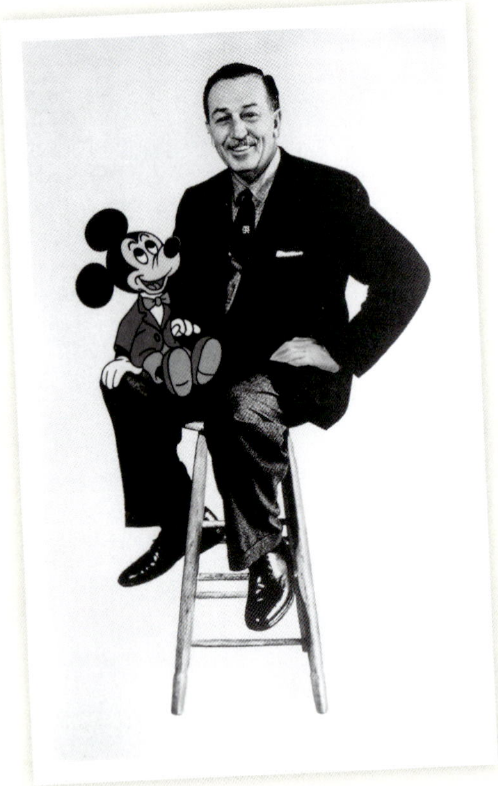

PUBLICITY SHOT OF WALT DISNEY AND MICKEY, 1958.

The fallout from Snow White changed all that. On the program for the feature film's wrap party, animator Ward Kimball—just for fun—tried drawing Mickey with more realistic, Dwarf-style eyes and cheeks. Soon Moore was using the technique on official model sheets. Mickey began to evolve: The new look—far from Mickey's beady-eyed barnyard roots—provided charm, nuance, and modernity.

In "The Sorcerer's Apprentice" segment of *Fantasia* (1938; released 1940), the eye-shift was realized in animation. Other shifts followed fast: By 1941, Moore's Minnie had her famous giant hair bow, and Mickey had slightly bulkier hands and feet. While not undermining the new realism, these touches added back a bit of exaggeration—for a slicker, bouncier look.

1940s AND BEYOND ANIMATION TIMELINE

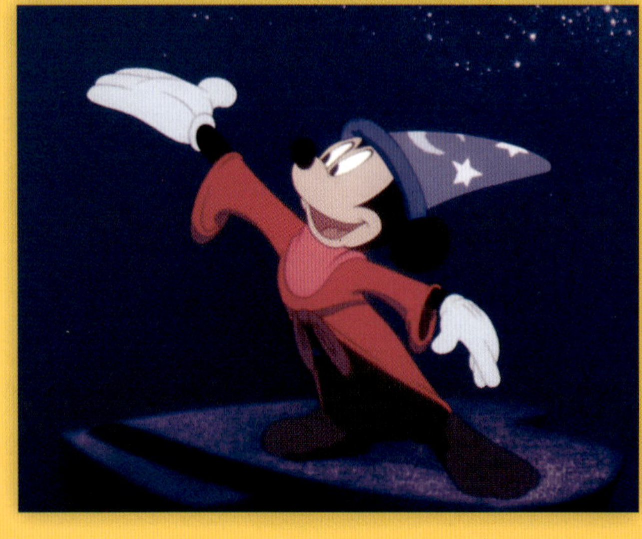

1940

THE SORCERER'S APPRENTICE FROM FANTASIA

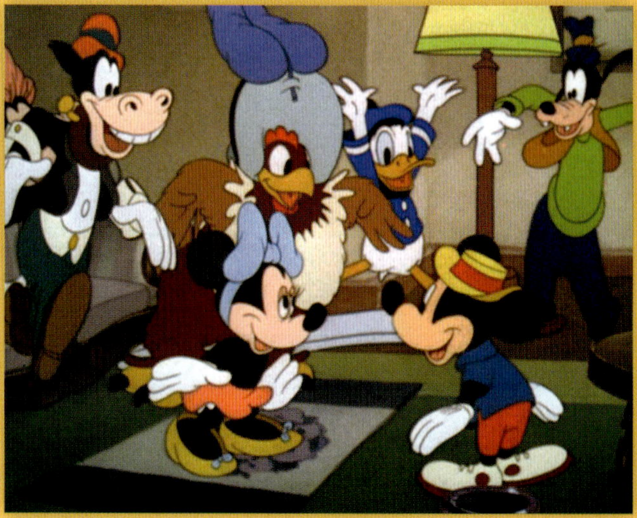

1942

MICKEY'S BIRTHDAY PARTY

The ever-clumsy Goofy was also given some bounce: the 1940s saw the Goof forego his earlier sleepy-eyed appearance, now rushing into clumsy hijinks with new bravado. But the real 1940s bravado belonged to Daisy Duck. Actually born as "Donna" in 1937, Daisy got her final name three years later—along with a classier, definitive wardrobe. Then, as now, Daisy's classy exterior hides the fact that her temper is almost as bad as Donald's. She is one of very few beings able to put him in his place!

The early 1940s Mickey, Minnie, and Goofy are the direct forerunners of today's models, first drawn in 1997 by creative director John Loter. Loter's Donald and Daisy, meanwhile, owe much to late 1940s designs by director Jack Hannah. But the intervening decades have also seen many other famous "looks" for the Standard Characters—because the Disney creative teams have never stopped experimenting.

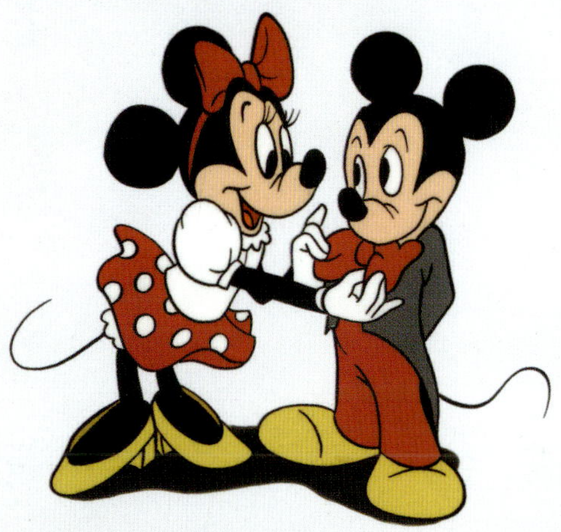

PUBLICITY DRAWING, 1980s

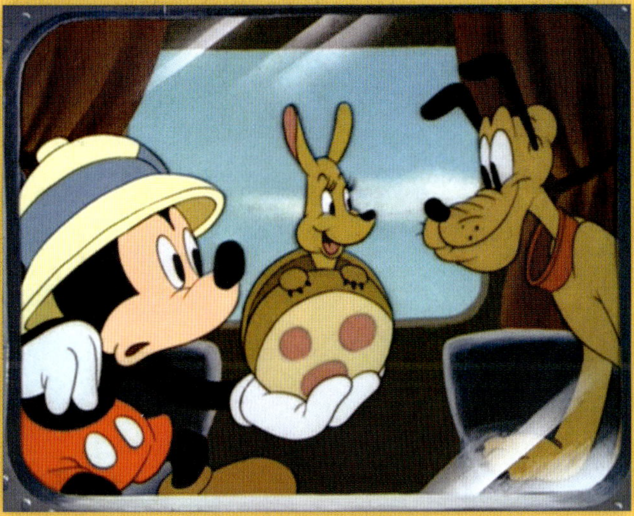

1943

PLUTO AND THE ARMADILLO
(LAST TIME MICKEY APPEARS IN HIS RED SHORTS UNTIL 1995)

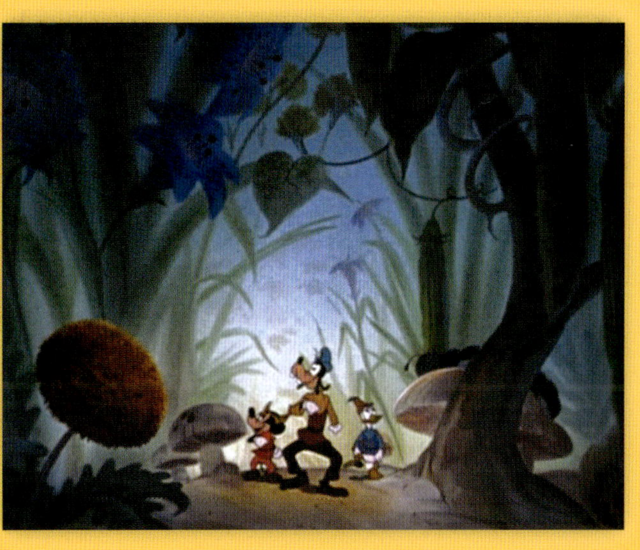

1947

MICKEY AND THE BEANSTALK
(FEATURED IN THE FILM FUN AND FANCY FREE)

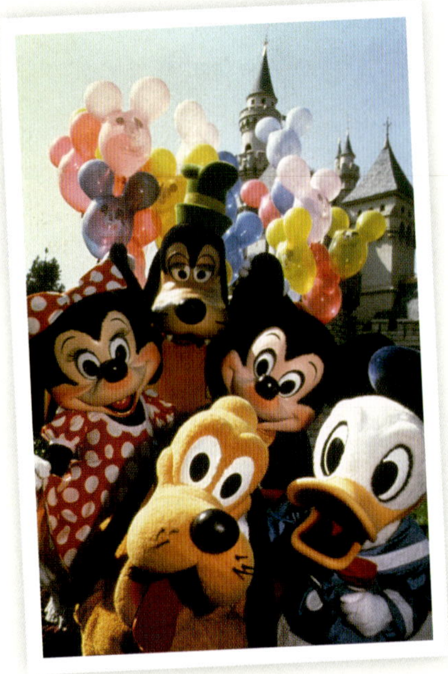

One 1940s Fred Moore design, for instance, gave Mickey and Minnie floppy ears that turned in realistic perspective. At the other extreme, 1950s TV commercials by animator Tom Oreb turned Mickey into a Picasso-like, pointy-nosed abstraction. Still other 1950s designs gave Goofy smaller eyes and nerdier, close-set buckteeth.

Then, of course, came the quintessential postwar Disney makeover: the "grown-up" Mickey Mouse, informally nicknamed "Mickey Ricardo" within the studio today. In 1950, *The Los Angeles Mirror* announced that our hero had "traded his old buttoned [shorts] for a well-draped suit and fancy bow tie. And between those famous big ears, the Mouse will sport a snappy fedora."[1] *The Mirror* called this Mickey's "new, hip appearance"—yet, as per his nickname, "Mickey Ricardo" owed more to the father figures of concurrent golden age TV sitcoms. In cartoons, he was almost exclusively cast as Pluto's bossy parent; in comics,

1940s AND BEYOND ANIMATION TIMELINE

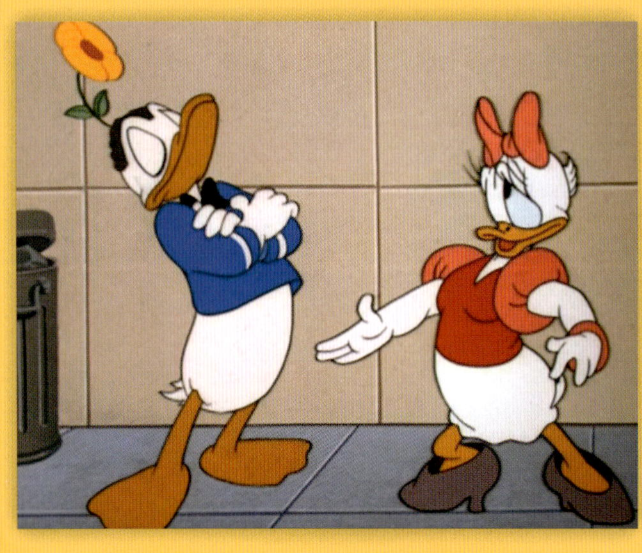

1947

DONALD'S DILEMMA
(DAISY DUCK'S MOST CELEBRATED PERFORMANCE)

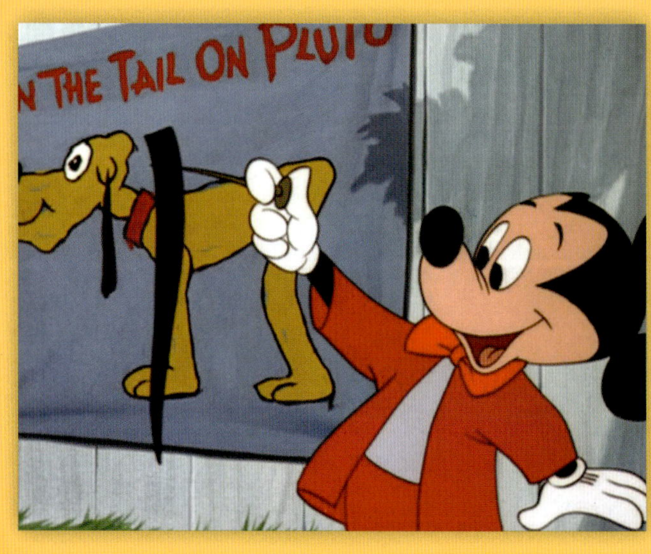

1952

PLUTO'S PARTY
(FIRST USE OF EYEBROWS ON MICKEY IN ANIMATION)

he became a serious-minded detective, a loose adult evolution of his youthful adventurer self. In that form, at least, the long-pants Mickey continues as a popular variant today; even if never, exactly, hip.

The classic, short-pants Mickey Mouse and his evergreen gang of Minnie, Donald, Daisy, Goofy, and Pluto are at once the most iconic versions of our cantankerous clan—and the longest lived. It's hard to even look at them without thinking of the adventures, the mischief, the frustration, and the outrageous humor they've shared with us over the years.

By drawing them ourselves, in their storied variations, we can forever send them on escapades anew.

[1] "In a 'Retail' Deal—It's a Comeback for Mickey Mouse." *The Mirror* (Los Angeles: November 18, 1950).

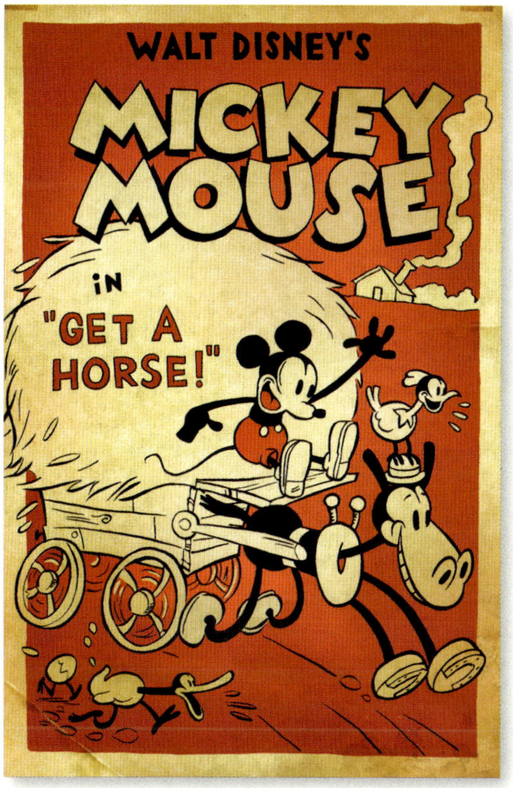

GET A HORSE! *PROMOTIONAL POSTER (2013).*

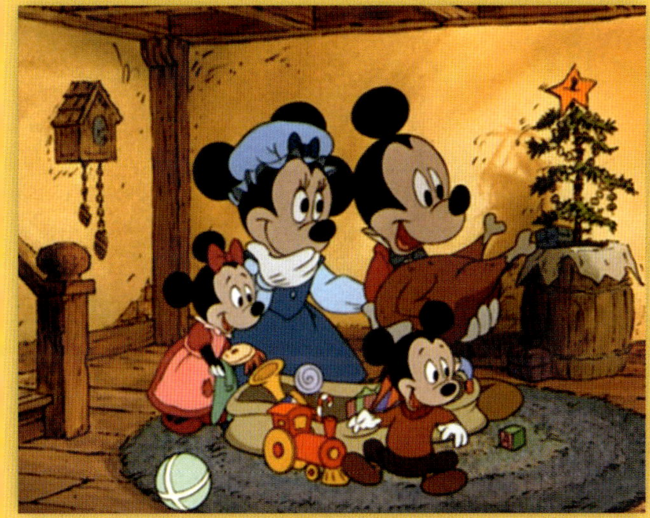

1983

MICKEY'S CHRISTMAS CAROL
(MICKEY'S FIRST SCREEN APPEARANCE SINCE 1953)

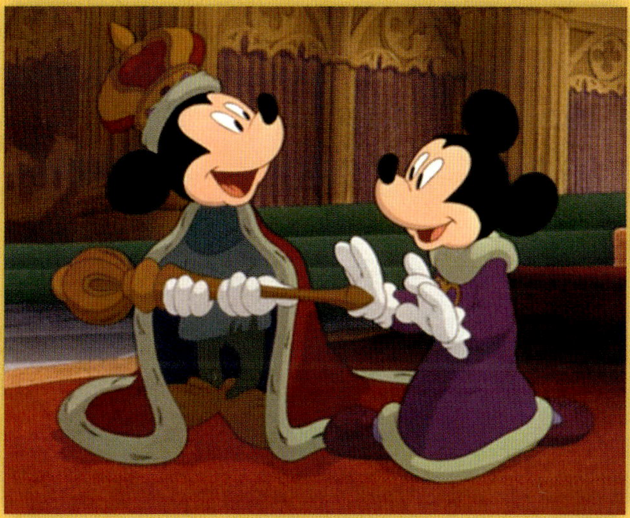

1990

THE PRINCE AND THE PAUPER

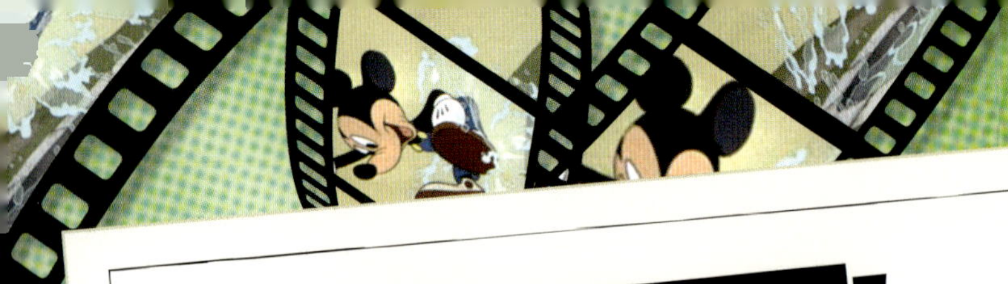

1940s

MICKEY MOUSE

THE LITTLE WHIRLWIND

1

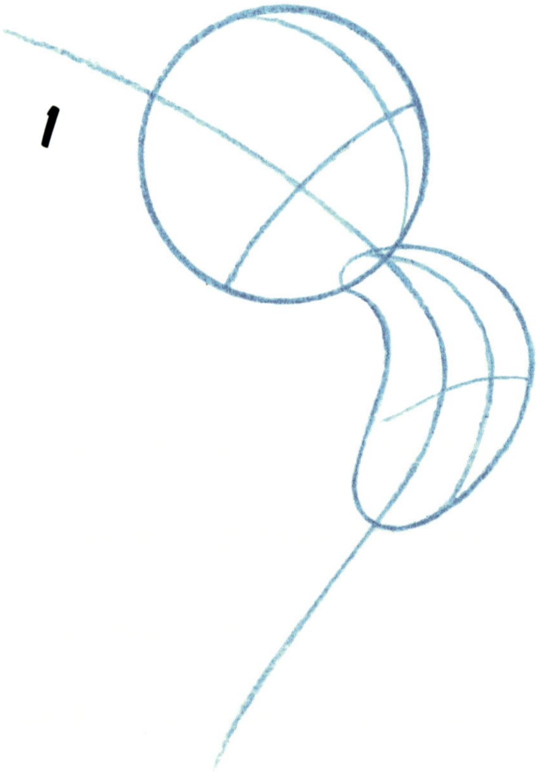

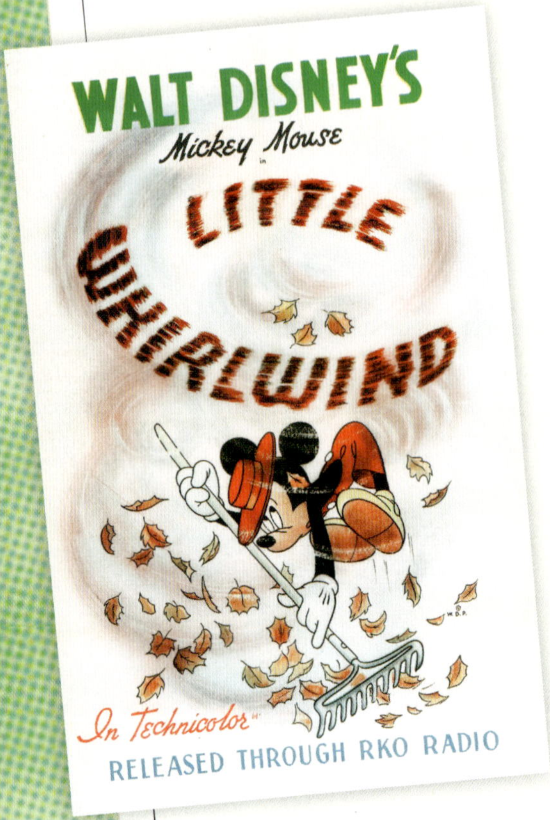

IMAGE COURTESY OF HERITAGE AUCTIONS.

FILM FACT

MICKEY'S PATIENCE AND DETERMINATION ARE PUT TO THE TEST IN THIS SHORT WHEN HE BATTLES A HUMANIZED BABY TORNADO AND ITS GIGANTIC, DANGEROUS "MAMA."

2

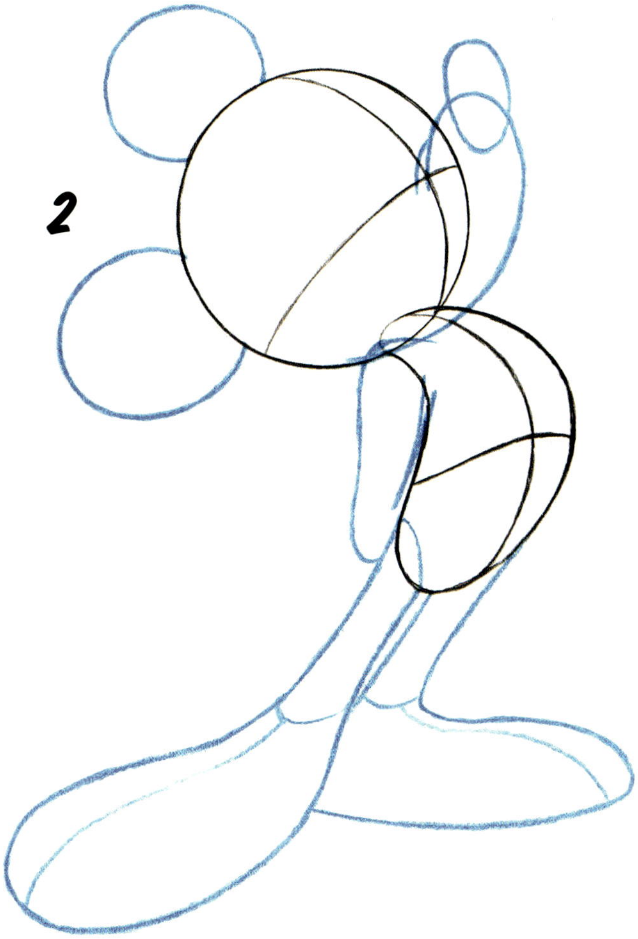

3

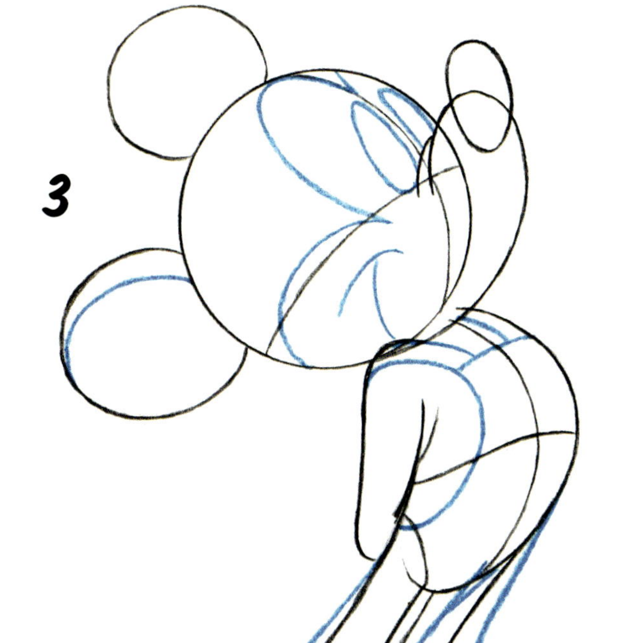

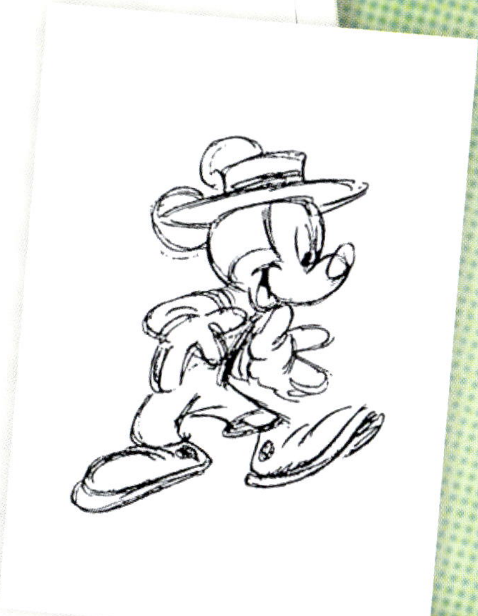

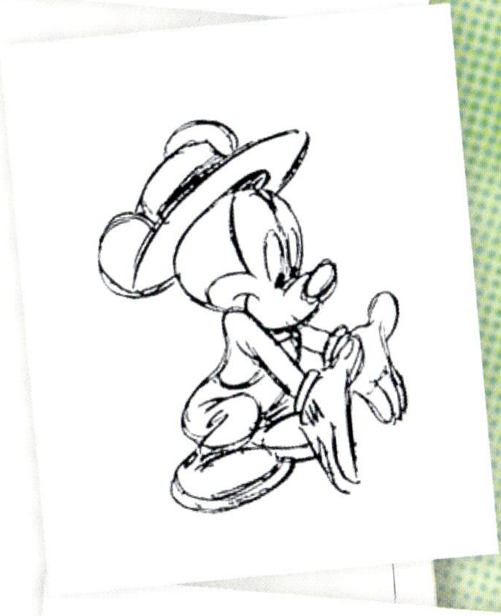

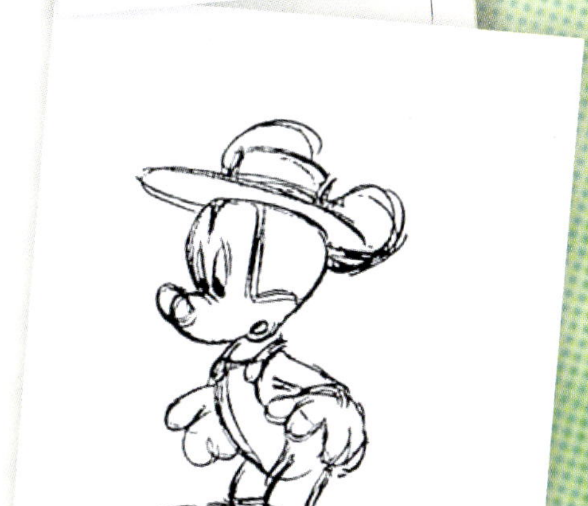

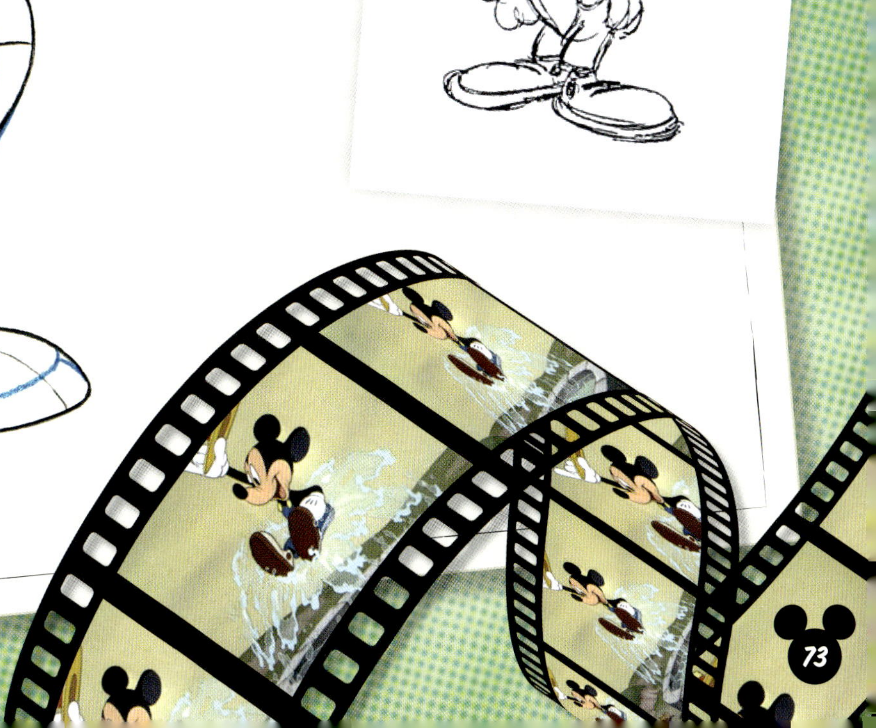

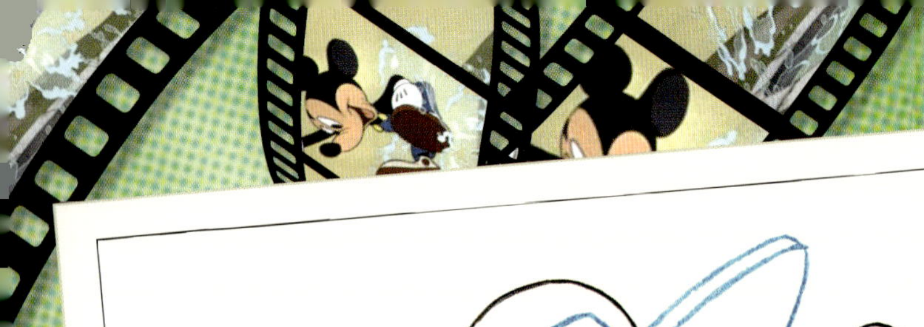

4

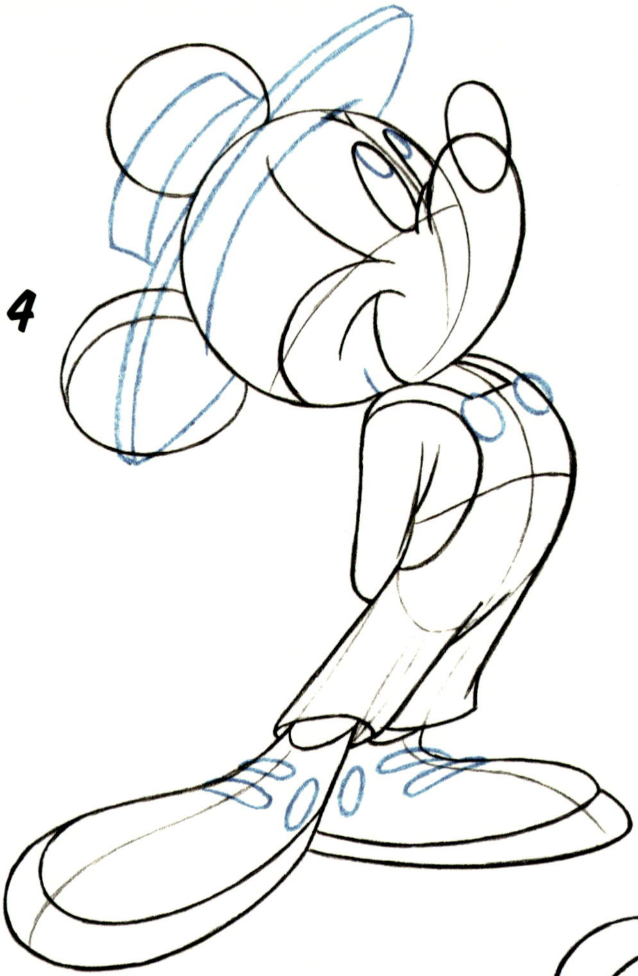

THE LITTLE WHIRLWIND MARKED THE DEBUT OF MICKEY'S NEWLY UPDATED EARS, CHANGED TO WORK IN PERSPECTIVE, AS WELL AS A SLIMMER BODY AND LARGER HANDS AND HEAD.

5

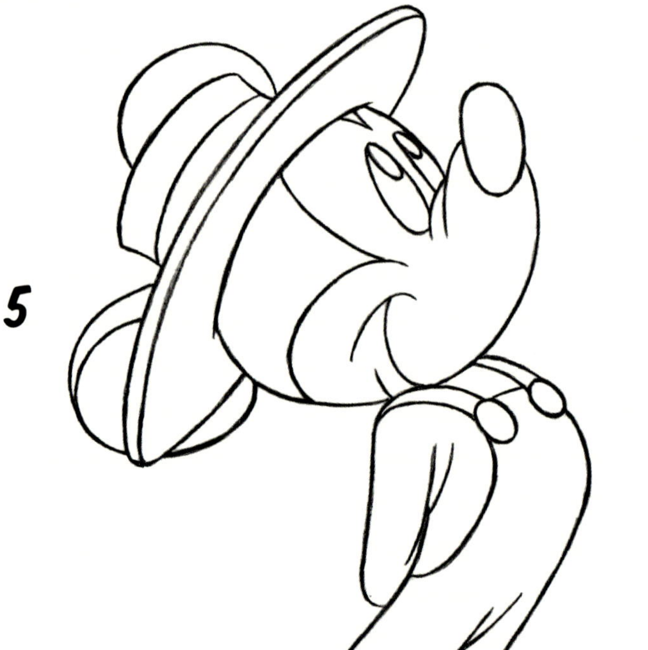

6

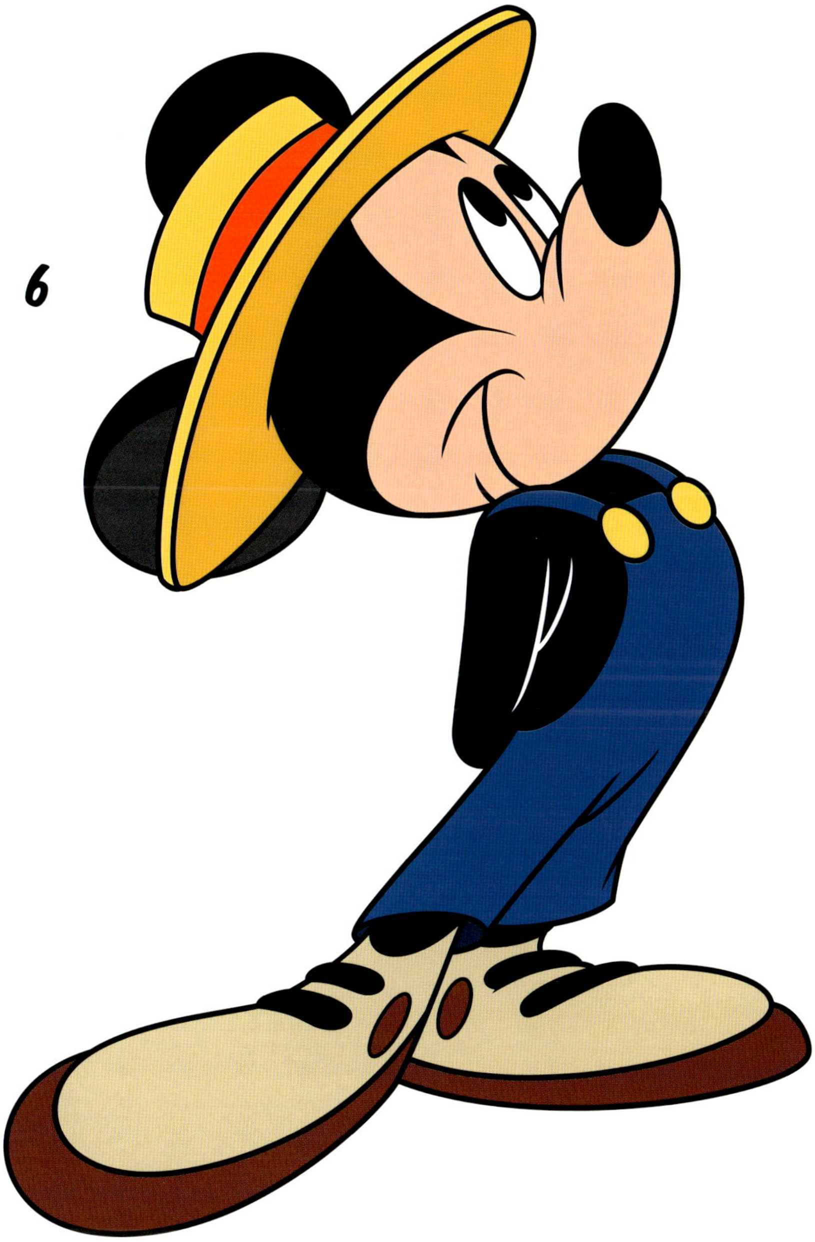

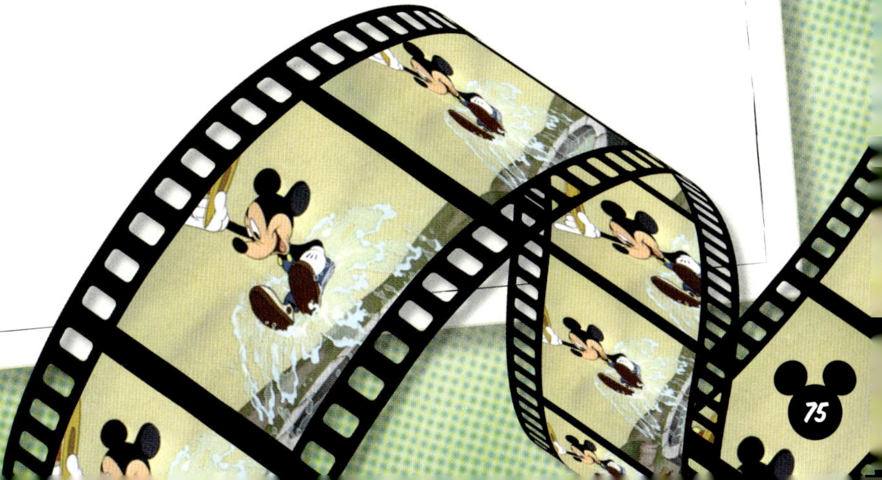

1940s

MICKEY MOUSE

SORCERER'S APPRENTICE

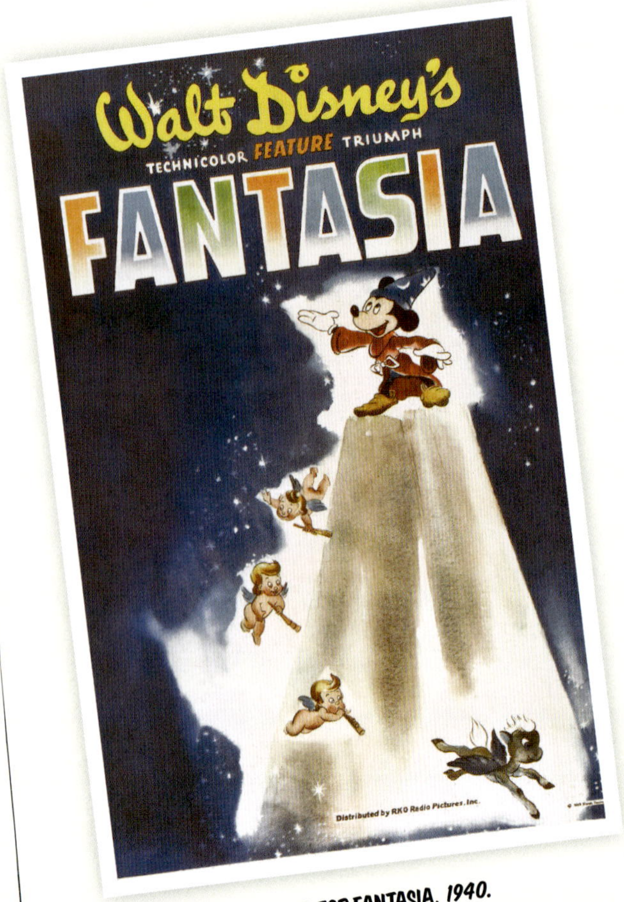

PROMOTIONAL POSTER FOR FANTASIA, 1940.

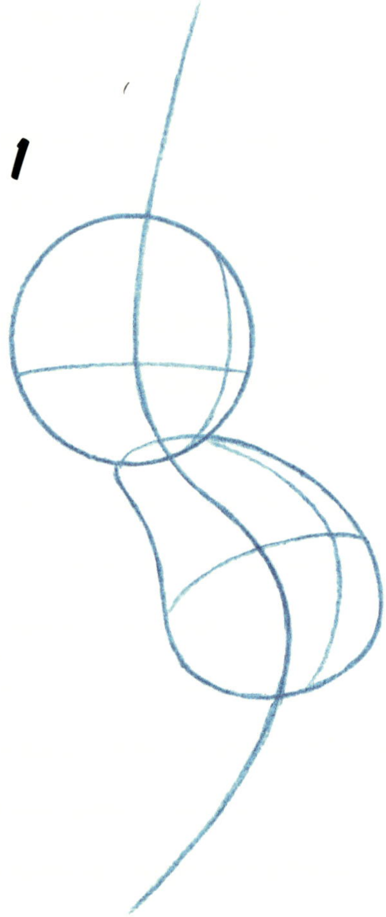

FILM FACT

"THE SORCERER'S APPRENTICE" STORY IS BASED ON A LEGENDARY GERMAN POEM BY GOETHE, IN WHICH THE EPONYMOUS HERO TRIES SOLVING PROBLEMS WITH HIS MASTER'S MAGIC AND GETS IN OVER HIS HEAD. IN DISNEY'S VERSION, THE SORCERER IS NAMED YEN SID; TRY SPELLING IT BACKWARDS.

2

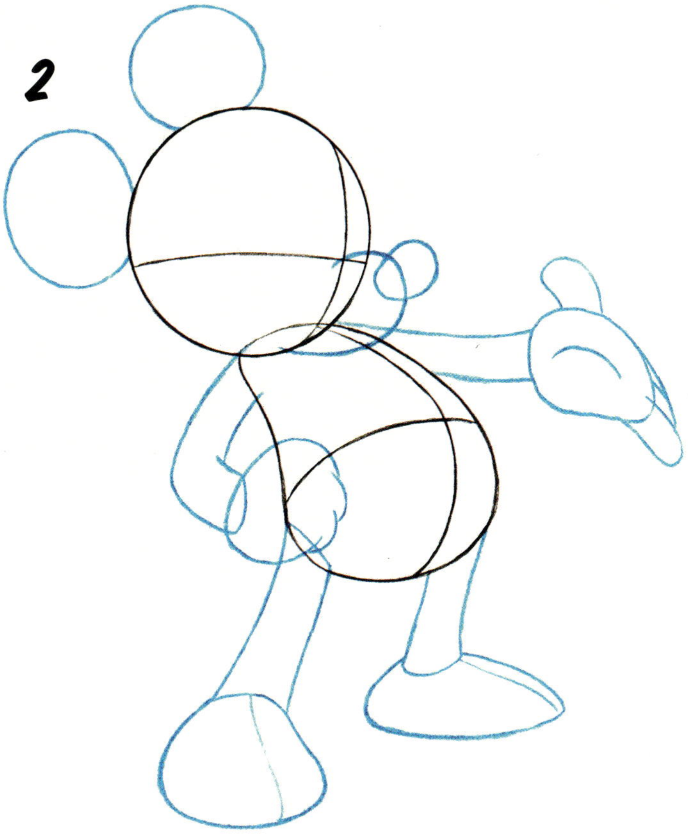

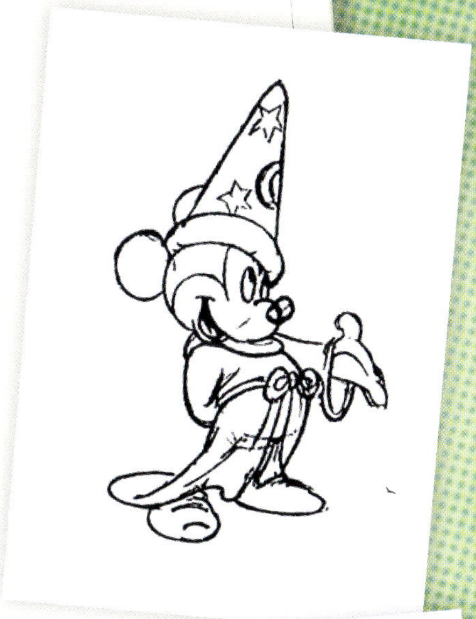

3

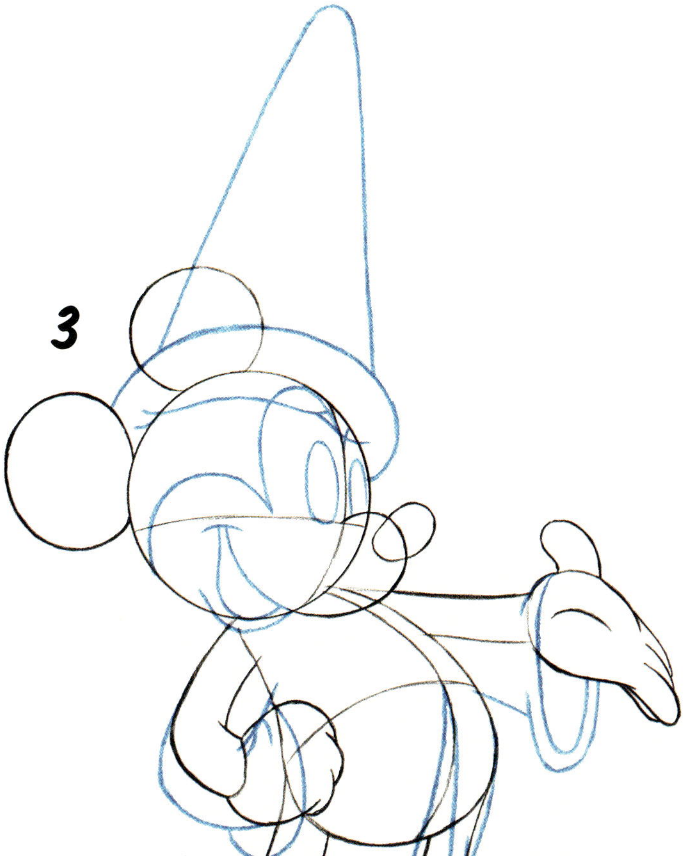

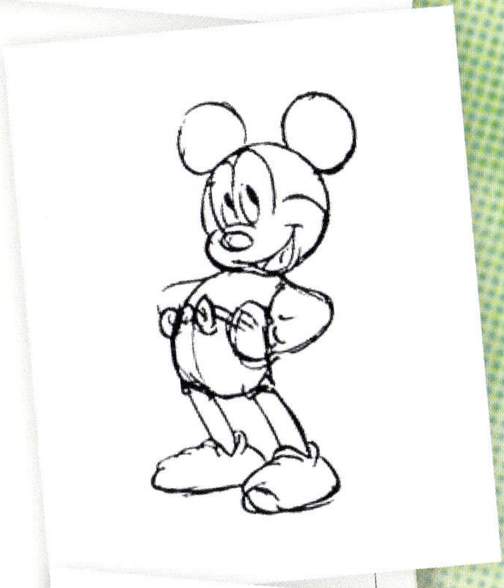

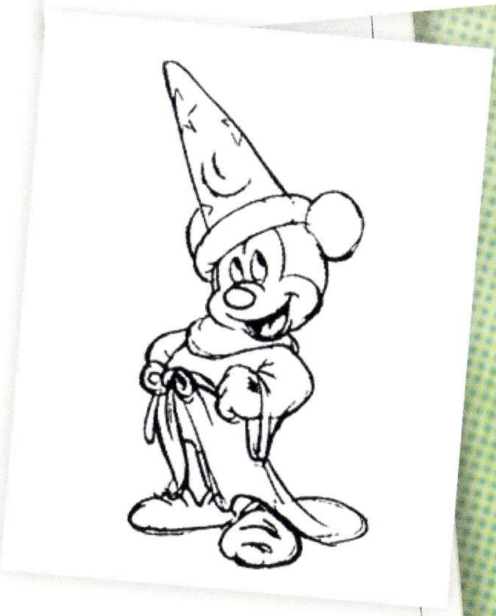

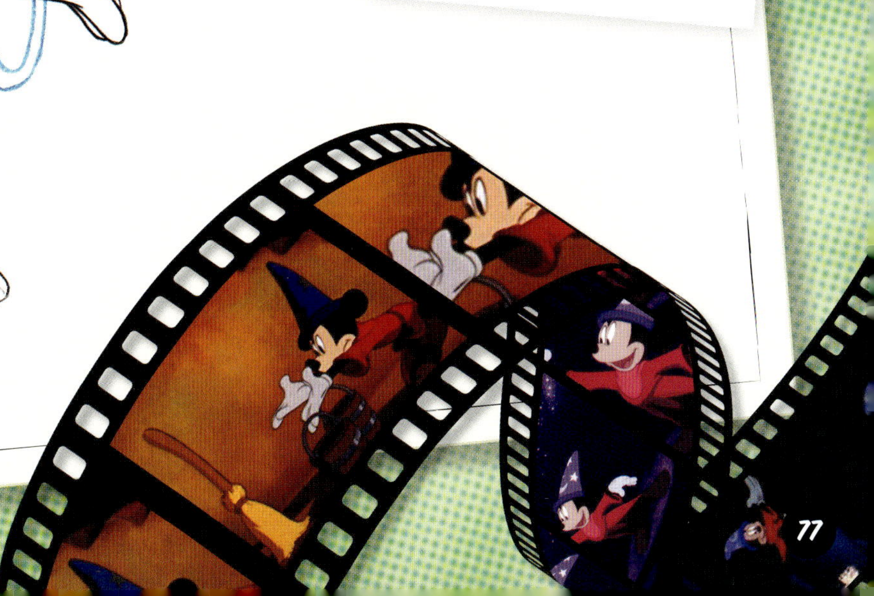

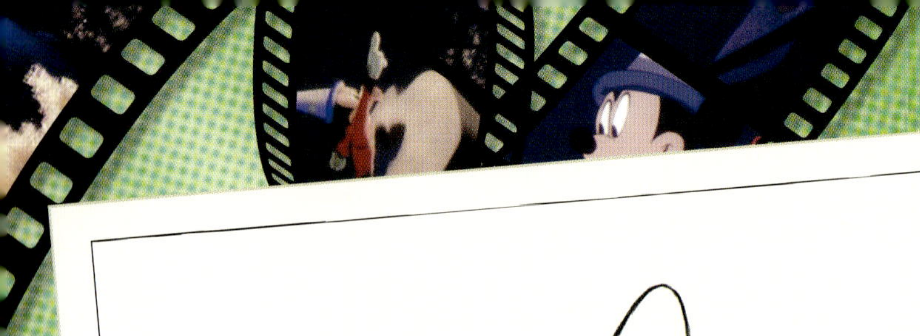

THE VERY FIRST USE OF MICKEY'S NEW EYE DESIGN WAS ON THE PROGRAM FOR THE SNOW WHITE AND THE SEVEN DWARFS WRAP PARTY IN 1938 (OPPOSITE). MICKEY'S MODERN DESIGN WAS ANIMATED FOR THE FIRST TIME IN "THE SORCERER'S APPRENTICE" IN 1940.

4

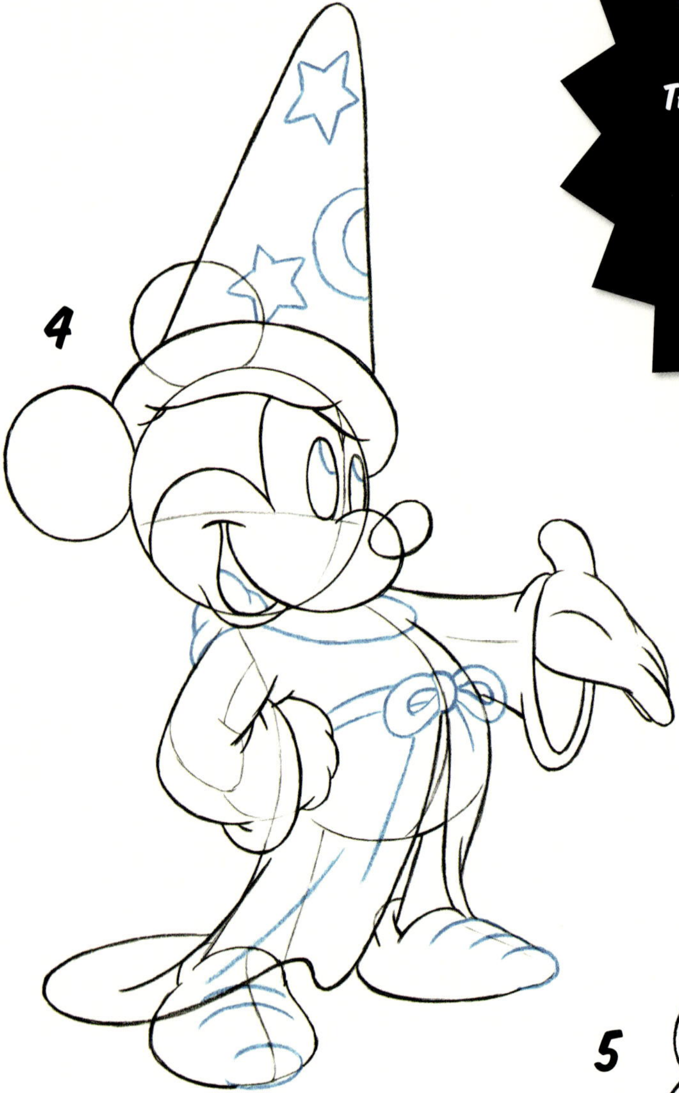

5

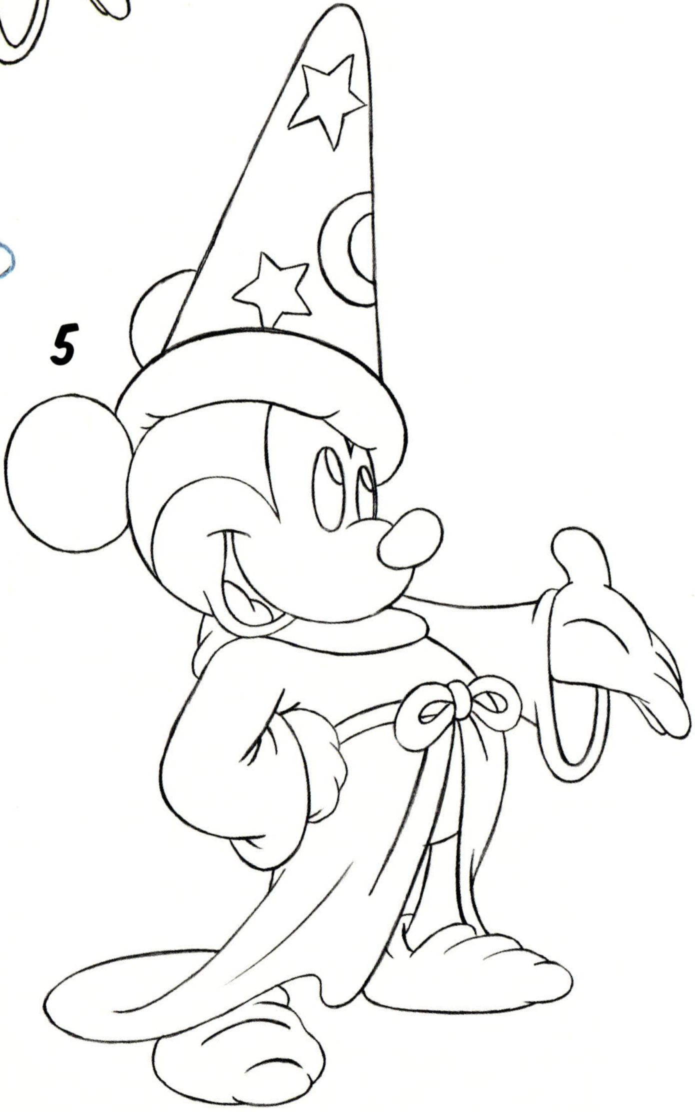

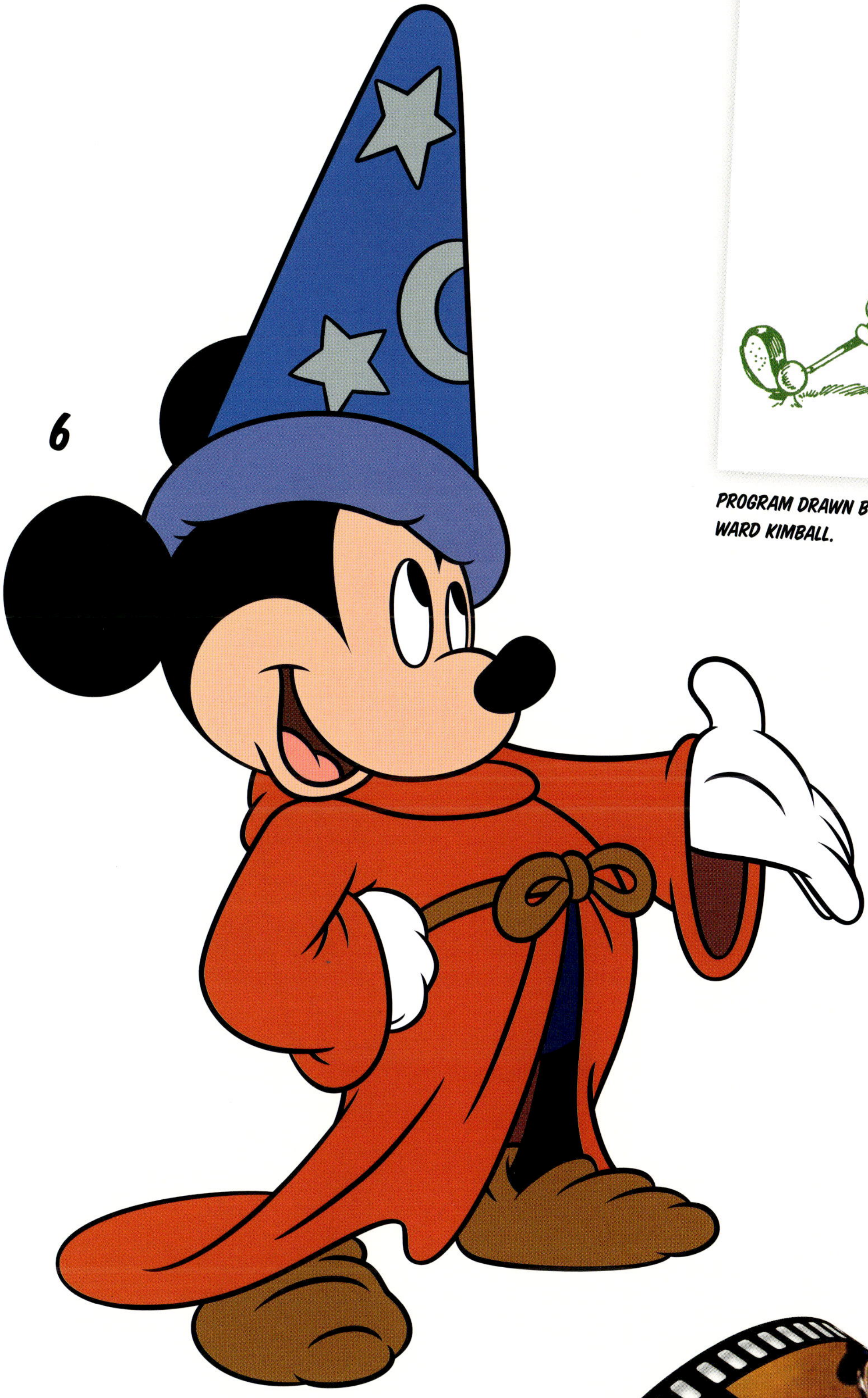

6

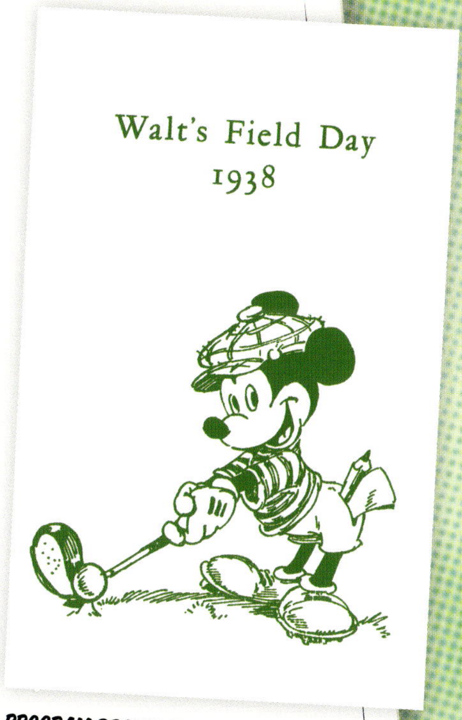

PROGRAM DRAWN BY WARD KIMBALL.

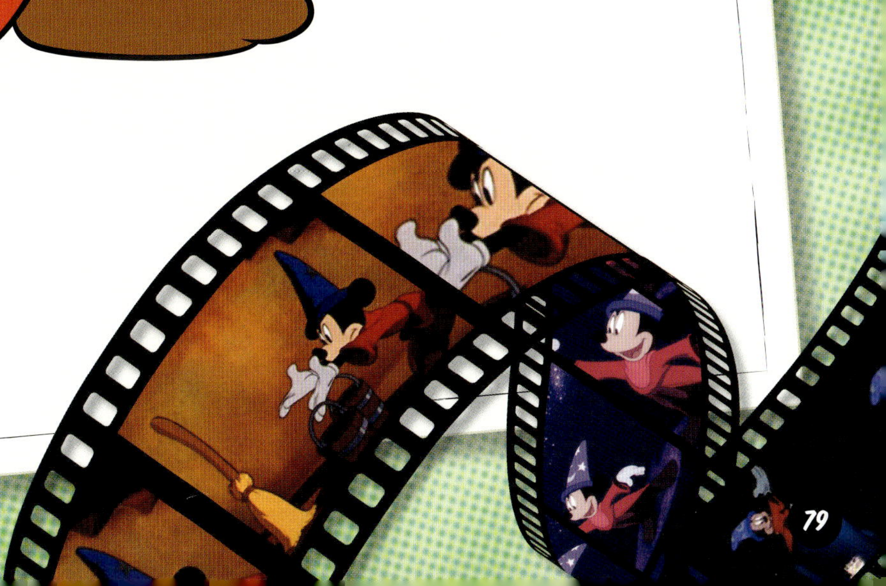

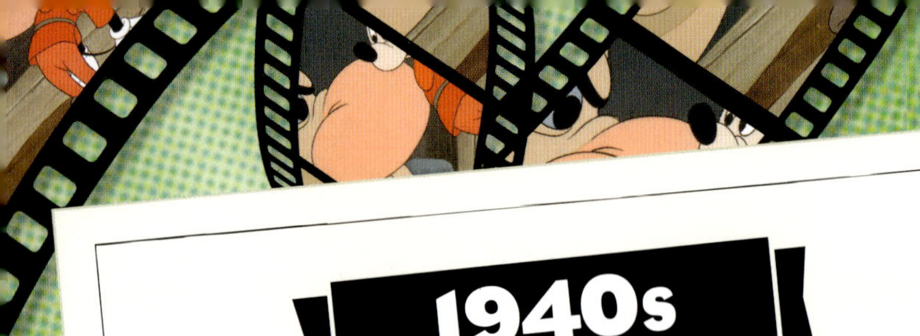

1940s

MICKEY MOUSE

MICKEY AND THE BEANSTALK

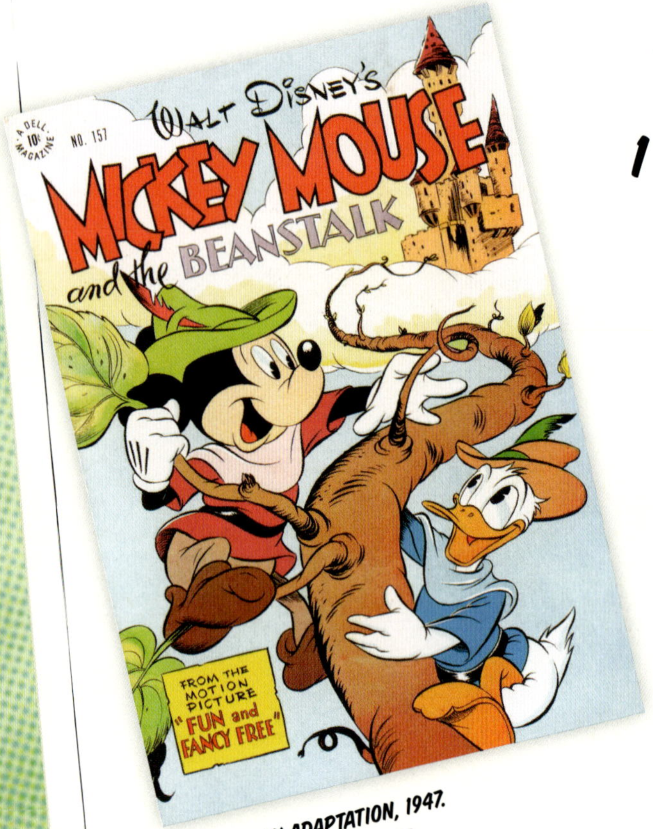

COMIC BOOK ADAPTATION, 1947.
ART BY HARVEY EISENBERG.

1

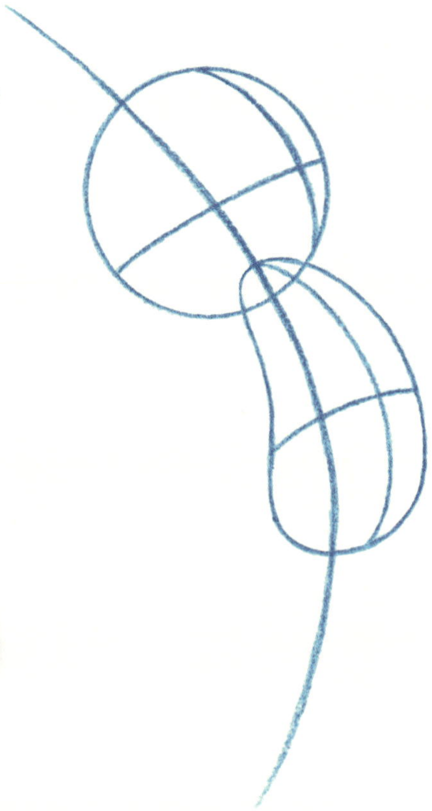

FILM FACT

AS DISNEY'S ADAPTATION OF THE FAMOUS ENGLISH FAIRY TALE JACK AND THE BEANSTALK, "MICKEY AND THE BEANSTALK" WAS THE FINAL TIME WALT DISNEY HIMSELF VOICED MICKEY MOUSE IN FILM ANIMATION.

2

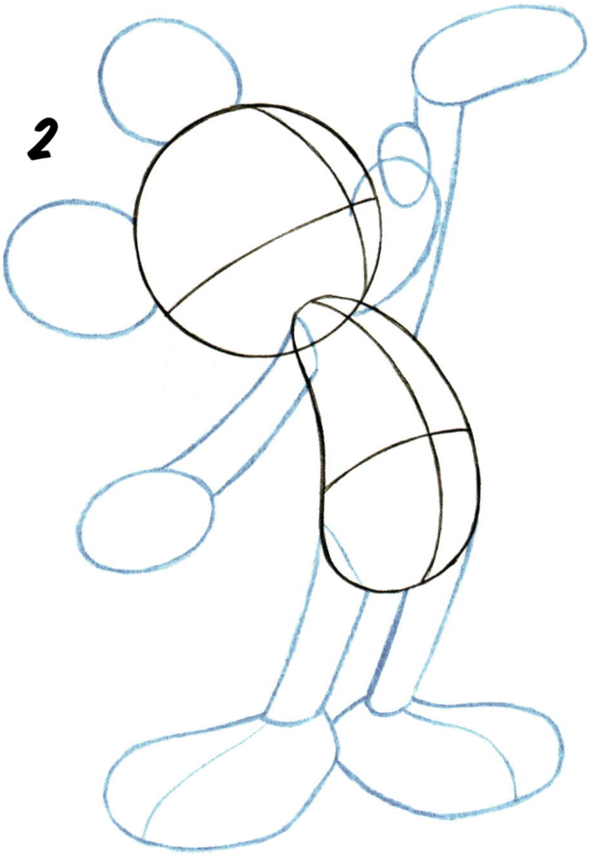

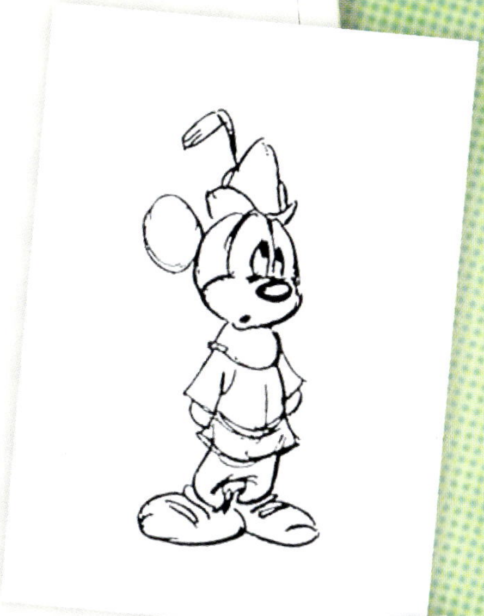

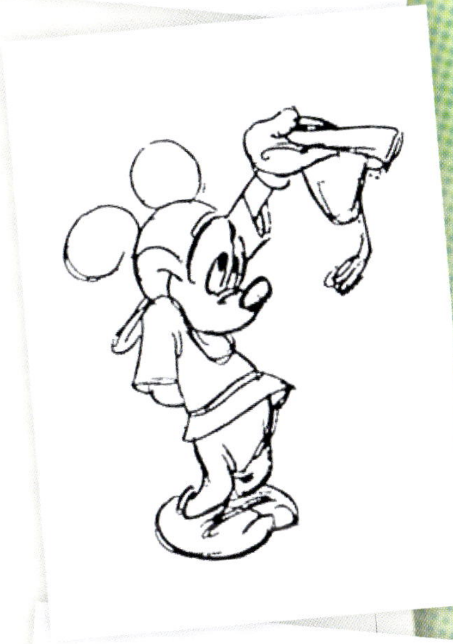

3

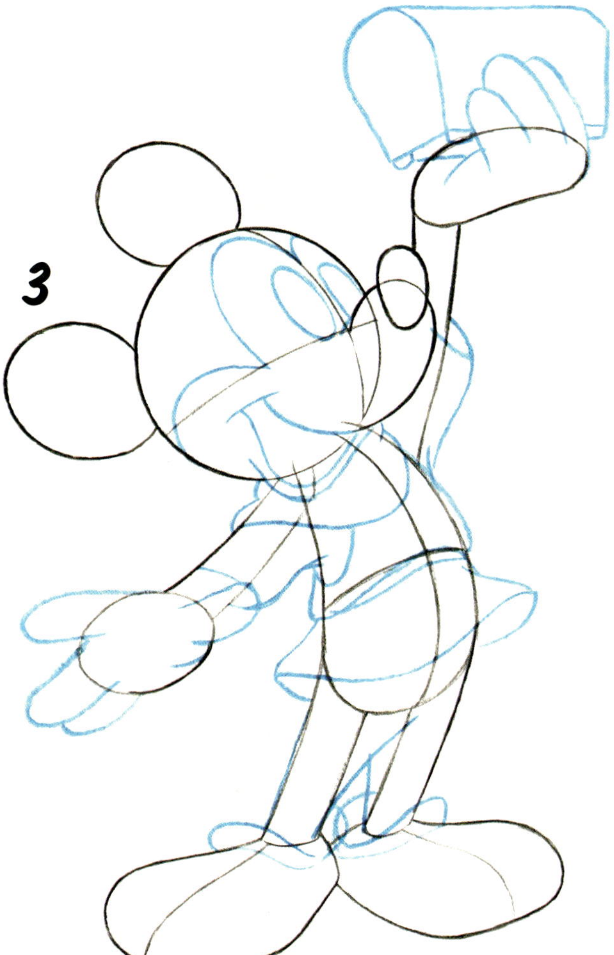

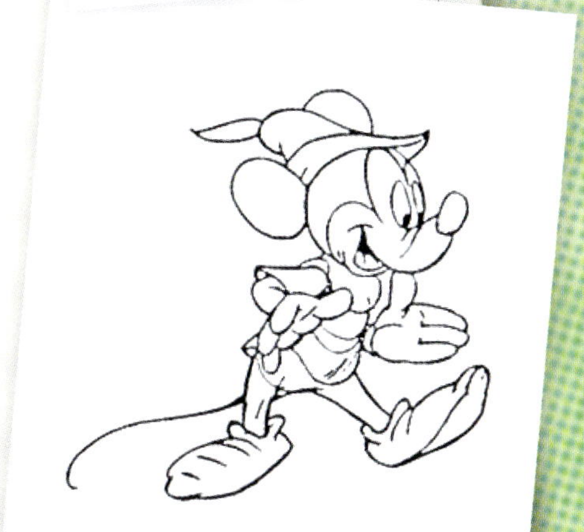

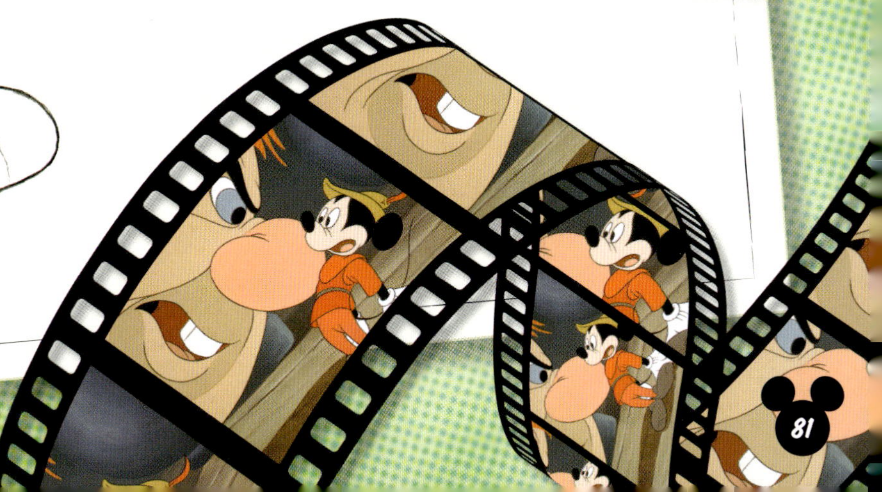

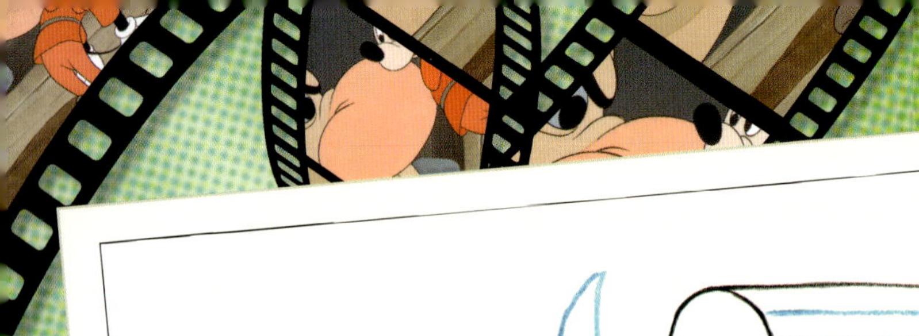

4

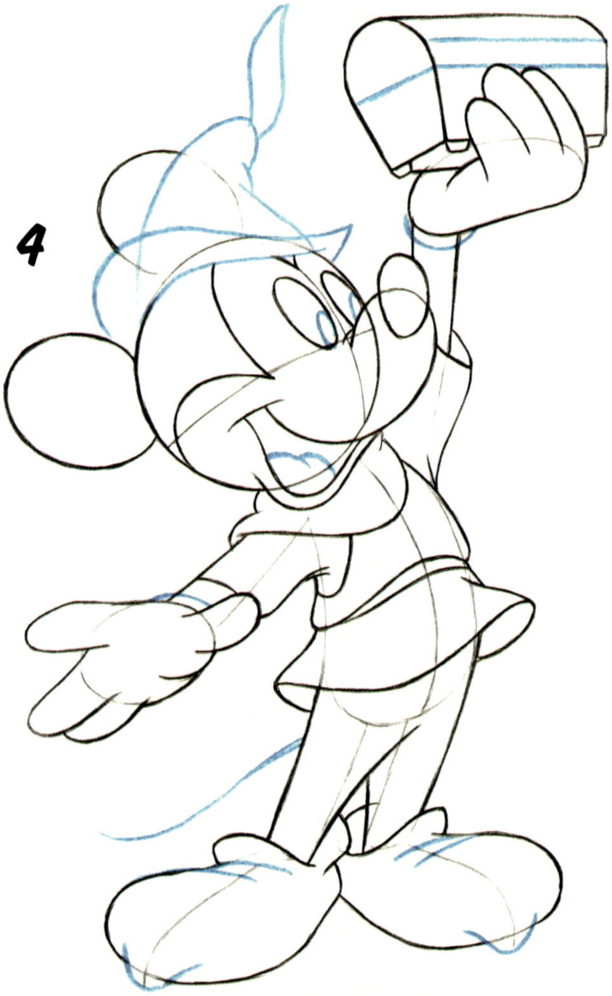

"MICKEY AND THE BEANSTALK" WAS COMPLETED AS A FEATURETTE-LENGTH FILM, BUT HAD EARLIER BEEN PLANNED AS A FEATURE—WITH SOME EXTRA CHARACTERS WHO WERE LATER DROPPED, SUCH AS QUEEN MINNIE AND A WIFE FOR WILLIE THE GIANT.

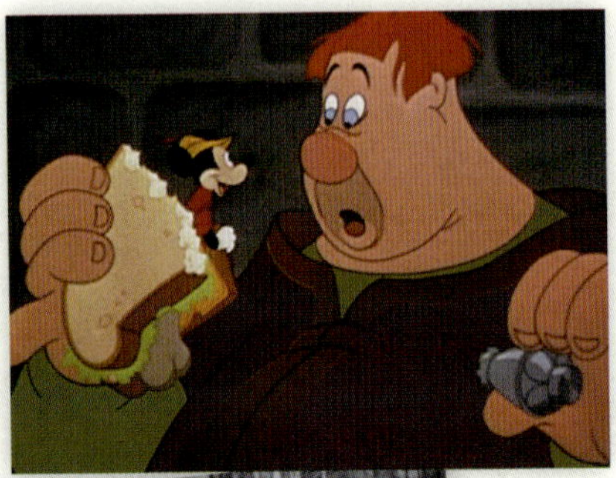

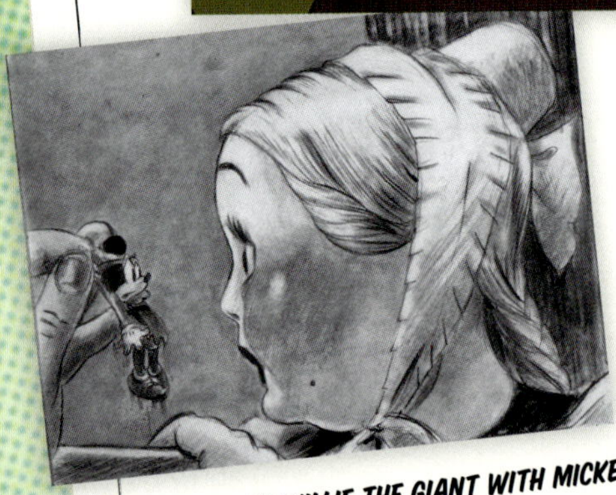

(ABOVE) WILLIE THE GIANT WITH MICKEY. (BELOW) LATE 1930S STORYBOARD FOR AN UNPRODUCED SECTION OF "MICKEY AND THE BEANSTALK," FEATURING WILLIE THE GIANT'S WIFE.

5

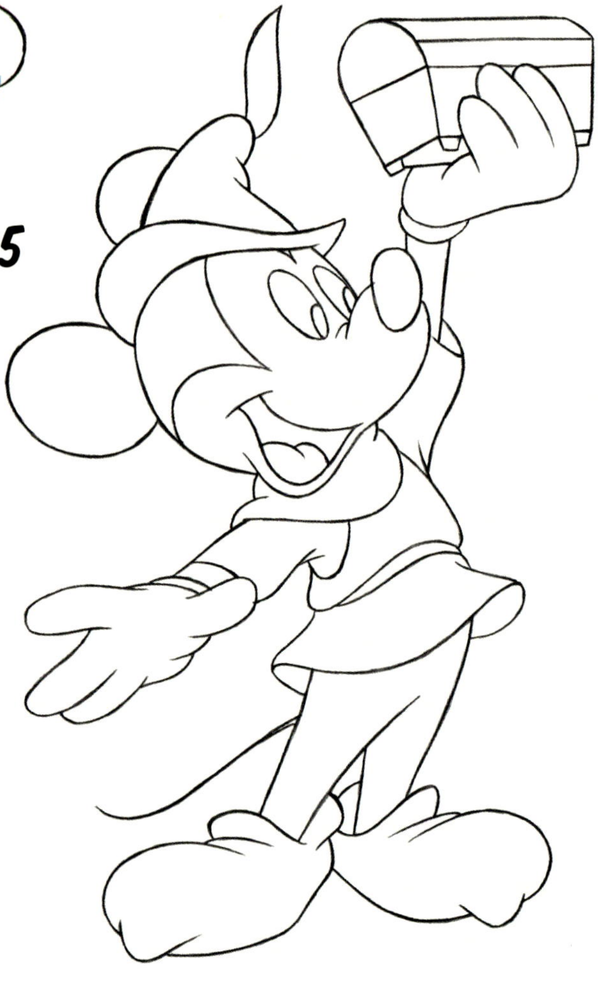

6

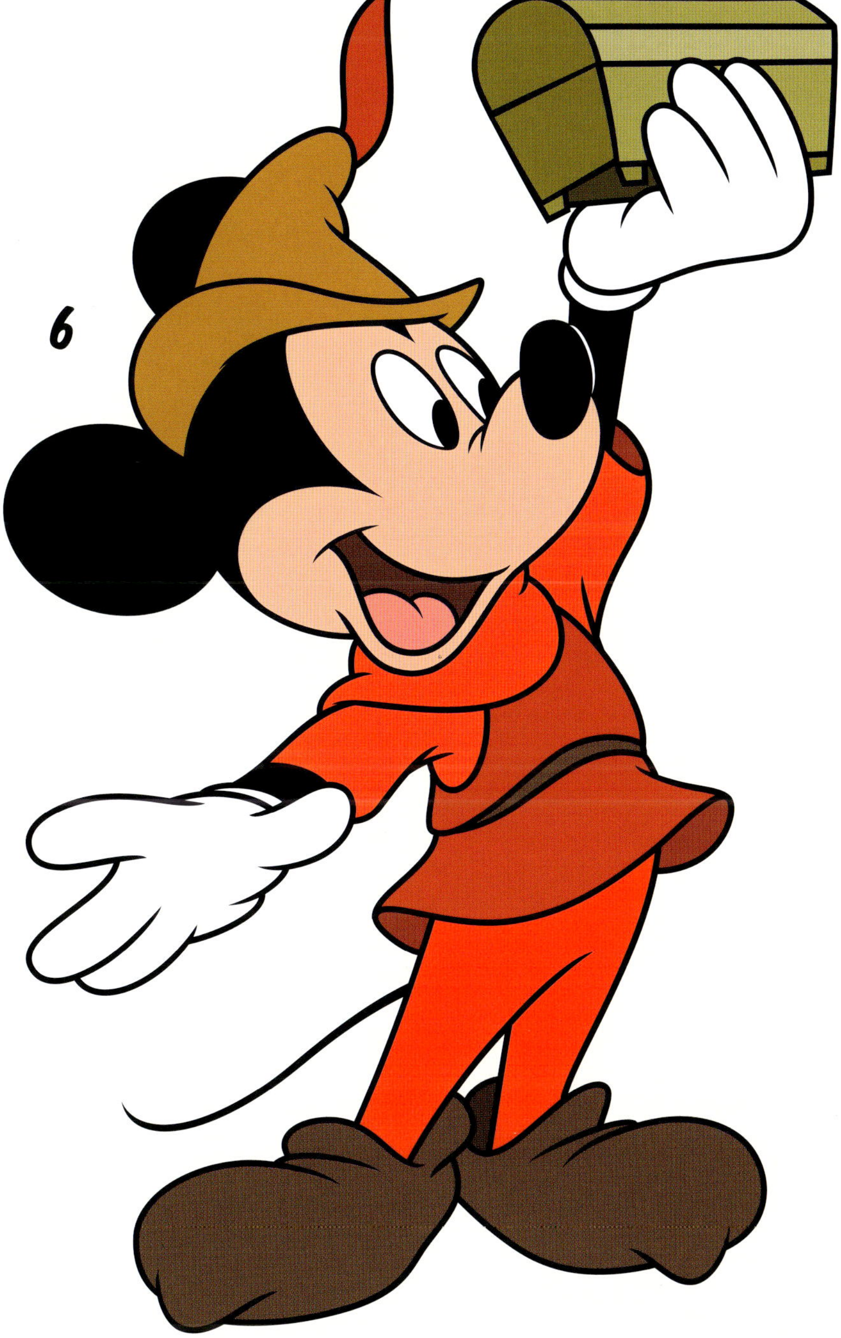

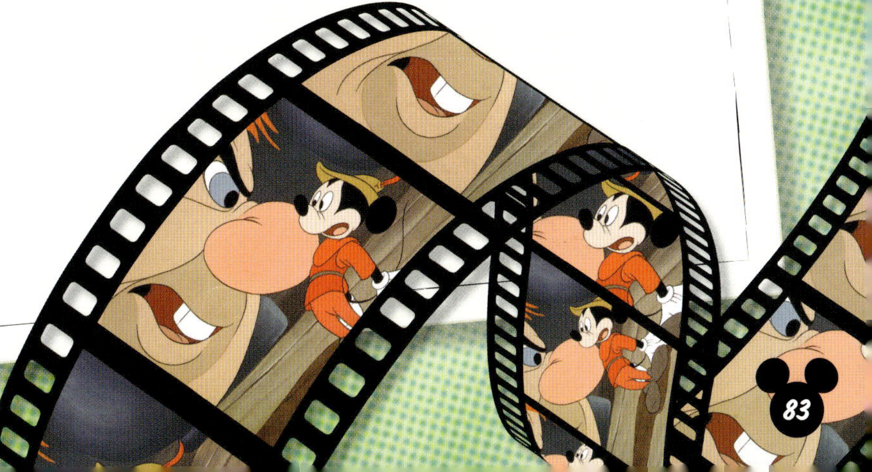

INSIDE STORY

A MOUSE OF MANY HATS (AND CAPS AND CLOAKS...)

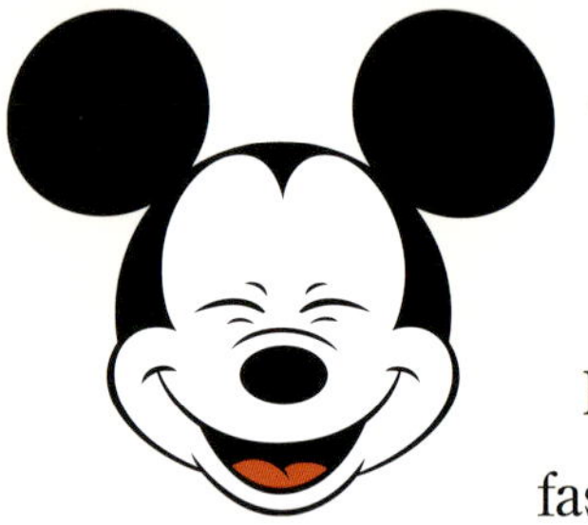

LIKE ANY GREAT ACTOR, MICKEY MOUSE has enjoyed a number of costume roles—and built up quite the wardrobe. His numerous classic outfits are fascinating (and fun to draw!) in their own right.

Mickey's wardrobe also has a special distinction: Some of it predates its wearer! *Mickey Steps Out* (1931) and *The Little Whirlwind* (1941) cast Mickey as a romantic ne'er-do-well in a jaunty straw hat; *Ye Olden Days* (1933) gave him a medieval Tyrolean cap. But neither chapeau really started with Mickey. They were worn earlier by Oswald the Lucky Rabbit and other silent-era

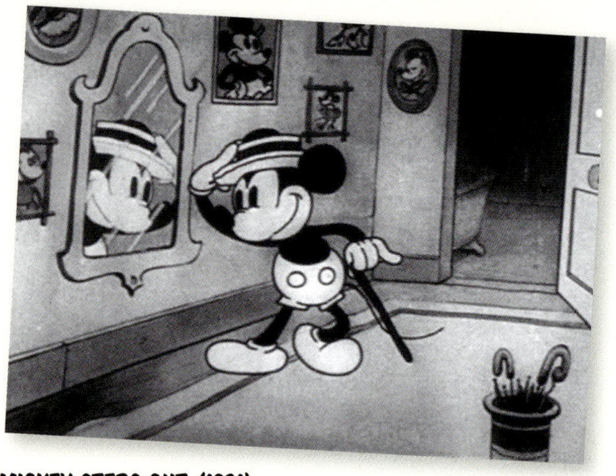

MICKEY STEPS OUT (1931)

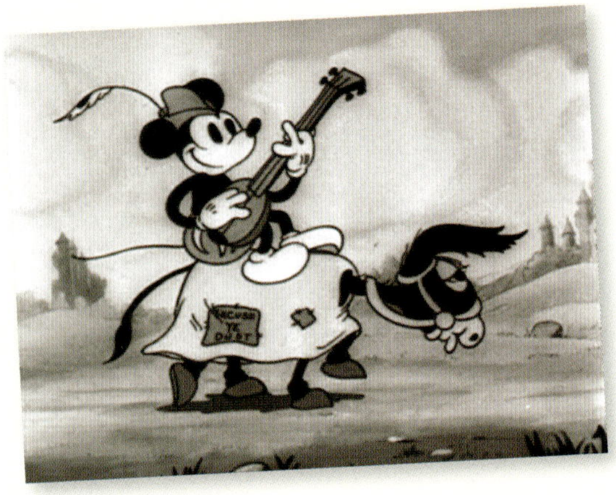

YE OLDEN DAYS (1933)

BELOW: SEVERAL OF MICKEY'S VARIED DESIGNS (LEFT TO RIGHT: LATE 1930s, 1997, 2013).

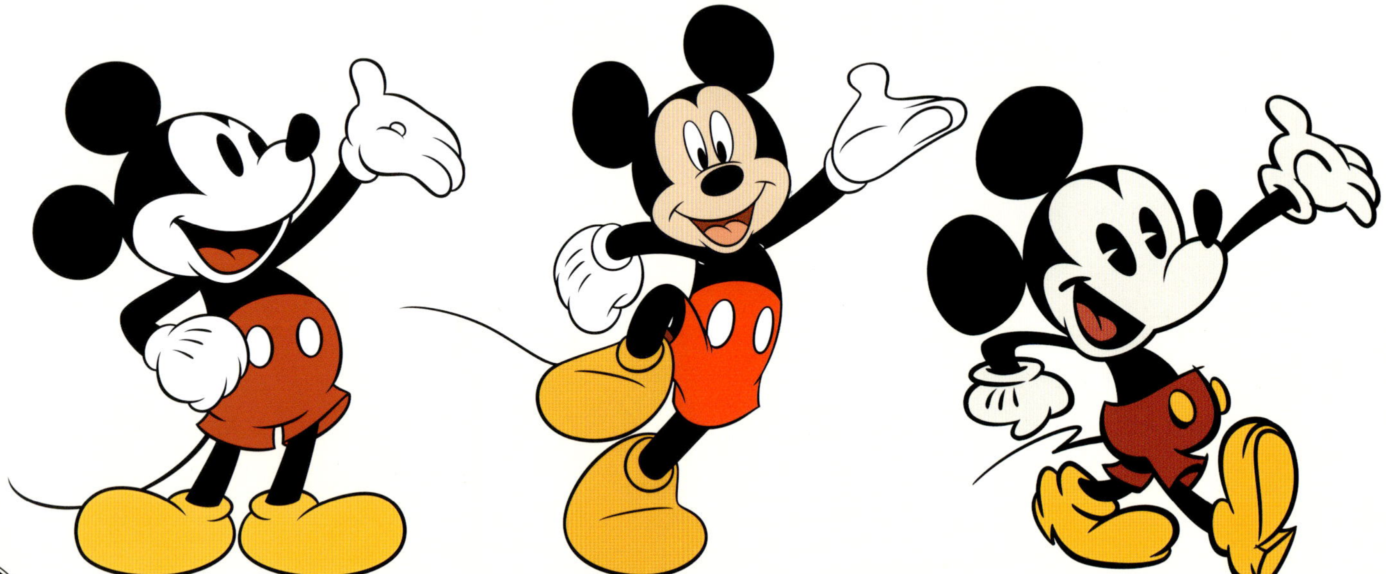

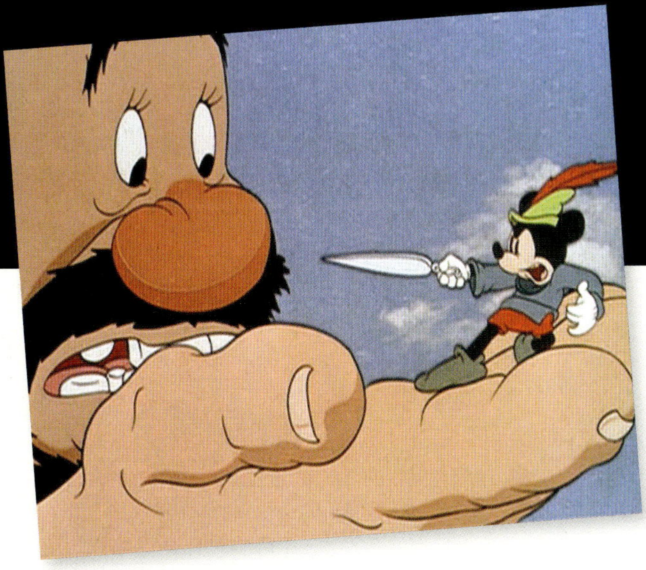

BRAVE LITTLE TAILOR (1938)

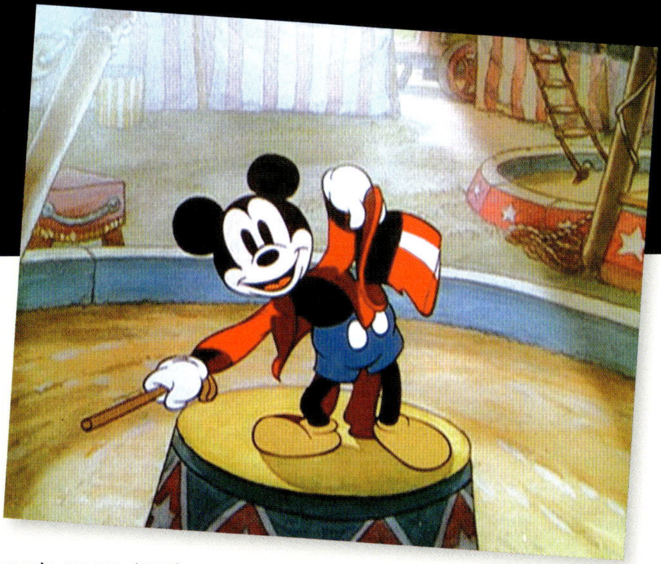

MICKEY'S CIRCUS (1936)

Disney stars, marking them less as character-specific costumes and more as studio shorthand for certain themed roles. By carrying them on, Mickey made them lastingly iconic.

The Tyrolean cap, for instance, was seen again in *Brave Little Tailor* (1938); again in the "Mickey and the Beanstalk" segment of *Fun and Fancy Free* (1947)—and even today, in modern Mickey shorts with an Old World theme.

Other iconic outfits, of course, were uniquely Mickey's from their moment of inception. "The Sorcerer's Apprentice" segment of *Fantasia* (1938; released 1940) gave Mickey the pointy blue magic hat that is still synonymous with spellcasting. And for *Mickey's Circus* (1936), our hero wore flashy ringmaster's gear that *almost* survived a dunk in the seal tank.

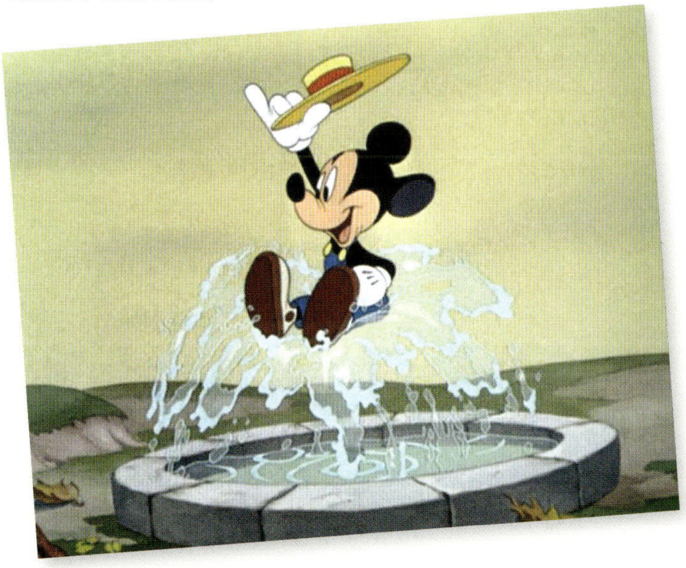

THE LITTLE WHIRLWIND (1941)

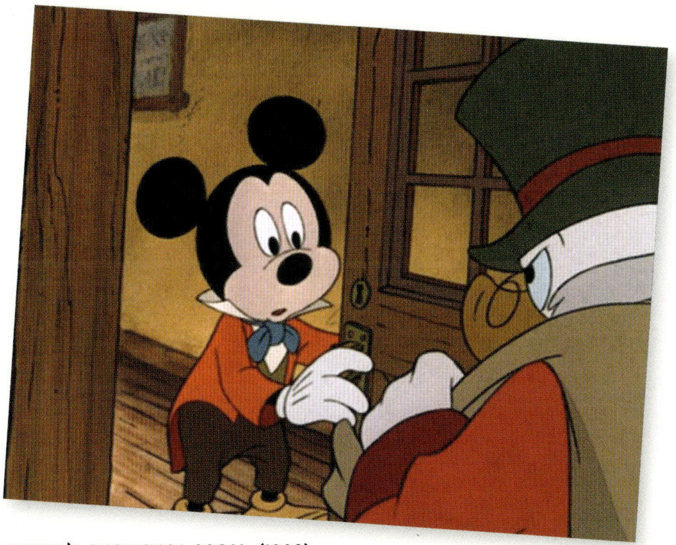

MICKEY'S CHRISTMAS CAROL (1983)

MICKEY 1950s-1980s

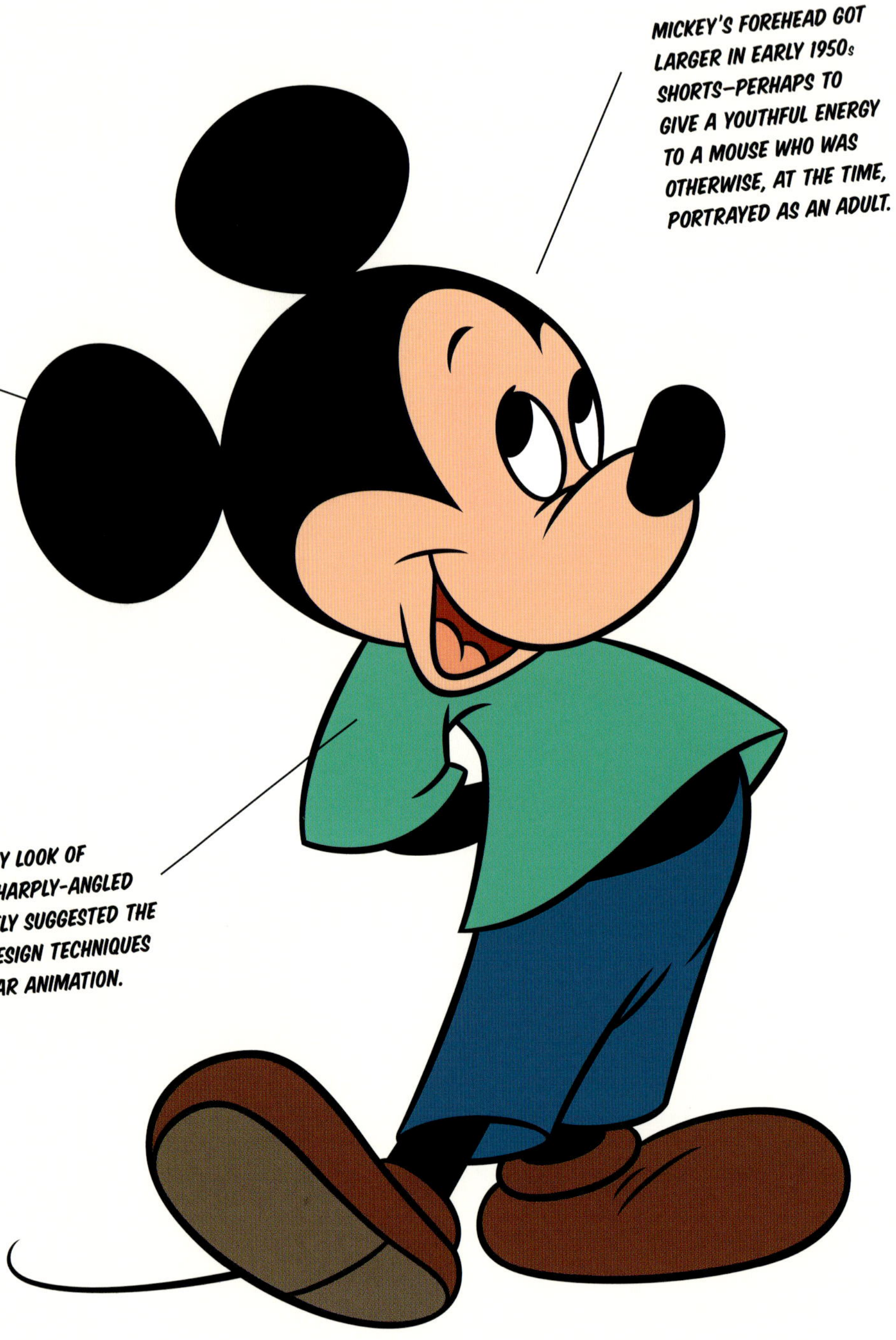

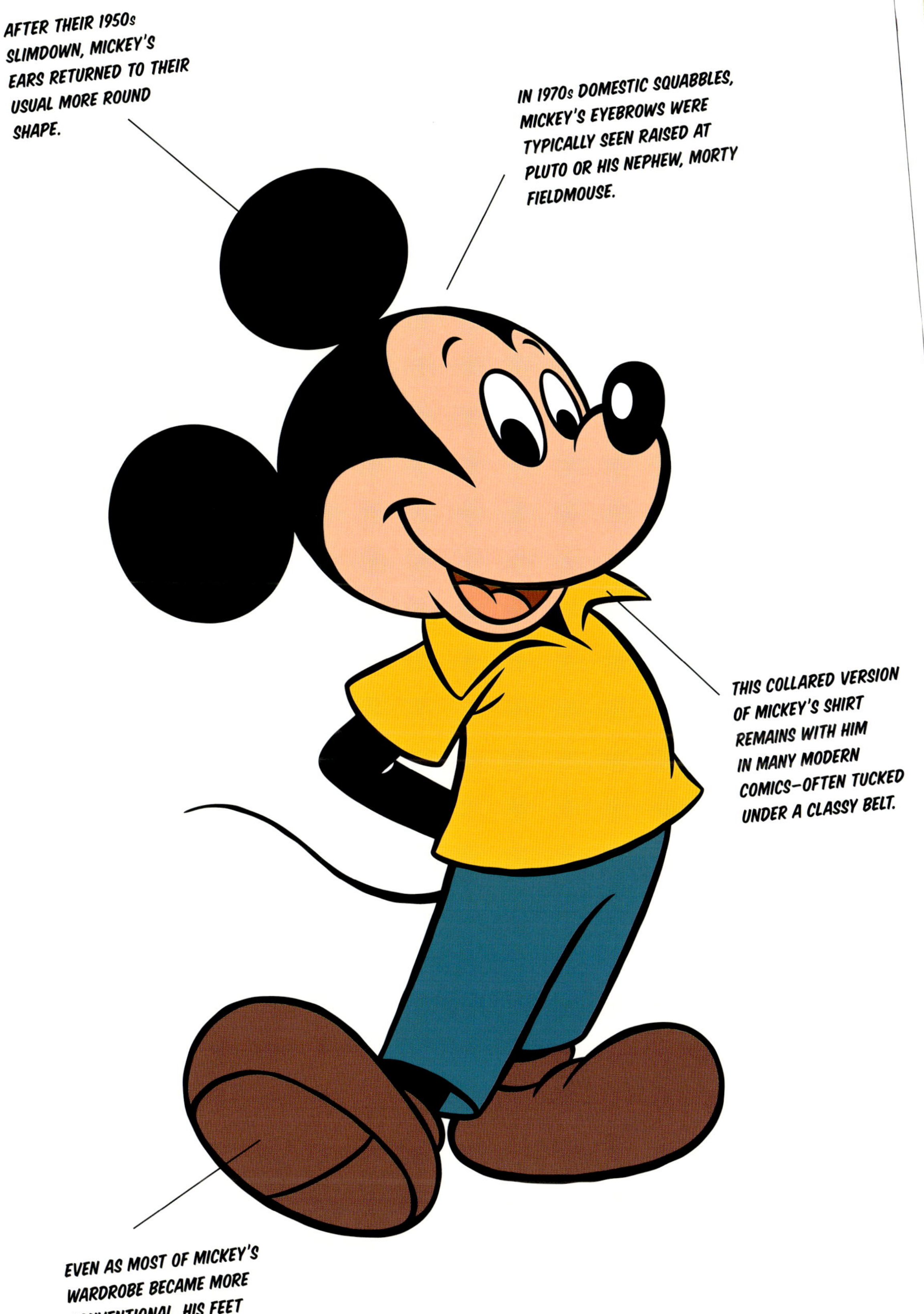
AFTER THEIR 1950s SLIMDOWN, MICKEY'S EARS RETURNED TO THEIR USUAL MORE ROUND SHAPE.
IN 1970s DOMESTIC SQUABBLES, MICKEY'S EYEBROWS WERE TYPICALLY SEEN RAISED AT PLUTO OR HIS NEPHEW, MORTY FIELDMOUSE.
THIS COLLARED VERSION OF MICKEY'S SHIRT REMAINS WITH HIM IN MANY MODERN COMICS—OFTEN TUCKED UNDER A CLASSY BELT.
EVEN AS MOST OF MICKEY'S WARDROBE BECAME MORE CONVENTIONAL, HIS FEET FELT BEST IN HIS PUFFY 1930s OXFORDS...AND STILL DO!

CONTEMPORARY

MICKEY MOUSE

HEAD POSE

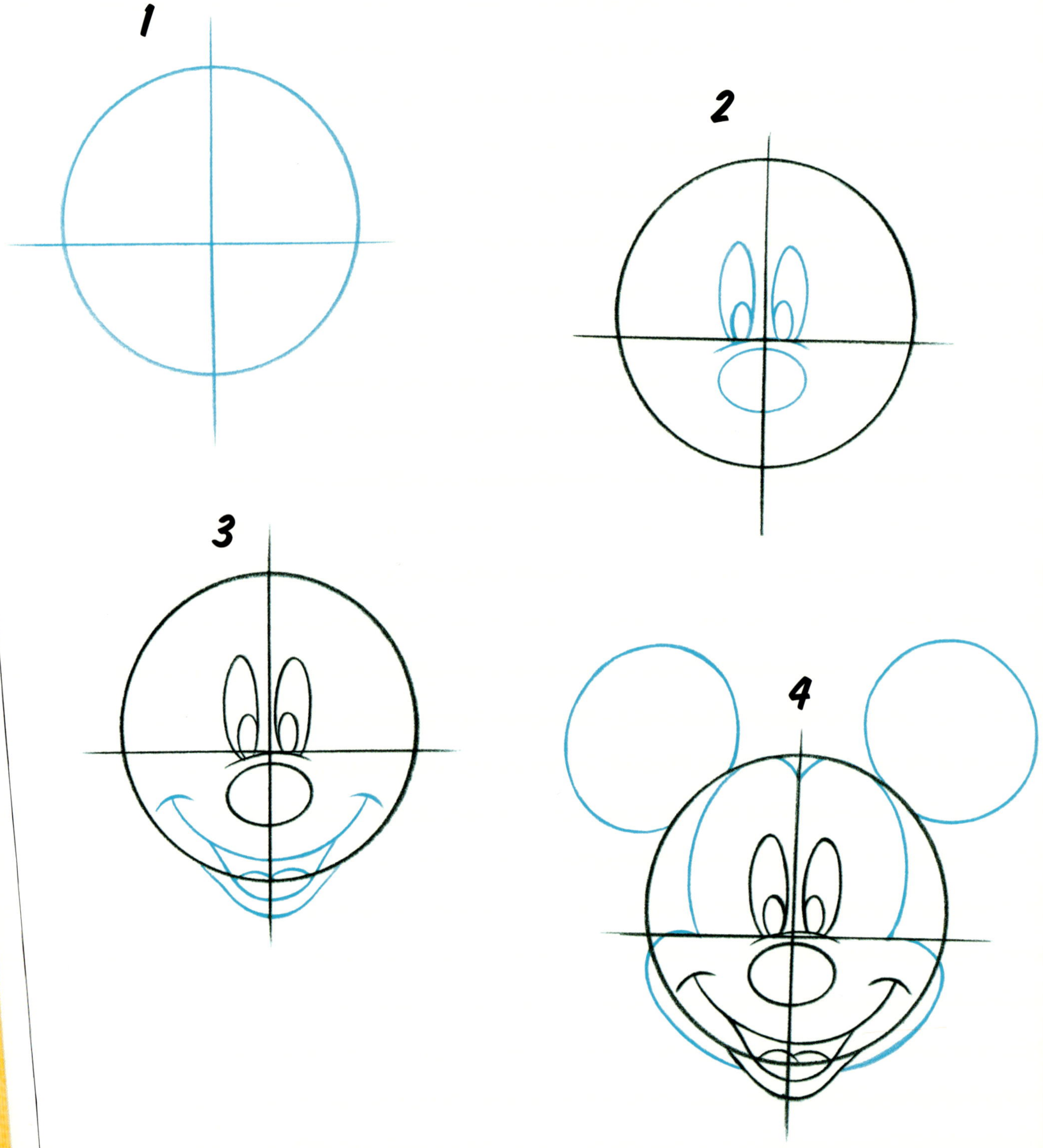

5

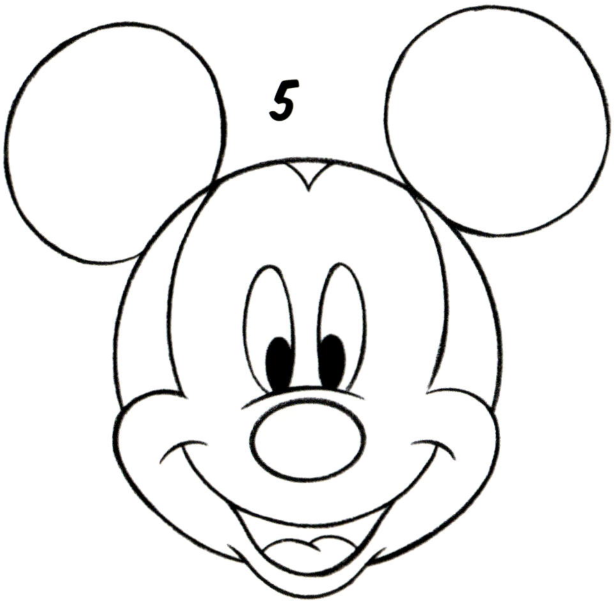

6

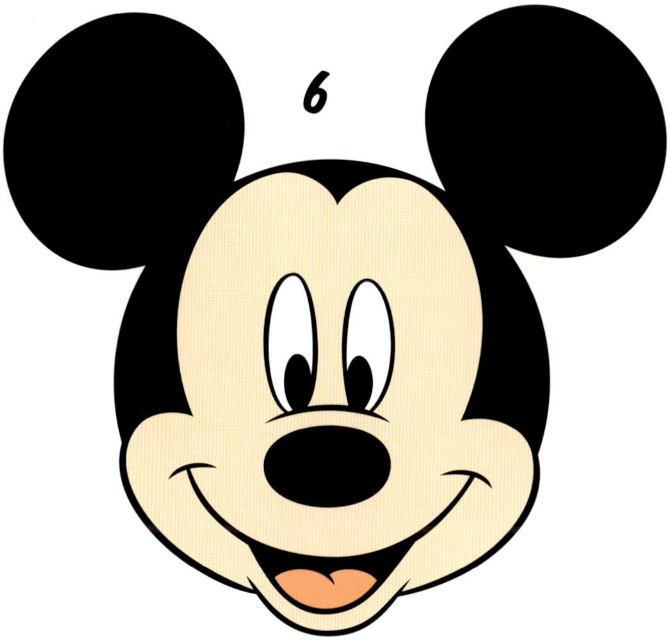

MICKEY'S EXPRESSIONS

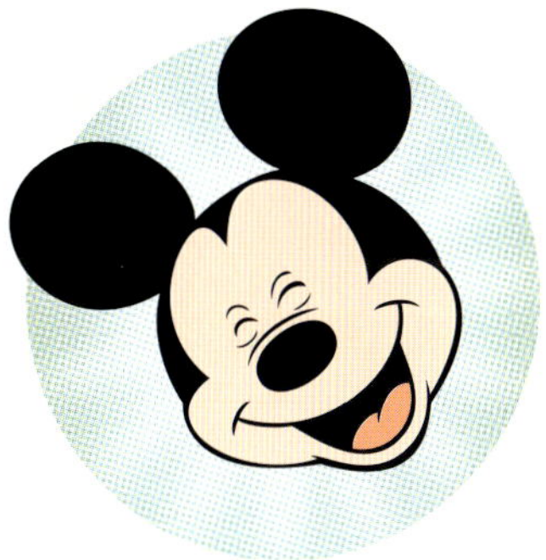

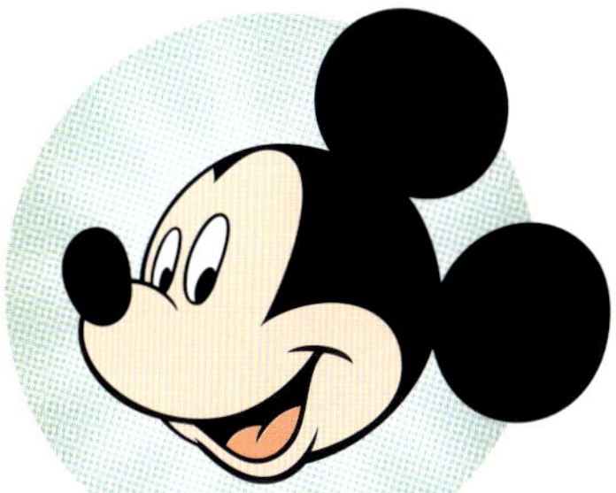

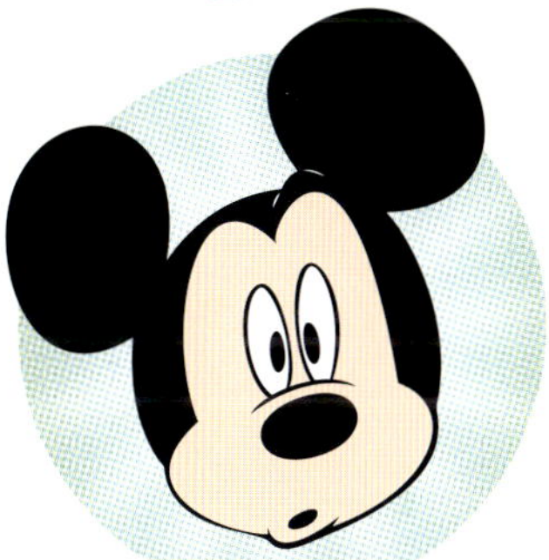

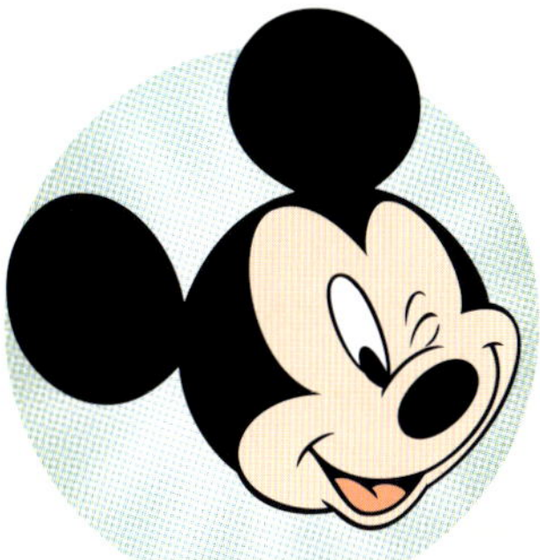

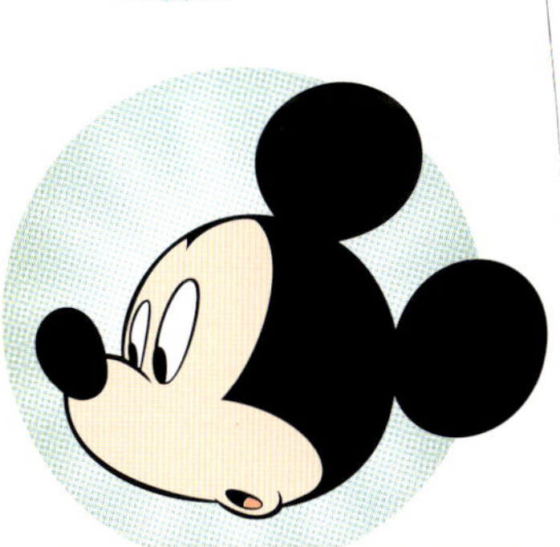

CONTEMPORARY

MICKEY MOUSE

BODY POSE

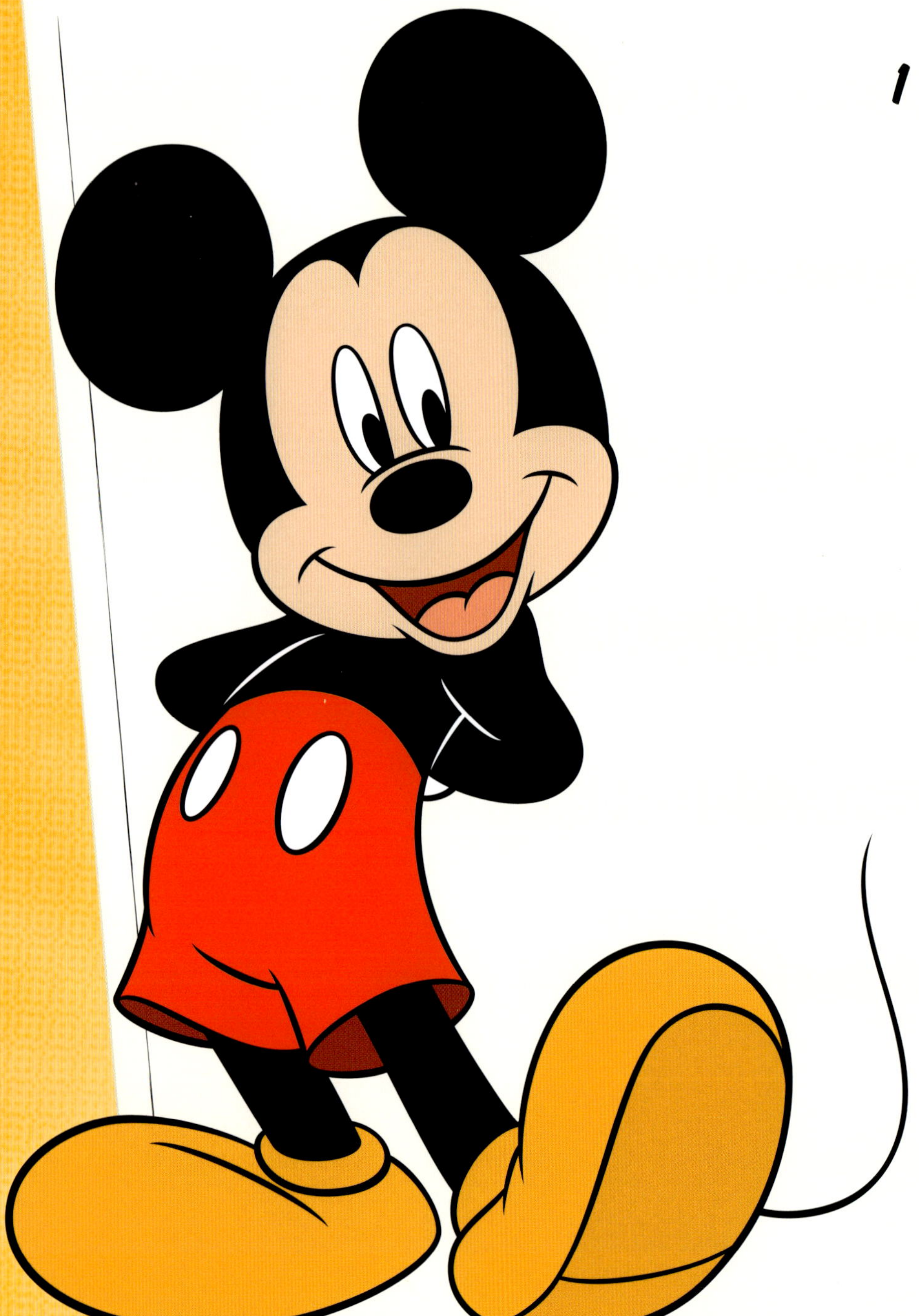

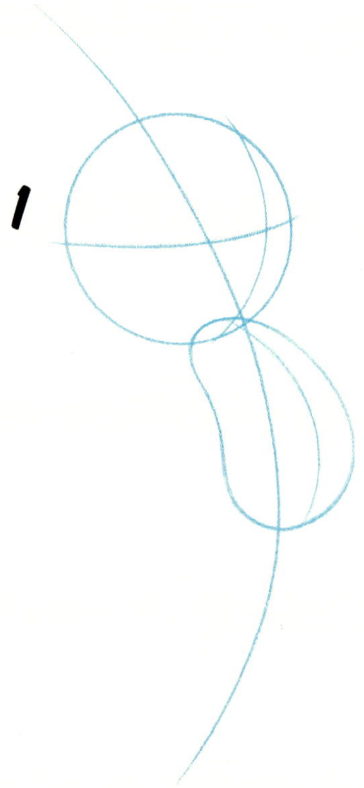

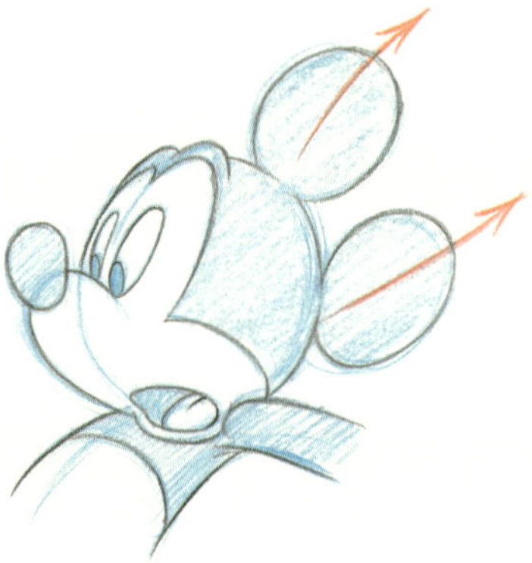

WHEN MICKEY IS SURPRISED, HIS EARS GO UP.

2

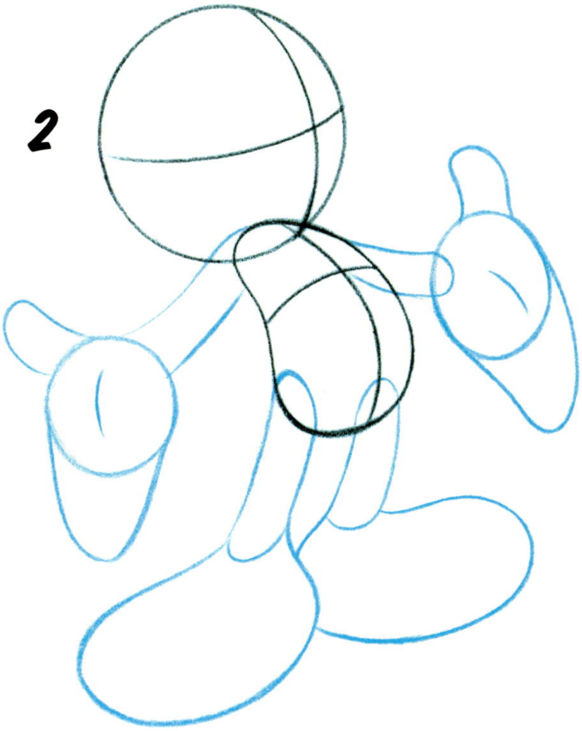

3

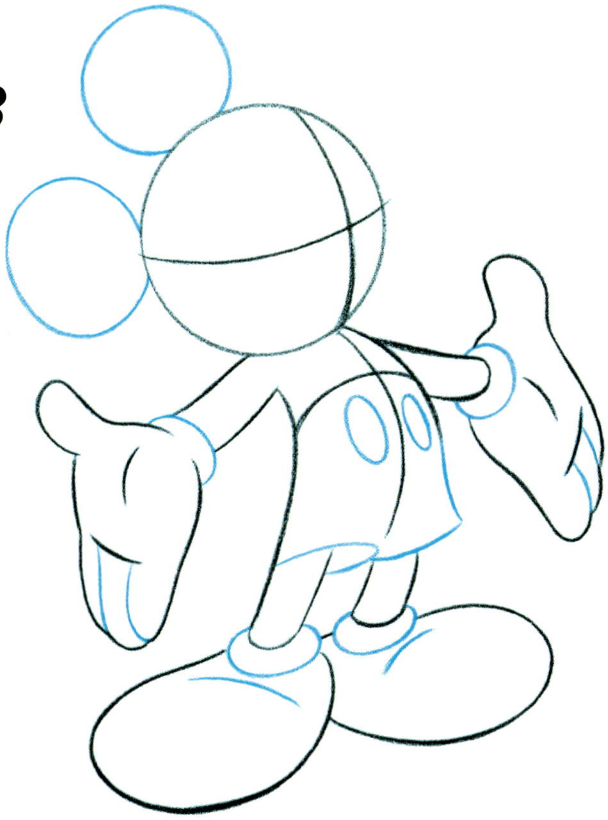

MICKEY'S POSES

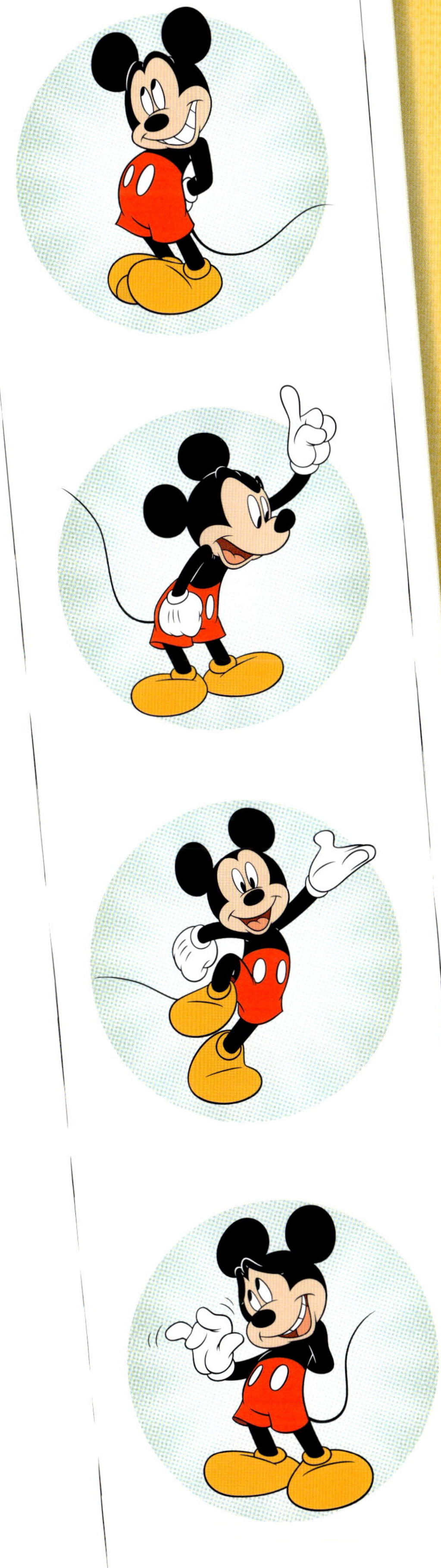

4

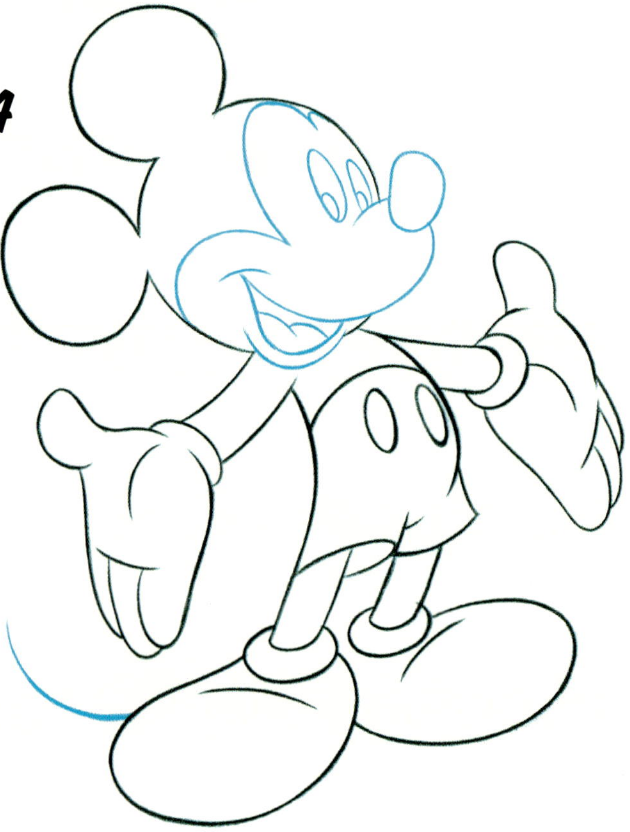

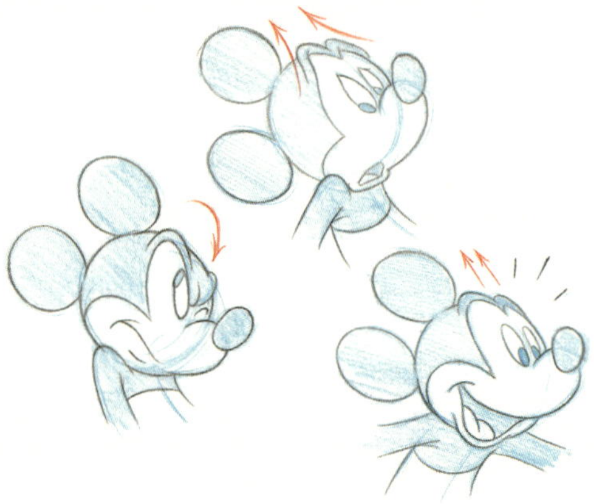

MICKEY'S EYEBROWS CAN SHOW HOW HE'S FEELING.

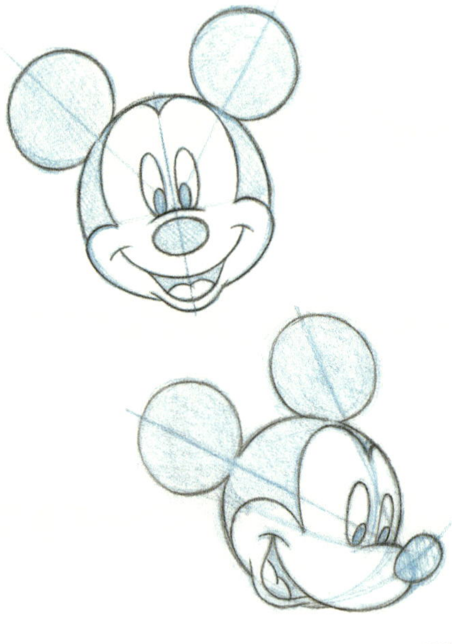

YOU CAN ALWAYS SEE BOTH OF MICKEY'S EARS, NO MATTER WHICH DIRECTION HIS HEAD IS TURNED.

5

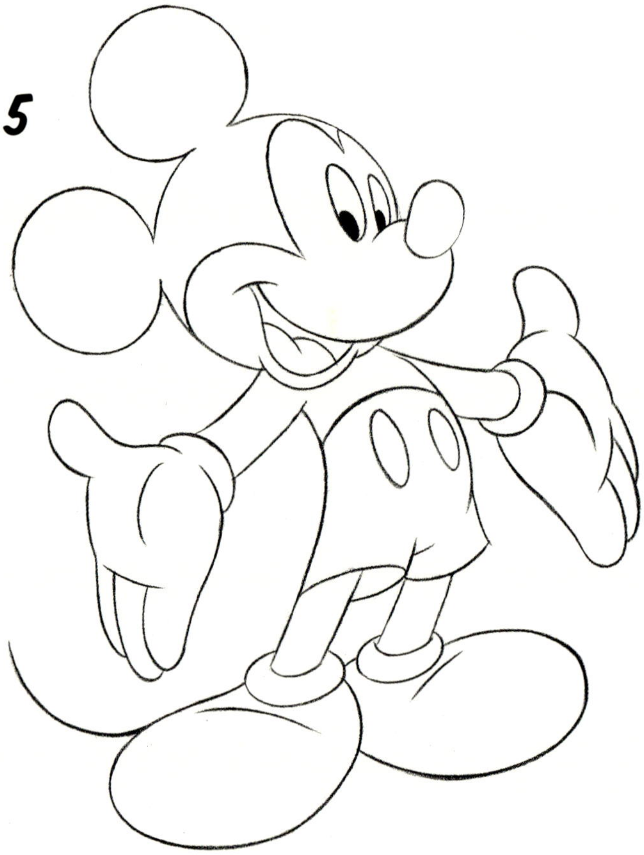

MICKEY'S POSES

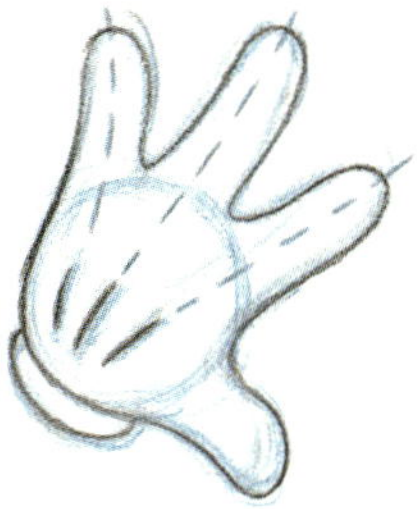

WHEN THE TOPS OF MICKEY'S HANDS SHOW, BE SURE TO ADD THE STITCHING LINES TO HIS GLOVES!

6

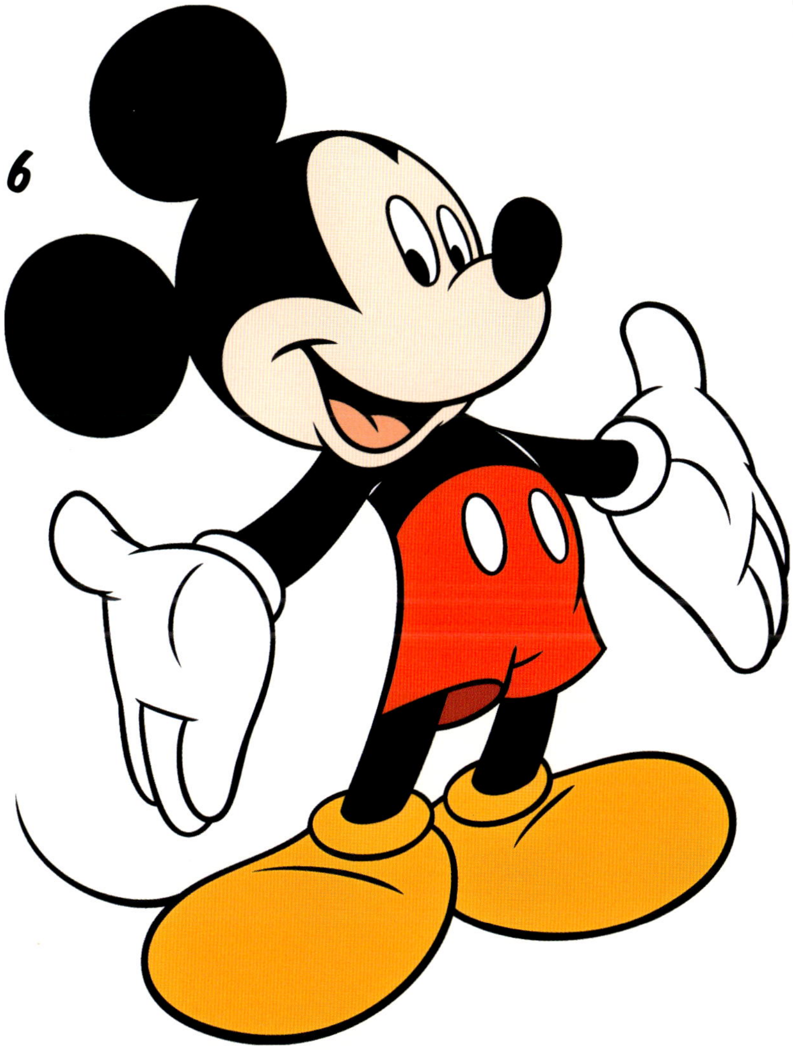

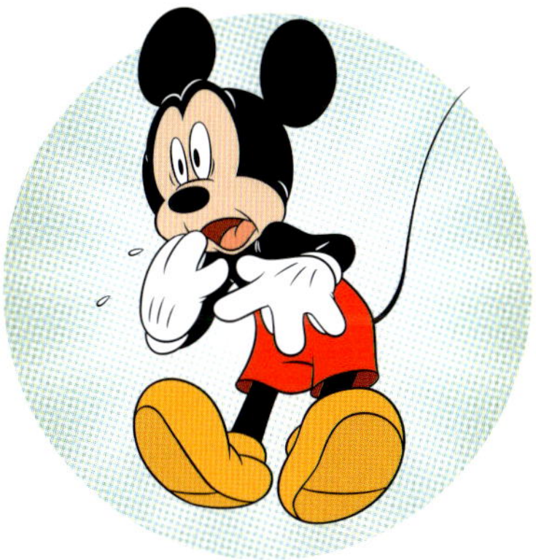

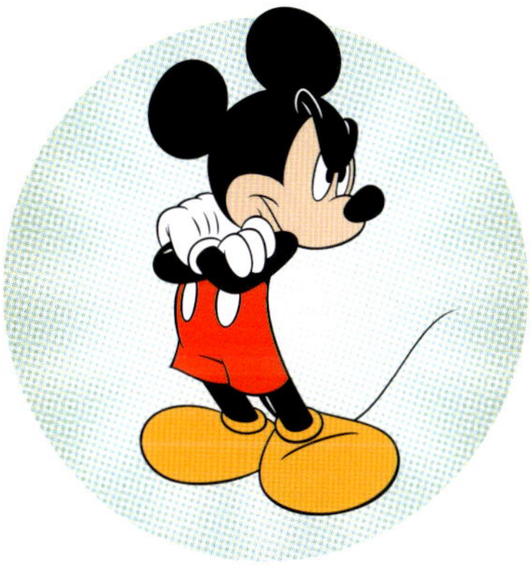

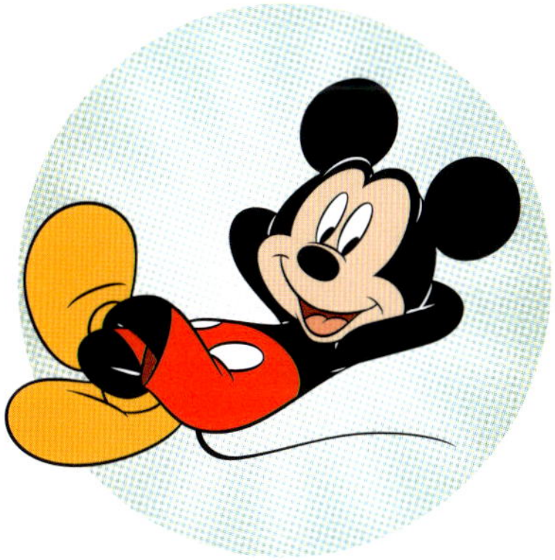

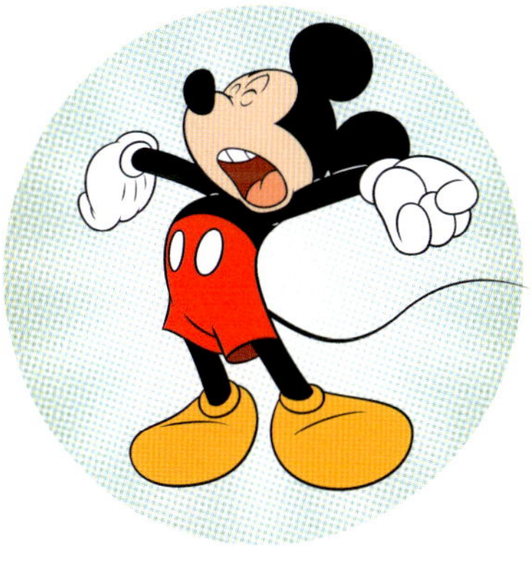

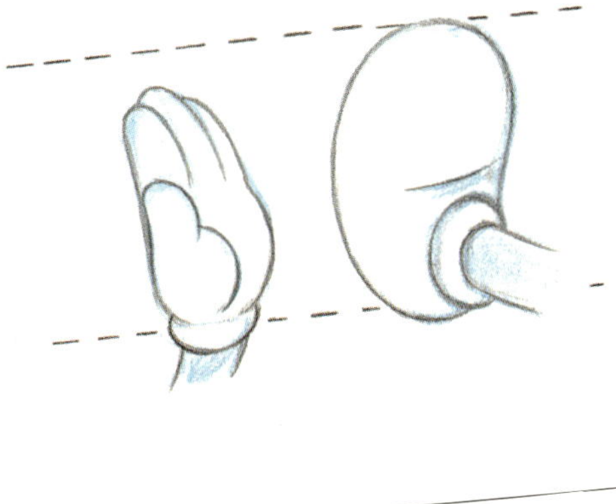

MICKEY'S SHOES ARE SLIGHTLY LONGER THAN HIS HANDS.

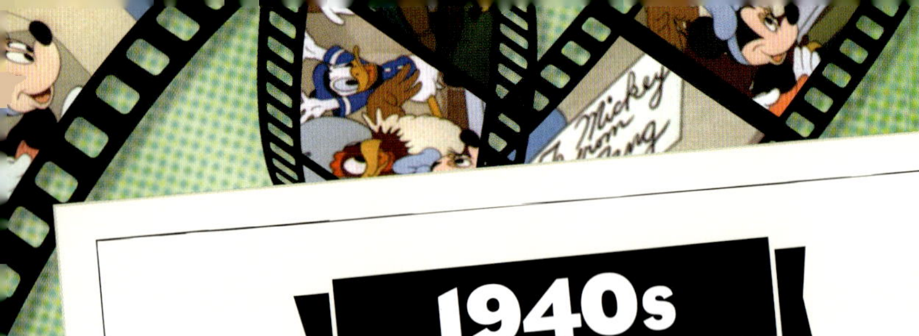

1940s

MINNIE MOUSE

MICKEY'S BIRTHDAY PARTY

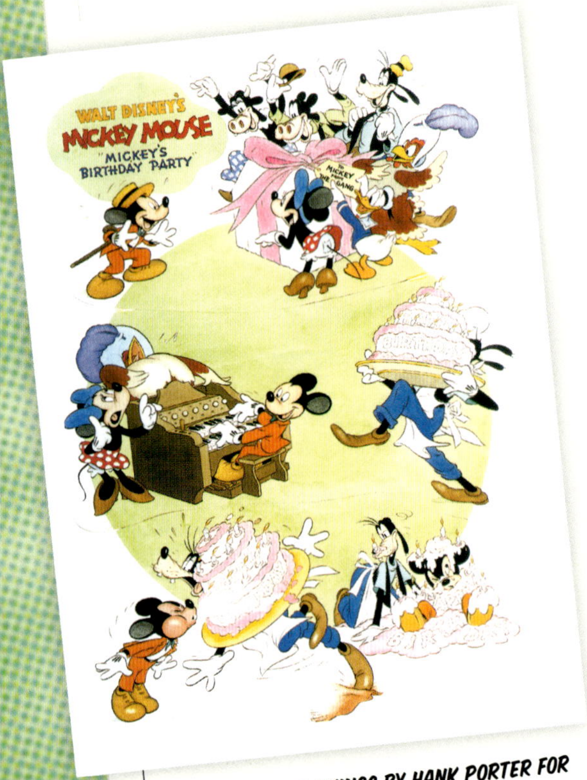

PUBLICITY DRAWINGS BY HANK PORTER FOR MICKEY'S BIRTHDAY PARTY (1942).

1

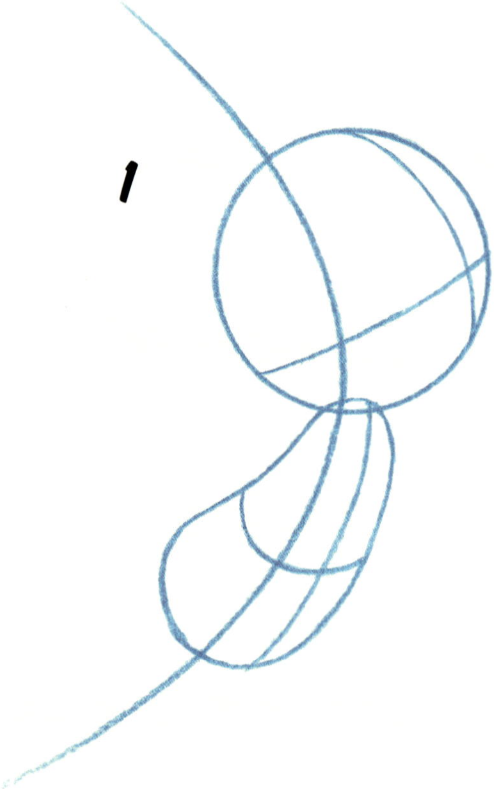

FILM FACT

MICKEY'S BIRTHDAY PARTY (1942) WAS A COLLABORATIVE EVENT THROWN BY MINNIE WITH DONALD, GOOFY, AND THEIR FRIENDS CLARABELLE COW, HORACE HORSECOLLAR, AND CLARA CLUCK. THE CARTOON REUSED SOME ELEMENTS FROM THE BIRTHDAY PARTY (1931), AN EARLIER MICKEY SHORT WITH THE SAME THEME.

2

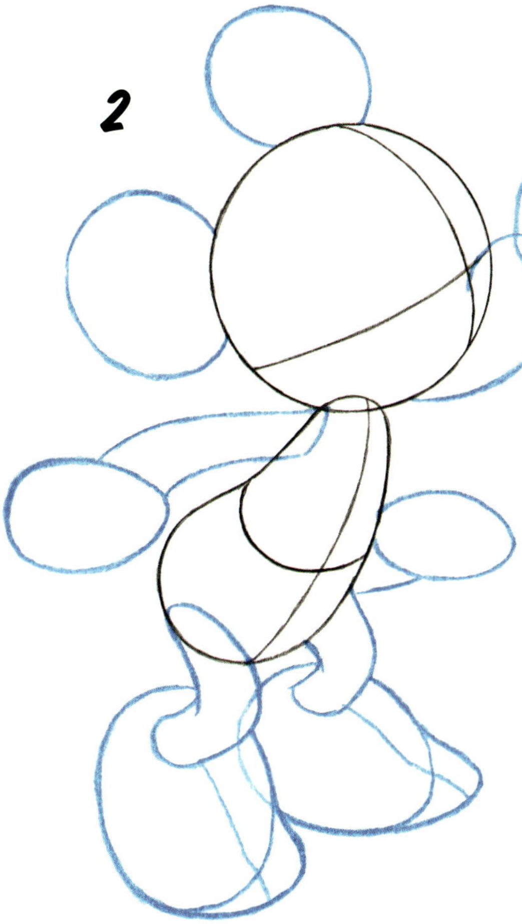

3

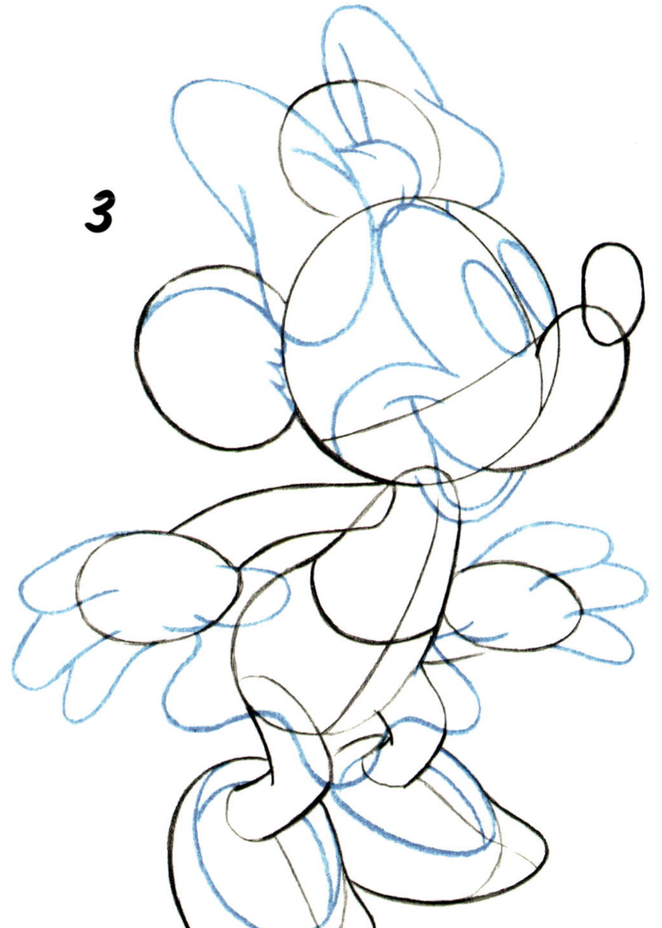

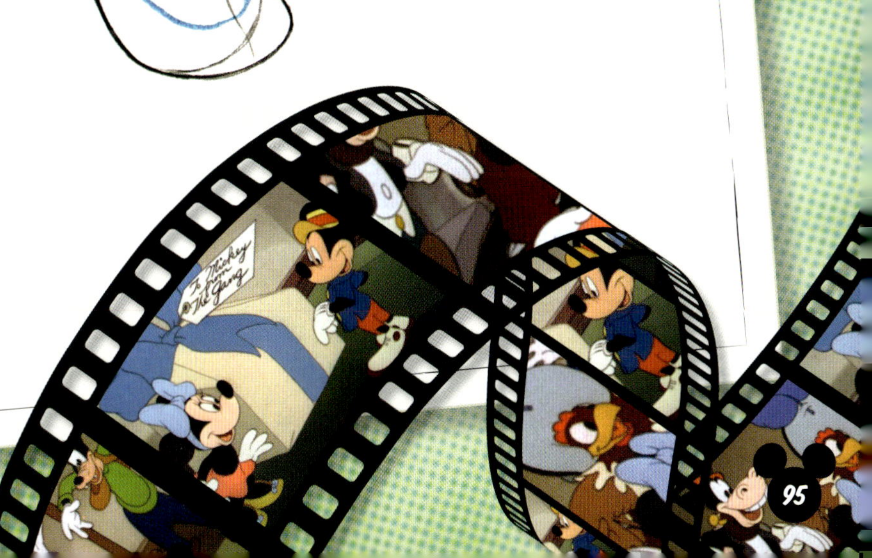

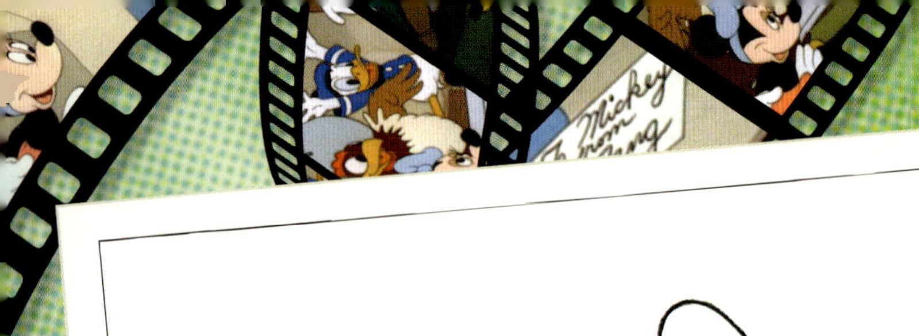

4

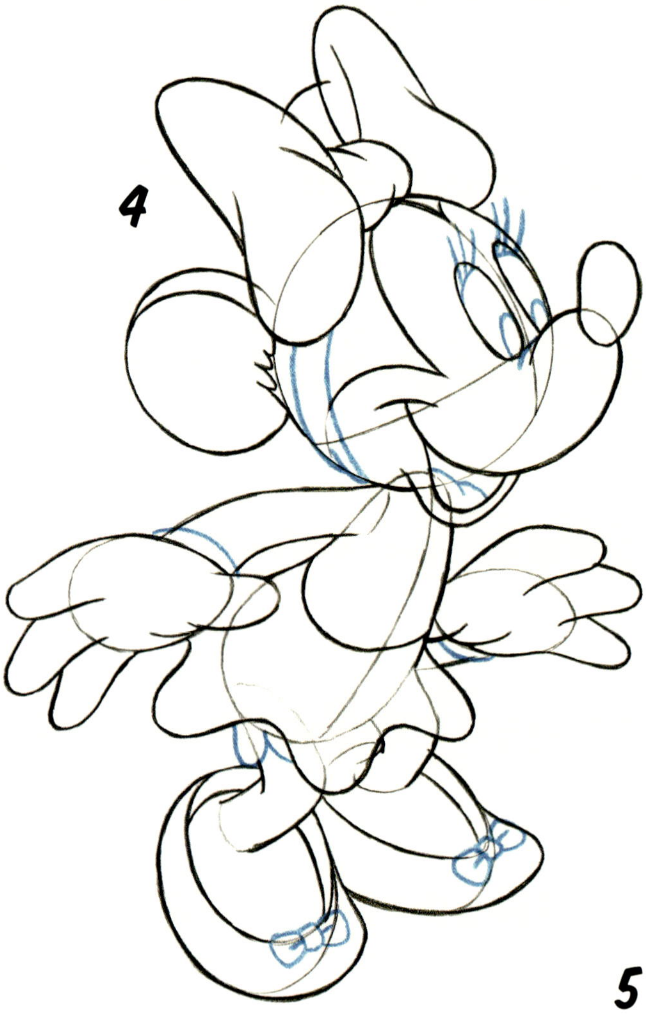

5

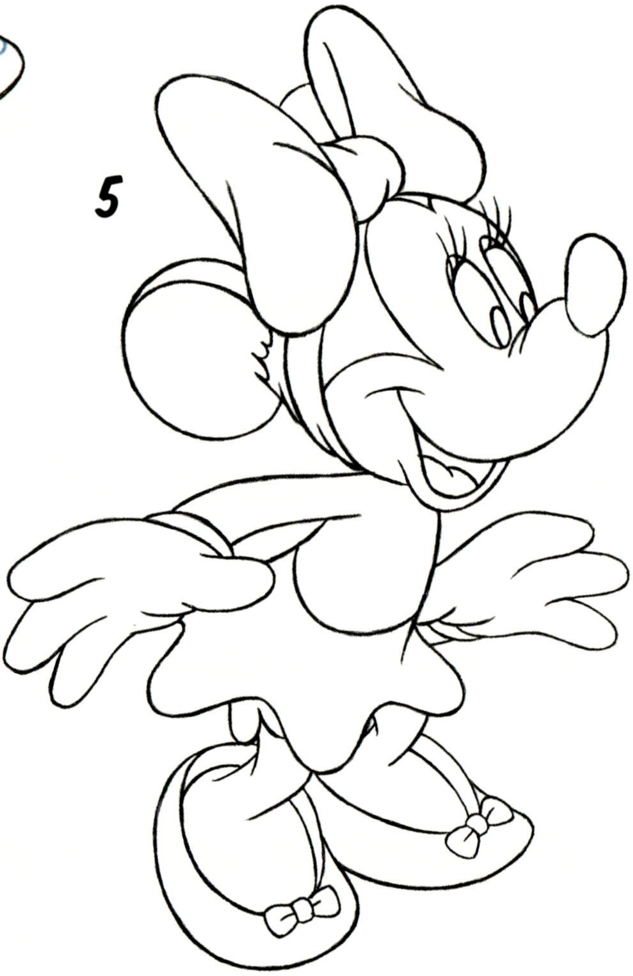

6

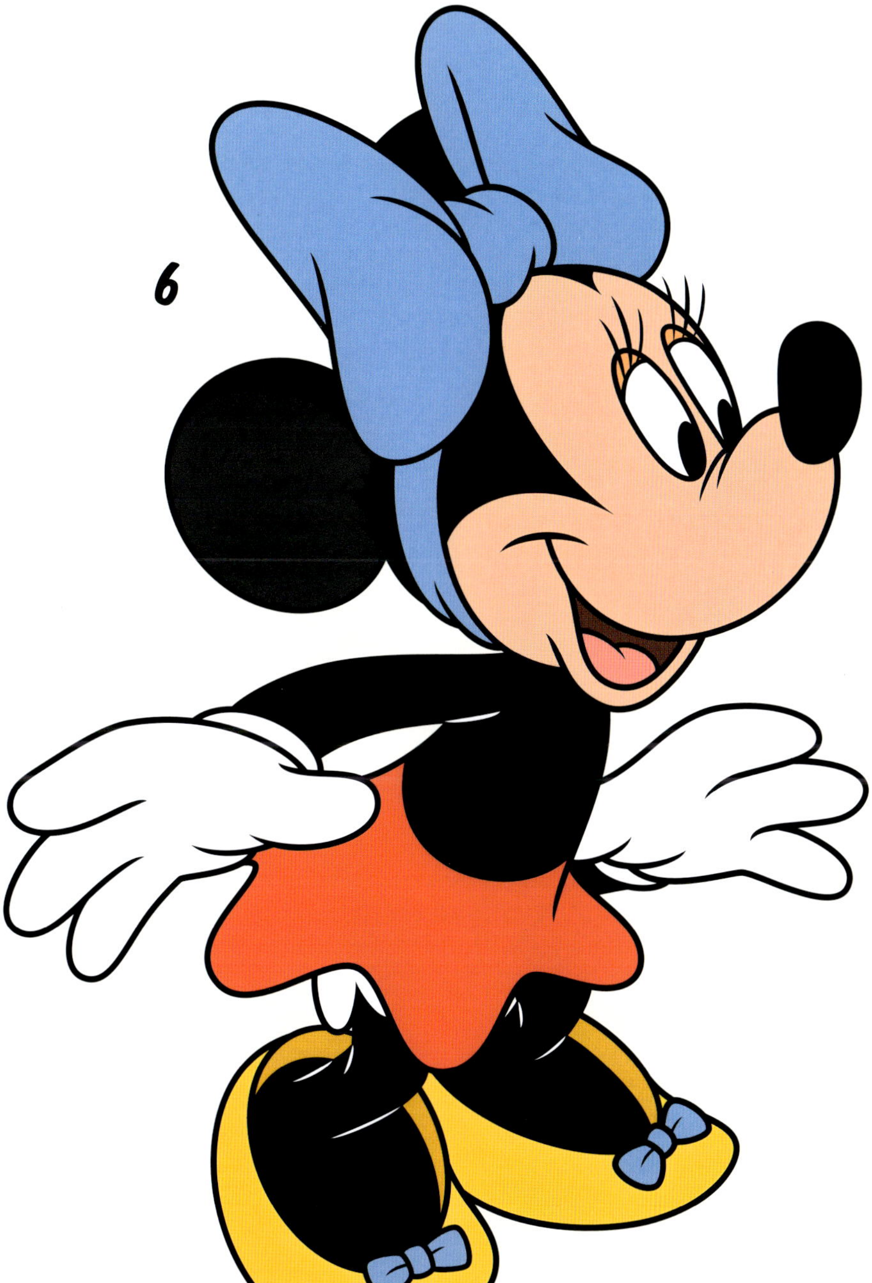

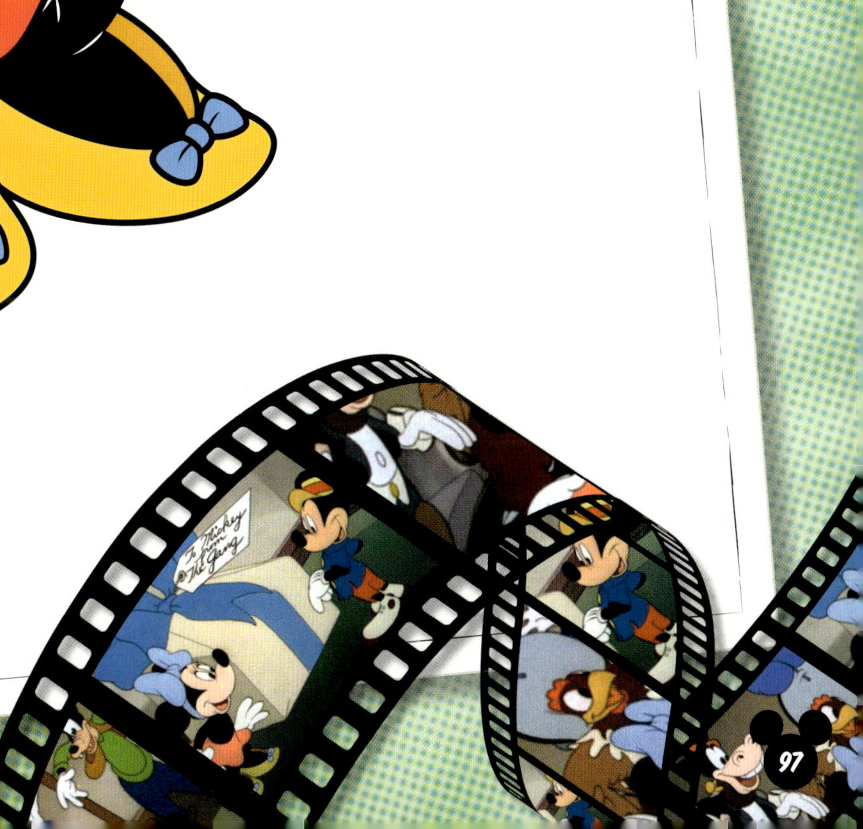

MINNIE 1950s-1980s

THIS 1950s MINNIE HAS HER WIDE EYES OPEN—BUT ANOTHER POPULAR PERIOD LOOK SHOWS MINNIE'S EYELIDS AT FLIRTY HALF-MAST.

A POINTIER BOW SUGGESTS THE ANGULAR STYLE OF 1950s ANIMATION.

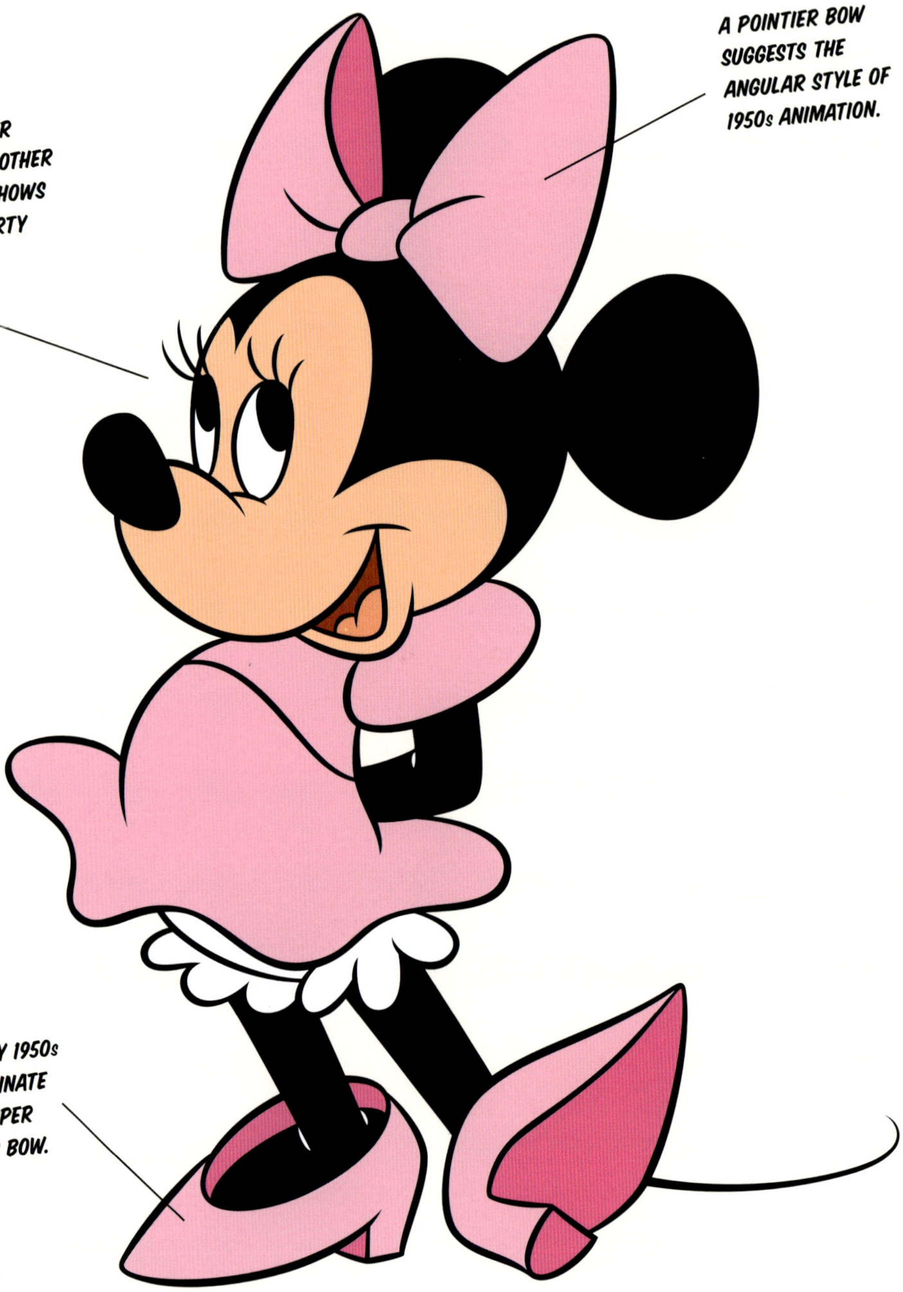

A SUPER-POINTY 1950s SHOE TO COORDINATE WITH THE SHARPER ANGLES OF HER BOW.

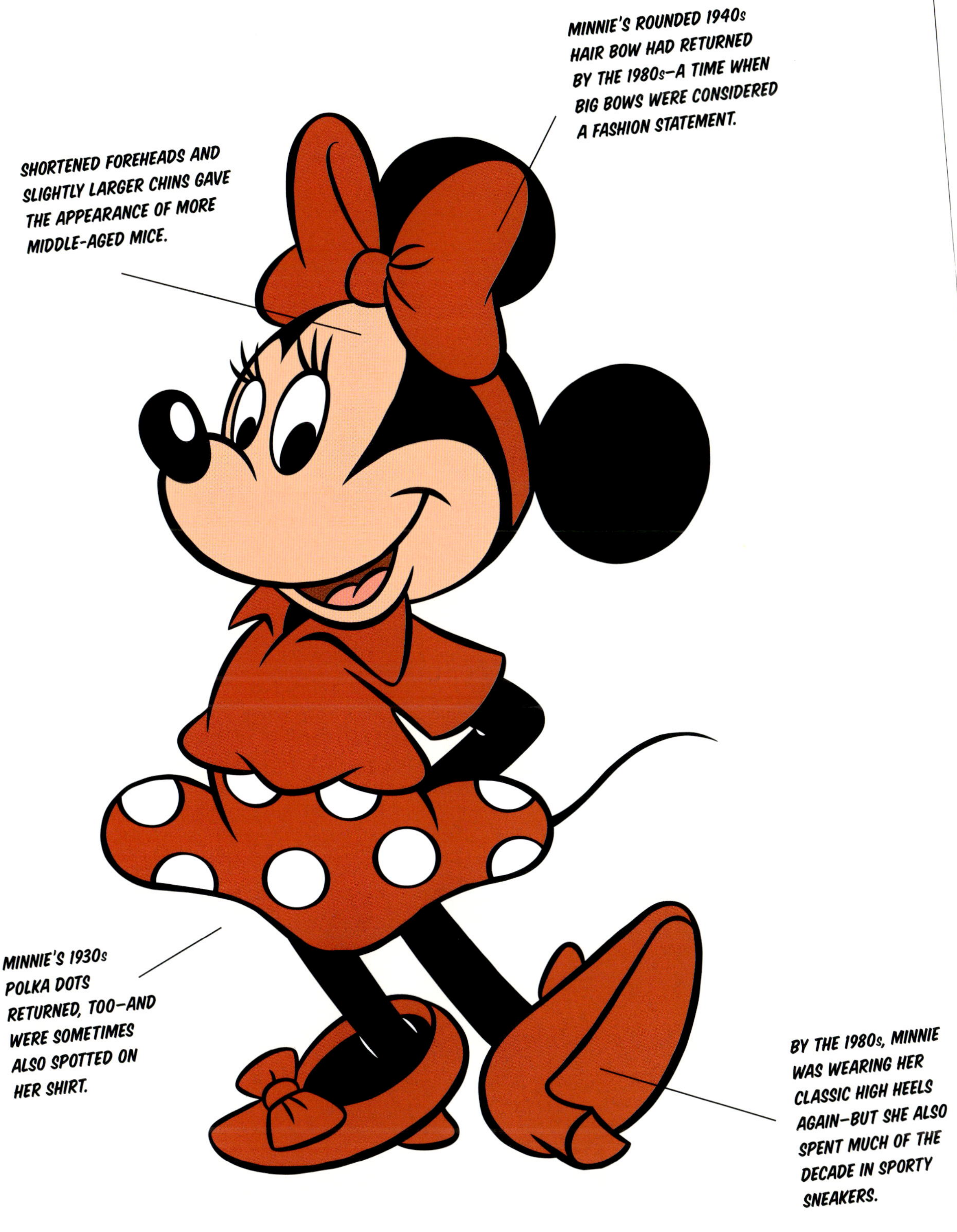
MINNIE'S ROUNDED 1940s HAIR BOW HAD RETURNED BY THE 1980s—A TIME WHEN BIG BOWS WERE CONSIDERED A FASHION STATEMENT.
SHORTENED FOREHEADS AND SLIGHTLY LARGER CHINS GAVE THE APPEARANCE OF MORE MIDDLE-AGED MICE.
MINNIE'S 1930s POLKA DOTS RETURNED, TOO—AND WERE SOMETIMES ALSO SPOTTED ON HER SHIRT.
BY THE 1980s, MINNIE WAS WEARING HER CLASSIC HIGH HEELS AGAIN—BUT SHE ALSO SPENT MUCH OF THE DECADE IN SPORTY SNEAKERS.

INSIDE STORY

TOTALLY MINNIE: A PASSION FOR FASHION

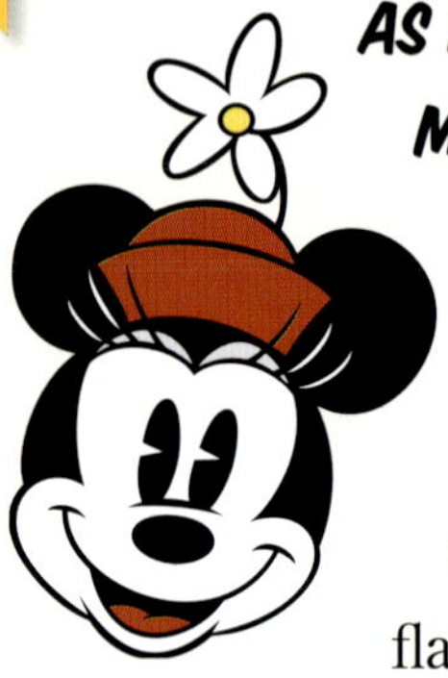

AS NOTED EARLIER, MINNIE MOUSE WAS BORN AS A STYLISH, CUTTING-EDGE FLAPPER—and then the Depression hit. In the midst of nationwide poverty, flaunting fancy clothes wasn't the thing to do. So Minnie's showy top hat made way for an unassuming pillbox; her fashion-plate top was replaced with a natural covering of her own black fur.

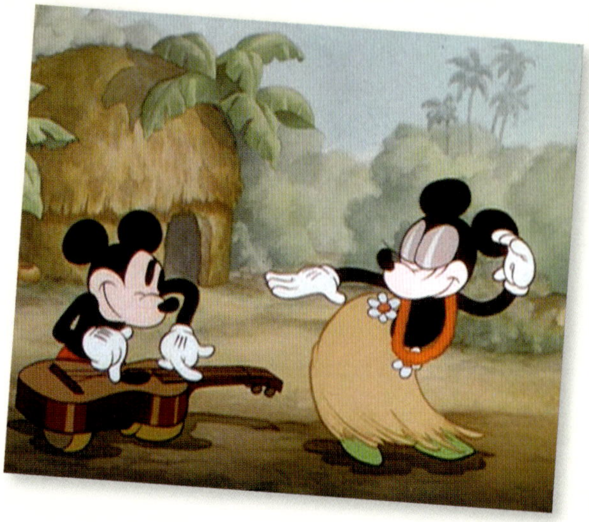

HAWAIIAN HOLIDAY (1937)

But America recovered—and so did Minnie. While more modest, our heroine was still just as brainy and creative—and some splendid new styles began to show. *Ye Olden Days* (1933) and *Brave Little Tailor* (1938) gave Minnie a billowy princess ensemble. *Hawaiian Holiday* (1937) showed her in a tropical lei. *Mickey's Surprise Party* (1939) replaced Minnie's pillbox hat with her famous puffy hair bow. And *First Aiders* (1944) gave her a fetching nurse's ensemble.

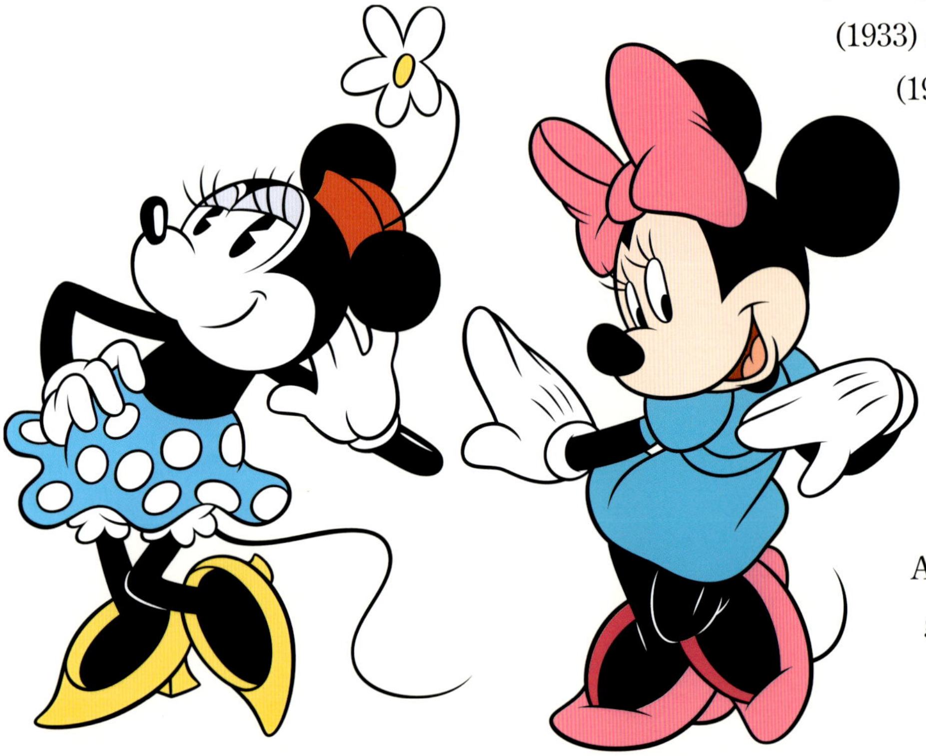

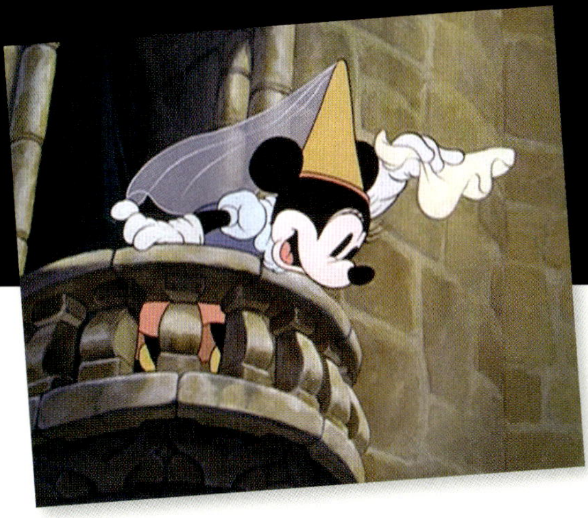

BRAVE LITTLE TAILOR (1938)

Recent decades have seen Minnie rise to modern fashion challenges—from the costume jewelry and bold colors of 1986's "Totally Minnie" merchandise[1] to a slick bandleader's uniform in TV's "Mickey Mouse Works" (1999). Even Minnie's hair received an up-to-date low-cut makeover for *Mickey, Donald, Goofy: The Three Musketeers* (2004).

But hey! The old pillbox hat resurfaced in 2013's recent series of Mickey Mouse TV shorts—which just goes to show that fashion trends really do cycle around again and again!

[1]Bob Thomas, Associated Press. "Minnie: no longer content to be quiet as a mouse." *Philadelphia Inquirer* (April 24, 1986), C8.

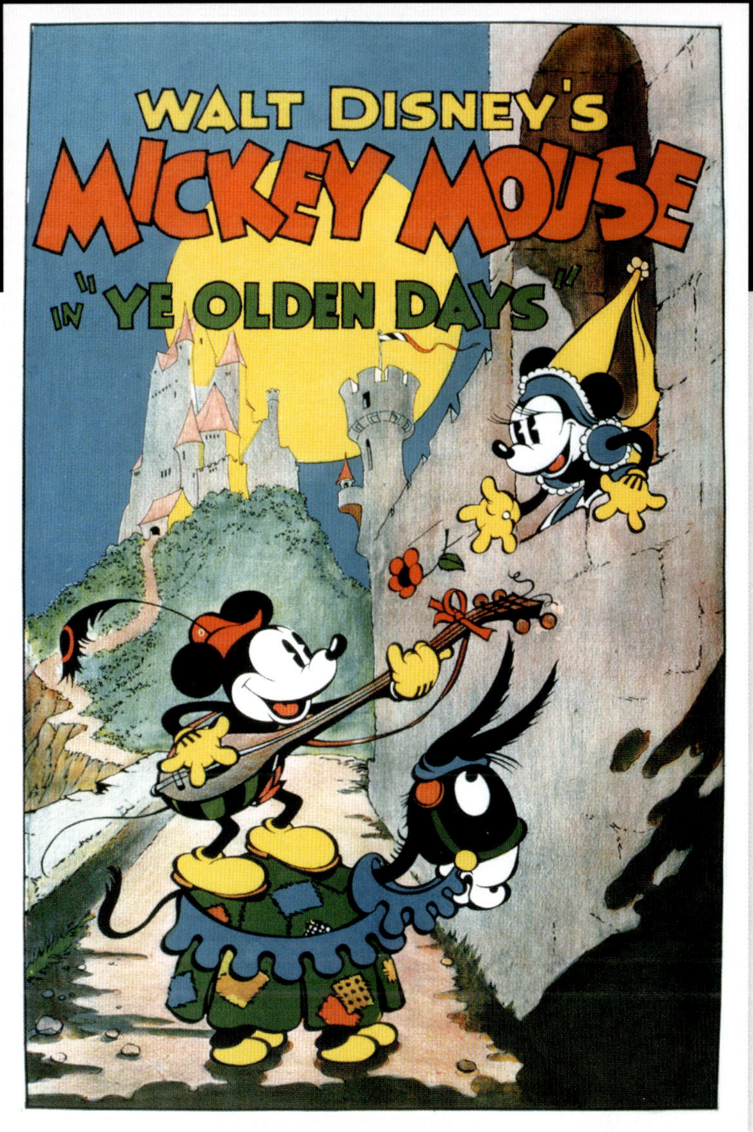

YE OLDEN DAYS (1933)

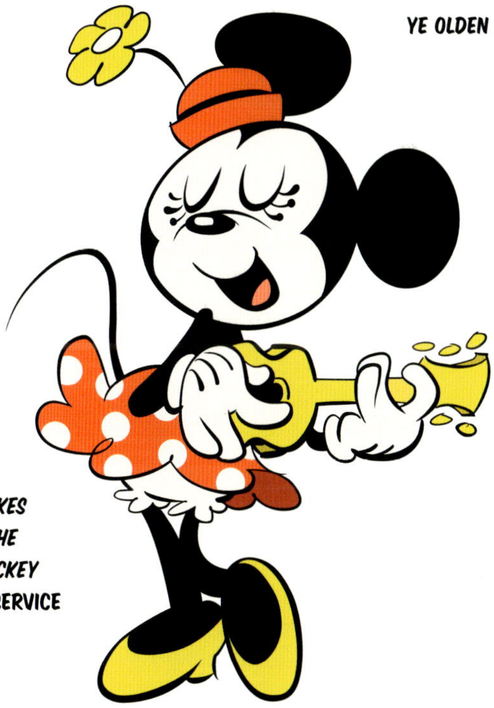

MINNIE MAKES MUSIC IN THE RECENT MICKEY SHORT NO SERVICE (2013).

CONTEMPORARY

MINNIE MOUSE

HEAD POSE

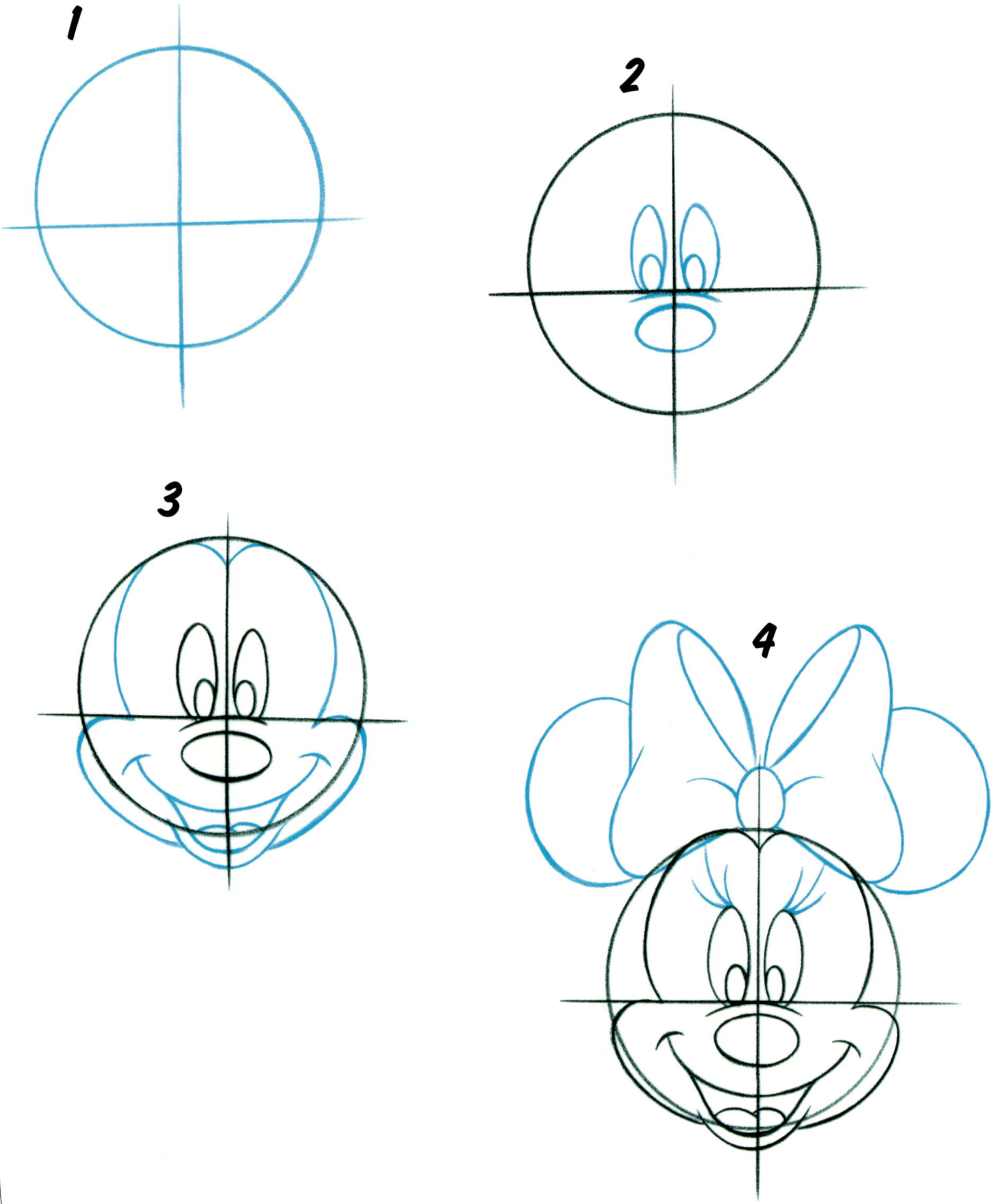

5

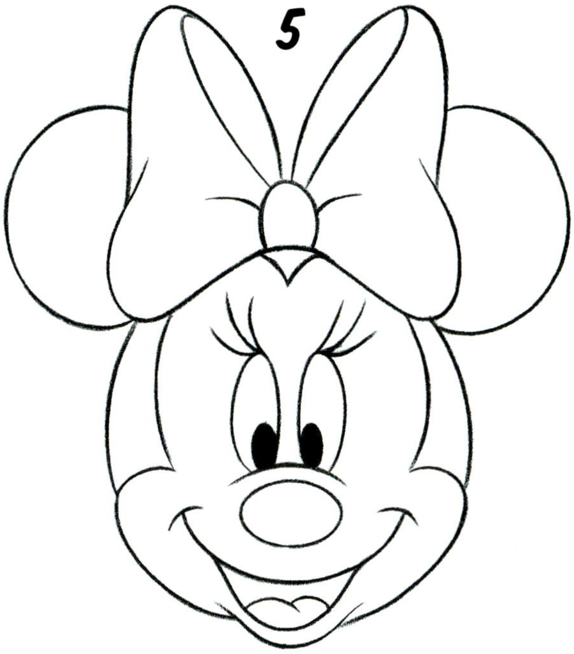

6

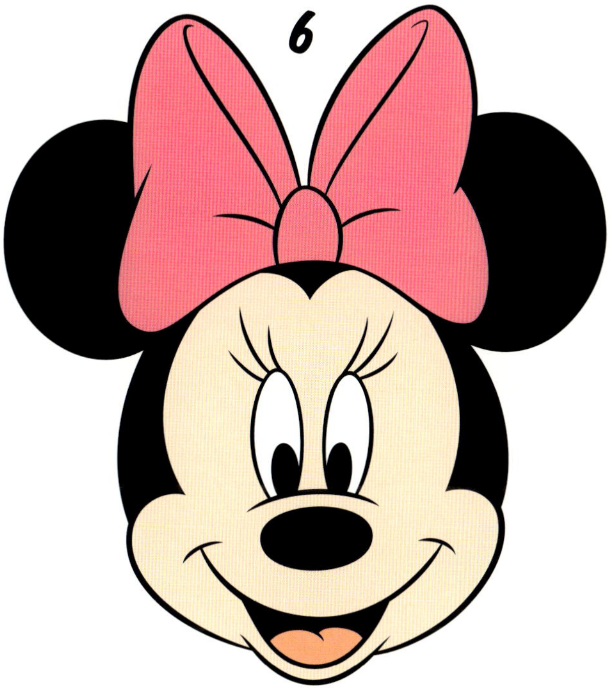

MINNIE'S EXPRESSIONS

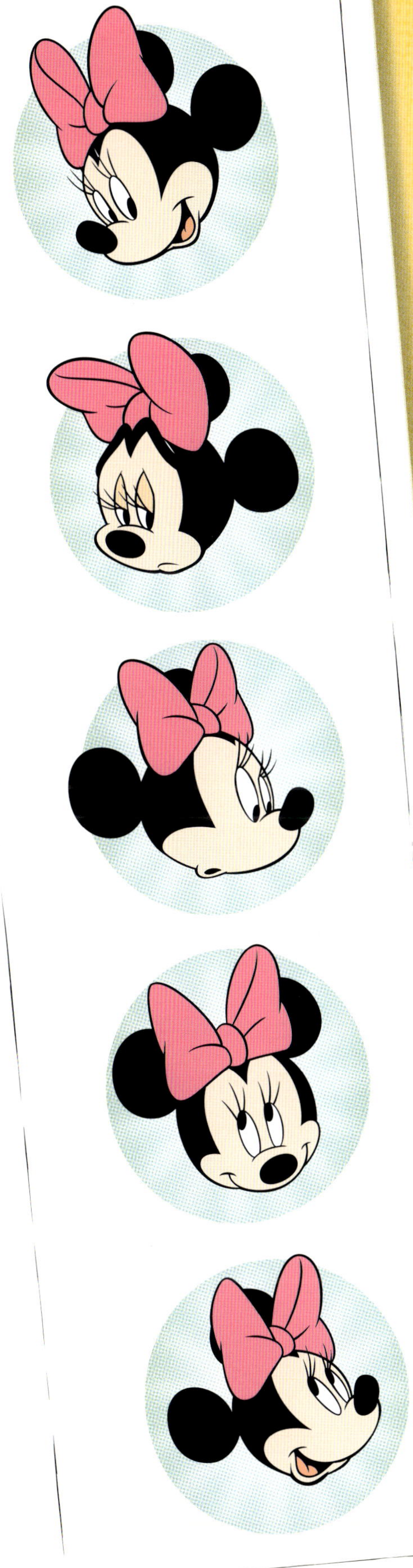

CONTEMPORARY

MINNIE MOUSE

BODY POSE

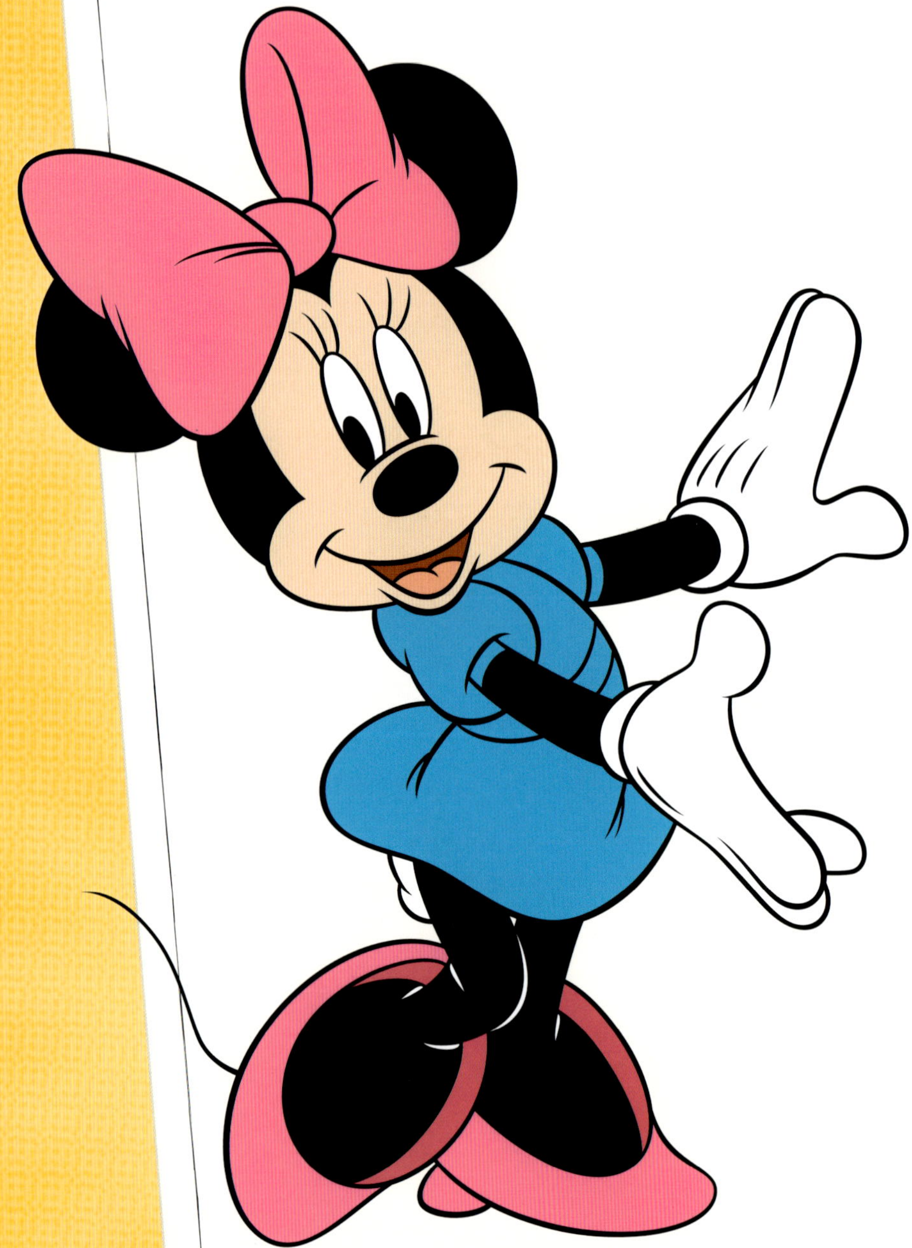

1

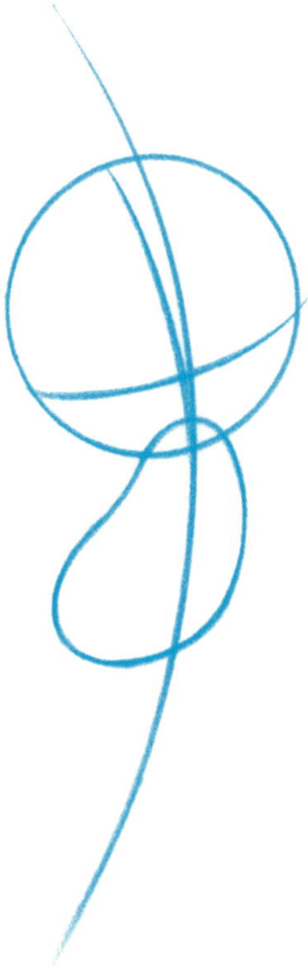

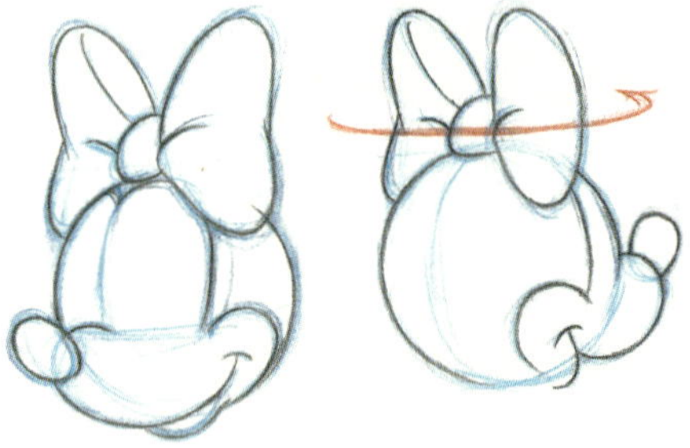

MINNIE'S BOW IS LARGE AND FULL IN FORM. IT BENDS BACK SLIGHTLY IN PROFILE OR REAR VIEWS.

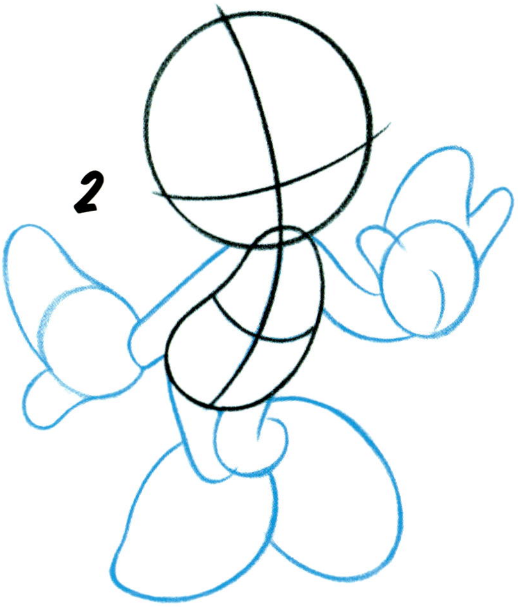

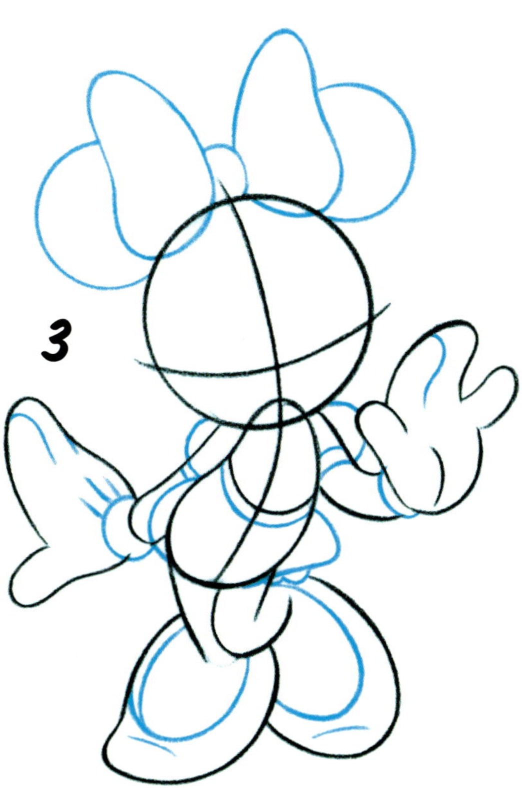

MINNIE POSES

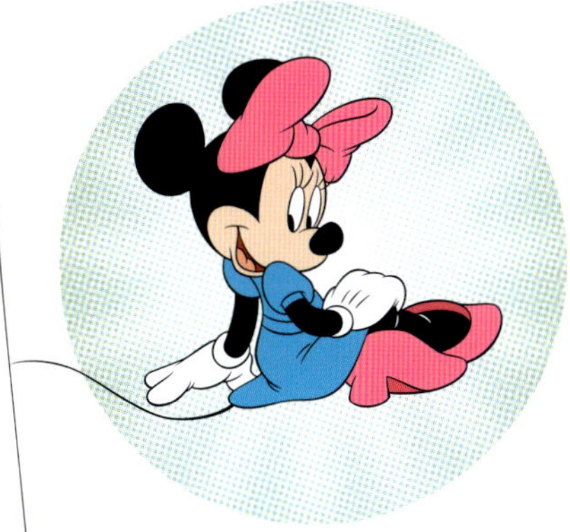

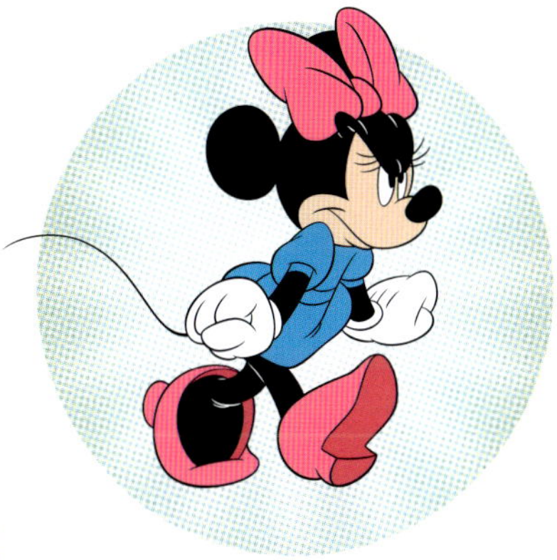

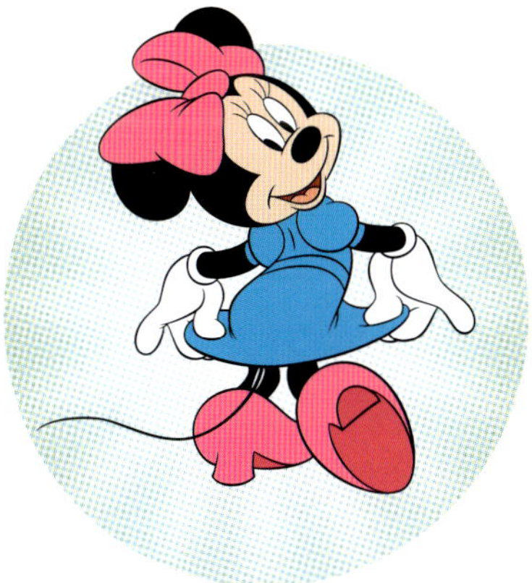

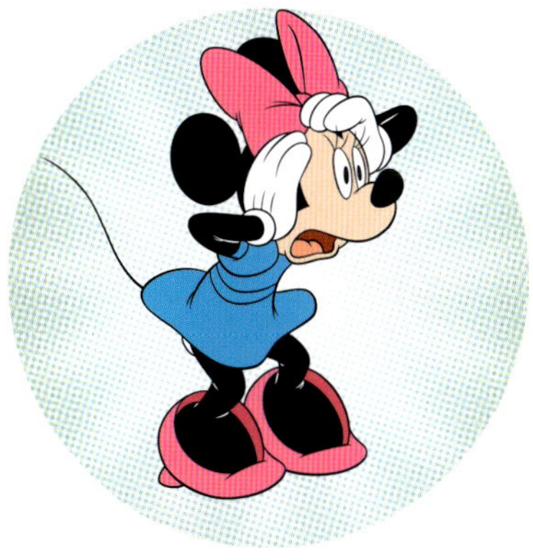

4

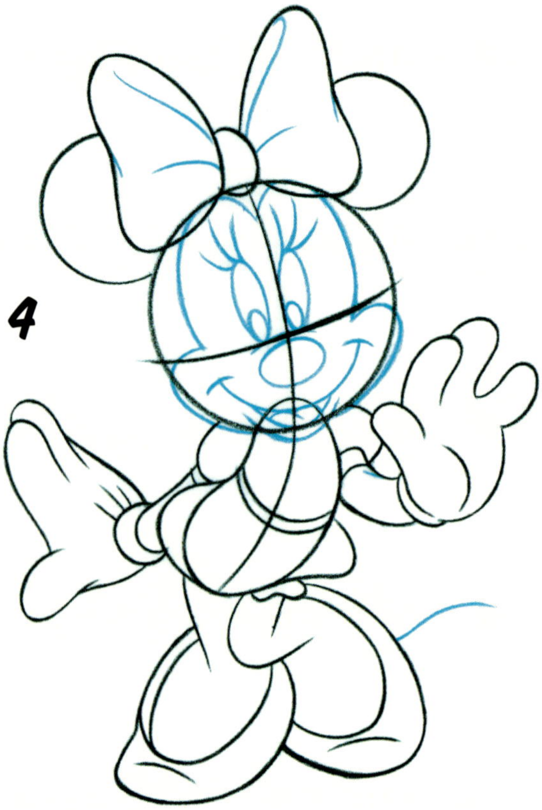

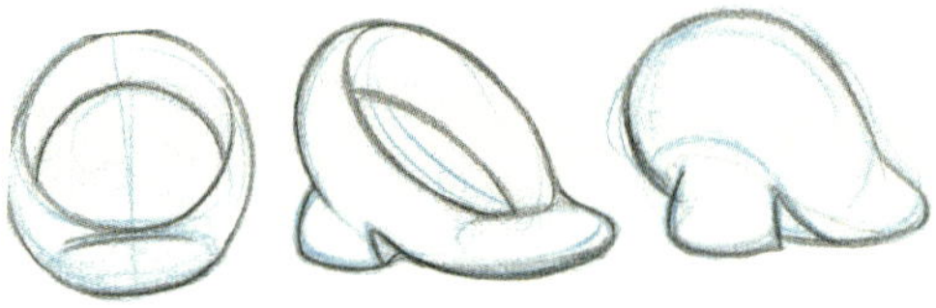

MINNIE'S SHOES HAVE A WIDE, POINTED TOE AND THICK, HIGH HEELS.

5

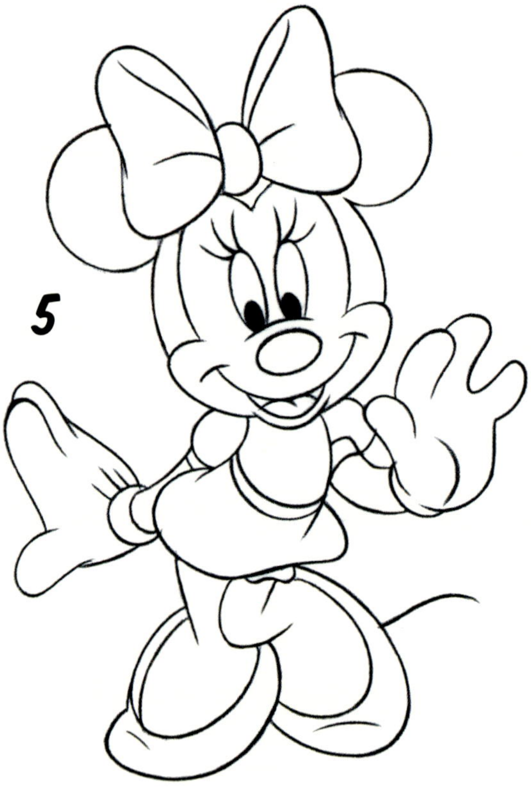

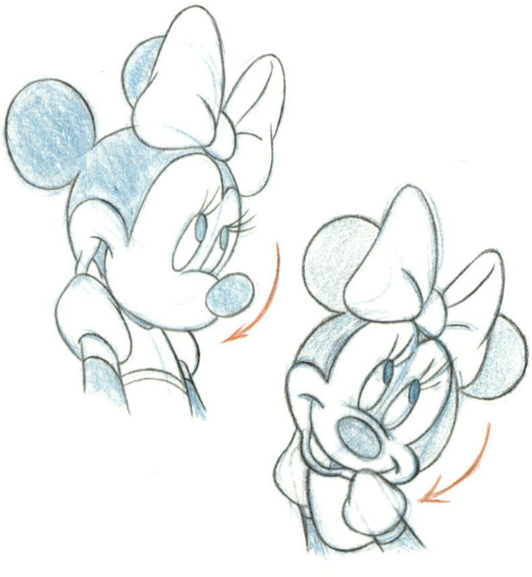

YOU CAN CHANGE MINNIE'S EXPRESSION BY TILTING HER HEAD.

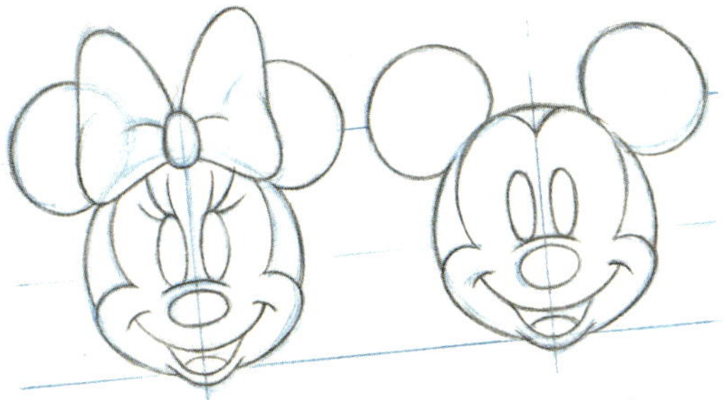

MINNIE'S HEAD IS SIMILAR TO MICKEY'S, BUT MINNIE'S EYES ARE SLIGHTLY LARGER AND WIDER, AND HER OPEN MOUTH IS SLIGHTLY SMALLER.

6

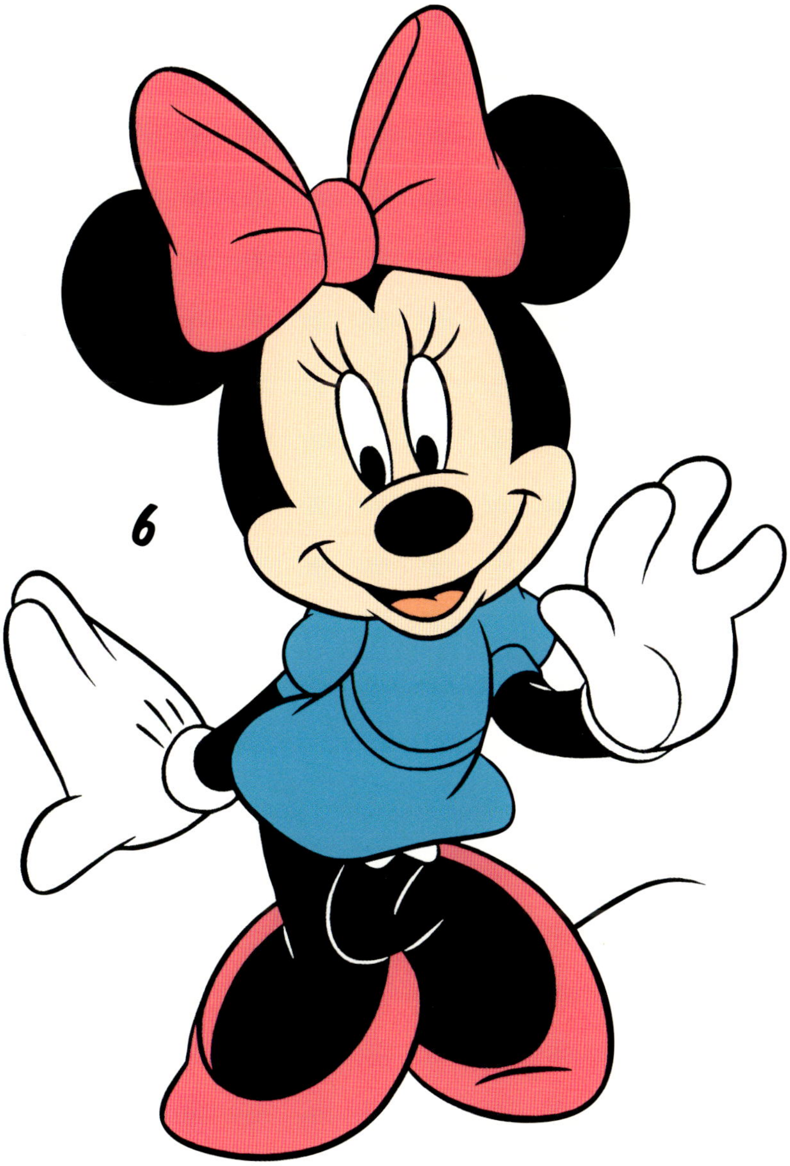

MINNIE POSES

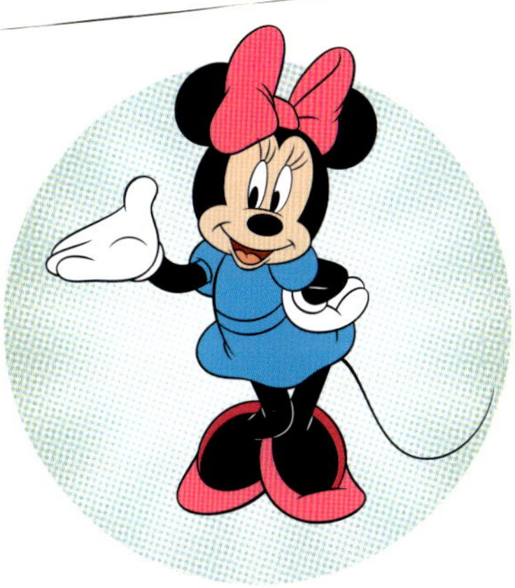

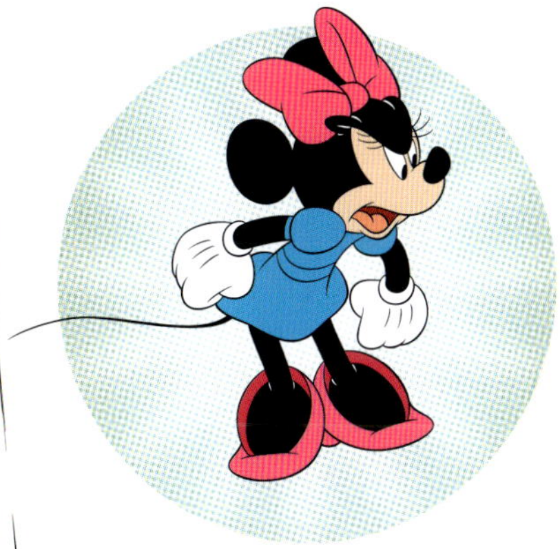

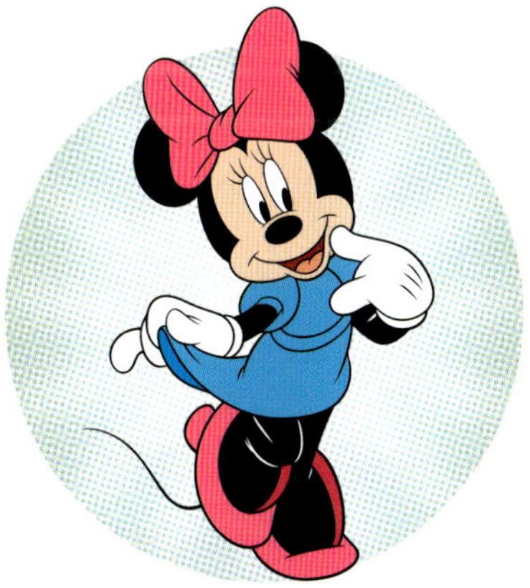

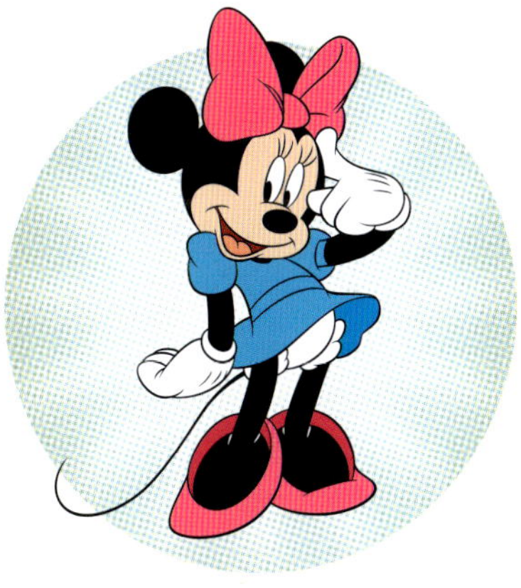

CONTEMPORARY

DONALD DUCK

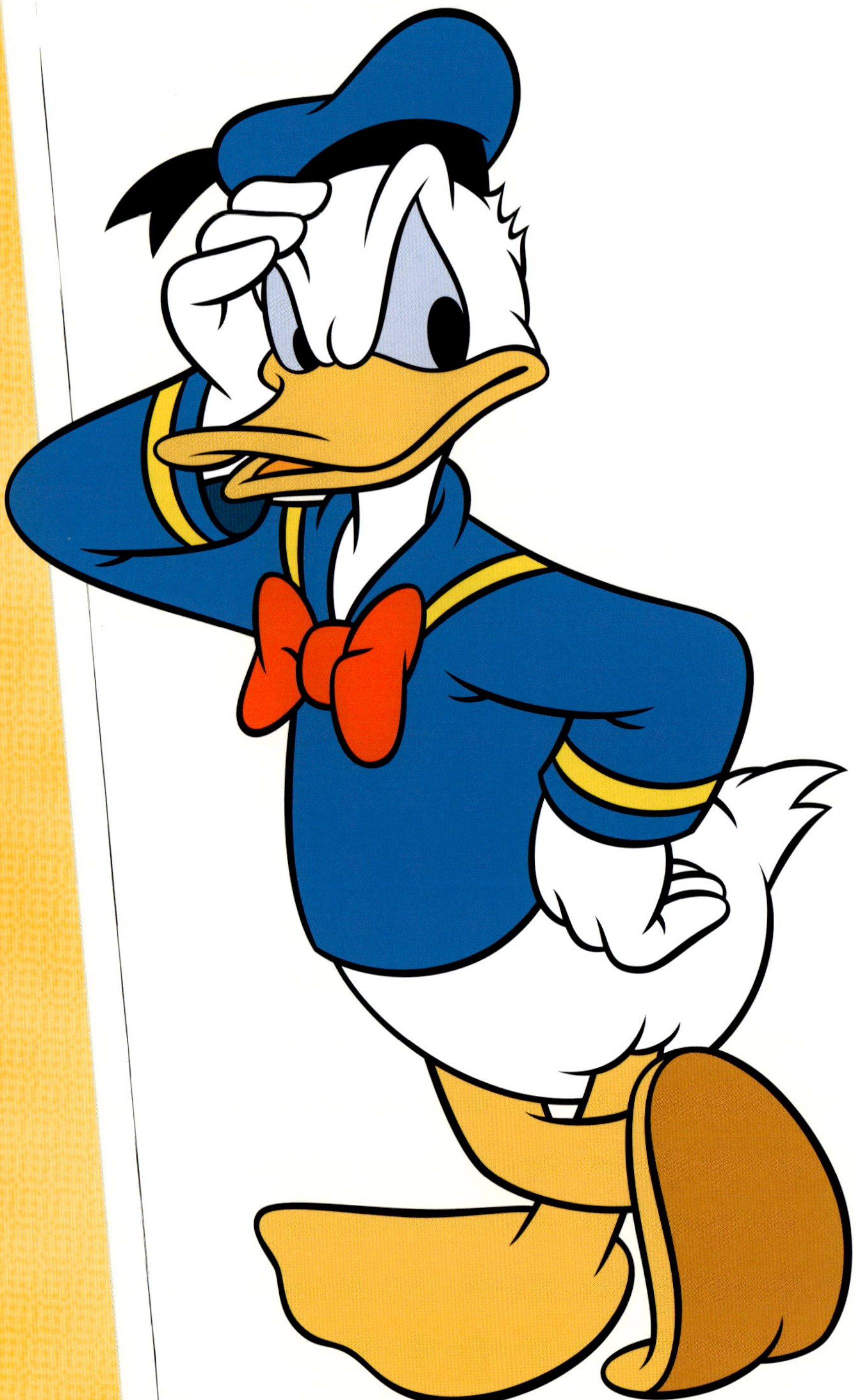

1

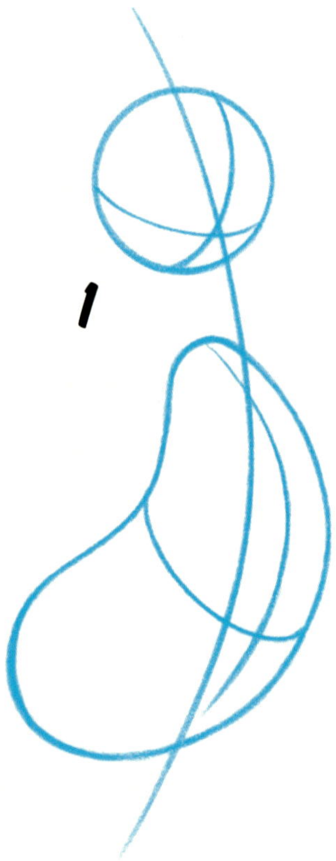

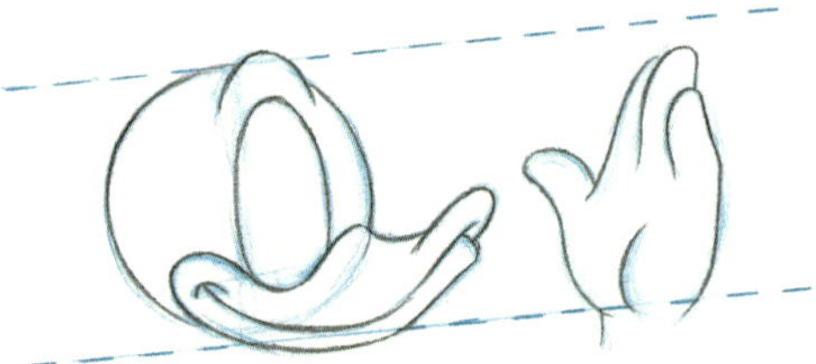

DONALD'S HANDS ARE ALMOST AS LONG AS THE HEIGHT OF HIS HEAD.

DONALD POSES

2

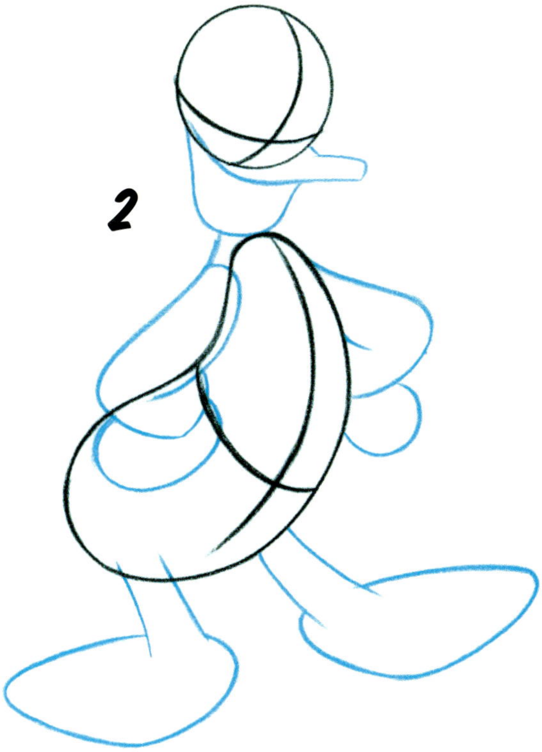

3

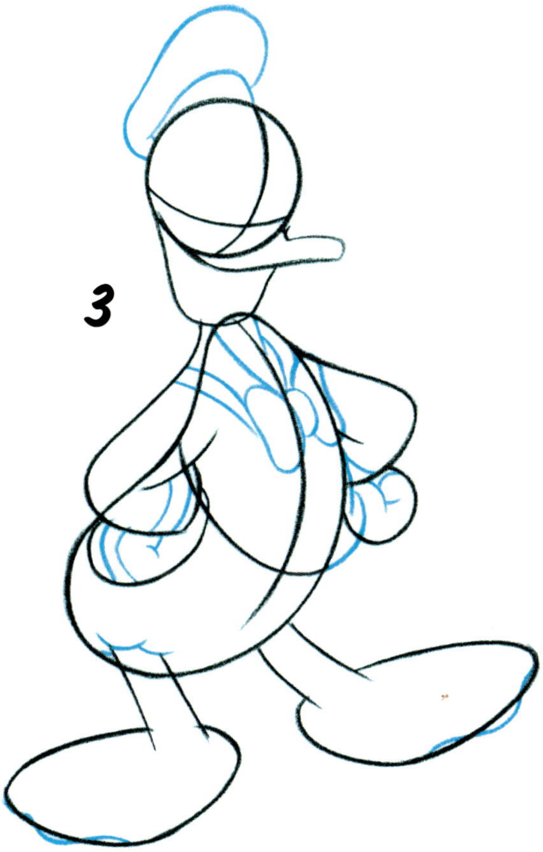

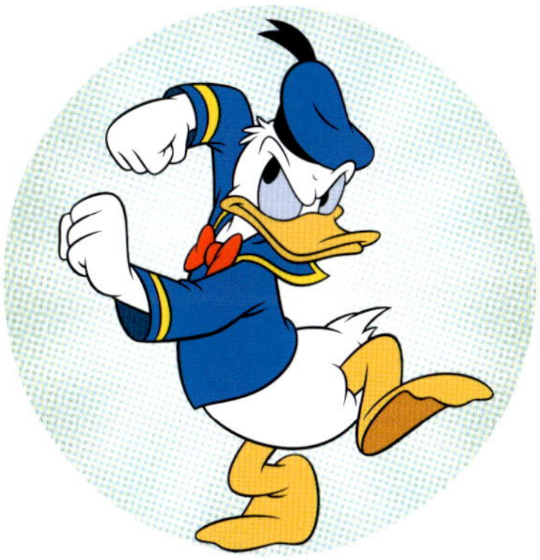

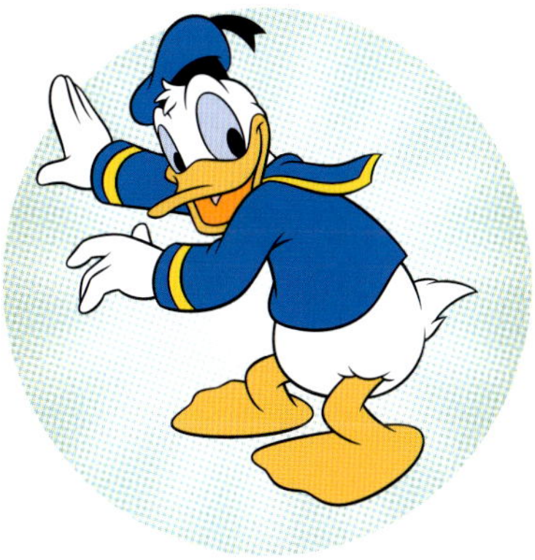

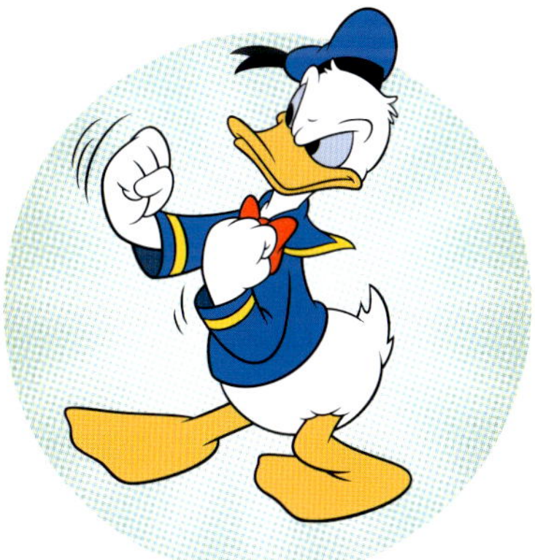

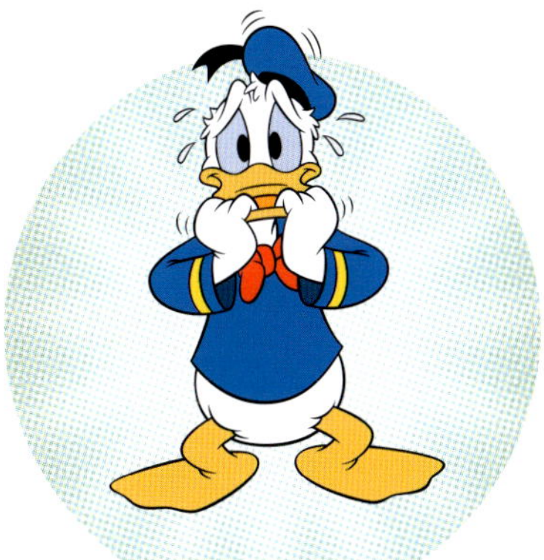

4

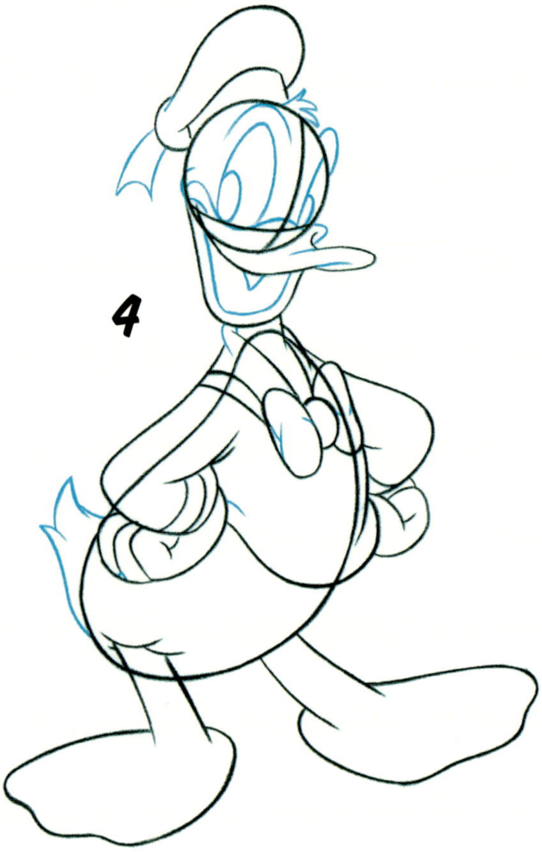

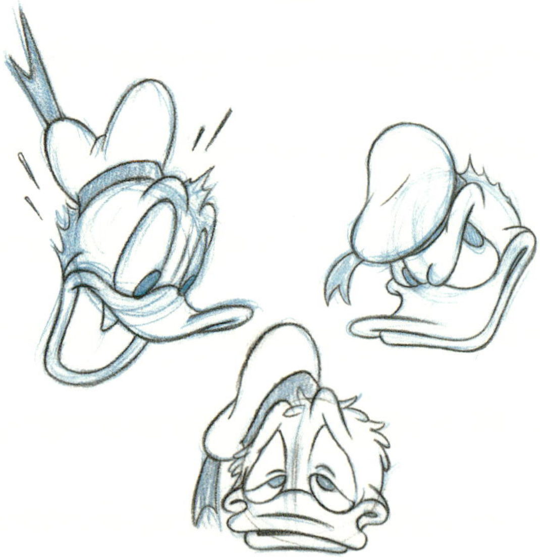

DONALD'S FACE CHANGES WHEN HE'S IN DIFFERENT MOODS.

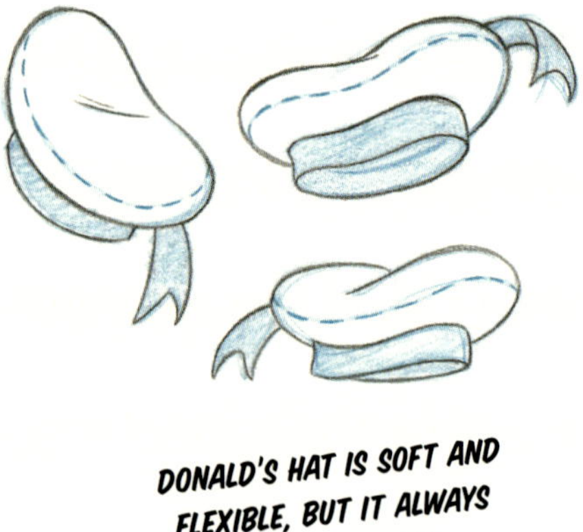

DONALD'S HAT IS SOFT AND FLEXIBLE, BUT IT ALWAYS HOLDS ITS SHAPE.

5

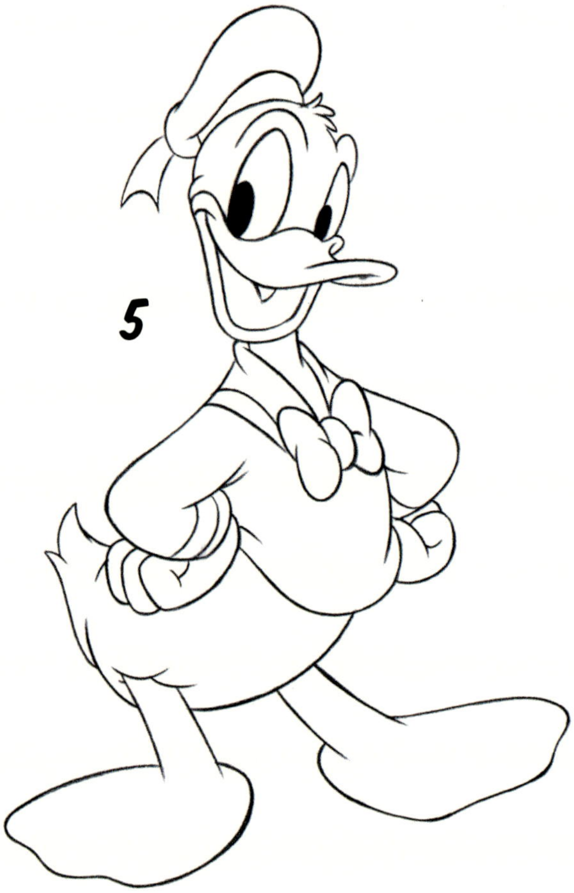

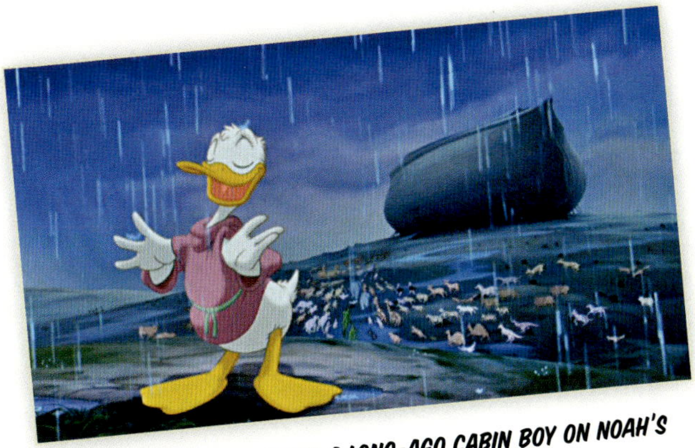

MODERN-DAY DONALD PLAYS A LONG-AGO CABIN BOY ON NOAH'S ARK IN FANTASIA 2000 (1999).

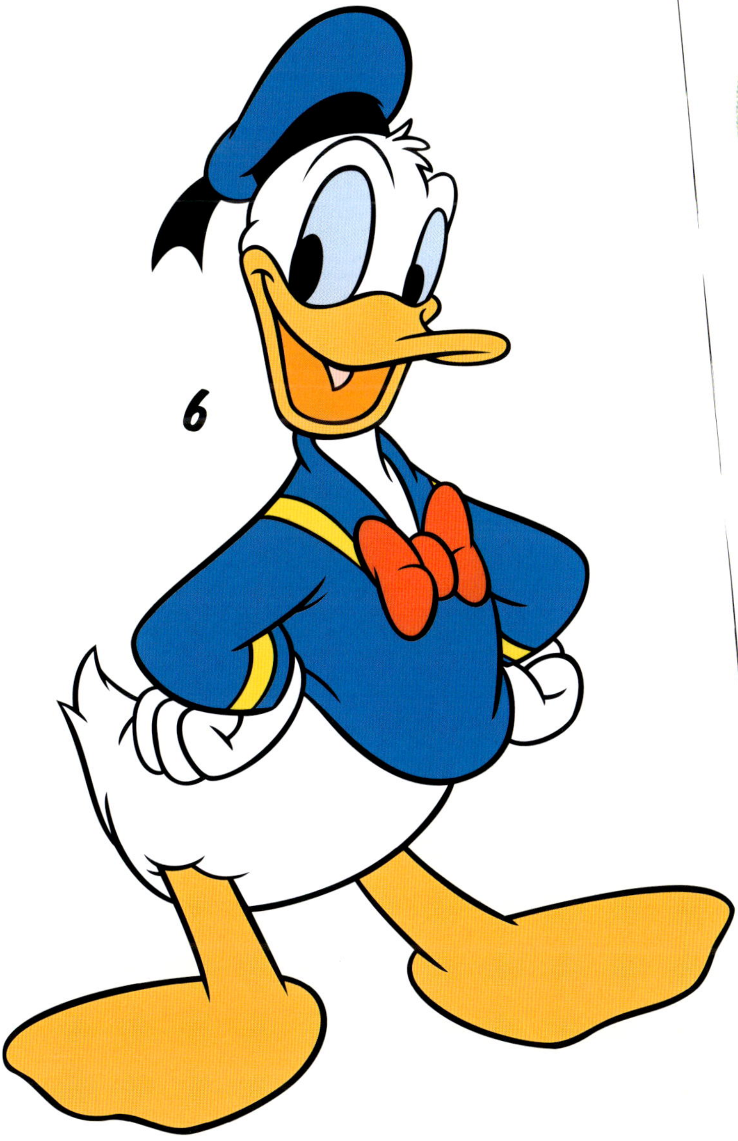

6

DONALD POSES

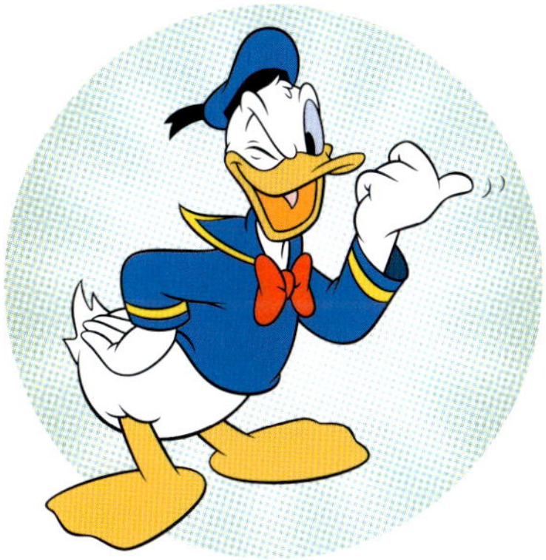

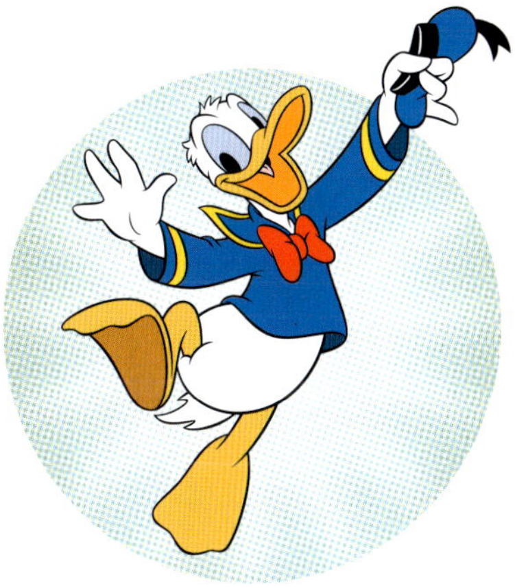

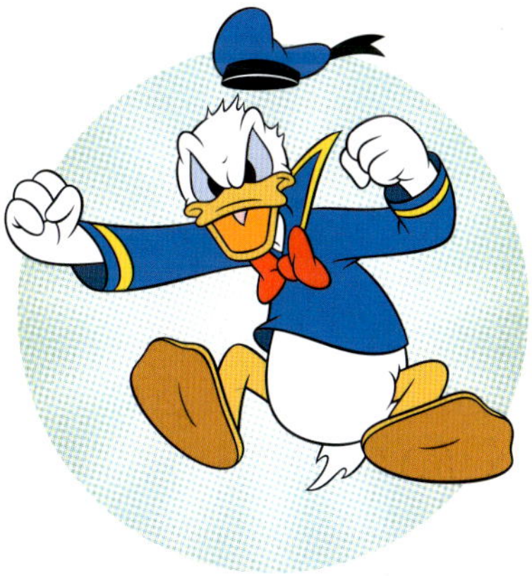

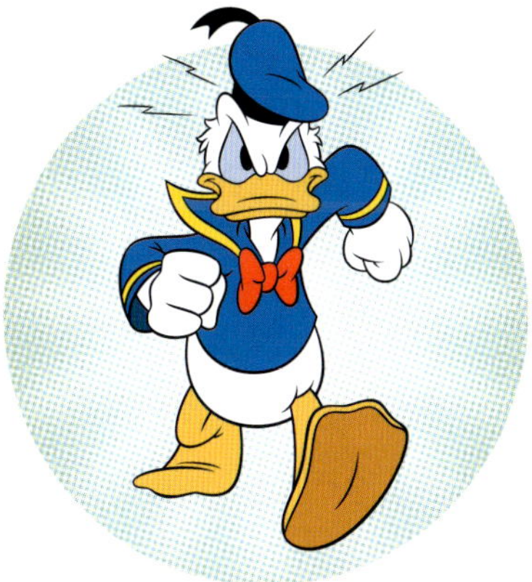

CONTEMPORARY

PLUTO

1

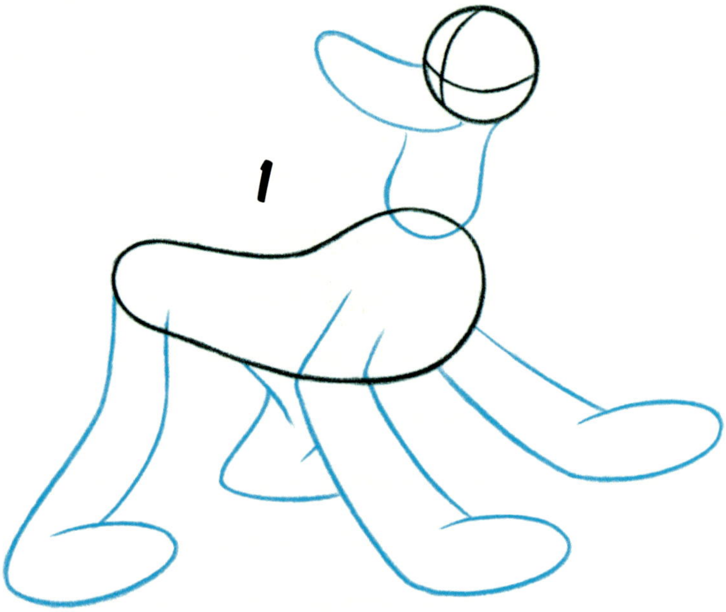

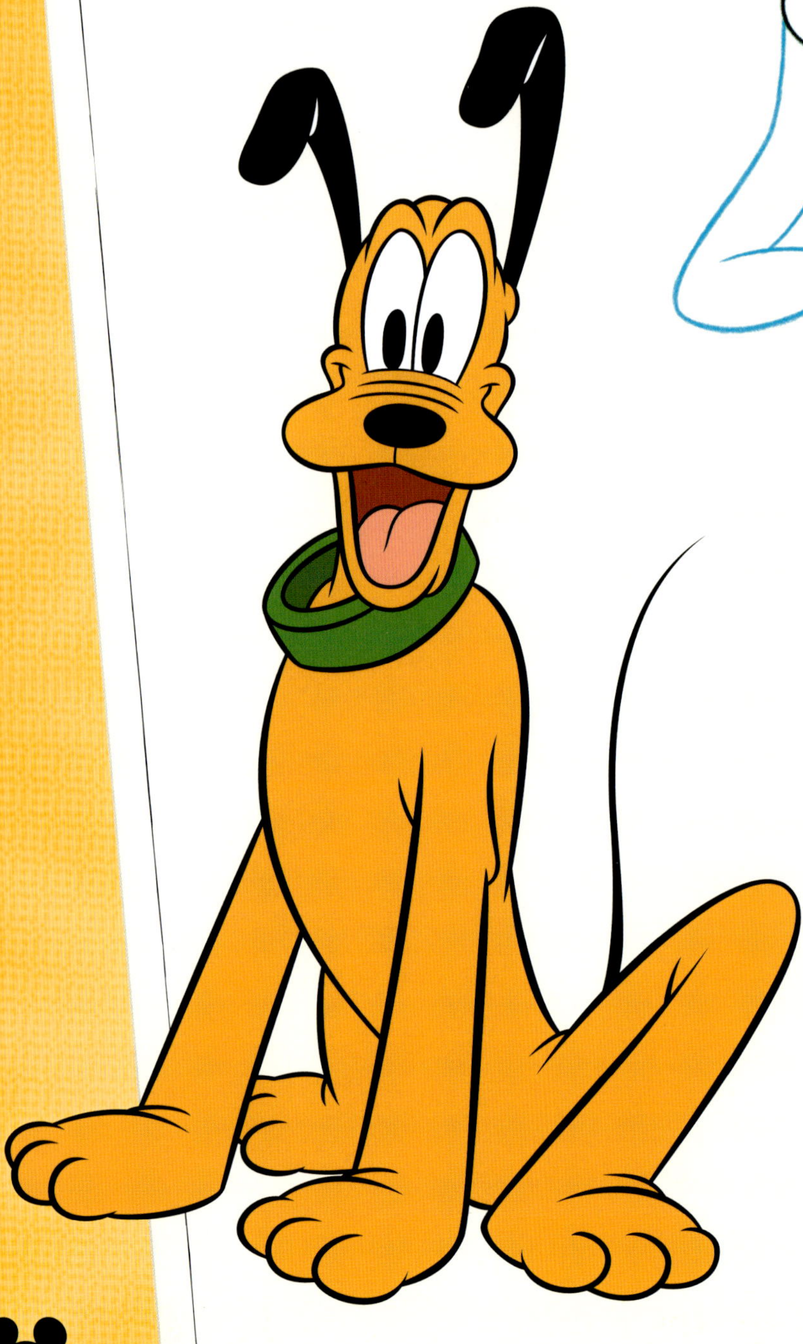

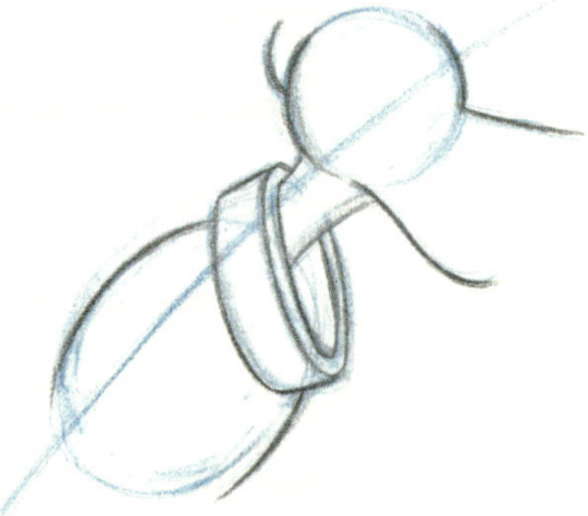

HIS COLLAR HANGS LOOSELY AT THE BACK OF HIS NECK.

PLUTO POSES

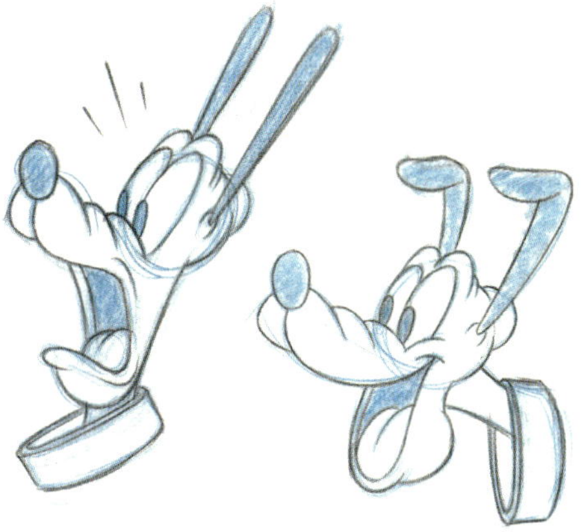

PLUTO'S EARS CAN ACT
TOGETHER TO ACCENTUATE
A MOOD OR AN EXPRESSION.

2

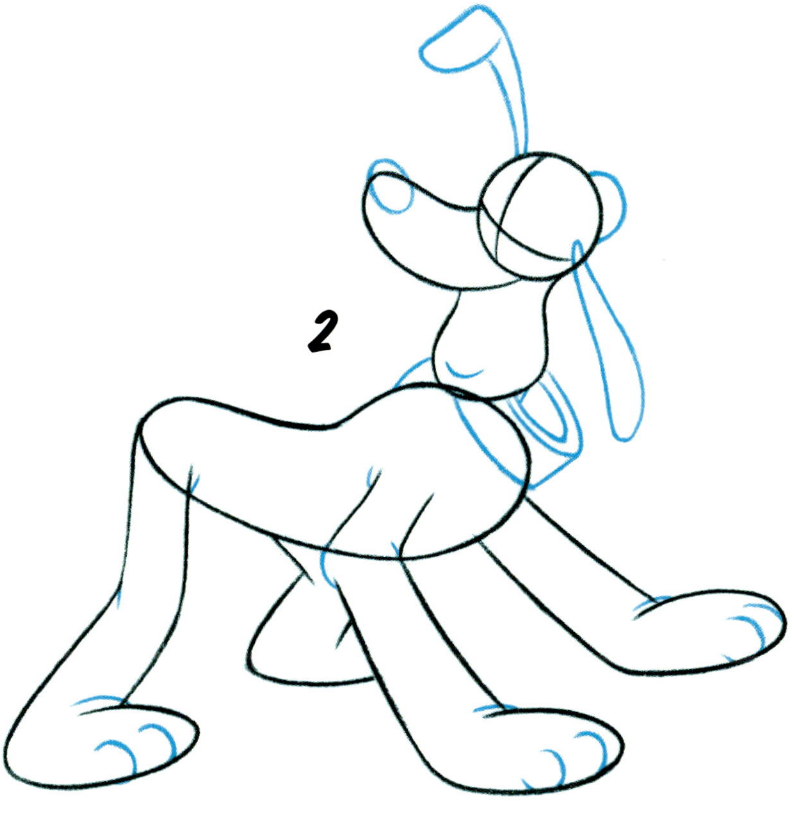

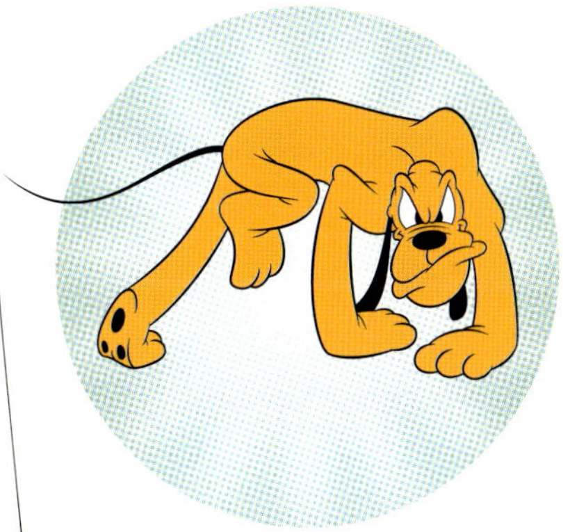

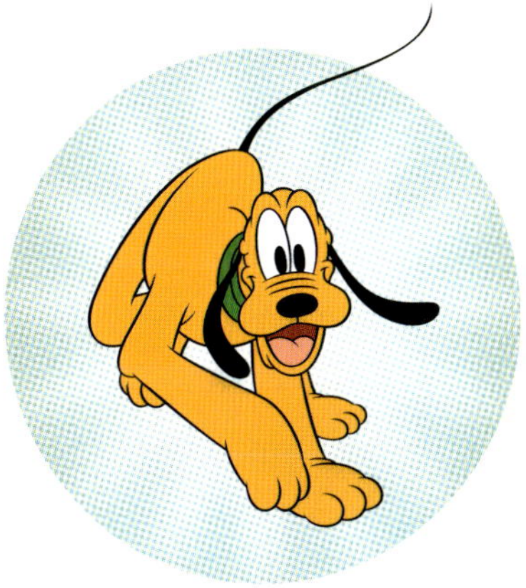

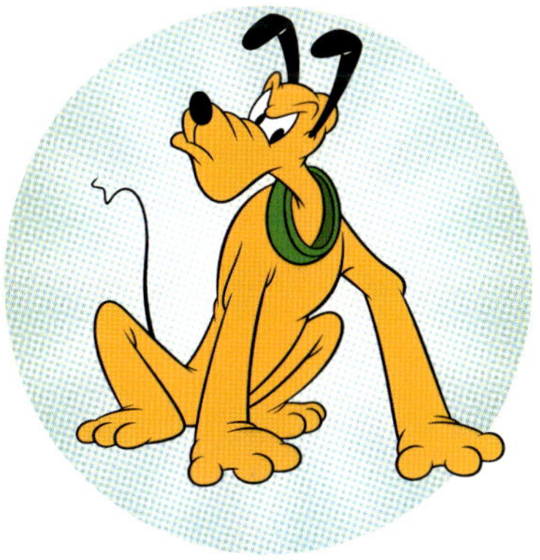

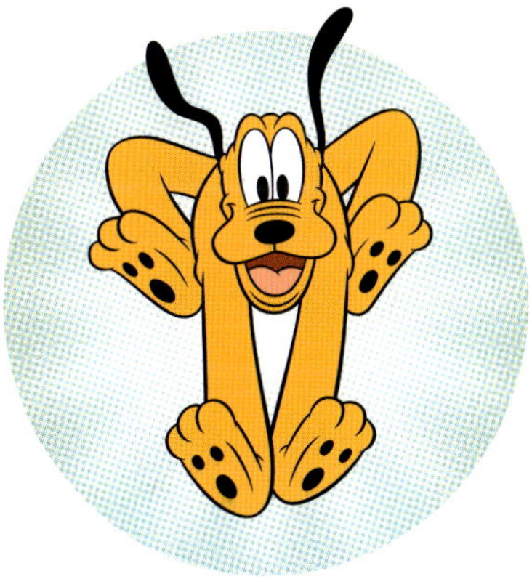

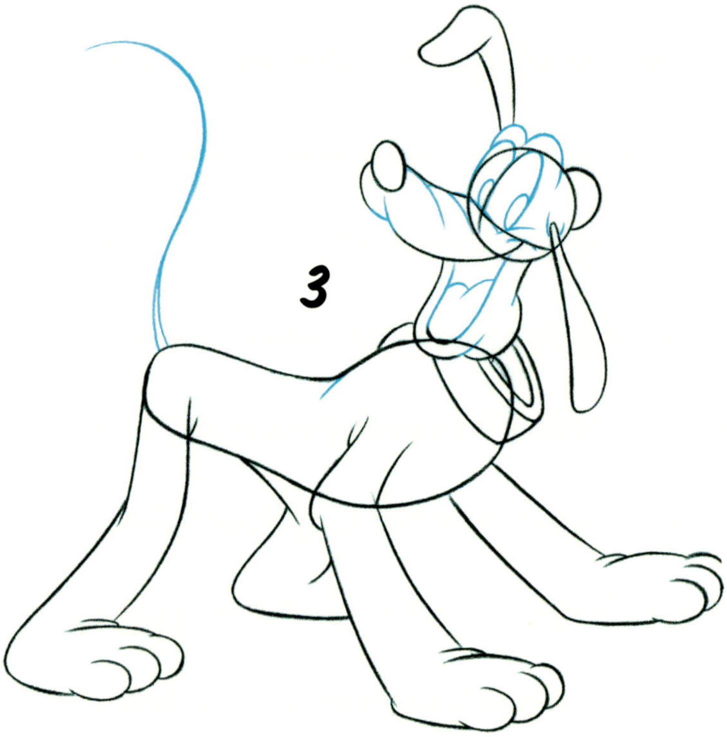

3

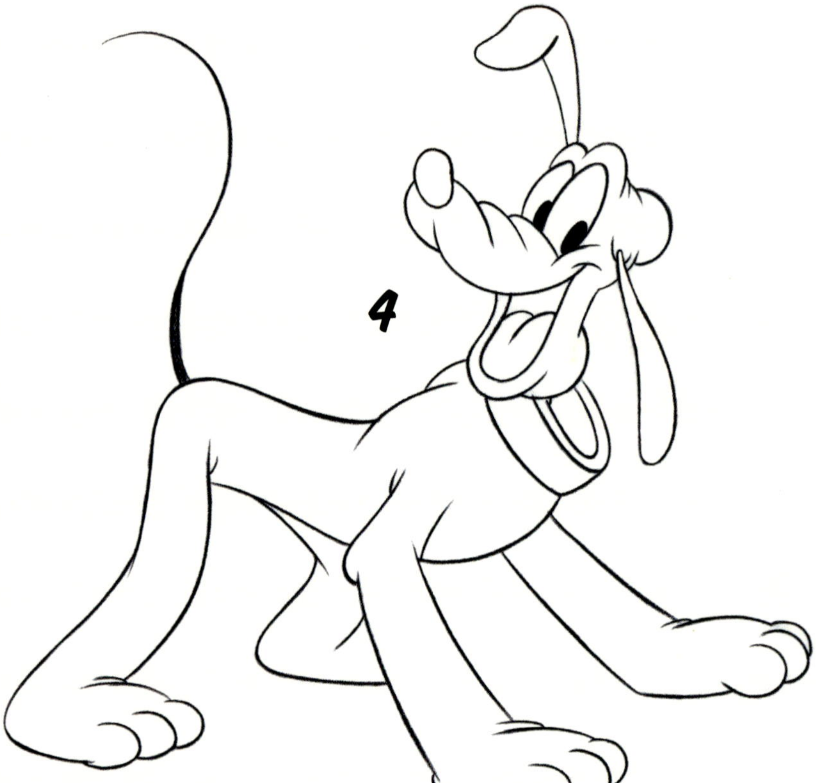

4

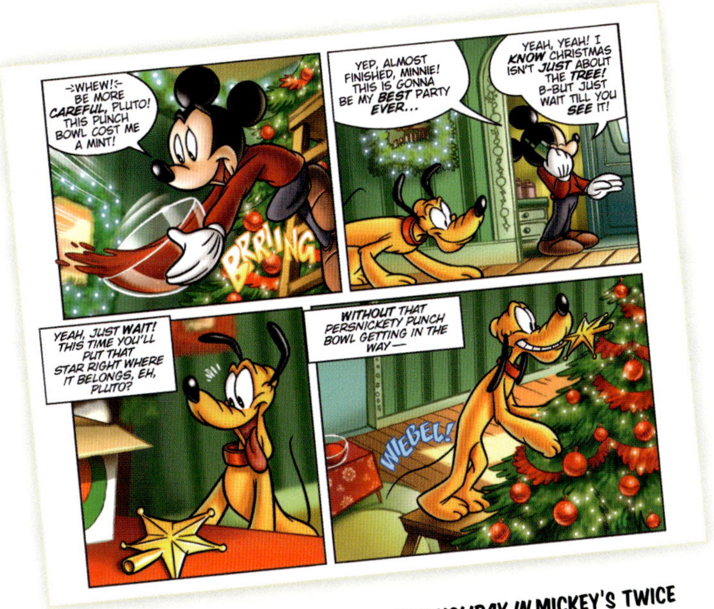

MODERN-DAY PLUTO CAUSES AN UNHAPPY HOLIDAY IN MICKEY'S TWICE UPON A CHRISTMAS (2004), HERE IN ITS COMIC ADAPTATION. ART BY DANIELA VETRO, FEDERICO MANCUSO, AND PAOLO CAMPINOTI.

5

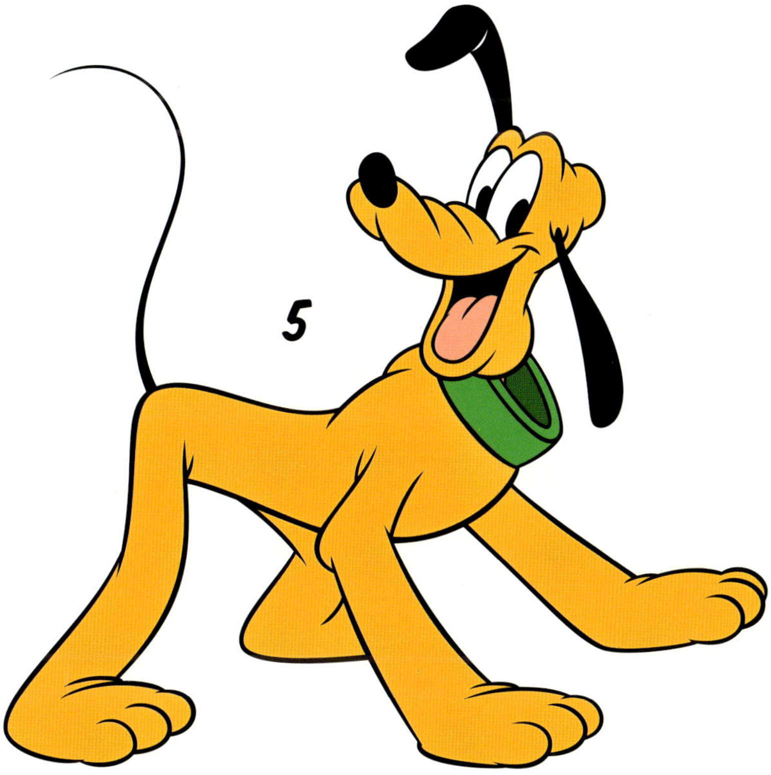

PLUTO POSES

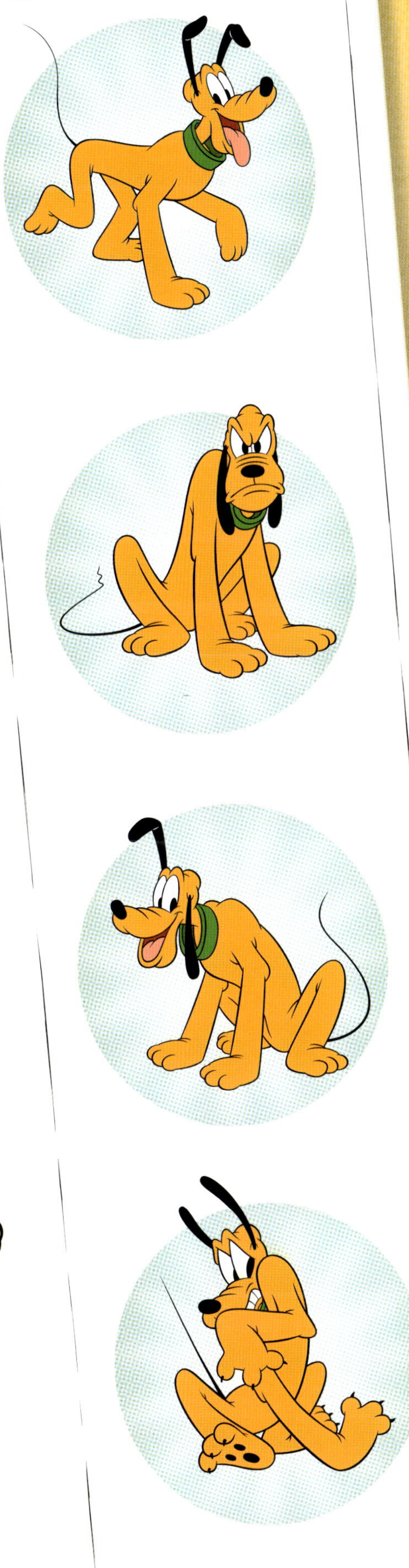

CONTEMPORARY GOOFY

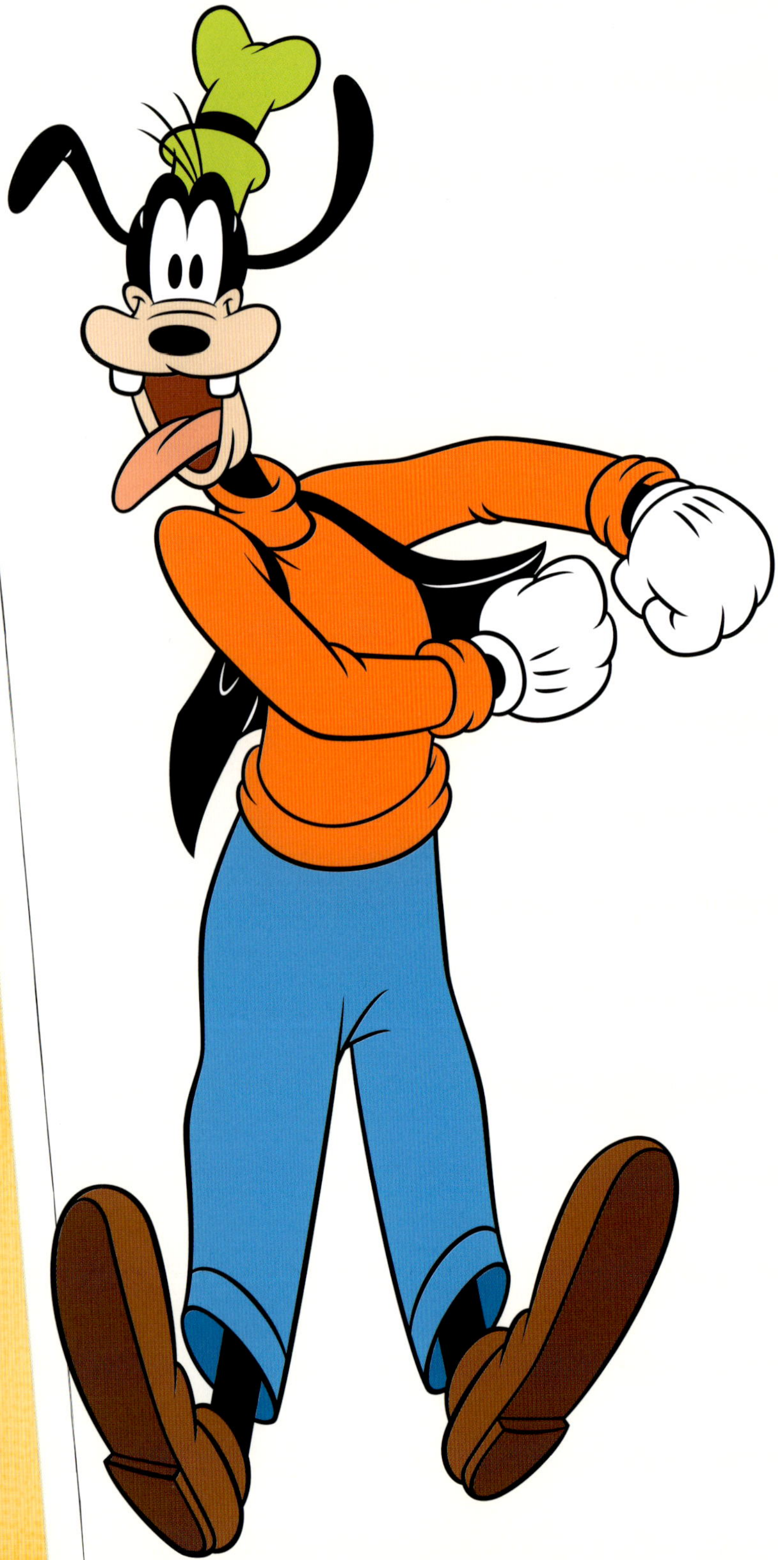

1

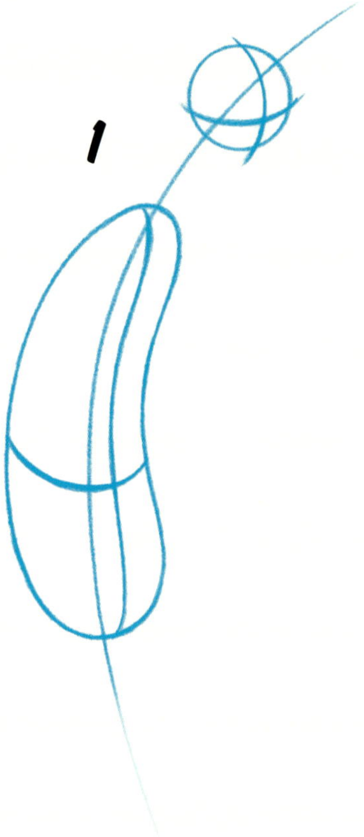

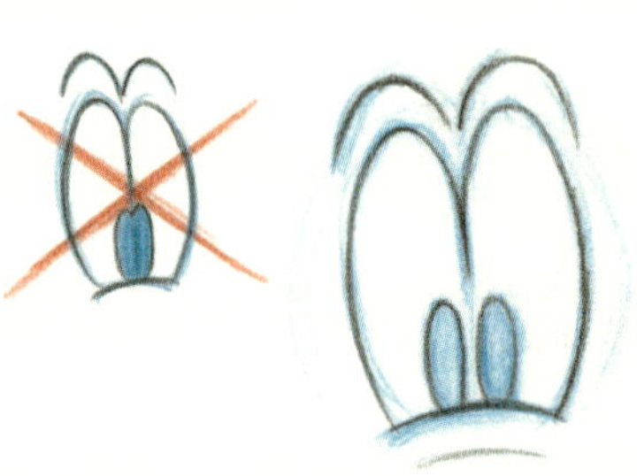

NOTICE HOW THE WHITES OF GOOFY'S EYES TOUCH EACH OTHER. JUST MAKE SURE YOU KEEP HIS PUPILS SEPARATE.

2

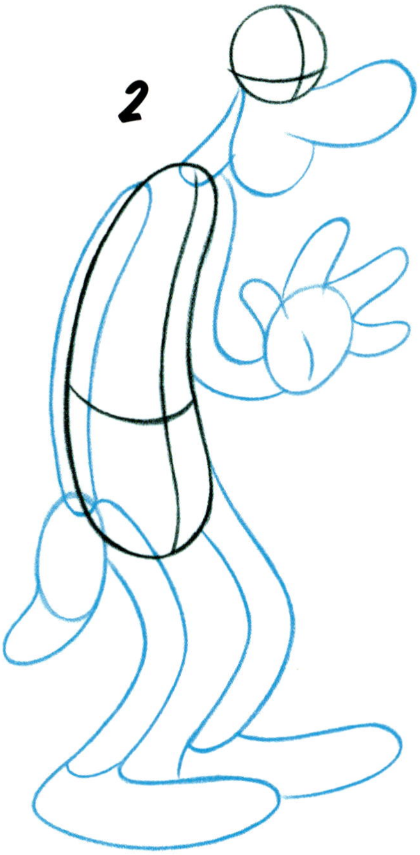

3

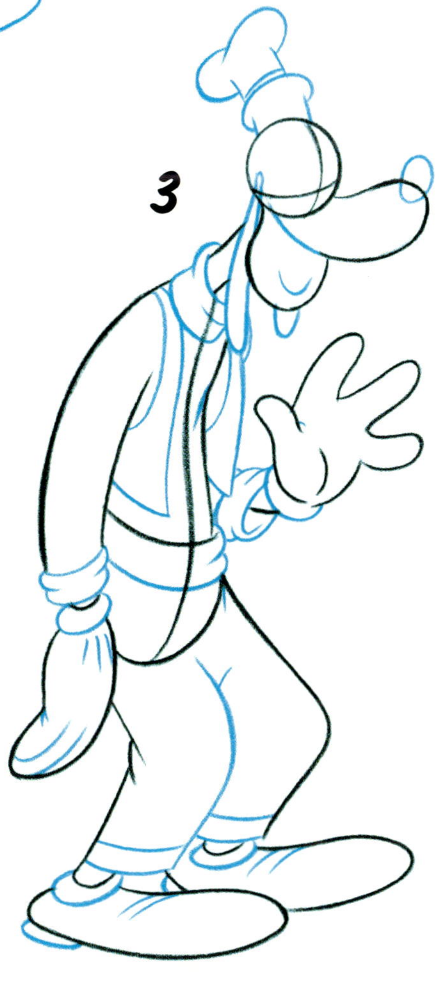

GOOFY POSES

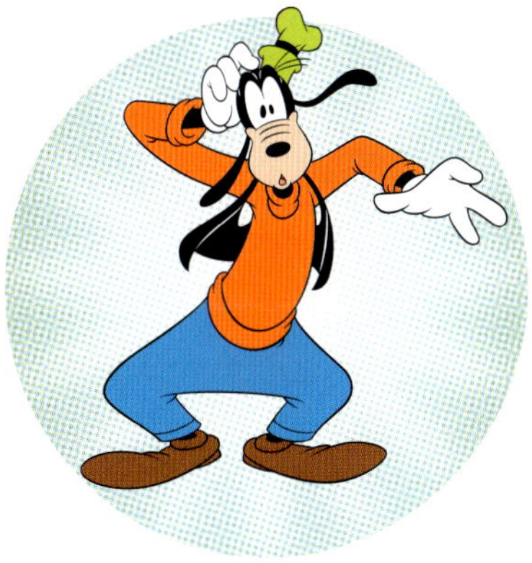

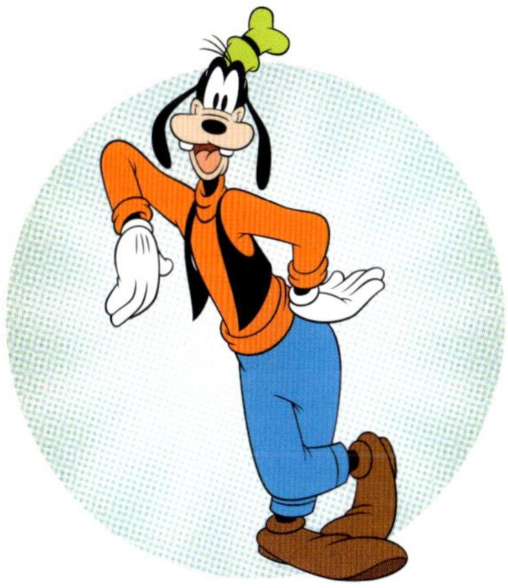

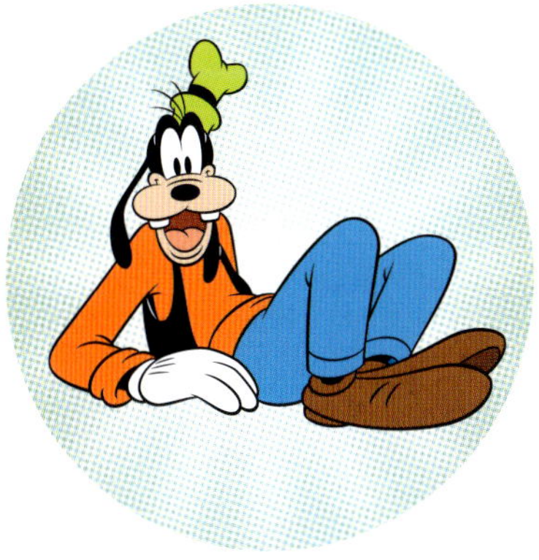

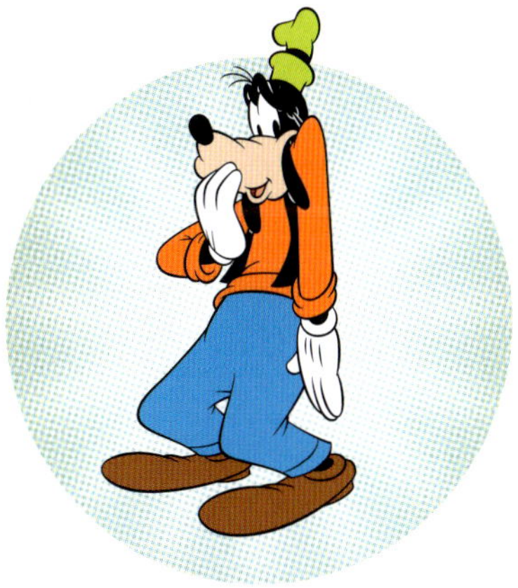

4

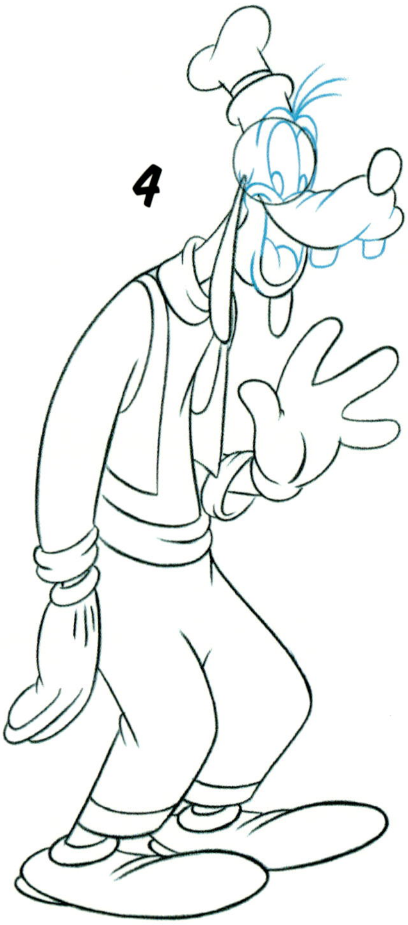

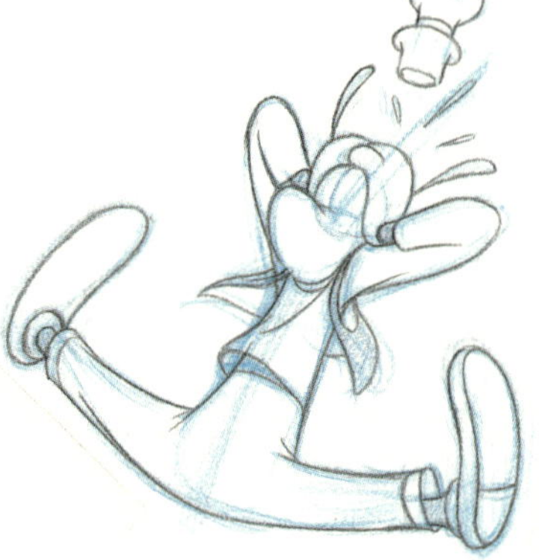

USE GOOFY'S ENTIRE BODY TO ACT OUT A MOOD OR ACTION.

5

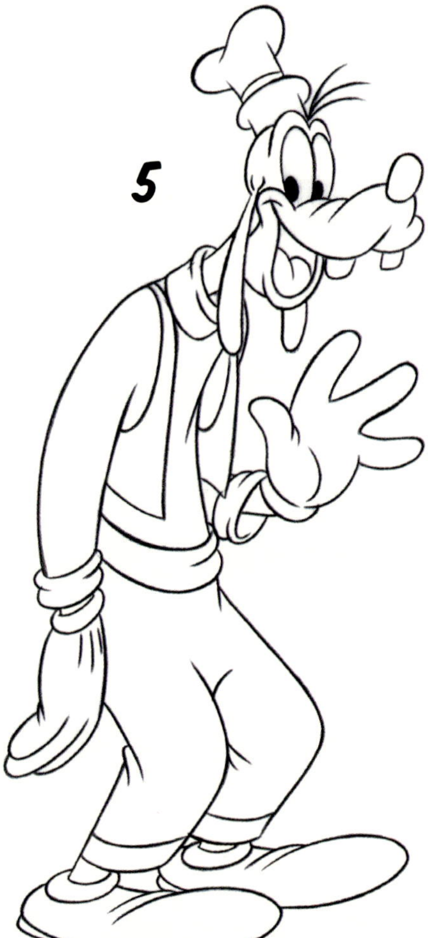

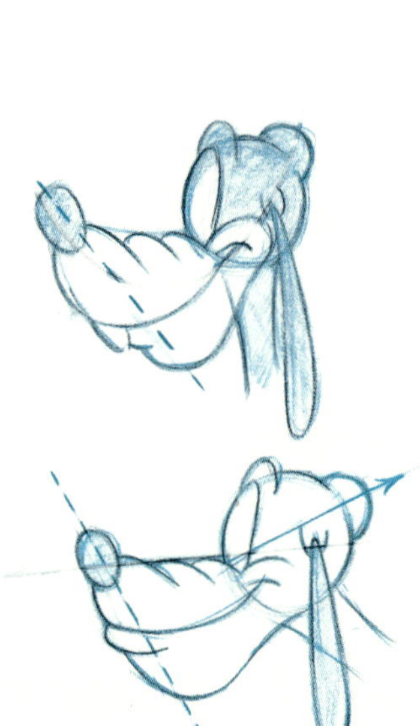

GOOFY'S HEAD IS SIMILAR TO PLUTO'S.

6

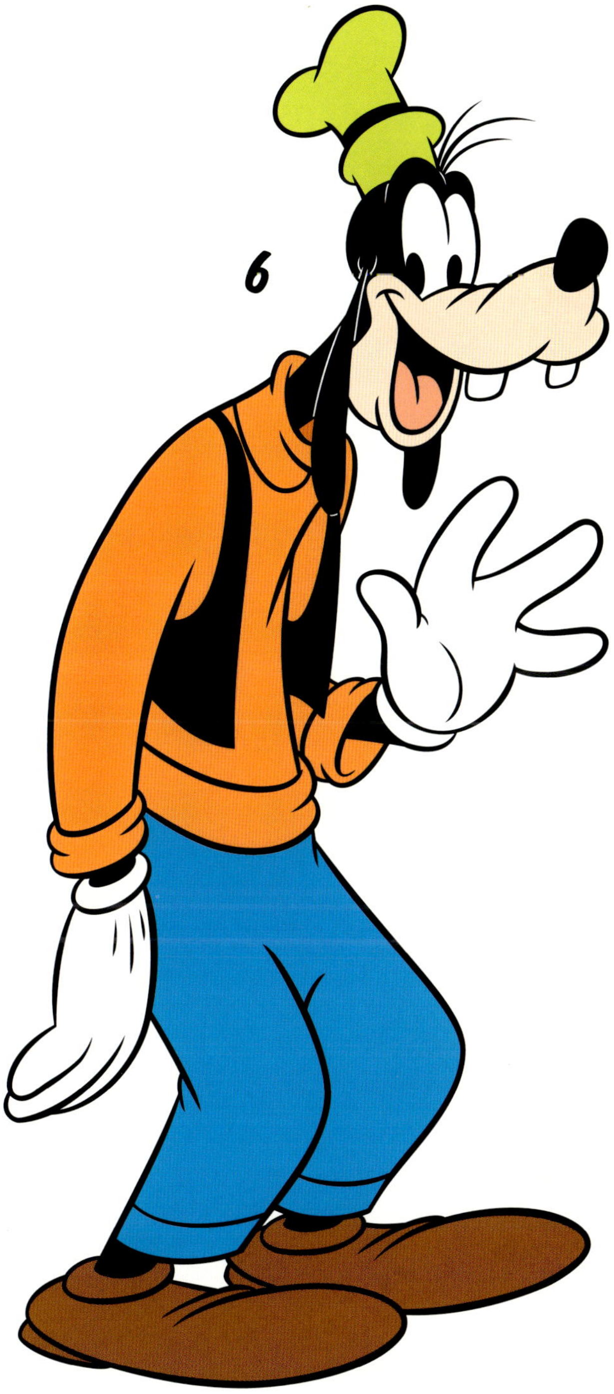

GOOFY POSES

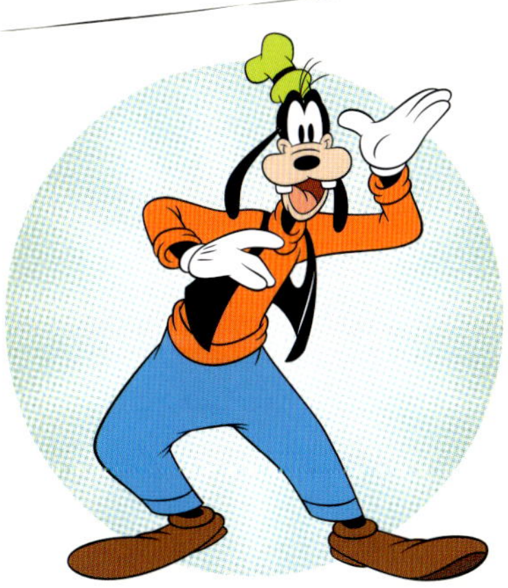

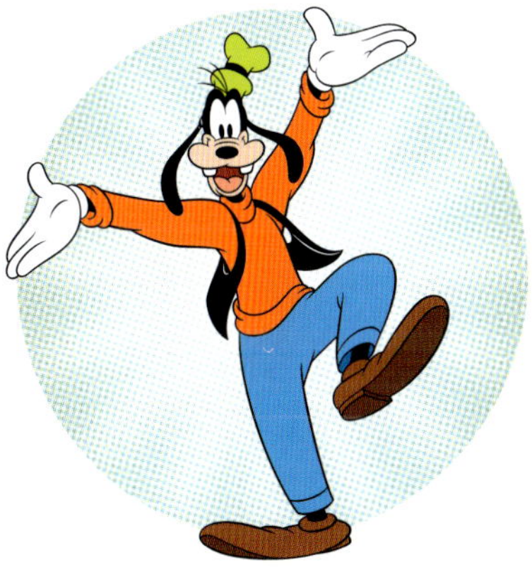

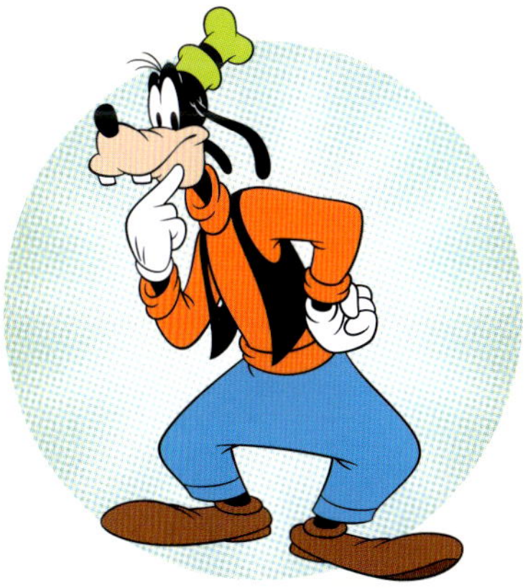

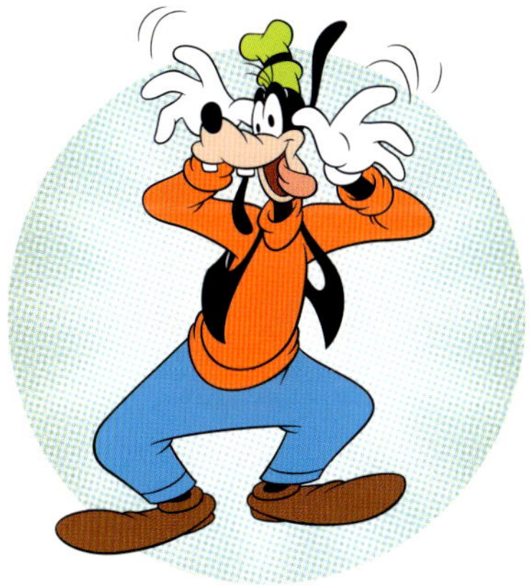

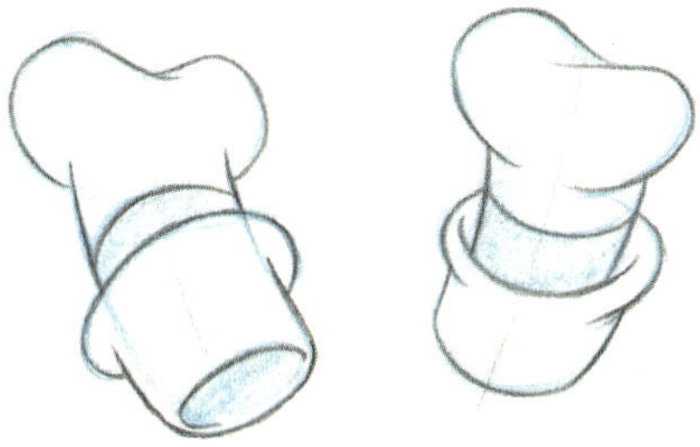

GOOFY'S HAT IS ABOUT 1 HEAD LONG. IT'S SQUISHY LOOKING AND LEANS TO ONE SIDE.

1940s

DAISY DUCK

EARLY APPEARANCE/ MR. DUCK STEPS OUT

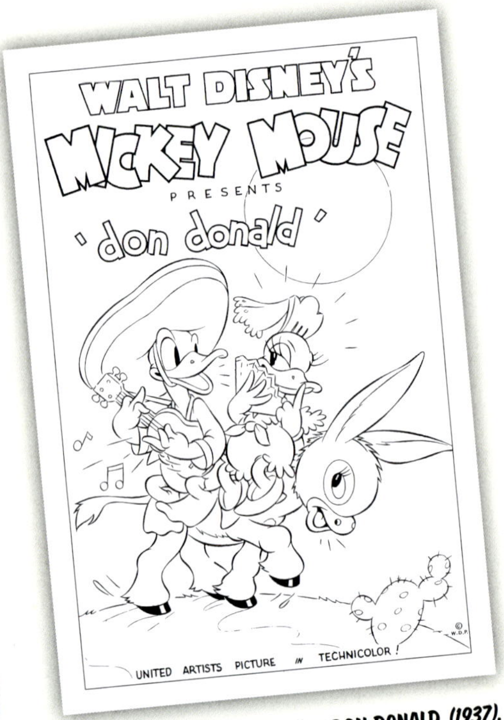

DAISY DEBUTS AS "DONNA" IN DON DONALD (1937). PROMOTIONAL POSTER DRAWN BY MANUEL GONZALES.

1

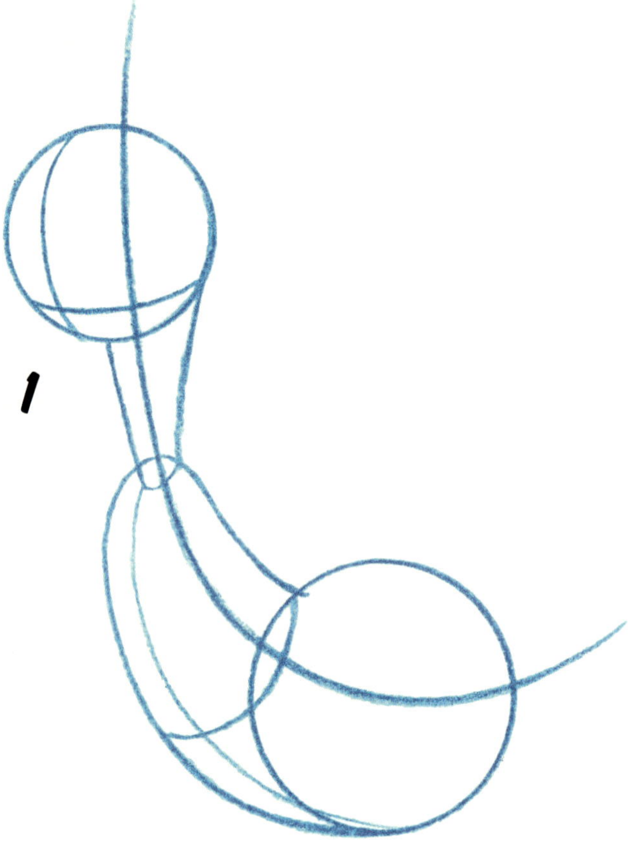

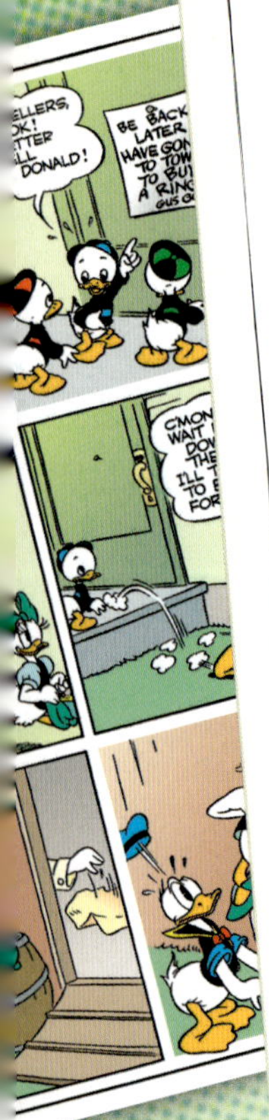

PERSONALITY PLUS

DAISY DUCK IS SASSY YET SOPHISTICATED. SHE HAS IMPECCABLE MANNERS (MOST OF THE TIME!) AND A PASSION FOR THE FINER THINGS IN LIFE.

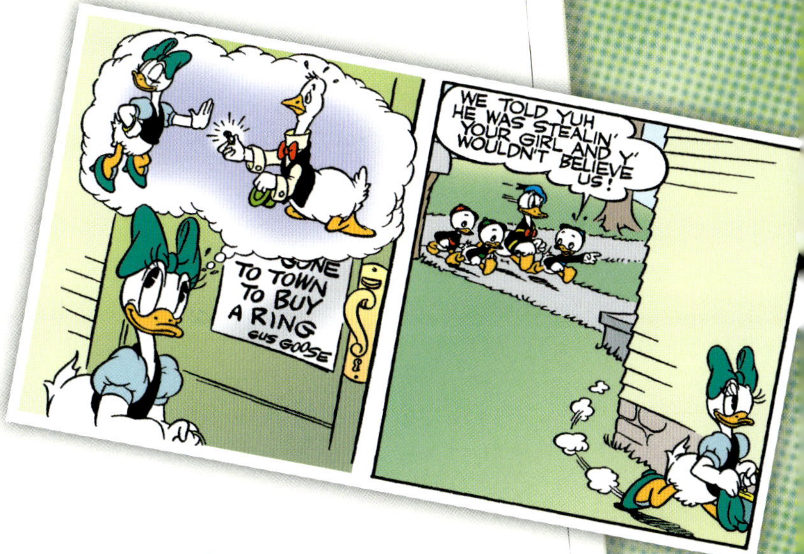

2

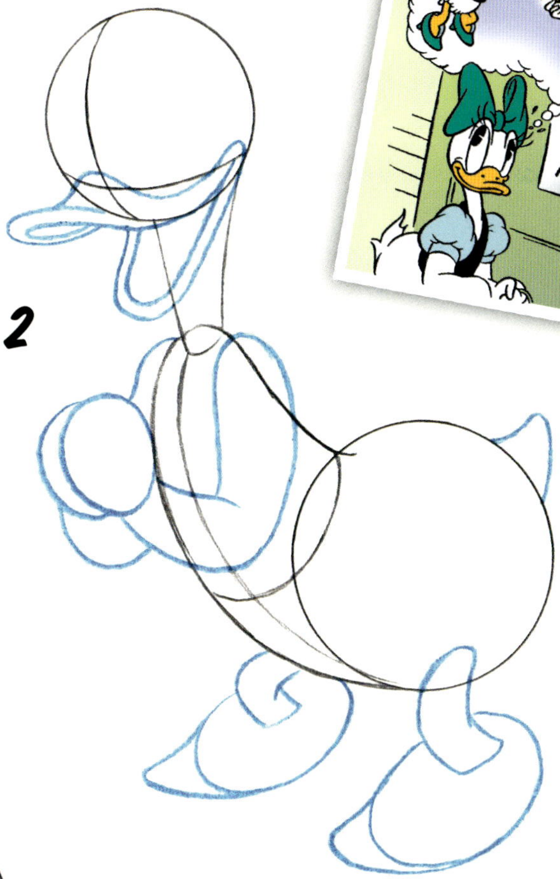

3

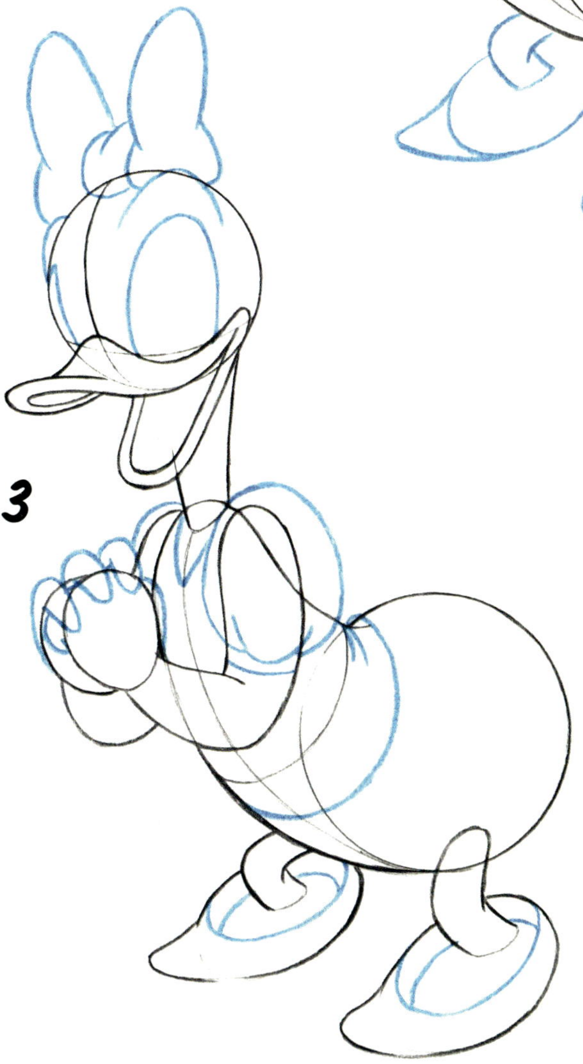

DAISY DUCK FIRST APPEARED AS "DONNA DUCK" IN THE 1937 FILM SHORT DON DONALD. HER REAL NAME WAS FIRST USED IN MR. DUCK STEPS OUT (1940).

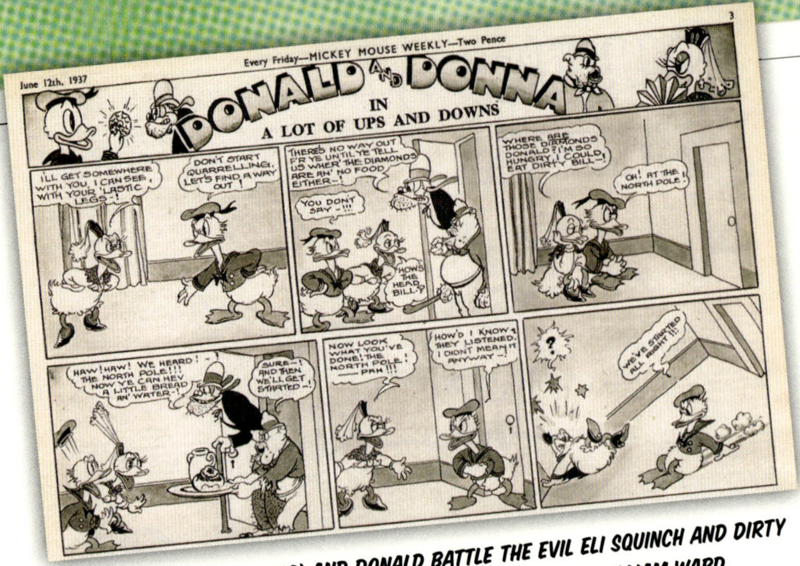

Daisy (then called Donna) and Donald battle the evil Eli Squinch and Dirty Bill in a classic British Disney comic from 1937. Art by William Ward.

4

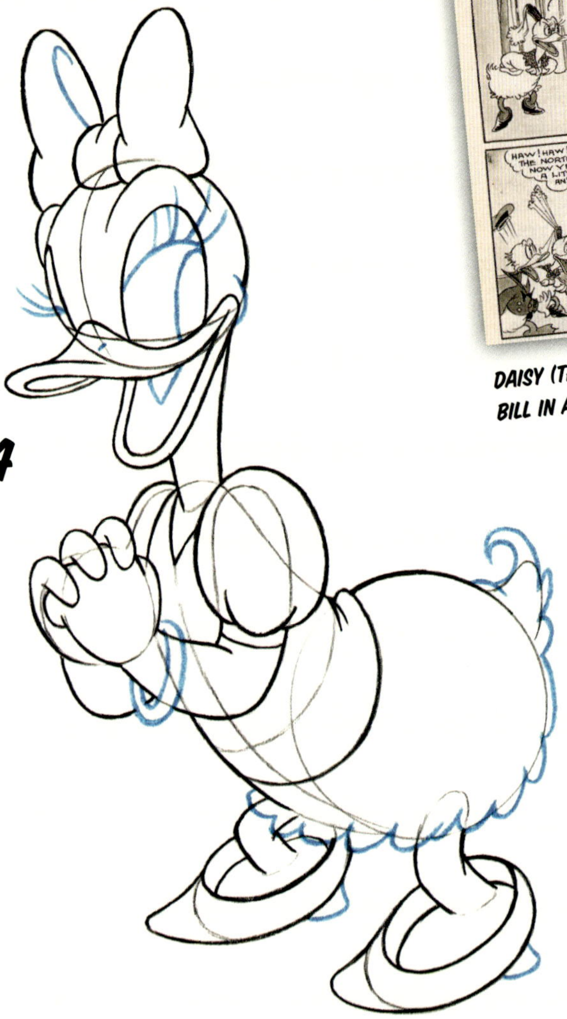

5

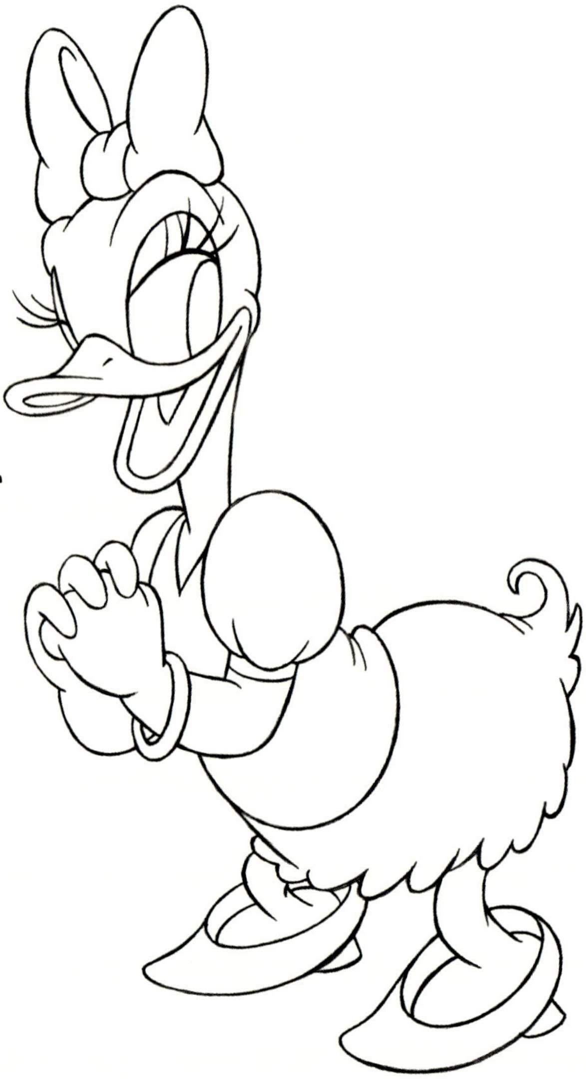

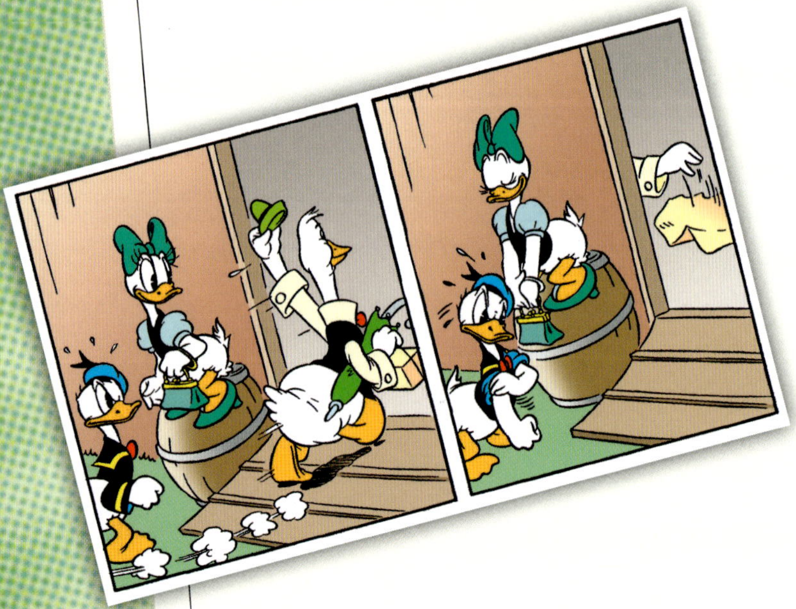

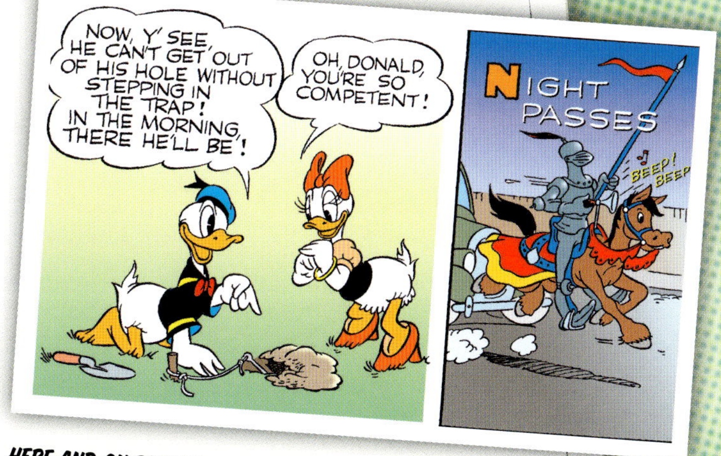

HERE AND ON PAGE 121: EARLY-1940s DAISY AND DONALD SUNDAY COMICS WRITTEN BY BOB KARP AND DRAWN BY AL TALIAFERRO.

6

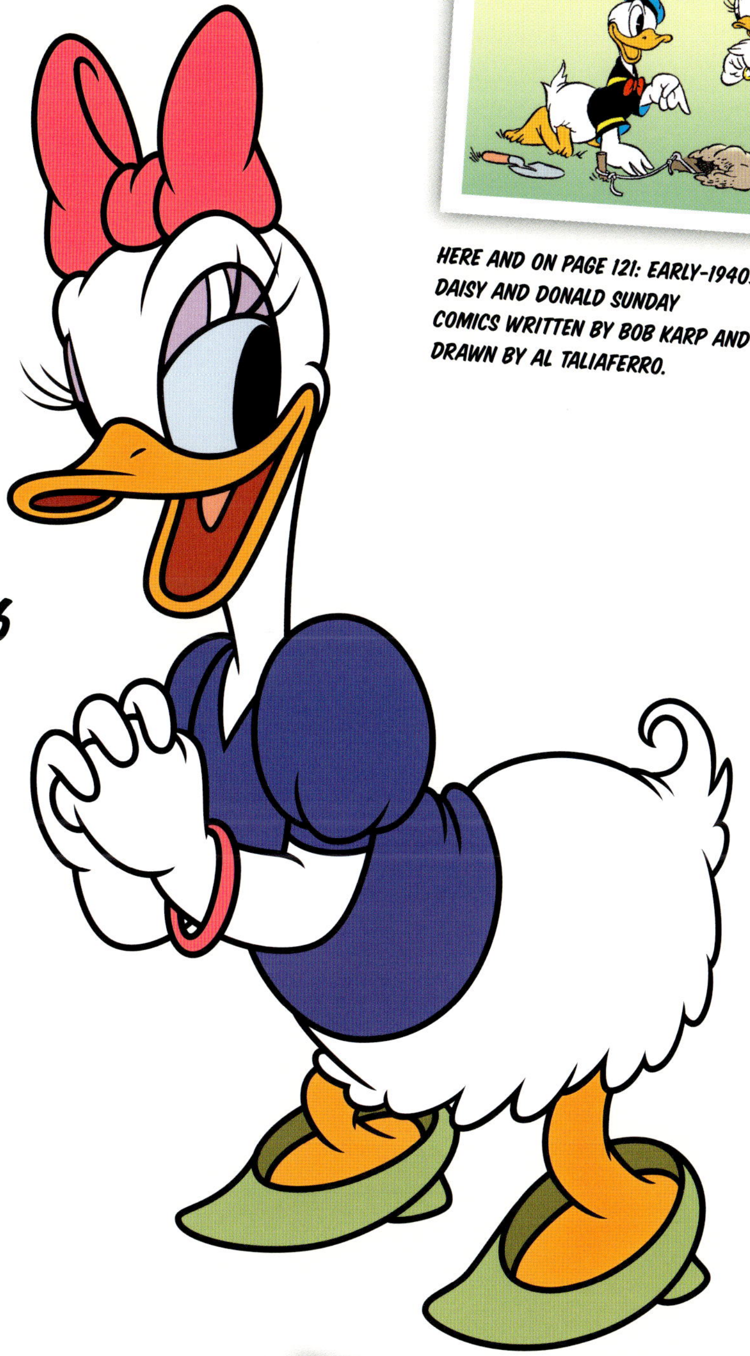

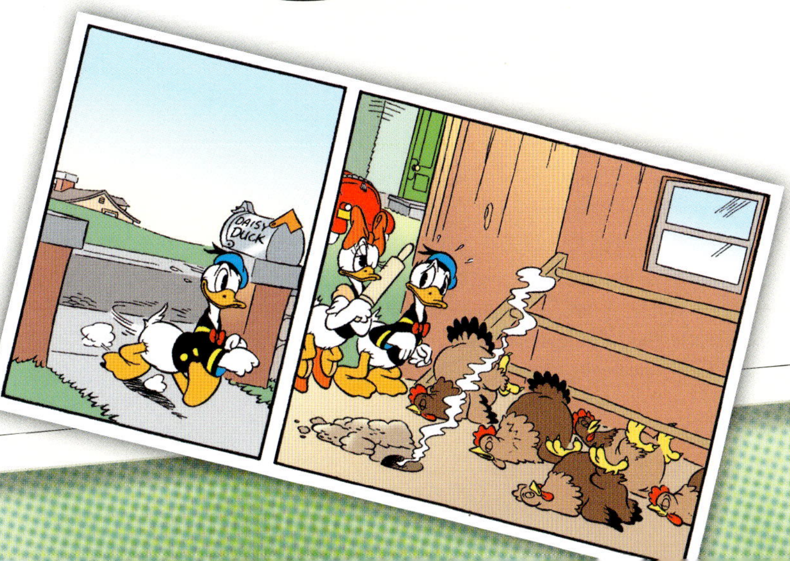

CONTEMPORARY

DAISY DUCK

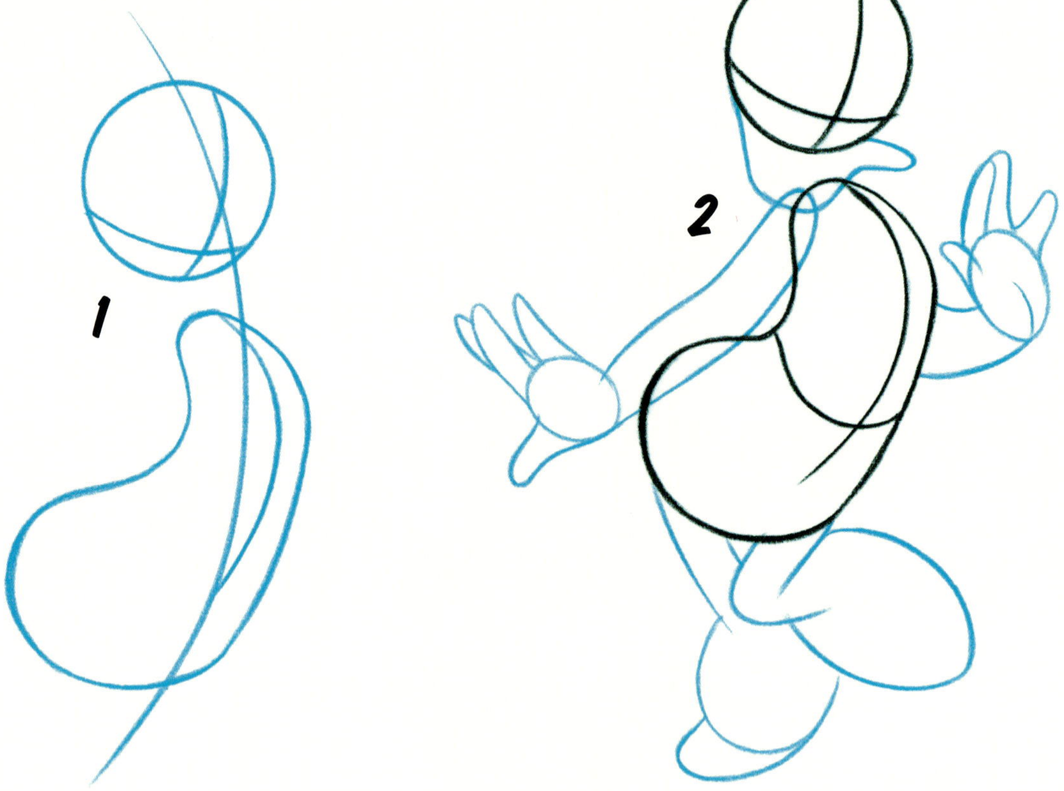

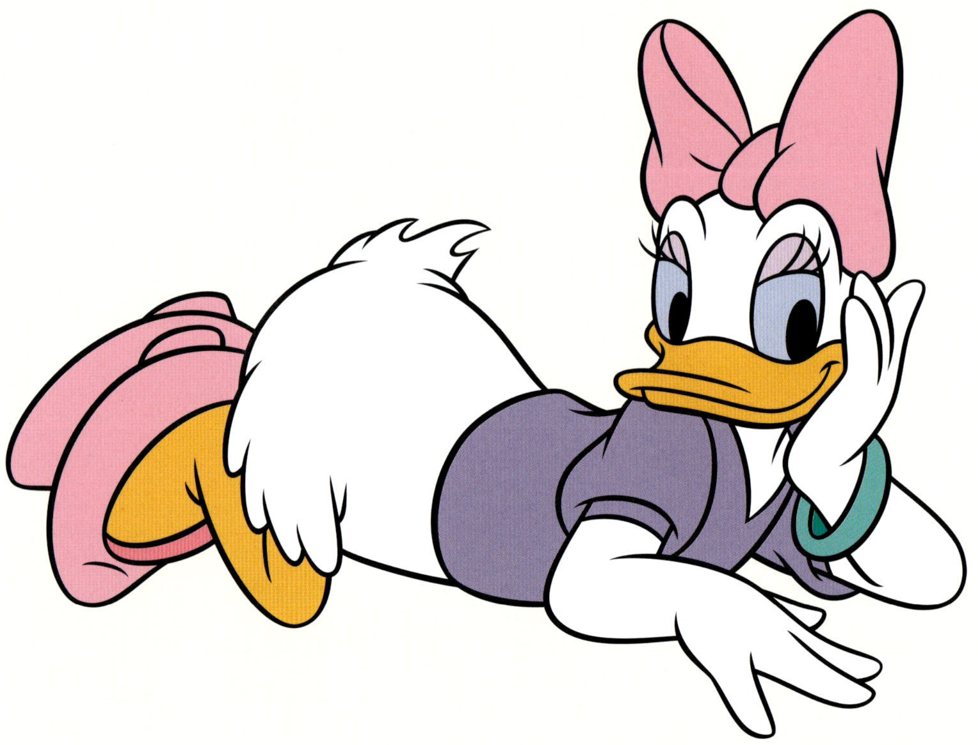

DAISY POSES

3

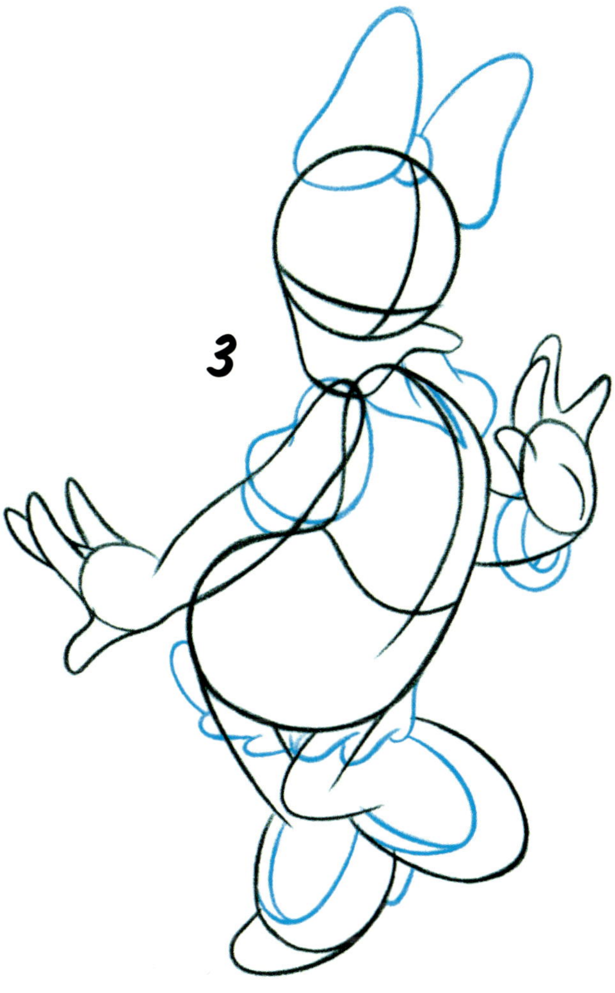

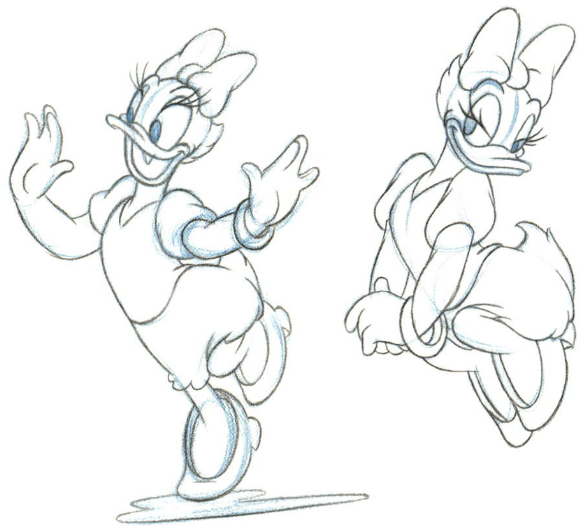

If you curve or tilt Daisy's body and head, she can look flirtatious, happy, or surprised.

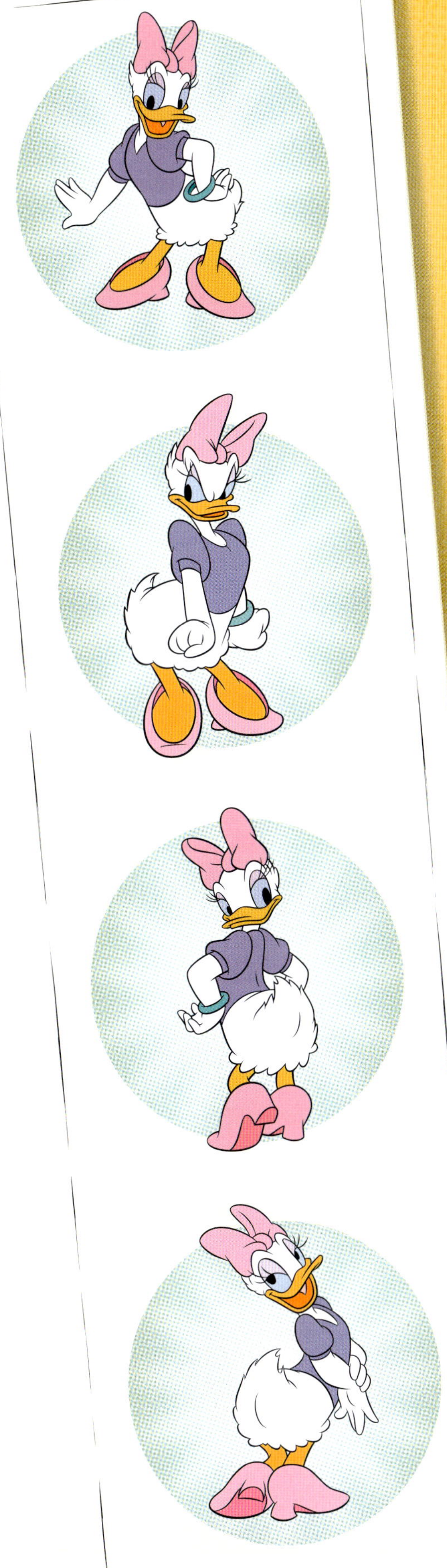

4

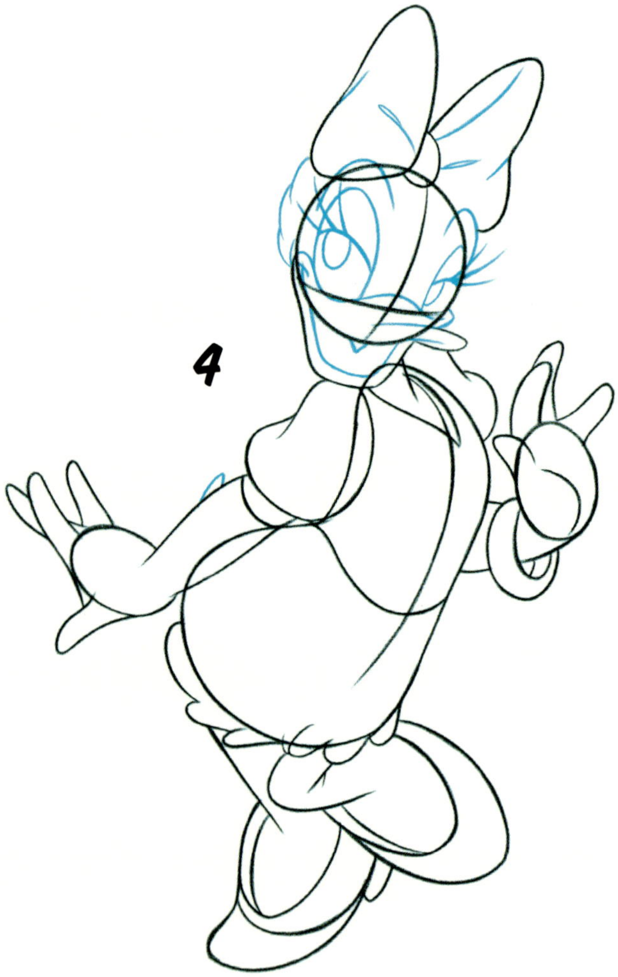

DAISY'S BRACELET HANGS LOOSELY FROM HER LEFT WRIST.

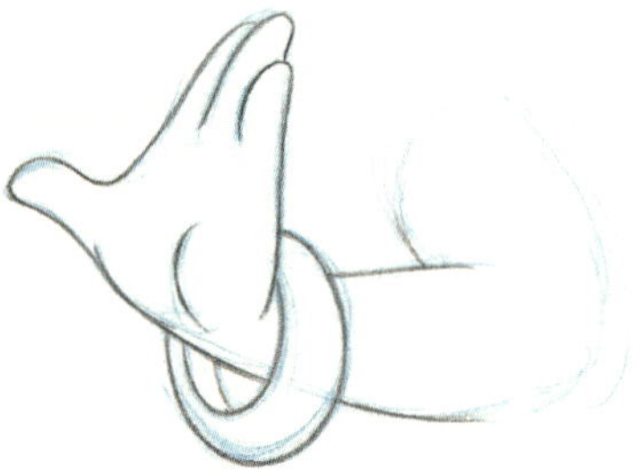

5

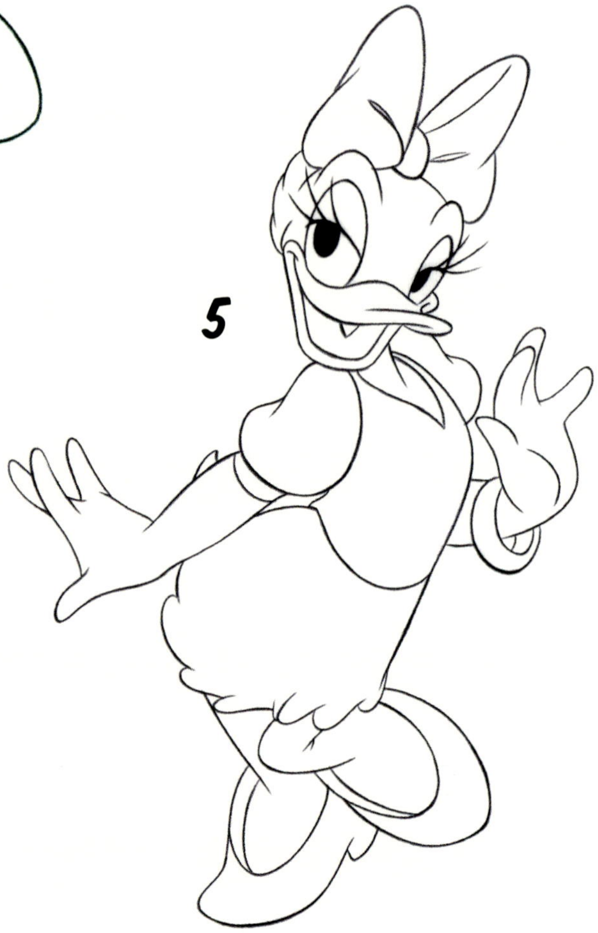

DAISY POSES

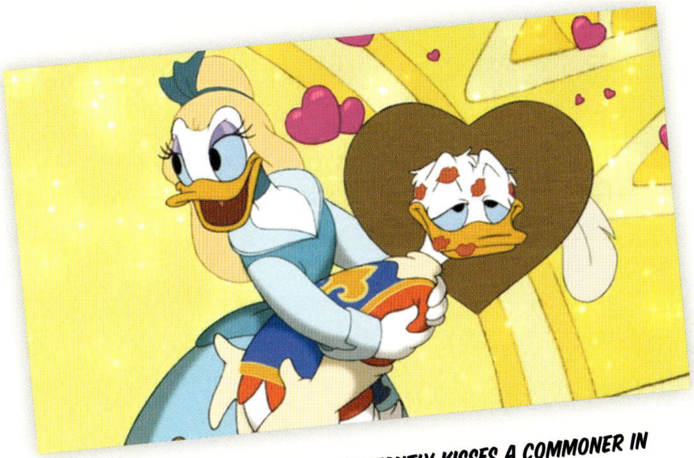

ROYAL LADY-IN-WAITING DAISY RELUCTANTLY KISSES A COMMONER IN MICKEY, DONALD, GOOFY: THE THREE MUSKETEERS (2004).

6

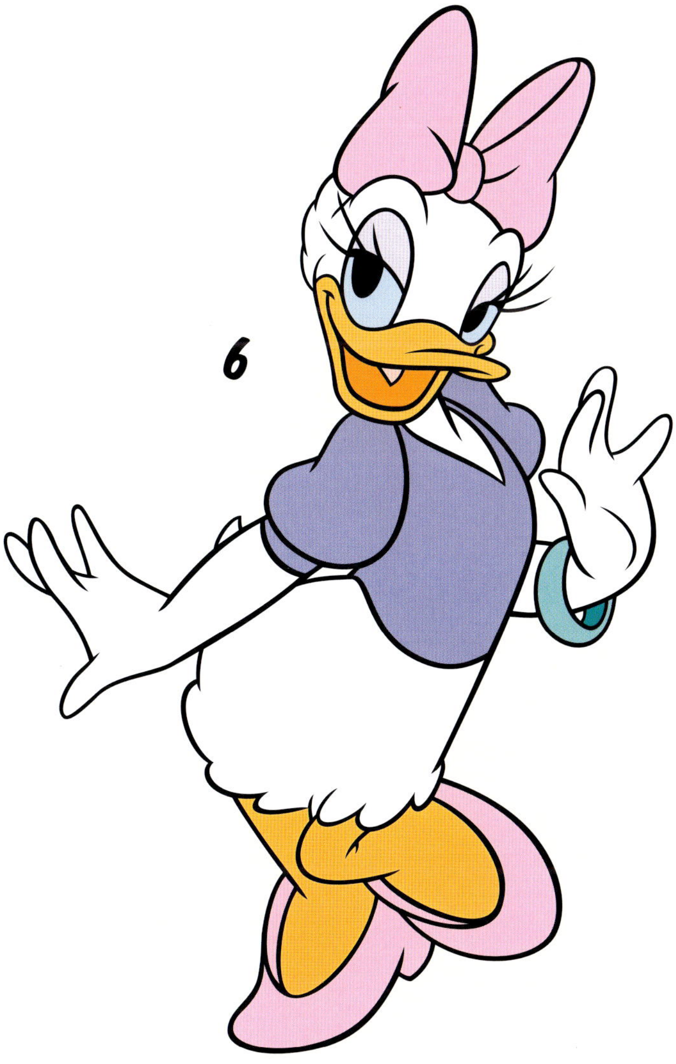

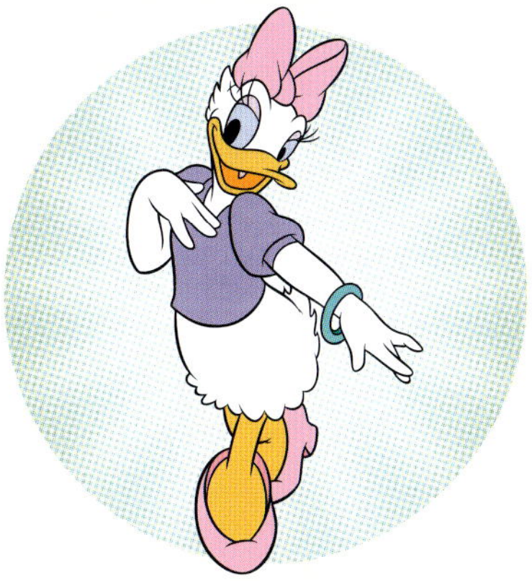

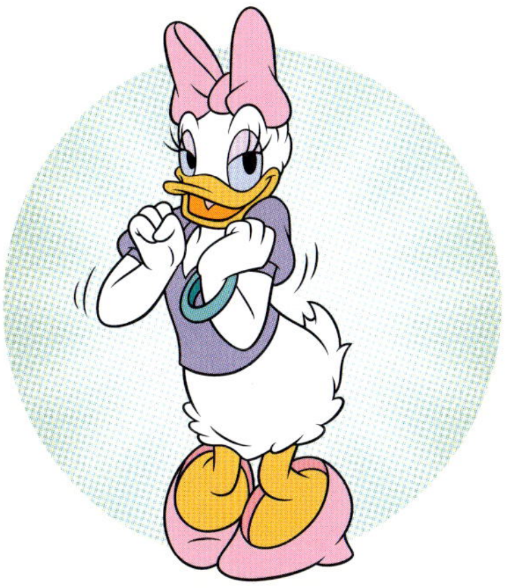

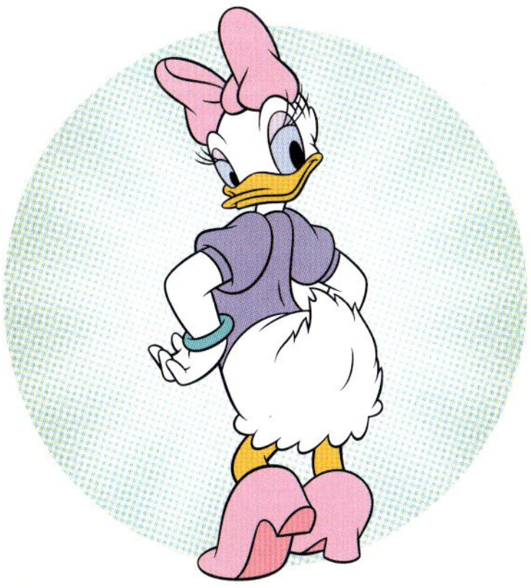

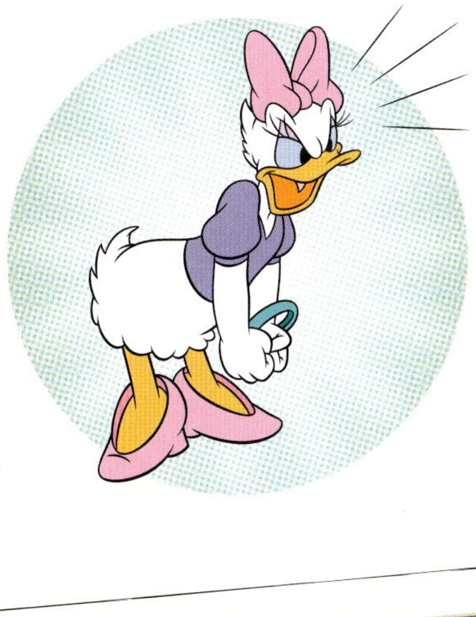

MICKEY & MINNIE TODAY

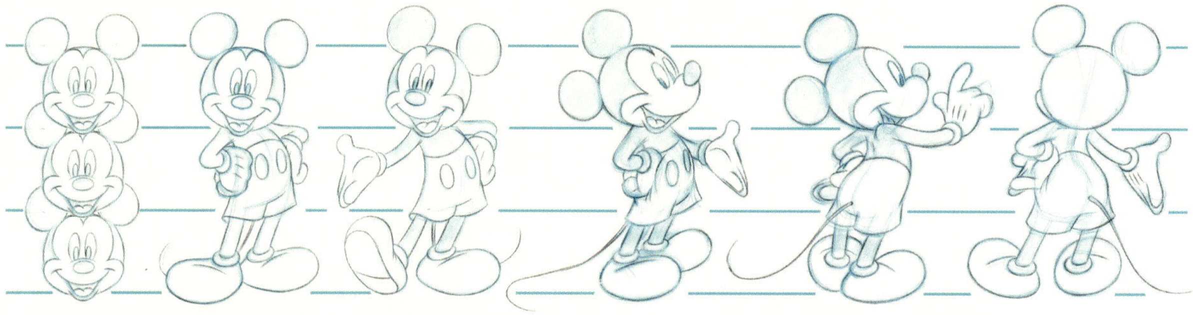

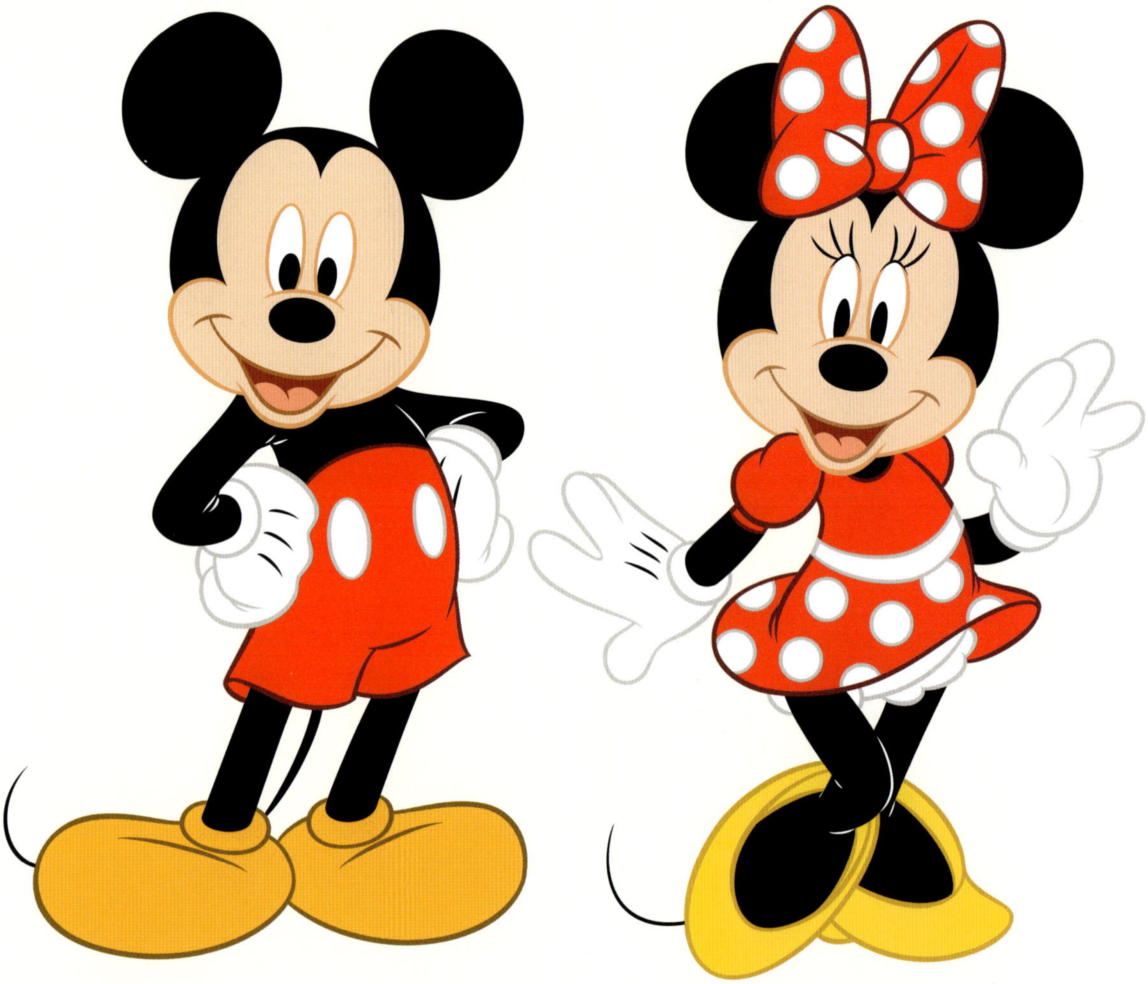

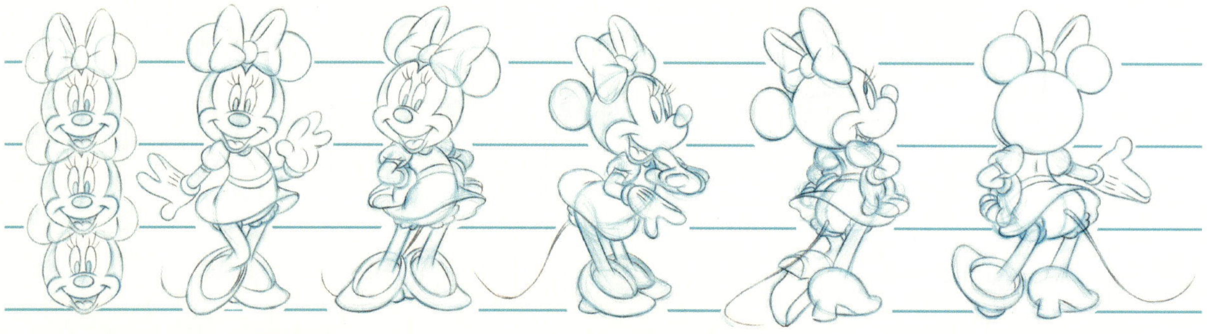

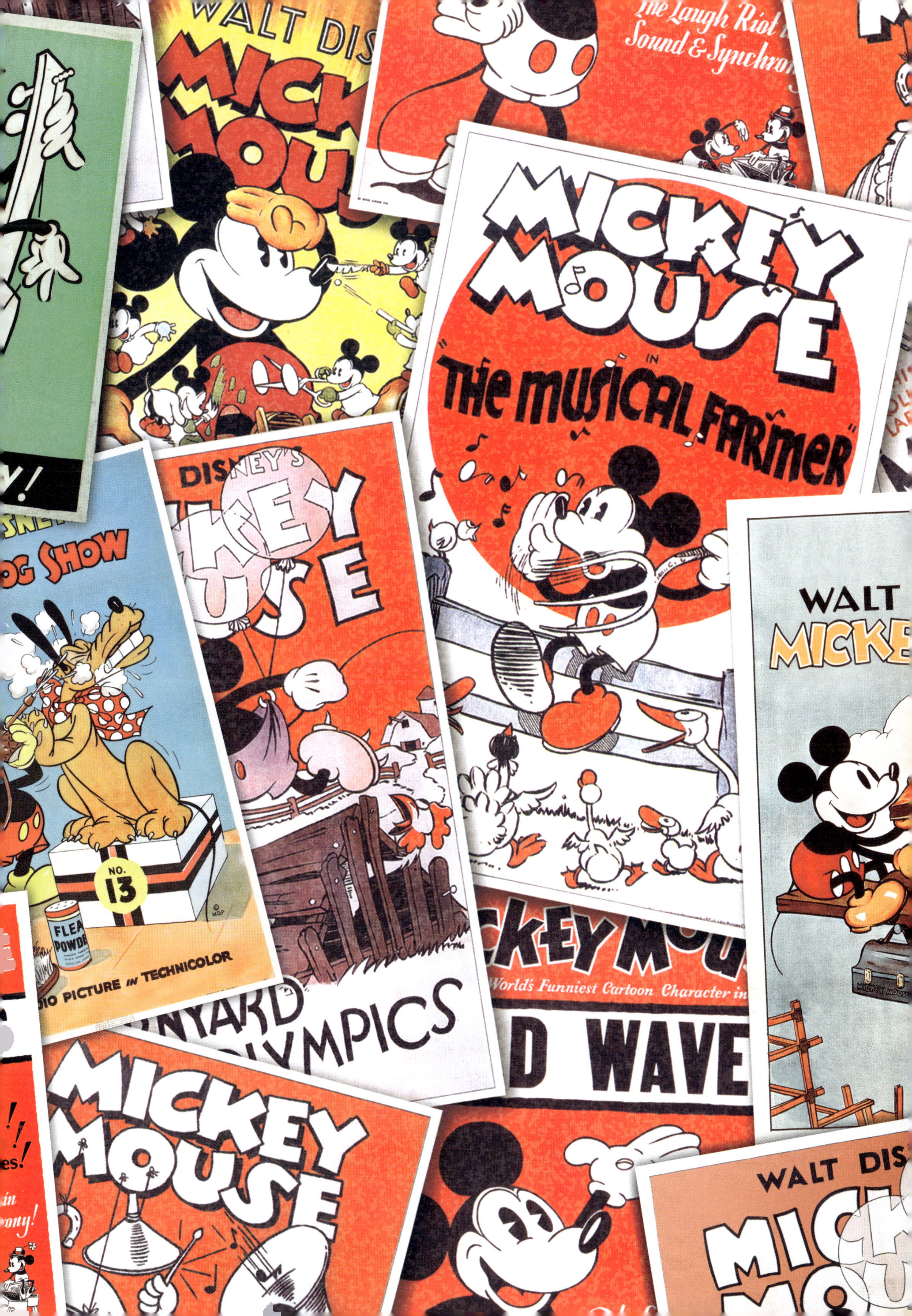

WALT DIS
The Laugh Riot
Sound & Synchron
MICKEY MOUSE
IN
"THE MUSICAL FARMER"
DISNEY'S
OG SHOW
NO. 13
FLEA POWDE
DIO PICTURE IN TECHNICOLOR
NYARD
YMPICS
CKEY MOU
World's Funniest Cartoon Character in
D WAVE
WALT
MICKE
MICKEY MOUSE
MICKEY MOUSE
WALT DIS

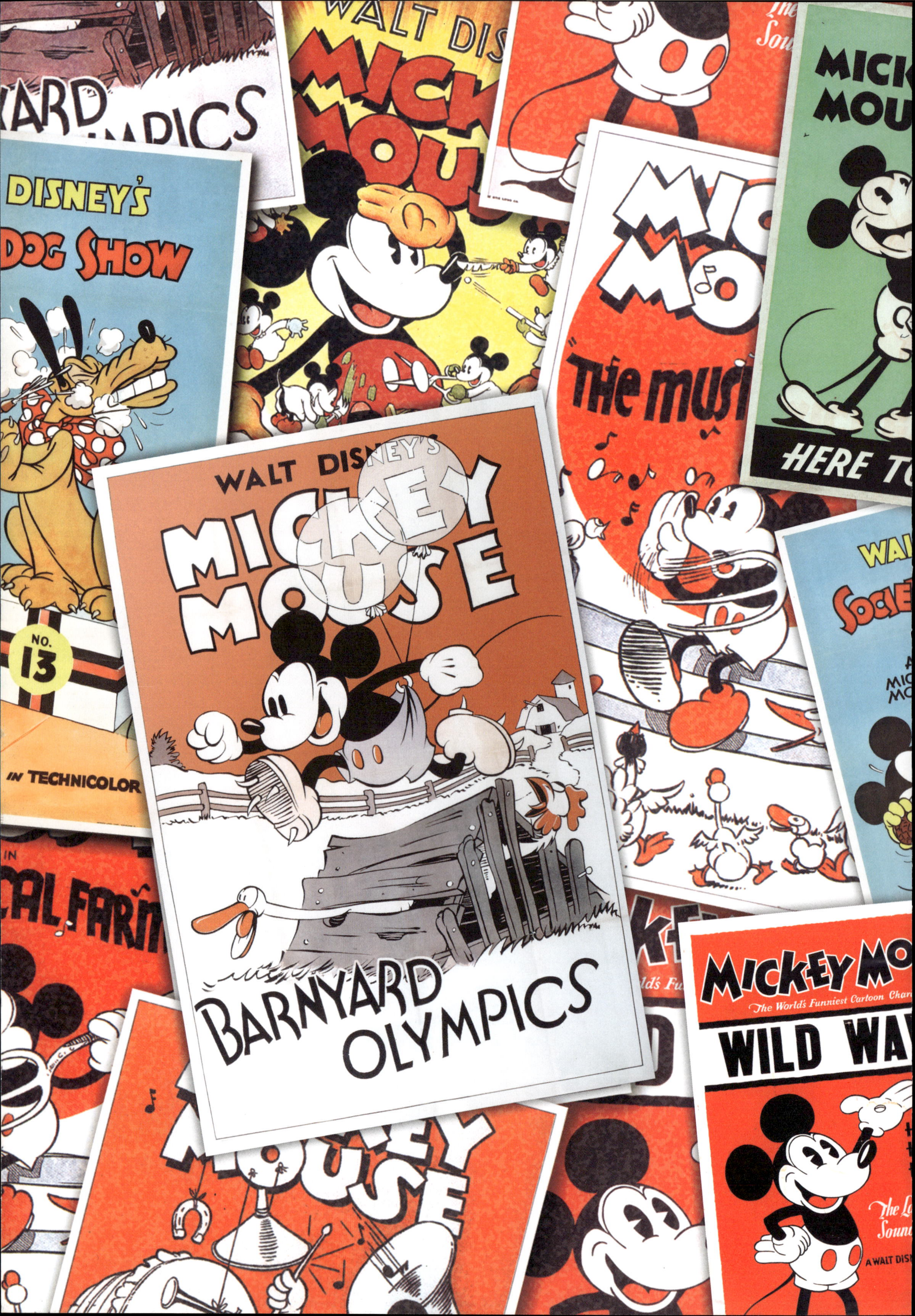

DISNEY'S
DOG SHOW
NO. 13
IN TECHNICOLOR
WALT DISNEY'S
MICKEY MOUSE
BARNYARD OLYMPICS
"THE MUSI
HERE TO
MICKEY MO
The World's Funniest Cartoon Chara
WILD WA